The
Illustrated Digital
Imaging Dictionary

THE ILLUSTRATED DIGITAL IMAGING DICTIONARY

Daniel Grotta &

Sally Wiener Grotta

McGraw-Hill, Inc.

New York   San Francisco   Washington, D.C.   Auckland   Bogotá
Caracas   Lisbon   London   Madrid   Mexico City   Milan
Montreal   New Delhi   San Juan   Singapore
Sydney   Tokyo   Toronto

Library of Congress Cataloging-in-Publication Data
Grotta, Daniel, 1944-
    The illustrated digital imaging dictionary / Daniel Grotta and Sally Wiener Grotta.
        p.   cm.
    Includes index.
    ISBN 0-07-025069-3
    1. Image processing—Digital techniques—Dictionaries.
    2. Computer graphics—Dictionaries.   3. Photography—Digital techniques—
Dictionaries.   4. Computer art—Dictionaries.
    I. Grotta, Sally Wiener. 1949-   . II. Title.
    TA1509.G76   1997
    621.36'7'03—dc21   97-36149
                                  CIP

1 2 3 4 5 6 7 8 9 0   DOC/DOC   9 0 2 1 0 9 8 7

ISBN 0-07-025069-3

*The sponsoring editor for this book was Scott Grillo, the editing supervisor was Sally
Glover, and the production supervisor was Sherri Souffrance. It was set in New Caledonia
by North Market Street Graphics.*

Printed and bound by R. R. Donnelley & Sons Company.

 This book is printed on recycled, acid-free paper containing
a minimum of 50% recycled, de-inked fiber.

McGraw-Hill books are available at special quantity discounts to use as premiums and sales
promotions, or for use in corporate training programs. For more information, please write
to the Director of Special Sales, McGraw-Hill, 11 West 19th Street, New York, NY 10011.
Or contact your local bookstore.

To the days of Milne and Pooh,
Poe and Tolstoy,
Johnson and Craigie

And to our mothers—Edith and Cecile—who read to us,
Taught us to love language
And to delight in the magic of words that communicate

Acknowledgments

Writing a dictionary, which defines a whole new language that continues to change as we write, has been an enormous undertaking, one which we could not possibly have accomplished without the generous help of many people and companies.

For their support, generosity of time and guiding expertise, our heartfelt praise goes to Katrin Eismann (Praxis), Jeff Mace, John Macintosh (American Film Institute), Jerry Magee (Kodak), Bob McKeever (Kodak), Jay Munro (*PC Magazine*) and Steven Ross (Columbia University).

Our sincere thanks for material and information to: Sonya Schaefer of Adobe Systems; Keri Walker of Apple Computer; Jayme Curtis and Doty Hunter (formerly with Apple); Suzanne Stewart of Alexander Communications; Kari Bencha of Corel; Mark Stroble of Fargo; David Beigie, John Metzger and Joe Runde of Kodak; Lynn Stadler of Macromedia; Kristina Keyes (formerly of MetaTools); Chip Partner of Safer Associates; Jen Jones and R. J. Rogers of Tektronix.

Also, to the following companies for their permission to reprint screen captures, images, photographs, pictures from stock libraries and other illustrations related to their products: Adobe Systems, Apple Computer, Corel Corporation, Eastman Kodak, Fractal Design, MetaTools, Macromedia and Micrografx.

Of course, our gratitude for their patience and faith in us and in this book to Brad Schepp and Scott Grillo, our editors.

And thanks, especially and always, to Noel and Edith Wiener for their unconditional love and abiding friendship.

If we have left anyone out, please forgive us. The hour is late. You know who you are and how much we appreciate you.

Introduction

Sally and I first got involved in digital imaging in the summer of 1991, the week before Kodak inaugurated its famed, but ill-fated, Center for Creative Imaging in Camden, Maine. As a professional photographer (Sally) and writers (both of us), we already knew about the exciting potentials of this new technology. Now, finally, it was in a form (on the desktop) and in a price range (not stratospheric) that we would be able to incorporate into our studio. Since then, our studio has grown to include numerous computers (Macs and PCs), scanners (film and flatbed), film recorders, printers, storage devices, filmless cameras, etc., as well as our tried-and-true repertory of traditional film-based professional equipment.

That growth didn't come without its full complement of problems, but that was offset by the excitement of new creative challenges, our curiosity, and our love of both pictures and words. Early on, we discovered that digital imaging has, like most disciplines, professions and secret societies, a language of its own. It's a language that freely, almost casually, borrows words from the fine arts, prepress, typography, advertising, the computer industry, photography, mythology, science fiction novels, movies, childhood nonsense and just about everywhere else. Some of the jargon and nomenclature sounded quite familiar, but alas, the specific digital imaging definitions didn't correspond to anything we knew, or thought we knew. Other definitions are completely altered from their original meanings, or they are so twisted as to be unrecognizable. We even found words whose meanings are rooted in archaic, but rather logical thinking—you know, the last definition in the *Webster's* listing, which was previously so seldom used as to sometimes be marked (obs) for obscure or obsolete.

In our quest to master the technology, we had to learn the language. That meant exploring fields that we never had entered. For instance, in that first year, we had no idea what two important professional graphics arts terms carried over to digital imaging meant: *trapping* and *choking*. To us, trapping meant setting snares for small animals, and choking referred to murder by asphyxiation or starting a car by restricting the flow of air to the carburetor. Another example is a seemingly self-explanatory term like *unsharpen*. The first time we heard it, we erroneously assumed that it meant to blur, or make an image less sharp. Actually, unsharpen is a filter that sharpens an image.

Since language is the key to entering a field and becoming an initiate into its mysteries, we plodded on, through nearly incomprehensible software and hardware documentation, written by technocrats whose first language often seemed to be binary, not English. It was, at first, excruciatingly difficult. We used considerable trial and error, trying to define words in context and frequently asking those more experienced and knowledgeable about the meaning of specific words and phrases. Had there been a digital imaging dictionary available, we certainly would have used it often.

That was back in the early part of the decade. Since then, Sally became a recognized digital artist; we have written numerous articles and reviews on the subject, given lectures, done consultations, and, of course, authored *Digital Imaging for Visual Professionals*. And, yet, though we are now considered experts in the field, we are still often surprised and challenged by the new turns the language can take. To us, that sense of always having to learn, exploring new ideas, techniques and terms is what makes life so fascinating—and sometimes frustrating.

After we had finished our book, *Digital Imaging for Visual Professionals*, we looked back on our bewilderment, and then mastery of imaging terms, and realized that it didn't have to be as difficult as it had been for us. Why should others have to plod through, guessing at words, when what they really want to do is get on with their imaging? That's when we suggested to Brad Schepp, our editor at McGraw-Hill, that our next book should be a digital imaging dictionary. We wanted it to be a fun and interesting work, just as the field is. Rather than simply listing dry definitions that would be technically correct and accurate, we would informally explain what the words meant in relation to how they are actually used and how they affect the way an imager works. In addition, whenever possible, we would illustrate the terms with screen shots, drawings and photographs. Agreeing that there was a need, and sensing a rapidly growing market, McGraw-Hill enthusiastically supported our project.

When we first proposed the *Illustrated Digital Imaging Dictionary*, we had projected defining a maximum of 500 words and terms. That's because we intended to exclude simple computer-related terms, like *RAM*, *ROM* and *operating system* (which we thought we could safely assume were already known), as well as nearly useless (to the imager, that is) technical jargon like *SAA*, *deblock* or *peek & poke*. However, market research showed that many potential buyers of our dictionary were not only imaging novices, but relative computer newcomers. So, rather than force them to consult two dictionaries to define both imaging and computer terms, we decided to include basic computer words. We still resisted including technical buzzwords and comparatively obscure terms, on the grounds that the relatively few users who would be required to know their meaning were already familiar with those words anyway. It would just be confusing to the rest of us.

Based on an estimate of 500 terms requiring approximately 130,000 words to define, we initially projected that we would be able to research and write the entire dictionary in a single two-month stretch. That was a wild underestimation of the number of words needing definitions, and a very unrealistic assessment of our time. Ultimately, the dictionary included closer to 1,000 words, and took us almost a year to complete (with frequent, periodic interruptions to write numerous magazine articles and reviews, buy an old Masonic hall for our home and studio, move 18 years of personal and professional possessions, give lectures and seminars on digital imaging and filmless photography, etc.). It also proved far more difficult than simply spinning definitions from our knowledge and experience. The most common words, such as those for software tools which are used daily, proved to be some of the more problematic to define. Frequently, we would have to consult or reference documentation, third-party books and trade publications to explore the whys and wherefores of a single definition. For instance, we spent literally hours researching the specific difference between a Bezier and a spline curve, including making a number of phone calls and e-mail messages to friends who are expert in the field. Another unexpected problem was the continuing evolution of the language of digital imaging. As soon as we had defined some words, they had developed new, additional meanings. And yes, the two of us occasionally argued, and ultimately compromised over minutiae, including whether to split infinitives to make a definition more readable and accurate (but grammatically incorrect).

Finally, here it is. We hope that this dictionary will be useful, entertaining and enlightening, for novices and experts alike. We've written it as a browse book as well as a reference work, which can be picked up at random and enjoyed for the sake of language. We have attempted to bold any words used in definitions which are, themselves, defined elsewhere. Hopefully, that will encourage you to explore our dictionary.

Of course, we're the first to admit that, despite our best efforts and the wonderful assistance of friends who volunteered as unpaid technical readers, there are undoubtedly many errors of commission and omission. After all, this is only a first edition. Therefore, we're in uncharted waters and have the grave responsibility of defining the language of a comparatively new field which is not only very inventive visually, but also verbally. So, if something we have written about is inaccurate or incomplete, or if we've left out some words that every imager should know, please tell us, and we'll try to correct it in the next edition. For, there certainly will be periodic updates, because imaging nomenclature grows and changes so frequently. Scarcely a week goes by that we don't hear or read a new word or term that sends us scurrying to find out what it means.

Thank you for your interest and support. We hope that you will find this dictionary a frequent friend and an indispensable reference work. Happy imaging!

Daniel Grotta & Sally Wiener Grotta
Pixel Hall, Newfoundland, Pennsylvania
e-mail address: dgrotta@ptd.net

The
Illustrated Digital
Imaging Dictionary

About . . . is a pulldown option or button that gives information about the currently active program. Included in this information may be the active program's serial number, which may be required for receiving authorized **technical support** over the telephone. In Windows, it may also reveal information about **system resources** or how much memory is free. Similarly, on a Mac, you can use the **Get Info** command to find out details such as allotted memory and the version of a program.

Absolute position refers to a specific spatial relationship in which there is an exact correlation between objects, between a mouse or stylus movement and the related movement of a cursor on the monitor, or between tools. For instance, when a **clone** tool is set at absolute, then the distance between the **source point** and the **destination point** remains constant, at all times.

Absorptive color, also called **subtractive color**, is the scientific term to describe color pigmentation in which white is the

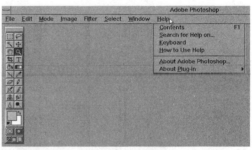

ABOUT A

ABOUT B

About: In *Windows* programs, the About option in the Help *pulldown* menu **(A)** usually opens up a box **(B)** that will provide you with valuable information regarding the active program.

absence of color and black is made by combining all colors. It is the opposite of **additive color**, in which black is the absence of light and white is made by combining red, blue and green color. Absorptive color deals with reflected, as opposed to transmitted, light, and with dyes, inks and pigments rather than pure light. Most desktop printers and printing presses use an absorptive **color model** in which the primary color pigments are **CMYK** (Cyan, Magenta, Yellow and blacK—a *K* is used in BlacK so that it won't be confused with the primary color Blue). On the other hand,

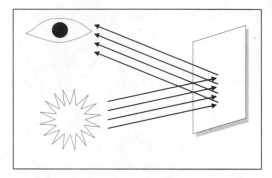

Absorptive color: Absorptive color is created by light that bounces (or is *reflected*) off a surface (such as a piece of paper) into the eye of the viewer.

computer monitors use an **RGB** additive color model. This difference in the way color is defined by monitors and printers is a major source of the **color management** problems inherent in digital imaging.

Accelerator board is a computer peripheral that plugs into an **expansion slot** inside the computer. It will speed up the computer, a particular component (such as the drive controller), or specific software functions such as **Rotate, Size** or **Unsharpen**. Accelerator boards operate by shifting some of the workload from the **CPU** to high-speed **coprocessors** or **DSP**s that act only on specific hardware or software. Accelerator boards are particularly useful in boosting productivity in **image editing programs** like **Photoshop**, or in reducing the time it takes to load or save a file from a **hard drive**.

Accelerator chip is almost the same thing as an **accelerator board**, but it's a single chip or crystal that clips onto the **CPU** or plugs into a socket designed to accommodate such a chip. Sometimes, it is also called a "fixed function" processor, since it cannot process instructions as a CPU can.

Access time is the time required to find a particular file on a **hard drive** or **CD-ROM** drive. It's a measurement of speed and performance—the lower the access time (which is usually expressed in milliseconds, or ms), the faster the drive. At the time of this writing, a typical hard drive may have an access time between 9 and 13 ms, and a 24X CD-ROM drive may have an access time between 125 to 150 ms.

Acquire is a command that is found in the File **pulldown menu** of most **imaging** programs. It is used for **uploading** pictures, usually from a **scan-**

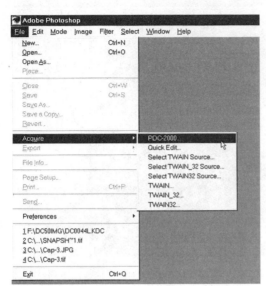

ACQUIRE A

ACQUIRE B

Acquire: The Acquire command brings pictures into *imaging software* (such as *Picture Publisher* or *Photoshop*), using *external hardware*, such as a *scanner* or a *filmless camera*. For it to work, you have to install that device's software (*plug-in*) correctly and, following instructions, link it to the imaging program. Then, like the Polaroid PDC-2000 camera shown here in our Acquire menu **(A)**, your device will display as an option on your screen. Or, **(B)** if the device is TWAIN-compliant, you will be able to select it from among all of the TWAIN devices installed on your computer. In either case, the Acquire command gives you direct control over the way the picture will be *imported* into the program.

ner or **filmless camera**. To see your input device (camera or scanner) on the Acquire menu, you first have to install it and its software **driver**, which is often (but not always) a **TWAIN-compliant** (industry-standard) driver.

Acrobat is a program from **Adobe Systems** for exchanging and displaying graphics or information in the form of a desktop published document without requiring the recipient to have the **application program** or **fonts** that created the original file. For example, you can create an image in **Photoshop**, insert it into a **Ventura** file, save the document in the Acrobat format, send or transmit that file to any Mac or PC, and then view it without having Photoshop or Ventura installed on that computer. Without Acrobat, the recipient's computer, if it could read the file at all, would reformat the margins, fonts and other design elements, so that the user wouldn't see exactly what you created. It's a good way of displaying your work, sending a newsletter, sharing promotional material, and so forth. However, the recipient must have an **Acrobat** reader (software) to be able to see the file. By the way, since it is for viewing only, you don't have to be seriously concerned about possible theft or misappropriation of images—the resolution is usually too small for quality reproduction.

Active: Though there are three pictures open on this desktop, only one can be active at any one time. You know at a glance that the Leaf picture is the active one, because its title bar is a different color from the title bar of the other two. You can usually set up the colors that your computer will use for Active and Inactive windows, according to your own personal *preferences*.

Active Window is exactly what it says it is, the window, screen or frame on your monitor that is currently selected. The active window is often framed with shading or color on top that differentiates it from nonactive or background windows. Whatever command, filter or other edit you invoke will affect the active window. So, it is important to always be aware of which image or window is the active one.

Actor is any object that can be made movable by an **animation** program. For instance, a ball that is made to bounce across a screen is an actor, as is the dog that chases it.

Actual Color is the precise numerical value of the color of any **pixel** in either **RGB, HSB, CMYK**, or other **color model**. In some image editing programs, the only way

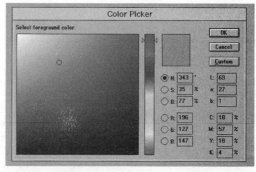

ACTUAL COLOR A

ACTUAL COLOR B

to determine the Actual Color mode is to use the **eyedropper tool** to pick up the color and then look in the **Color Palette** for the RGB or CMYK value. In other programs, such as Photoshop, there are **Information** tools that will provide similar data. Another name used for both the eyedropper tool and the information tool is **Color Probe**. Finding the actual numeric value of a color is important for exact color matching, regardless of how the colors appear on the monitor.

Adapter refers to any device that is modified, enhanced or configured so that it will plug into, activate or work with another device. For instance, a **gender changer** is a plug that connects two male or female cable connectors, or a **VGA** adapter is a plug that connects an Apple computer to a standard VGA monitor.

Adaptive is an **indexed color** table option. When **24-bit color** is converted to **256**

Adaptive: You'll want to reduce the number of colors in an image, if you are planning to display it on a system that doesn't support 24-bit color. This is especially true of the Internet, where, even if the accessing computer can read 24-bit color, it will slow the transmission down. The command to reduce the number of colors from the 16.7 million of 24 bit to the 256 of indexed color is usually found in a Convert . . . command in a pulldown menu. That will open up a dialog similar to this one, in which the adaptive option is chosen.

ACTUAL COLOR C

Actual Color: When you select a color from the *palette* or *picker* in most *imaging programs*, you can choose to use the numbers (or percentages of *primary colors*) rather than trusting your eyes to pick the correct, exact color that you need. For instance, in this Color palette **(A)**, which is set to *RGB* colors (but could be changed to other *color models*), you can mix the primary colors of red, green and blue by moving the sliders under the numbers you want chosen. In this Picker **(B)**, the color chosen is expressed in equivalencies of four different color models: *RGB, HSB, LAB,* and *CMYK*. In addition, some *raster* (pixel-based) programs, like *Photoshop*, have an *Info* palette **(C)**. When the Info palette is opened, anytime you put your cursor into your picture, it displays the numbers defining the color of the pixel on which the cursor rests.

colors, millions of colors are reduced to the hundreds by **mapping**. Mapping assigns a range of colors from the 24-bit information to a single color in a palette of 256 colors, according to a **color table**. The adaptive color table attempts to assign substitution colors that most closely resemble the original ones, in the hope that there will be little or no discernible difference between the two versions of the picture. Sometimes, it works.

ADB is short for Apple Desktop Bus, but it actually describes the Macintosh and PowerMac **port** into which a keyboard, mouse, **digitizing tablet**, etc., is plugged.

ADC, or **Analog-to-Digital** converter, is a chip, chips, device or plug-in board that convert **analog** signals to **digital data**. All **scanners** and **filmless cameras** use either built-in ADC chips or an external device with ADC capability to convert captured analog signals (everything in the noncomputer world, including photographs, is analog information) into the zeros and ones that make up digital information (the only type of data computers can recognize and use).

Additive color, also called **RGB color**, is light in which the addition of pure red, green and blue is white, and the absence of light is black. Additive color is light that is transmitted directly to the viewer from an illuminating source such as a computer monitor, a 35mm transparency, or the sky. It is the opposite of **absorptive** (aka **reflective** or **subtractive**) color, in which the absence of pigment is white and the combination of pure cyan, magenta and yellow is a muddy black. (Because chemical pigments such as paint are never pure, black is usually added to the mix to get darker, more saturated colors.)

Most of what we see in the real world is absorptive color, such as the light reflected from a wall, car, piece of furniture, or photograph printer onto paper. Conversely, much of what we see in the computer world is additive color. Remember, monitors display additive color (because they are pumping electrons and photons directly from a picture tube to your eyes), while printers output absorptive color (because you are viewing a nonilluminating object that is illuminated by a light source, such as the sun, a strobelight, or a lightbulb).

Numerous **color management** schemes and technologies are used to try to more accurately convert additive to subtractive color for printing out a picture from a computer.

Add is a **blend mode** and **channel operation** command that combines the color values of pixels that are layered or painted one on top of the other. It is the opposite of **subtract**, in which the pixel values of the one are subtracted from the other.   SEE color plate 2.

Add-on is an adjective that describes a piece of **software** or **hardware** that is meant to be added onto or attached to another **program** or **device**. The add-on cannot function without the primary software or hardware that it augments. For instance, **special effects filters** are added onto **graphics software** to extend the special effects available in the program.   SEE **Plug-in.**

Add noise is a **filter** that adds random **pixels** to an **image**. It's a special effect that creates color or monochrome mottling on an image. The degree of Add Noise can be varied tremendously, from a subtle, barely discernible effect, to an image that looks as though it were painted in pointillist style by an impressionist painter.

Add: The Add command (sometimes also called *Additive*) adds the values of each pixel of the original and the pasted on or layered picture together, to come up with the values of the new composite. This usually lightens the picture. (See also color plate 2.)

ADD NOISE A   **ADD NOISE B**   **ADD NOISE C**

Add noise: Noise is usually added to pictures to give them the look of a grainy photograph, to soften them or to attempt to create an artistic sense of the color dots that make up the image (as in a pointillist painting). It is also useful when compositing two pictures together, to blend the differences between them more fully. Here, the photograph of a smooth faced child **(A)** is given a soft grainy appearance **(B)** by setting the Add Noise filter at 39 with a Gaussian (irregular) rather than uniform distribution **(C)**.

Address describes the exact location where specific information, especially about a particular device (such as a **scanner**), is stored. It's usually expressed as a **hexadecimal** number (such as A20F). Addresses can be important in **imaging** because every device attached to the computer is found at a specific address, and if your computer is told to look for that device at the wrong address, or if a device's address conflicts with another one, it may work improperly or not at all. However, most installation programs scan the computer for existing hardware addresses and will automatically select an unused one.

In **e-mail**, an address is the location of a person, company or other communicating entity. For instance, when we send a column to one of our editors over the **Internet**, we send it to his e-mail address, just as we would send a mailed letter to his physical street, city and state address.

There are other computerese definitions for address, but these are the two most relevant to **imagers**.

Adobe is one of the most important software companies specializing in **imaging** and **desktop publishing** for the **Mac, PC** and other computer platforms. Among its better-known products are **Photoshop, PageMaker, Illustrator, Acrobat** and **PostScript**.

Adobe Type Manager, or **ATM**, is Adobe Systems' **utility** for managing **PostScript** or **TrueType fonts**. ATM is included as part of many Adobe programs, is sold as a separate utility, or is bundled with many **image editing, desktop publishing** or **illustration** programs. It's used primarily to create "on-the-fly" (or quick, on-demand) fonts for the screen at any size, to eliminate **aliasing** (or "**jaggies**") on screen fonts (type displayed on the monitor), and to output PostScript files on non-PostScript printers.

Advanced photo system   SEE **APS**.

Air is the empty, unused white space on a page. Everything you see in this book that isn't type or an illustration is air. In **desktop publishing**, the amount of air on a page is a design consideration, since a too dense layout is hard to read and is usually unappealing. On the other hand, too much air can be wasteful and visually boring.

Airbrush is a software tool that mimics the effects produced by a graphic arts compressed, air-powered airbrush. That is, it's a **mouse-** or **stylus**-driven swathe of ink or color (which can be adjusted from fine to coarse) that is "sprayed" over portions of an image. Depending on its **opacity** (which the user can usually vary), the airbrushed section can either completely cover whatever image is underneath or simply add a barely discernible touch of color. Most frequently, airbrush is used to eliminate unwanted defects and blemishes (such as a mole on the face of a model) or to create a soft-looking part of an image.

Alert is when the program informs the reader in some manner that something selected is either unavailable or not possible. For instance, a color alert graphically shows, usually by flashing, when a selected color (such as a metallic red or iridescent blue) cannot be printed by the presently selected printer. The user then has the option of choosing another color that can be printed, or checking to see whether the equivalent

Airbrush: The airbrush stroke (on the bottom) is soft edged and somewhat transparent. Compare that to the oil brush stroke on the top. For obvious reasons, airbrush tools are often used to create the appearance of shadows (as well as to paint a soft image or remove imperfections from a photograph).

color automatically selected by the program will be acceptable. An alert may be a visible, readable memo that pops up on the screen, some sort of visual information (such as blocked-out areas on a picture) and/or an audible sound.

Algorithm denotes a specific piece of **software** programming code designed to solve a problem. Algorithms are used to accurately **compress** and **decompress** image files, rapidly convert **analog** information to **digital** data, sample **32-bit** color down to **24-bit** color, define a **filter** or **special effect**, etc. Algorithms are invisible to the user and simply the way a program or **subprogram** achieves something. However, some algorithms are better than others, so sophisticated digital artists sometimes make choices regarding which tool, command or effect to use, based on their knowledge of how the underlying code works.

Alias/aliasing refers to the appearance of unwanted visual information produced by imperfections or limitations in hardware or software.

In **digital imaging** and **desktop publishing**, aliasing most often refers to the "**jaggies**" phenomenon that occurs when digital data are displayed on a screen or printed out.

For instance, the curve of an *O* may have jaggies or stair-stepping-like ridges where you expect a smooth curve. SEE the illustration at the **Antialias** definition.

Aliasing can also refer to **noise** or **artifacting**, which is the creation of random pixels where none should be.

In graphics arts, aliasing can be undesirable visual effects, such as **moiré patterns** that occur when a **screen angle** is improperly set.

With digital cameras and scanners, color aliasing is the misalignment of RGB data in such a manner that the colors don't look right.

Most aliasing can be eliminated or greatly reduced by adjusting software **parameters**, using software **anti-aliasing** options, changing positions or options, or using the proper hardware.

Another definition for the word *alias* is an **icon** on the Mac **desktop** that is created by the user to point to (or start up) a program, whose icon would otherwise be hidden in a **folder**.

Align refers to the positioning of objects, images or type in relation to each other or some other abstract position, such as the left margin of a page. In some programs, align is a command used to "snap" text, images or objects to a specific location or object on a page layout.   SEE **Justify**.

Aligned screens is a graphics arts term for the proper positioning of 4 separate **CMYK halftone screens** at identical angles. This helps produce

ALIGN A

ALIGN B

ALIGN C

ALIGN D

Align: *Align* and *Justify* commands are used to line up objects or text in relation to each other or the page. **(A)** The circle is aligned to the center of the box. **(B)** The circle is aligned to the inside center/top of the box. **(C)** The circle is aligned to the inside center/left of the box. **(D)** The circle is aligned to the inside bottom/right of the box.

optimum reproduction quality while minimizing unwanted **artifacts**, such as **moiré patterns**.

All is a command that allows the user to select everything in an image, layer, scene or document (for editing, moving, printing, etc.). In many programs, using the All command places a **marquee** or border around the objects, layer or image. Usually, the All command is found in the **Select** pulldown menu, **selection palette** or wherever the program has its **selection tools**.

All point addressability in some programs is the term used to describe a situation in which the user is able to place all selected text and images anywhere on a page. The opposite occurs when images, charts, text or whatever must be placed into specific boxes or **windows** on a page.

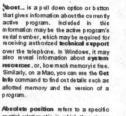

About... is a pull down option or button that gives information about the currently active program. Included in this information may be the active program's serial number, which may be required for receiving authorized **technical support** over the telephone. In Windows, it may also reveal information about **system resources**, or, how much memory is free. Similarly, on a Mac, you can use the **Get Info** command to find out details such as allotted memory and the version of a program.

Absolute position refers to a specific spatial relationship in which there is an exact correlation between objects, between a mouse or stylus movement and the related movement of a cursor on the monitor, or between tools. For instance, when a **clone** tool is set at absolute, then the distance between the **source point** and the **destination point** remains constant, at all times.

Absorptive color, also called **subtractive color**, is the scientific term to

and printers is the source of the **color management** problems inherent in digital imaging.

Accelerator board is a Mac or PC peripheral that plugs into an **expansion slot** in the computer. It will speed up the computer, a particular component (such as the drive controller), or specific software functions, such as **Rotate**, **Size** or **Unsharpen**. Accelerator boards operate by shifting some of the workload from the **CPU** to high-speed **co-processors** or **DSPs** that act only on specific hardware or software. Accelerator boards are particularly useful in boosting productivity in **image editing** programs like **Photoshop**, or in reducing the time it takes to load or save a file from a **hard drive**.

Accelerator chip is almost the same thing as an **accelerator board**, but it's a single chip or crystal that clips onto the CPU or plugs into a socket designed to accommodate such a chip.

Alley: The space between columns of text on a printed page is called an *alley*. Your alley needs to be large enough to make a clear demarcation between the columns, without leaving too much *white space* for the page design.

Alley is a printer's term that describes the space between columns on a page layout. In most layout programs, the width of the alley or the dimensions of the columns may be adjusted manually, numerically or automatically, to make them wider or thinner.

Allocate resource is the command certain programs use when either the user (manually) or the computer (automatically) must select and reserve a particular resource, such as **RAM** or **hard disk** space. For instance, hard drive storage space is typically set aside as a **buffer** area to be used for **virtual memory** (when the computer has reached its limit of RAM, or electronic memory, and uses the hard drive to mimic RAM). Allocate resource is often used for reserving a specific memory **address** for a hardware device, such as a graphics board, so it will work properly without being accidentally overwritten by another device's software that wants to use the same address.

Alpha is the name of Digital's high-speed **RISC CPUs** used to power its Alpha-class computers. While not **Pentium** compatible, Alpha computers can run the **Windows NT operating system** and **Windows** software at speeds equal to or greater than Pentium systems. Alpha computers have not made much of a penetration in the professional graphics market, despite

Alpha channel: In this Photoshop Channels palette, you can see representations of the composite RGB image, the color channels (red, green, and blue), and four masks or alpha channels (#4, #5, #6, and #7). Where the alpha channels are white is the area that the mask will let through. Where an alpha channel is black, that portion of the picture is masked off, when that mask is activated. An alpha channel can be saved with a picture without affecting anything in the picture. To use the mask, the alpha channel or selection has to be loaded and active.

their excellent performance speeds, because of the greater price and fears of hardware and software incompatibilities.

Alpha channel is the **channel** that is used to store noncolor information about a picture. Most often, this information can be a **mask**, or it may contain data about the levels of transparency, illumination or texture. Technically, it's the top 8 bits of a 32-bit RGB image file, in which the red, green and blue channels are the bottom 24- bits of information. However, some programs allow you to have more than one alpha channel. Every alpha channel that is saved with an image file increases the size of that file and slows down processing or editing speeds.

Alpha software   SEE **Beta software**.

Alphanumeric refers to any combination of numbers and letters that make up words or codes. An example of an alphanumeric is R2D2.

Alternate key, or ALT, is found on PC and other **platform** keyboards (but not on the Mac). It is often used in conjunction with other keys to invoke commands, tools, etc. Or, it may be used with a mouse click or other monitor-based action to constrain or modify that action. When you see ALT in **documentation** or in **hot keys** memos, it is telling you to hold down the alternate key while doing something else. For instance, ALT + S means that you should hold down the Alternate key while you press the S key.

Ambiance refers to a property of light that appears to be omnipresent, without a single defined source. It is also referred to as *incidental light,* or it may be a combination of different light sources within an image, such as a room lit by sunlight, fluorescent lamps, and spotlights. The ambient light in your imaging room is an important influence on monitor display colors and illumination. That's the reason it affects the **calibration** of monitor **gamma** values. Ambient can also be an option in programs that allow you to define light sources and types.

Amiga is the name of a now-discontinued computer system that once competed with Macintoshes and PCs. It was designed as an inexpensive but surprisingly powerful graphics workstation, especially for **multimedia** applications in which the final output was to be broadcast on television or displayed on a computer monitor. Its hallmark was being able to quickly switch from **RGB digital** mode to **NTSC analog** mode, with appropriate **resolutions** for each.

Amiga HAM (Hold And Modify) is a file format used by Amiga computers that packs, or compresses, 12 bits of data into 6 bits. It is generally used for low resolution images.

Amiga IFF (Interchange File Format) is used to transfer 24-bit image files to and from Amiga computers. IFF also supports 24 bits per color channel, or 72-bit files, for use in Amiga's **Video Toaster** system. However, PC and Mac image editing programs that read or write IFF files work only in 24-bit mode, not 72-bit mode.

Analog (which is short for analogous, or similar to) is the moniker given to anything and everything in the real world. In graphics, it refers to a continuous, seamless sweep of color, tone, and/or other variable information.

Computers work in **digital** (just zeros and ones) only. But televisions display analog information. This key difference between TV (or video) and computer monitors requires a conversion between digital and analog data according to where the editing will be done and where the pictures will be displayed.

Think of analog as a ramp of information and digital as steps, or analog as a light dimmer switch and digital as a switch that is either on or off, with nothing in between.

Analog camera, or **still video camera**, is considered to be the opposite of a **digital camera**. However, though the term *digital camera* is often bandied about, technically speaking, all cameras, **filmless** and film, actually capture analog information only from the real world. Digital cameras convert that data into the zeros and ones that a computer can read. But analog filmless cameras send the analog information to an external device (through a **frame**

grabber board or a conversion box) to turn it into digital data. Therefore, the difference between an analog and a digital camera is not the kind of information they capture, but the kind they **export**. Digital cameras tend to produce images better suited for printed reproduction onto paper, while still video cameras are most efficient when the ultimate display medium is electronic (such as a multimedia presentation on a computer monitor or television set). This is because video cameras use an **interlace** scan—that is, they display half the image with the first scan and the rest of the image on the second scan. Because each frame consists of two scans made about one-fifteenth of a second apart, any motion between the scans will cause a blur. In contrast, digital cameras capture images at one take, so that there is no possibility of blur from interlaced capture.   SEE **ADC** and **Analog-to-digital**.

Analog-to-digital refers to the process of converting real-life **analog** signals into **digital data** that the computer can recognize, store and manipulate. For instance, **scanners** read analog visual information, turn it into digital data, then feed it to the computer. SEE **Analog, ADC** and **Analog cameras**.

Anchor point(s), also called **node(s)**, are the fixed or defining points of a line or a curve, specifically when drawn with a **Bezier** or a **spline** tool. Anchor points remain stationary as the line or curve is drawn or flexed. They are used in conjunction with **segments** (the line, curve or path between 2 anchor points), **direction** or **control points** (which define the direction that the line or curve is going), and **endpoints** (the points at which lines are ended or finished).

Angle of rotation is the degree to which an object or image is rotated in a specific direction, using the rotation tool or command. It is often expressed as a number on an *x/y* axis or a degree within the 360 degrees of a circle.

Animation is the illusion of continuous movement of objects, drawings and other nonphotographic images on a computer

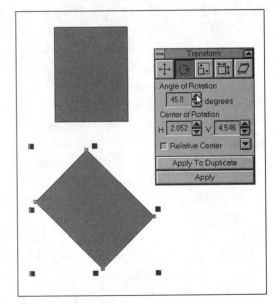

Angle of rotation: The lower rectangle has been rotated 45°. Notice also, that this CorelDRAW dialog (like many others of its type) allows you to change the location of the center of the rotation and, if you wish, to apply the rotation to a new duplicate of the object rather than to the original.

monitor, television set or motion picture screen. It is created by rapidly projecting a series of frames, each one slightly different from the other but drawn in such a way that the motion is advanced slightly in each succeeding frame. The human eye cannot distinguish individual frames when projected faster than 15 frames per second (fps), which is the minimum speed most animation programs allow. Standard 16 and 35mm film is shot at 24 fps; American television (**NTSC**) is projected at 30 fps; Japanese and European television (**PAL**) at 25 fps; most computer animation at 30 fps.

ANPA stands for the American Newspaper Publishers Association. The ANPA is very active in developing standards and specifications related to desktop publishing layouts for newspapers.

ANPA colors are approved for use in newspaper printing and may be selected from a commercially available **swatch palette** and incorporated in most **image editing** and **desktop publishing** programs.

ANSI is short for the American National Standards Institute, an organization that develops and promulgates standards for all sorts of industries, including many computer hardware and software standards. These include standards for software escape and control codes and screen drivers for positioning and controlling the cursor. ANSI screen drivers work on PCs only when the following line is loaded into the **Config.sys** file: DEVICE=ANSI.SYS.

Anti-alias is a command, option, or **algorithm** that smooths the circular or angular edges of an object (image, type, etc.) and helps to eliminate **jaggies** (bumpy,

ANTI-ALIAS A

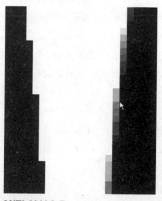

ANTI-ALIAS B

Anti-alias: The *O* on the left has the jaggies, but the one on the right appears to have a smoother edge because it was formed with anti-aliasing turned on. Look at the magnified section **(A)** to see how this illusion is achieved. Rather than have the absolute black and white of the jaggies, an anti-aliased curve has a softening *gradient* between the edge and the background. To the naked eye, it looks neater and better formed.

staircase-like edges). It averages the colors at the edge of the line, creating a smoother transition to the background. For instance, if you have black type on a white background, anti-aliasing would introduce a gray (or several levels of gray) along the edge of the type. The human eye interprets this as a softer, less jagged, more natural line or curve. Used correctly, it doesn't affect the sharpness of the line, but if overdone, it can cause some blurriness.

Most illustration and image editing programs, as well as most printers, have built-in anti-aliasing options or **algorithms**.

Append swatches is a **color palette** command that allows the user to add colors that have been previously saved in a file to the current choices of colors in the **palette**. Other programs achieve the same thing by using the command **load**.

Apple is the name of a computer manufacturing company that produces a wide variety of desktop and laptop systems. Among its many products, Apple specializes in graphics-oriented, **workstation**-like systems specifically suited for **image editing, desktop publishing** and **CAD/CAM** functions.

Apple Color Picker is Apple Computer Company's color wheel used for selecting or changing **foreground** or **background** colors. Available in a variety of programs, the Apple Color Picker can select from **RGB** or **HSB** color models.

Apple Desktop Bus   SEE **ADB**.

Apple key is found on the Mac keyboard and is often used in conjunction with other keys to invoke **hot keys**. Or, it may be used with a tool, command or other monitor-based action to modify or **constrain** that action. The apple key is often depicted as an apple icon. Or, it may be called a **command** key.

Applet is a mini-application, usually a **utility**, designed to perform a specific task. It may come in a collection of applets, which are often packaged as part of a full-size program or **application**.

AppleTalk is Apple Computer Company's built-in **network port** designed to **interface** with other computers, printers, etc. AppleTalk is generally far slower and more limited than other built-in or add-on network systems, such as **Ethernet**, but it's easy to set up and maintain. Because of its slow speed, AppleTalk is rarely the port of preference for serious **imaging** or **desktop applications**.

Application is a program designed to accomplish certain tasks, such as **word processing, desktop publishing, image editing,** or **databases**. It differs from **system** software, which are designed to service everything to do with a computer's **operating system**, and from **utilities** software, which are programs devised as tools to assist in the smooth operations of the computer or the running of an application program.

Application error is one of the most dreaded messages that can flash on your computer screen. It occurs when something goes wrong within the program you are running, causing it to fail. At that point, the program must be closed and reopened, or in some instances, the computer must be shut down and restarted. Application errors usually occur when the programming code of a particular application conflicts with other code running in the background (the **operating system**, a **device driver**, etc.). The computer does not know how to resolve these overlapping codes, so it shuts down and freezes.

Apply image is a command that allows **channel** information from one **image** (the **source document**) to be applied to another (the **target document**). It's a **channel operations** command for compositing information from two or more channels (or pictures) together into a single channel (or picture).

APS (Advanced Photo System) is a film-based camera system that was introduced in 1996 to compete with the growing market in amateur **filmless cameras**. It uses 24mm film, which is much smaller than the traditional 35mm. However, the quality of the film is brighter, with finer grain. And the cameras are set up so that the user can choose, at will, between three different picture sizes: 4×6, 5×6 (for wide angles) or 3.6×10 inches (for panoramas). There are other advances and new developments related to APS, but what is important to digital imagers is its easier integration with the computer.

Arbitrary Rotate is a command in which the user specifies the **angle of rotation** in a **dialog box**. It is invoked by typing in a number between 0 and 359.9 degrees and indicating whether the rotation is clockwise or counterclockwise. This is in opposition to **free rotate**, in which the user **interactively** turns the selected item or area by pushing on the corners of a **bounding box** or **selection handles**, which surround that object.   SEE **Angle of rotation** illustration.

Arbitrary Map is a **gamma curve** option that allows the user to edit the curve by just pushing points on the curve in whatever direction. This can create some bizarre and interesting effects or other more subtle ones—depending

Arbitrary map: Though the *gamma* of a picture usually functions and is edited as a curve, an arbitrary edit (which here in Corel PhotoPAINT is called *free hand*) allows the user to pull at individual points on the curve and move them in any direction on the graph. This can create some unusual and bizarre effects. But in the hands of an experienced imager, it can also be used for very subtle changes to the picture.

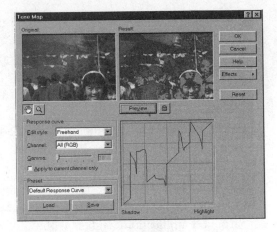

on the degree of editing. As the curve changes, so will the colors or tones in the image.

Arc is a **vector** draw tool that creates an open curve. The arc usually looks like an incomplete circle or ellipse, but it may actually be any curved shape that has **endpoints**. It is also called an **open path**.

Arc tool is a **vector drawing tool** that can create portions of circles or ellipses.

Architecture, when used in a computer context, refers to the particular design of a computer, its components, or even its software. For example, you will read about **motherboard** architecture, **bus** architecture, **firmware** architecture, etc. **Open architecture** is the term that describes specific hardware or software whose manufacturer has published technical specifications that allow **third-party** companies to develop and market **add-on boards** or **plug-in** programs that will improve performance or extend the capabilities of their product. When an imaging program uses open architecture for its **filter** plug-ins, then a wider variety of special effects available from various manufacturers can be used with that program. Many **bitmap** or image editing programs conform to Photoshop-compatible open architecture

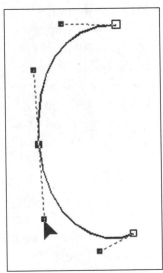

Arc: In some *draw* programs, there is a specific *primitive* tool for creating arcs. Others use *Bezier* or *spline* curve tools (such as pictured here) for the purpose.

for their plug-ins, which means they can use filters sold by MetaCreations, Xaos and other companies.

Archival, as the name implies, refers to the permanent, safe storage of images and documents, usually in the form of files. Archival files are usually saved to **removable storage media** like **SyQuest** or **Jaz** cartridges, or **tape drives** like **DAT** or **QIC** formats.

Various problems are associated with archiving files. One is fidelity, or the accuracy of the **data**. This generally is not a problem with true **digital** devices, but it can be with **analog** recording devices like QIC tape, in which the media can stretch or shrink, and the recording level can affect the play-back quality. Another problem is permanency, or how long will a file last before the media begin disintegrating and will experience data dropouts. Tape is said to have a useful life of 1–5 years only. **Floppy disks** and traditional magnetic media are said to have a useful life of 5–10 years. **Magneto-optical** (MO) and **CD-ROM discs** are said to have a useful life of 10–100 years.

Access speed and convenience are considerations when archiving. Tape is **discrete**, which means it moves in only two directions, so it must be wound or rewound to the specific area where the required data are, a process that can take several minutes, depending on the device, the length of the tape, etc. Disks and discs are **random access** devices that can quickly locate data within seconds or even **milliseconds**.

Another consideration is cost. At the time of this writing, tape is the cheapest archival storage, with CD-ROMs coming in next, MOs being more expensive, and removable drives costing even more. To determine the cost of media so that you can compare the different technologies, calculate the per **megabyte** cost.

Area composition is a **desktop publishing** term for positioning text and **images** onto a **page** that will be reproduced mechanically or electronically to make a **plate** for a printing press.

Array cameras or **array backs** are **filmless** devices that use a superimposed array or sandwich of red, green and blue filters to capture color pictures. Most real-time **filmless cameras** are array-type devices.

Arrowhead is a pointer symbol that shows where your cursor is on the monitor.

In **illustration** programs, arrowheads are types of lines that may be drawn and customized.

Also, in desktop publishing, it's a typographical symbol.

Depending on the **application program** being used, an arrowhead's size, shape, color and direction usually can be modified.

Artifact refers to unwanted lines, dots, splotches and specks in images that appear during scans or other image editing processes. Producing some artifacts is almost unavoidable, but better equipment and more optimized software can greatly reduce the number and severity of artifacts.

Ascender describes lowercase letters that rise above the height of other letters. The letters *b, d, f, h, k, l* and *t* all have ascenders. The opposite of ascender is **descender**: *g, j, p, q* and *y* all have descenders. Most desktop publishing programs automatically adjust for ascenders and descenders, though they have command options for adjusting line height to make the ascenders and descenders look good while staying within a set format.

Arrowhead: In many circumstances the location of your *cursor* on the computer screen is indicated by an arrowhead. (In some programs, you can set your cursor to look like the tool that is being used, or like a circle that represents the size of that brush.)

ASCII is short for American Standard Code for Information Interchange and refers to the universal codes for the most commonly used printable letters, numbers and punctuation, as well as certain control codes. For instance, the ASCII decimal code for capital *T* is *116,* for small *t, 74.* ASCII is also called *text mode,* since this is the format in which many character-based messages are transmitted via **modem**. Because it is very slow and cumbersome by modern standards, the ASCII format is never used to store or transmit graphics.

Aspect ratio is the relationship of height to width. For instance, a single frame of 35mm film is approximately 1×1.5 inches, and therefore has an aspect ratio of 1:1.5.

Aspect ratio is frequently used in image editing programs when the user is changing the file size but wishes to retain the same proportions. When you don't constrain image size changes to the original aspect ratio, your picture may look stretched or squashed, as though it's being viewed through a funhouse mirror.

Aspect ratio is also an important consideration when printing an image. Maintaining the aspect ratio of 35mm's 1:1.5 when output on a device

ASPECT RATIO A

ASPECT RATIO B

Aspect ratio: When the original proportions of the height and width of a picture aren't maintained during an enlargement or reduction in the size of the picture, you can end up with distortions. Notice how the very slim model **(A)** can be made to look as though she had more flesh on her **(B)** by ignoring the rules of aspect ratio. Similarly, a baseball can be made to look like a flat flying saucer, or a skyscraper can be made to look less soaring and more squat. In just about all Image Resize dialogs, there is some manner of locking in the aspect ratio, to assure that it isn't changed.

capable of printing onto 8.5 × 11 inch paper means that part of the image will be **clipped**, or cut off, or printed at a relatively smaller size.

Asynchronous refers to a specific method used to move or transmit information. As its name implies, the data are moved irregularly, according to the accompanying bits that are used to start and stop the flow.

Asynchronous Transfer Mode, or ATM, is a relatively new high-speed data transfer protocol for networks. It has the capability of moving data faster than **token-ring** and **Ethernet** network protocols. It has absolutely nothing to do with **Adobe's ATM**, which is a utility for managing typefaces, nor with the bank ATMs that dispense money if your account isn't overdrawn.

ATM SEE **Adobe Type Manager** or **Asynchronous Transfer Mode**.

Attribute has two distinct meanings. In the computer world, attribute refers to the characteristics assigned to a specific file, i.e., date created, if it is a **read-only** file, etc.

In the graphics world, it refers to the condition of a font, i.e., bold, italicized, etc.

And, then, in general, the attributes of any item, picture, object, etc., refer to those options and/or details that are associated with and/or attached to it.

Audiovisual is an almost obsolete term used to describe the simultaneous presentation of visual and audio information, such as a movie clip with sound. In the computer world, audiovisual has been replaced by the term **multimedia**.

Authoring is the process of developing tools or applications that can be used to create programs or data. It's more than just programming; it's the creative design of tools that will then influence the creative use of computer code. Most users are not involved in the programming level of authoring but can use higher level (less complicated) authoring tools to develop **CD-ROM**s, **multimedia** presentations, and so forth.

Auto- When the prefix auto is used in any **image editing, desktop publishing** or **illustration** program, it generally means that a specific task—such as making a **mask**, filling in colors, adjusting **levels**—is left to the software and the computer rather than done manually by the user. Auto functions are generally easier and faster than manual adjustments, but may not do exactly what is desired (such as drawing an accurate outline around a particular object). After all, computers are just dumb machines and can't make the kind of creative or illogical decisions at which human beings excel.

AutoCAD is a high end drawing **CAD/CAM** program geared primarily toward scientific/engineering/medical users who need precision in creating **models, renderings**, schematics and other computer-generated illustrations.

Autodesk is a company that markets relatively expensive **CAD/CAM, multimedia** and **3-D modeling** programs for artists and illustrators who need or prefer complexity and precision.

Auto erase is a command that some programs have in which the user is able to delete or remove areas or objects and replace them with either a user- or program-defined object, color or area. For instance, in **Photoshop**, the user can remove an area of color and replace it with the **background** or **foreground** color.

Auto levels is an automatic adjustment to **levels** or **histograms** that some programs provide. Essentially, it evens out the percentage of **pixels** that are dark to those that are light, and those that are midtone. It creates an even balance between contrast and brightness that may or may not be appropriate to an image. For instance, if you have a photograph of a sunset, using auto levels can sometimes make it look as though it were taken at noon. Still, it is a very quick and useful method for adjusting many over or underexposed pictures.

Auxiliary storage is an infrequently used phrase that has been commonly replaced by the term **external storage devices**. These are self-powered boxes that plug into the computer and provide additional permanent data storage. Among the most commonly used external storage devices are **external hard drives, CD-ROM drives, MO** (magneto-optional) **drives, SyQuests, Bernoullis, DAT drives**, etc.

AVI is short for Audio Visual Interleaved and is a **Windows multimedia** file format. AVI files contain visual data that are combined with audio data, producing animations that may include music, spoken words or sound effects.

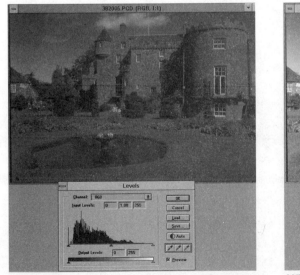

AUTO LEVELS A

AUTO LEVELS B

Auto Levels: The original picture **(A)** has a *histogram* that shows a lack of highlights and shadows. (Notice that there are no spikes in the graph at either far end.) Using the Auto Level command **(B)** redistributes the pixels from the brightest possible highlight to the darkest shadow, so that there are pixels representing all levels of light. *(Photo from the Corel Stock Photo Library. A Corel stock image.)*

Background, as its name implies, refers to the image or document that is inactive, in the background. No changes can be made to it unless and until it is brought to the **foreground** or made **active**, which is usually done by clicking anywhere in the image or document window.

Background also denotes that some calculation, save, load, print or other function is being performed automatically while you are working on something else.

In fact, background can mean several things, depending on the word that comes after it—as in **background layer** and **background program**. Usually, it refers to things happening on the computer which the user cannot directly affect, unless whatever is in the background is somehow brought to the **foreground**.

Background color is the underlying user-selected color that covers the screen

Background: All of the pictures opened up here in *Photoshop*—except the Portrait of the little girl—are background pictures, *images* or *windows*. That is because only one image can be *active* or in the *foreground* at any one time, and that is the picture that can be edited. The *title bar* of the foreground picture (which is white here and says *Portrait.JPG*) is almost always a different color than the background ones (which are all gray in this example). To bring a background image to the foreground, just *click* on it, or choose it from the Windows *pulldown menu* at the top of the screen.

when in **DOS, Windows**, or **System 7.x** or **8.x**. It is usually selected from among 8, 16 or 256 different colors.

The background color in an imaging program also refers to that color which may fill an empty **canvas** or the color that will be revealed when you use the **eraser** tool. It may be changed by clicking on the square of color that represents the background color and choosing from the color palette, which, in a **24-bit color** program has **16.7 million colors**.

Background layer is the bottom **layer** in picture files that are made up of layers. For instance, in a picture of a dog flying through the sky, the background would probably be the sky. In some programs, the background layer can be edited by turning it into the active layer, simply by clicking on it in the **layer palette** (which keeps track of all the layers in a picture). In other programs, the only way to edit a background layer is to copy it to another layer (usually the one directly above the background), or to create a new empty background layer, which would make the old background a normal (editable) layer.

Background printing occurs when a program spools or dumps data to the printer, or to a hardware or software **buffer** in such a way that control of the computer quickly returns to the user. Most operating systems and many application programs allow the user to set preferences that will permit background printing. There's usually a small price for being able to print in the background: reduced speed. The computer must periodically interrupt what you are doing in the foreground to process information in the background, and this can momentarily slow things down. But the faster your **CPU** and the more **RAM** your system has, the less noticeable that slow-down will be.

Background color: The current *foreground* and *background* colors are often represented by two overlapping colors in this manner. Here, the white square is the background color, and the black is the foreground. In most cases, you can choose another color by just clicking on the square, which then opens up a *palette* from which to choose the new color. To revert to the default black and white, in some programs, you simply click on the tiny black and white squares that are, here, pictured below the foreground and background squares. And, if the software has a double-headed arrow, as this one does, click on it to reverse the foreground and background colors.

Background program is any program, utility or driver that automatically runs in the background. This ability to run a program in the background is referred to as **multitasking**, or the ability to do more than one task simultaneously. For instance, you could have a **Photoshop filter** running in the background while accessing the **Internet** in the foreground.

Backslash, in DOS, is the "\" character used to separate subdirectories or folders. For instance, the command to change to another directory is CD\, and a subdirectory in **Photoshop** used to store templates might be written C:\photoshp\templates.

It is also used on the **Web**, in **Internet** addresses.

But, in imaging, backslashes are somewhat archaic since most PC programs are **Windows**-based and don't use backslashes as part of the command nomenclature, and Macs don't use them at all.

Backspace is the key on PC keyboards that moves the cursor one space left. It is most frequently used for deleting the last character typed. The **delete** key on the Mac keyboard acts like the backspace key, unlike the PC delete which erases the next character rather than the last one.

Backup is the process of making an accurate, mirror copy of an entire file, image, folder, subdirectory or drive. Backups are generally used for security against a file, image, etc., being accidentally deleted, corrupted, overwritten or altered from its original state. Usually, backups are made to **removable devices** or **media**, such as **DAT tape, QIC tape, MOs, CDs, SyQuest cartridges** or **Zip** or **Jaz cartridges**.

Some programs make automatic backups of files when you edit and save them. Often, the **file extension** for these duplicate, interim files is .bak.

Bad block is an error message that occurs at **POST** (Power-On Self-Test), or computer startup. It refers to a specific block or **address** of **RAM**, or Random Access Memory, that is faulty or defective and cannot be used or accessed. While the message denotes a problem, most computers can automatically isolate, or map out, bad blocks (assuming there aren't too many of them) so that they won't be used. The best solution for bad blocks is to replace the errant memory chip or board.

Bad sector is an **operating system** error message that refers to a specific section of a disk drive that, for one reason or another, is bad and therefore unusable. If you have data stored on a previously good section that is suddenly reported bad, you may be able to recover some or all of that data by using a disk fix **utility**, such as Norton Utilities or MacTools. **Windows** and **System 7.x** and **8.x** come with utilities that can identify, isolate and lockout bad sectors so they can't be used. Nearly all hard drives have some small areas that are bad, but it's usually such a small percentage of the space that, once it is locked out, it doesn't affect your use of the drive.

.bak   SEE **Backup**.

Balloon help is a cartoonish bubble that contains short definitions or information about commands, tools and other on-screen items. When turned on, it appears on the screen when a user points with his or her mouse to something on the screen. It is **context sensitive** and can be turned on or off.

Banding is an undesirable side effect of an imperfectly **rendered gradient**. In layman's language, banding occurs when a **continuous tone** in an illustration or a photograph—such as the gradual and seamless transition from white to gray, or blue to green—doesn't print out or display on the screen as a continuous sweep. Instead, it appears as bars of colors with very distinct borders between them. This usually occurs because of highly technical problems with the applications program software, the printer, or the file format. Or, it may be caused by not specifying enough levels of transition (or **steps**) when defining the gradient or its printout.

BANDING A

BANDING C

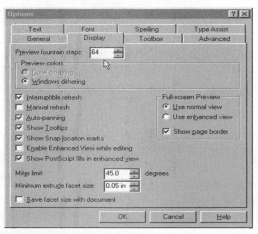

BANDING B

Banding: The first picture **(A)** shows significant banding, though the colors are meant to be a smooth *gradient* from white to black. But by increasing the number of fountain steps (or transitions between the colors) in the Corel-DRAW preferences **(B)**, the same picture no longer exhibits banding **(C)**.

BARREL DISTORTION A

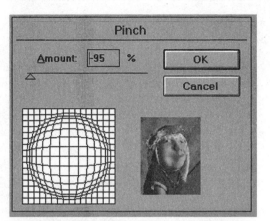

BARREL DISTORTION B

Barrel distortion: Barrel distortion is achieved using any of a number of different filters. Here, a negative setting of Photoshop's Pinch filter **(B)** turns this photo of a pretty girl **(A)** into a barrel distortion fun house-type of photo **(C)**.

BARREL DISTORTION C

Barrel distortion is a photographic term that describes the slight to moderate barreling, or expansion, at the center of an image that occurs when that image is reversed by an improperly designed or ground lens. It's like a funhouse mirror that makes you look round at the waist. Although usually an unwanted effect, some image editing programs feature a specific tool for creating and controlling barrel distortion effects.

Base alignment arranges a row of text on the same horizontal line, regardless of the letters' relative sizes or other characteristics.

Base font, also referred to as the **default** font, is the typeface automatically selected when a particular program loads in.

Base alignment: While the lower "aqua" (for water) is aligned normally, the upper one has all the letters aligned to a base line. That means that the *descender* (or tail) of the lower-case *q* is raised to fit the same alignment as those letters that don't have descenders. Be careful of base alignment, if any of your words have *p, q, y* or *g* in them—unless you are making a graphic design choice to have uneven placement of letters.

Baseline is the line, usually imaginary (though sometimes it is an actual line), on which type rests. It is also the point from which **ascenders** (letters with raised tails, such as *d, t, l*) or **descenders** (letters with tails that fall below the line, such as *g, p, q*) will rise or fall.

Batch file is a single file that, when activated, loads in several or a series of files or programs. Batch files, which either come as part of an applications program or can be created by the user, are convenient and time saving, since you don't have to manually open up each file. For example, a batch file could be set up that loads in **application** programs like **CorelDRAW8!** or **Fractal Design Paint**, and then a half-dozen image files that you are currently working on. Or, you may use a batch file to connect to your **e-mail** server (such as CompuServe or America Online), get and send all your mail, and disconnect—much more quickly and less expensively than doing it step-by-step, yourself.

Baud, or baud rate, is a measure of the speed with which one computer or peripheral (usually a **modem**, but sometimes a **filmless camera**) communicates with another computer or peripheral. Specifically, it refers to the number of data bits per second (**bps**) that are transferred. Most modems transmit at 28.8, 33.6 or 56K (the *K* is short for kilobytes) bps. Special high-speed **serial ports**, modems and filmless cameras can transmit data as fast as 500K. The important thing about working with baud rates is that the two computers or devices communicating with each other do so at the same speed. By the way, baud is named after the French inventor of the Baudot telegraph, J.M. Emile Baudot.

BBS is the acronym for Bulletin Board Service. A BBS is a computer attached to a **modem** or modems, and one or more telephone lines, which is equipped to automatically answer and interact with modem calls from outsiders. Many manufacturers and vendors maintain BBSs to give automated technical support; transmit **drivers, utilities, patches** and other software; take sales orders; and take messages from the caller. However, many BBSs are being replaced by Internet websites, which are faster, easier to maintain and can handle far greater traffic.

Behind mode paints or edits a **transparency** layer so that it appears that whatever color or effect you are applying is painted on the back of the transparency. It's the electronic equivalent of painting on the reverse side of glass or clear plastic.

Benchmark is a standard by which hardware and software performance is measured. Benchmarking is the process of establishing performance specs based on established standards. Testing labs will measure a computer's or peripheral's performance relative to a benchmark of standards that the lab or the industry has established.

Bernoulli drive is a removable storage device from a company called Iomega. Similar to a **Winchester**-type hard drive, the head (the component that reads and writes data) floats on a column of air (commonly called the Bernoulli effect, after the Swiss mathematician Jacques Bernoulli) over flexible disks encased in plastic cartridges. Bernoulli cartridges can store between 5 and 230 megabytes, and are often used by **service bureaus** as alternatives to the similar, but more ubiquitous, **SyQuest** drives and cartridges. Though used in the same manner, Bernoulli and SyQuest cartridges are not interchangeable, and each requires its own kind of drive to read and write data. Iomega's most popular drives, the **Zip** and the **Jaz,** are less expensive, higher density cartridges that have made Bernoullis all but obsolete.

Beta software refers to prerelease, not quite finished versions of commercial programs that are sent to users and reviewers for testing. The advantage to the user is the opportunity to try out software, for free, in working conditions, before it is commonly available. Often, beta testers are solicited for comments, criticisms and suggestions, giving them the opportunity to directly influence additions and improvements. The disadvantage is that most beta programs contain major bugs, or errors, that could cause the system to crash, or data to be lost. Beta testers are also required to keep a log of events and issue some sort of report on their experiences with the software, which can be tedious and time consuming.

By the way, alpha software is even more preliminary, and it is seldom available to anyone outside the development team. That is as it should be, because it is the buggiest and most problematic software of any. No one in his or her right mind would want to mess up their systems with alpha software, unless their jobs depended on it.

Bezier tool, also sometimes called the **pen tool** or **polygon tool**, is a precise method for controlling the rate and direction of an irregularly shaped curve of a line that is being drawn or traced. You create a Bezier curve by defining **anchor points** (places where the line starts, stops or changes), and then you manipulate them by pushing or pulling the points (or the tangent control lines that can be pulled out from them) with a mouse or stylus. At each point where the line curves, **control points** or **nodes** define the angle and sweep of the curve. It's the computer equivalent of a graphic artist's French curve. While the Bezier sounds complicated, it is a very precise drawing tool that is not difficult to master.   SEE **Spline, End nodes, Handles.**

Bicubic interpolation is a tool for **interpolating** or increasing the number or density of **pixels** (data) in an image. Interpolation is frequently used to increase file size, thereby boosting the dimensions and/or the **resolution** at which the image is printed out or otherwise **output**.

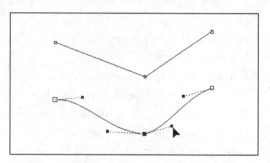

Bezier: In this illustration, both the upper and lower curves were created by a Bezier or pen tool and are defined by three points. In fact, the lower curve was actually created by duplicating the upper one. But in editing the lower curve, we pulled out the controls (the dotted lines) to force the lines between the nodes to follow a specific sweep that is defined by those tangential controls. The farther we pull the dotted line, the deeper the angle of the curve. The direction that we pull them sets the direction of the curve. Therefore, in a Bezier curve, the data associated with each node (or control point—and this example has three of them) defines how the lines between the nodes will behave. That information includes not only the position of the node, but also how you set the tangential controls for angle and direction of the line as it leaves the node. As it begins to approach the next node, the information associated with the second point will also affect the direction, sweep and angle of the line.

There are various methods of interpolating. Bicubic interpolation tends to produce the best, most precise interpolated images, though it is relatively slow. **Bilinear interpolation** is faster, but not as accurate. The fastest but least precise method used within commercial image editing programs is **Nearest Neighbor** interpolation. There are other types of interpolation, but they are usually found in high end programs or independent stand-alone programs.

As a rule, interpolated data is not as accurate as original data, which means that an image file that has been interpolated to boost its size may not be as sharp or well focused as one that was originally that size.

Bidirectional printer used to refer to **dot matrix, inkjet** or **daisywheel** printers in which the print head created letters or images with each backward and forward sweep.

Today, however, a bidirectional printer is a device that has the necessary circuitry for connecting it to a computer's bidirectional **port** by a special cable. That allows information to go in both directions along that connection—to and from the printer and the computer.

Big Blue is a colloquial expression for IBM and IBM products, such as "this computer was designed and manufactured by Big Blue."

Bilevel is a black and white **line art** scan with no grayscale or colors involved. It interprets **image** data strictly in **binary** form— that is, as zeros or ones, which are displayed as pure white and black.

Bilinear interpolation SEE **Bicubic interpolation**.

Binary are data that a computer understands— interpreted into zeros and ones. Actually, the computer can't handle any other kinds of information. It is able to process complex material only because it can go through so very many zeros and ones in such a short time. Therefore, any **data** (including **image** data) must first be converted to binary (or **digital**), before they can be assessed, manipulated, edited, opened, saved, etc., by a computer.

Bilevel: Scanning a photograph such as this one **(A)**, using a Bilevel setting, results in a black and white picture **(B)**, which has no grays or gradations of color. It is the same as *line art. (A Corel stock photo from the Corel Stock Photo Library.)*

BILEVEL A

BILEVEL B

Another definition for binary is one of the two most common ways of transmitting data over a **modem**: Binary is used for image and program files, while **ASCII** is often used for transmitting simple text files.

BIOS is short for Basic In/Out System. It's the instructions that the computer receives, usually from a chip on the **motherboard**, that informs it how the system is configured and what is directly attached—hard drives, floppy drives, keyboard, graphics type, etc. On PCs, the BIOS may be programmed or changed by the user, though it is usually configured at the factory or by the vendor. There's a special low powered **CMOS** memory chip that stores the system configuration and is protected for years by either an external battery clip that plugs into the motherboard, or by a battery soldered onto the motherboard. If you ever lose BIOS information and preference—i.e., if the computer won't boot because it can't find an attached hard drive—you probably need to replace the battery protecting the data on the **CMOS** chip.

Bisynchronous is a communications **protocol** used by devices such as a **modem** or printer in which both the sender and receiver must be absolutely synchronized before any data transmission can occur. The opposite of bisynchronous is **asynchronous**, in which the sender and receiver do not have to be synchronized before communications may commence.

Bit is sometimes used as an interchangeable word for **pixel** (picture element), which is a single dot of color and other image information that, when combined with thousands or millions of other dots, make up an image.

Actually, the bit is the smallest element that the computer can recognize and use. Short for *binary digit*, bits exist in two states: zeros or ones (or on/off, or plus/minus). When eight bits are combined, they form a unit called a **byte**. In math, a bit (with two possible states) arranged as a byte (eight positions) equals 2 to the 8th power, or 256 possible combinations. Those 256 combinations, to a computer, define different characters, numbers, command codes, etc. But the single bit is the basic building block.

Bit depth, also referred to as **bit resolution**, specifically refers to the number of bits that are used to represent black and white, **grayscale**, and/or colors in an image that can be displayed or printed.

1-bit depth can carry only a single bit of information about the image, so, ipso facto, it is either all black or all white.

8-bit depth (2 to the 8th power) means there are **256** possible combinations of either grayscale or color.

16-bit depth (2 to the 16th power) represents 65,536 possible color combinations.

And **24-bit** depth translates into approximately **16.7 million** different colors. Since the human eye is capable of distinguishing roughly 12–14 million different color shades and hues, 24-bit color depth most closely represents what we actually see in nature. That's why 24-bit color is also called **photorealistic** color or true color. Often, 24-bit color is referred to as 8-bits per color channel—that is, 8 bits for each primary color of red, green and blue.

In professional image editing, often files and devices capable of bit depths greater than 24 are used, such as 30-bit **scanners** or 48-bit **filmless cameras**. This raises the number of possible color combinations to the billions—far more than any output device (printer, **film recorder, imagesetter**, etc.) could reproduce. The purpose of this added bit depth is so that the software can select the best 8-bit per color channel set (which the computer can handle) for the finest possible color reproduction.

Bitmap is, literally, a map of all the bits (also referred to as dots or **pixels**) in an **image editing** or **paint program** file. Each individual pixel is assigned a specific location, **bit depth**, or characteristic (color, brightness and shades of gray). Thousands or millions of bitmapped pixels collectively comprise a single image.

Some programs also call a **1-bit** image a **bitmap image**, which can cause some confusion.　SEE **Bitmap display, Bitmapped files, Bitmapped images**.

Bitmap display is how each **bit**, dot or **pixel** is represented on the computer screen or monitor. Optimally, one dot on the image is directly translated into a single dot on the screen. But because **bitmapped files** may have a far higher **resolution** than the monitor is capable of displaying, the image on the screen may either be reduced in size, or only a segment or **window** of the image can be viewed at any one time. That's why, when one loads in a large bitmapped file, the initial image that comes up on the screen may be only a portion of the entire image. (The **zoom** or **magnification** tool may then be used to display the entire image.)

Bitmapped files formats, such as **TIFF, BMP, GIF** and **PICT**, are those that record each **pixel**, or dot, that specifically defines a **bitmapped** image. Because each individual pixel is mapped out, bitmapped files tend to be far larger in size than nonphotographic **vector** or **object-oriented** files (which are defined by mathematical formulas, or shapes, and not by specifically placed pixels).

Bitmapped fonts are fonts or typefaces in which each character is made up of many individual dots. In the era before **PostScript** equipped or compatible printers, bitmapped fonts were very common because they could be output by most types of desktop printers. However, each font took up lots of hard drive storage space, and print quality was marred by a phenomenon known as "**jaggies**" (the tendency for angled and curved lines to have a staircase-like look rather than a smooth line because of the square shape of the printer dots). So, bitmap fonts fell into disfavor when **vector** (mathematically defined) fonts became available and affordable. (Vector fonts use **anti-aliasing algorithms**, or software programming tricks, to virtually eliminate the jaggies.)

Bitmapped images are pictures or photographs made up of thousands or millions of **pixels**. Each element of the picture is a predefined dot that may be edited or changed globally (everything simultaneously), or pixel by pixel.

The number of pixels in a bitmapped image is called **resolution**. For instance, if there are 300 pixels per inch in a particular image, it is said to have a resolution of 300 ppi (pixels per inch).   SEE **Bitmapped files formats, Bitmap**.

Bitmapped programs are those **applications** that can open, edit, save and **output bitmapped images**. These include **image editing programs**, such as **Photoshop, PhotoDeluxe** and **Picture Publisher**, and **paint programs**, such as **Fractal Design Painter**.

Bit rate is the speed at which data are transferred, typically by a **modem**. SEE **Baud rate**.

Bit resolution is another way of expressing the number of **bits** per color channel. Photorealistic bit resolution is **256 colors** per **color channel**, which, when blended together (256 red × 256 green × 256 blue = 16.7 million colors), produce 24-bit **true color**. Another term for bit resolution is **depth resolution**.   SEE **Bit depth**.

Black body is an option in some image editing programs' **color tables**, which keeps track of replacement colors when a **24-bit image** (which has **16.7 million colors**) is reduced to only **256 colors**. The Black body option replaces the image's colors with those that mimic the stages of color changes as temperature rises in black objects to which heat is applied. For instance, a cool black body begins as black, and then, as heat is applied, it turns to red, orange, yellow and finally white hot. Other color table options include

Adaptive (which tries to **map** the replacement colors as closely to the original ones as it can) and **System** (which uses the 256 colors inherent in the computer's system software). SEE **CLUT**.

Black generation is the technical term printers use when they determine how much black must be added to the ink mix when the colors displayed on the monitor—Red, Green and Blue (**RGB**)—are translated into the cyan, magenta, yellow and black (**CMYK**) inks that are used by desktop printers and commercial printing presses. Theoretically, there should be a direct conversion from RGB to CMY, since they are opposites on the **color wheel**. However, in the real world of dyes, inks, toners and pigments, the RGB/ CMY conversion is less than perfect. To compensate for this, printers must add black ink to produce more accurate, crisper dark tones. That's the K (blacK) in CMYK. How much is added, and how, is called *black generation*. There are two methods of black generation: **undercolor removal** (**UCR**) and **gray component replacement** (**GCR**). Which one is more appropriate depends on the kind of paper the image is being printed on, the inks and the specific requirements of the printing press operator.

Blackletter is any **sans serif typeface** that is squared off on the top and the bottom.

Black matrix describes a **monitor** picture tube in which a black stripe is placed around the color phosphors to enhance the picture image.

Black matte is an option in image editing programs that allows the picture, selection or mask to be displayed against a black background. This makes the colors appear brighter and livelier. Its opposite is **white matte**. However, a neutral gray matte and background is generally preferred for realistic color display.

Black point is an **eyedropper** tool with which the user can identify the **pixel** that should be the darkest in the picture. Like its counterpart, the **white point** tool, it is a quick fix for adjusting imperfectly exposed photographs or for changing the **dynamic range**, or contrast, of an image. However, if users click on the wrong pixel, it can destroy image data. For instance, suppose they click on a dark gray pixel with the black point tool. Then, all pixels that are exactly the same lightness, and all other pixels from that point of lightness to the darkest in the picture, will be turned to pure black.

Blackout is the total loss of electrical power. Since computers need a continuous stream of electricity to operate, a blackout, even of a fraction of a second duration, can be catastrophic: The computer will instantly freeze, and whatever work you had open and not saved will be lost. There are two

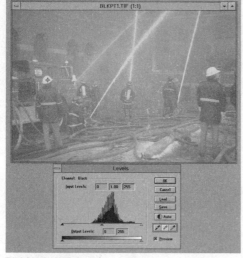

BLACK POINT A

BLACK POINT B

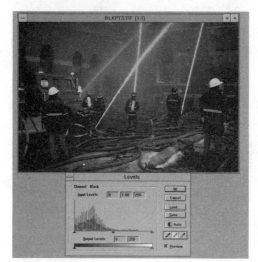

BLACK POINT C

Black point: The black point eyedropper can be found in several dialogs, depending on the software. In these examples, it is the left-hand eyedropper in the group of three, under the Auto button in Photoshop's Levels (or *histogram*) dialog. (The white point tool is the farthest right of the three.)

The first picture **(A)** is not well exposed. As you can see in the histogram, it is missing *pixels* in the *shadows* and *highlights*.

By clicking on the black point tool and then clicking in the darkest area of the picture that we could find (we do use the *Info* palette to assist us in our search for the right pixel), the picture can be made to look better exposed. But for our purposes, to create an even better photograph **(B)**, we also used the white point tool on the brightest point we could find in the picture. Note how the histogram now shows pixels in all areas of shadow, highlight and midtone.

But the black point and white point tools are very powerful. Be careful where you click with them. In the third picture **(C)**, we used the black point tool on a darkish area, rather than a darkest point. The result is a photograph that is too dark, with too many of the pixels turned to black, and all detail in the shadows lost.

important strategies to prevent data loss and work interruption due to black-out: frequent **backup** and attaching either an **SPS** or **UPS** battery to your system. Unfortunately, even the best **surge suppressor** or **line stabilizer** cannot counteract the effects of a blackout, although they are very useful in protecting your equipment and data during **brownouts**.

Bleed means extending text, photographs or illustrations to, or even beyond, the edges of the **page**, without showing any borders or **white space**. A partial bleed has 1, 2 or 3 edges that appear to run off the page, and a full bleed has no borders showing. Bleeds are used for visual and aesthetic effect. Full or partial bleeds may be obtained on some desktop printers by using a slightly smaller paper size than the printer expects to find. The other way to make a bleed is to use a paper cutter to trim off the white edges.

Bleed is also a variable option for certain image editing software brushes. When bleed is turned on, the color will blur beyond the edge of the brush, as though it were wet paint being applied to a textured paper (as with real world watercolor).

Bleeding occurs when the colors in an image run or leak outside their boundaries, something like crayoning outside the lines of a coloring book. It's either the byproduct of a glitch in the software or sometimes a malfunctioning graphics board, or it is a paint-brush option that can be turned on or off.

Blend has several meanings.

In **bitmap** or image editing programs, blend may be a **smudge** tool that produces a fingerpaint effect by smearing areas of colors together.

Blend may also be the name a program gives to its **gradient** tool or command, which creates a transition from one color to another in a seamless, gradual manner.

In a **vector, object-oriented** or **draw** program, Blend is a command that creates a multistepped transition between two shapes, so that they, in effect, **morph** into each other.

Blend mode is an option for **paintbrush, layer, channel operations** or other methods of laying down color onto a picture in **bitmapped** or **image editing** programs.

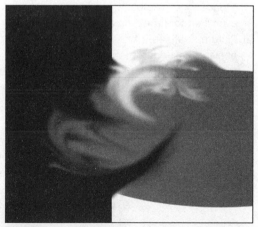

BLEND A

Blend: Using a *bitmapped* program's Blend or Smear tool **(A)**, we were able to smudge the colors between this rectangle and ellipse, in the same manner as if we were fingerpainting with the colors.

BLEND B

Blend: In *vector*-based *draw* programs **(B)**, you can create a blend or *morph* between two shapes. This example shows the initial two shapes—a rectangle and an ellipse. In the center is a 20-*step* blend between the two, in which the rectangle slowly reshapes itself and darkens its color, until it

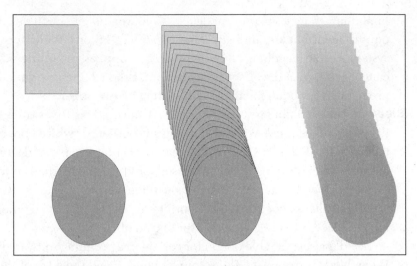

approaches and reaches the ellipse. And, on the right, is an example of what happens when you remove the outline of the original objects, before starting the blend—you can end up with an apparently seamless *gradient* between the starting and ending colors and shapes.

Blend mode: The blend mode options can usually be found wherever the tools that you are using are located. For instance, in Picture Publisher **(A)**, they are in a pulldown list in the ribbon bar above the work area, where other options for the active tool are found. And in Photoshop **(B)**, the blend mode options are in the brush palette (as pictured here) or in a similar pulldown list in the *Layers* palette. (See also color plates 2 and 3.)

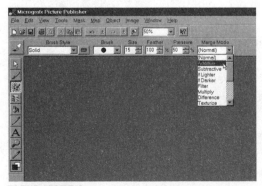

BLEND MODE A

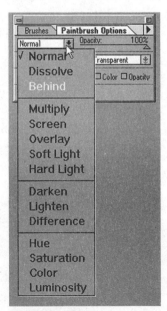

BLEND MODE B

By choosing among various blend modes, such as **darker, lighter, color** or **screen**, the user is telling the program how the pixels of the upper color or layer will combine with those of the lower color or layer. For instance, choosing the **color** (or **color only**) blend mode will result in the color of the upper layer (and not the **luminance, shadows, highlights** or substance) being laid on top of the lower layer. These are also known as **pixel value manipulations** or by the command **blend if**.   SEE color plates 2 and 3.

Block is a chunk of text or **pixels** in an image that is marked off and can be deleted, moved or altered by the user.

It's also a unit of data communicated in **binary** form over a **modem**.

Blockiness is an unwanted **artifact**, or the square representation of **pixels**, that sometimes appears in image files. Blockiness has any number of causes: random generation of the blocks of color by the input device, a too low resolution for the size of the display, too much compression/decompression leading to **data** degradation, and so forth.

Block move is the act of moving a block of text or a portion of an image from one location to another.

Blooming is an unwanted effect that can occur to a malfunctioning **monitor**, in which turning up the brightness also causes whatever is being displayed to expand in size. It also refers to an unwanted effect in digital photography when a **digital camera**'s **CCD** register is full of electrons (overexposed) and spill over into the next color.

Blue screen is a Hollywood-type special effects technique which photographs, films or tapes an object against a blue background. Then the blue is electronically removed and replaced with another scene. Even when another color is used (such as green, yellow or white—any color that does not occur in the outline or, sometimes, in the entire subject being photographed), the process is still often called *blue screen*.

It allows the user to quickly and easily **mask** the subject by defining a color range (i.e., the blue of the background), and then place the subject into any background desired. That's how Superman could be made to look as though he were flying through the Metropolis skyline. First, he was photographed in a studio. Then, using a blue screen–type technique, the studio background (including the cables that were holding him up) was removed, and the previously photographed skyline was put in its place.

Blue screening can be emulated by just about all **image editing programs** that have a **magic wand** or **color wand selection** or **masking** tool. Another version of the same technique is sometimes called *chroma key*.

Blur refers to a series of filters or tools that soften or blur the edges or areas of an image. It has the effect of reducing detail. In addition, a type of blur filter is used by some software to minimize or eliminate **noise**, scratches, dust, dirt and other unwanted artifacts on scanned-in images.   SEE **Gaussian blur, Motion blur** or **Radial blur**.

Blur More is a filter in which the degree of the blur effect can be increased by a specific increment.

Blur/sharpen is a tool that allows either blurring (softening edges to reduce detail) or sharpening (increasing clarity of edges for greater detail). It reduces detail by decreasing the **contrast** between edge-defining **pixels**, or enhances detail by increasing the contrast between pixels. In many programs that have blur and sharpen tools, the two opposites are controlled by the same **dialog** and/or **nested** into the same group of **icons**.

BMP is short for BitMaP, a **24-bit** Windows graphics file format. While not as hearty or versatile as the more commonly used **TIFF** file format, it has the advantage of being **device independent**. That means it can be easily printed out in almost any relevant program or by any printer without problems or prior conversions.

BNC, short for British Naval Connector, is a bayonet-type **coaxial** connector that extends from a computer's graphics board to the **monitor**. It differs from standard graphics cables in that the primary colors—red, green and blue—are assigned separate leads that connect to the monitor. Some BNC connectors also have separate connectors (for a total of 5 connectors) for the horizontal and the vertical hold. Supposedly, a BNC cable carries a stronger, better signal than a standard graphics cable, which translates into a more accurate color display on the monitor.

Board is the term used to describe the flat, thin square epoxy or fibreglass panel to which circuits, chips, resistors, capacitors and other parts and elements are plugged in, soldered on or otherwise attached. A board may be a device, such as an **expansion board, modem, graphics board, controller** or **accelerator**. The com-

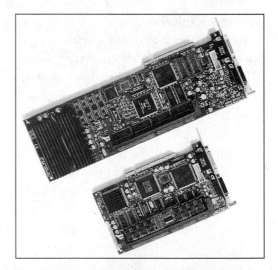

Board: There are any number of boards used in computers. Pictured here are a couple of Apple PC compatibility cards, which means, when one is plugged into an Apple, it can run Windows programs.

puter's main board is called the **mother-board**.

Boilerplate refers to any graphic or text that is repeated over and over again, such as the masthead of a magazine, a fancy company logo, the company motto or the first page design of a newsletter.

In databases, mailing lists, spreadsheets, etc., it is a **field** where a list of information, such as names and addresses, are automatically merged into a preset format.

Bomb is another word for **crash**, which means that the computer has frozen or the program running has ceased working. On the Mac, the bomb is an icon that appears when the user has an unrecoverable crash.

Boot, or **Boot up,** is the act of starting up a computer, program or file. It comes from the early days of computing, when a self-starting computer was said to be boot strapped, which was a takeoff of the colloquial "pulling yourself up by your own bootstraps."

Border refers to a stripe, lining, box, bezel, frame, etc., that surrounds or emcompasses an image and that draws attention to the image. Many borders consist of a solid ¼-inch white stripe or **margin** that surrounds an image, though borders may be of any size or color and may be decorative (such as ivy leaves or geometric shapes). Think of a border as a sort of picture **frame** or mat. In fact, in **imaging programs**, it is possible to create the illusion of a double or triple mat by laying borders or frames one on top of the other.

Bounding box is a user-drawn or tool-created rectangle that selects an area of an image to be edited, trimmed, sized or changed.

Border: Borders are often used to set pictures, much as a cut mat is used when framing a photograph. In fact, creative borders can be quite effective in replacing expensive double and triple mats. *(A Corel stock photo from the Corel Stock Photo Library.)*

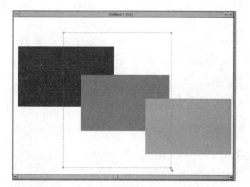

Bounding box: When we used the crop tool on this picture, it created the dotted lines around the area to which we plan to cut. Those dotted lines are a bounding box. Before double-clicking the crop tool inside the bounding box (to set the cut), we can pull on any of the four corner squares to reshape the box. Similar bounding boxes are used for rotation, perspective and other tools.

Tools that use bounding boxes include **resize, trim, rotate** and others. Bounding boxes usually have **handles** that can be **interactively** pushed or pulled to change the area, **size, orientation** or shape. The change (trim, rotation, resize and such) becomes set when the **mouse** or **stylus** is clicked within the box. There is often also a **dialog box** for defining precise changes by inputting numbers.

bps SEE **Baud rate**.

Break apart is a **vector** command that separates objects into their component shapes. For instance, a box is made up of a rectangle and lines forming two parallelograms. When that box is broken apart, the user can move and otherwise edit each of those three component objects independently.

Bridge is a device used in **networking**, or in connecting computers together, specifically in **LAN**, or Local Area Network systems, such as **Ethernet** or **token-ring**.

Brightness is the amount of light that is reflected from an object or an image, or transmitted from a source of light, to the viewer. But in a practical sense, it has to do with the visual impact of a picture. If it is bright as opposed to dark, there is more light in it than shadow. The brighter the picture, the more visible the detail. That is, unless an image is too bright, in which case all detail is washed out, as in a white fog. You will encounter Brightness in many software commands that affect the exposure of photographs or the relative level of light in any picture.

Brightness is also a fundamental component or property of color. For instance, in the **HSB color model**, color is defined by three components: brightness (the lightness or darkness), **hue** (the actual shade or wavelength of color), and **saturation** (the amount, strength, or **chroma** of color).

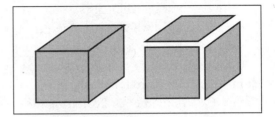

Break apart: This box can be edited as a single, *solid* object. But, after using the break apart command on it, the three component parallelograms that made up the box are independent objects and can be edited separately.

Brightness: As can be seen in this color palette that is using an *HSB color model*, brightness (B) is an important component of color. If the brightness were set at a lower number, the color would be a darker version of the same magenta, with the same *hue* and *saturation*. And, similarly, a higher brightness value would have created a lighter version of the same color.

Other color models include **RGB** (red/green/blue), which is used for transmitted light such as you see on a computer monitor; **CMYK** (cyan/magenta/yellow/blacK), which generally relates to pigments, dyes or inks that printers use on paper; and **L*a*b**, a model that attempts to define consistent color standards regardless of what device (printer or monitor) is being used. SEE **Color management, Dynamic range, Gamma curve**.

Brightness/contrast is a command in some graphics programs used to adjust the **tonal range** or **dynamic range** of a picture. Because of the direct rela-

Brightness/contrast: As can be seen from this series of pictures, brightness is the measure of light in a picture, and contrast is the measure of difference between the *highlights* and *shadows*. Therefore, when brightness is reduced, the overall amount of light is lowered. But when contrast is lowered, it decreases both light and shadows. Similarly, an increase in brightness casts light into both the highlights and shadows—potentially washing out the shadows. But an increase in contrast increases the values of both highlights and shadows. Quite often, the ideal setting for this dialog involves setting both the contrast and the brightness, to offset and complement each other.

tion of brightness to contrast, the two should usually be adjusted relative to one another to achieve optimum image quality.

The Brightness/contrast command is not the same as a **histogram**, which is the graphical representation of the relation between brightness and contrast in a picture, as well as a statistical analysis of how many pixels in the picture fall where within the continuum between the darkest and lightest points.

Brownout, also called a dip or power dip, occurs when the electrical power to your computer is momentarily reduced. Brownouts, when combined with **power peaks** or **spikes**, are called *dirty power* and can be very harmful to your computer. It may even cause your computer to freeze, in which case any unsaved data would be lost. That's because the most sensitive parts of a computer react to very tiny power fluctuations and can be damaged or even destroyed with prolonged repetitions. In fact, experts estimate that up to 90% of all computer problems are caused or exacerbated by dirty power.

Brownouts can occur anytime—indeed, it's estimated that in some areas, over 100 mini-brownouts occur each hour—and last from a few milliseconds to an hour. They're caused by a number of local conditions, usually by turning on a refrigerator, air conditioner or some other appliance. But the most serious brownouts happen outside, such as when the electric company goes on or off the national grid, or even during very hot days when the regional power draw is enormous and the electric company reduces the voltage to prevent a system-wide power failure.

Most computers' power supplies have capacitors that can deal with many brownouts—usually, the bigger the power supply, the larger the capacitor. However, the best way to prevent the ravages of brownout is to buy a good (expensive) **surge suppressor** or, better yet, a **line conditioner** or **UPS**. Inexpensive units either can't help with severe brownouts, or wear out within a few months and cease to offer any real protection.

Browser is a type of program that allows the user to browse, or navigate, though streams of information. Browsers are most commonly used in **hypertext** (unstructured databases) programs and, of course, the **Internet**.

Some **imaging** programs call certain types of **palettes** or **dialog boxes** browsers, specifically those in which the user may browse through and choose among options related to picture elements, commands and/or tools.

Brushes are software tools that turn your **mouse** or **stylus** into a painting tool, so that you can stroke color onto your picture. In some programs, there are only a few options related to the brush (such as size, and hard or soft edge).

Other software provide a wide range of options that may include levels of opacity/transparency, number and spread of bristles, unusual and/or user-defined shapes, amount of bleed, **natural media emulation**, etc.

Brush options is the command and/or **dialog box** for controlling the size, shape and **attributes** of creating, defining and selecting **brushes**.

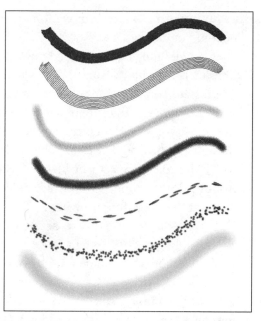

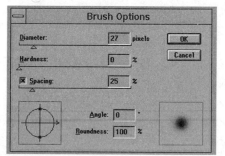

BRUSH OPTIONS A

Brushes: Depending on how the brush options are set, a single brush stroke can create widely different effects.

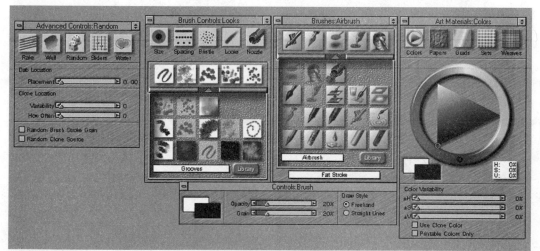

BRUSH OPTIONS B

Brush options: (A) Most programs offer more limited brush options than Painter, such as in this Photoshop dialog. **(B)** Fractal Design Painter has some of the most varied and variable brush options of all *image editing programs.*

Brushes pallette is a type of **toolbox** or **dialog box** that may contain (depending on the program you are using) all the commands and options for creating, defining and selecting **brushes**.

Bubblejet is a printer technology in which heated droplets of ink from tiny nozzles are sprayed onto paper creating the appearance of solid, seamless images or type. On most bubblejet printers, if you put a magnifying glass on the paper, you would see that, in reality, the printer has created that illusion by spraying tiny dots of color. This is unlike **dye sublimation** printers in which the colors are actually blended. Bubblejets are also commonly called **inkjet** printers (though technically, inkjets are different because they may not heat the ink before spraying).

Buffer is a dedicated **hardware** or **software memory** reservoir designed to appreciably speed up certain processes or functions. It holds a space open within memory that can be used by your computer when it is running software. In some programs, software buffers may be adjusted to balance speed gain with memory capacity. While generally beneficial in boosting performance, sometimes buffers can actually slow things down or even cause computers to behave erratically. Turning them off (if possible), flushing (emptying) them or changing their size usually eliminates any problems. A type of buffer is the **scratch disk**, which is an area of **RAM** or hard drive space used to temporarily hold **image data** that is being edited or processed.

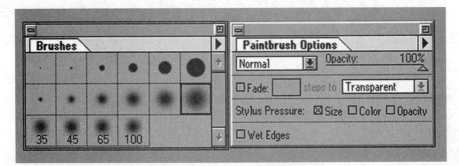

Brush palette: The brush palette is the area in the program where the user chooses the size and behavior of the brush, much as a traditional painter chooses a color from a paint palette. As you can see in these brush palettes from Photoshop (which are usually nested together), the palette is different from the *brush options*, in that the palette uses already defined brushes. The options *dialogs* allow the user to define new brushes. (However, some programs may use these names in different ways.)

Build refers to the specific version of **alpha** or **beta** software. For instance, a reviewer or a participating artist testing an important program may receive Build 125 on Tuesday and Build 126 on Friday. It's the way the manufacturer and the user keep track of exactly which version is currently installed.

Bullet is a graphic arts term for any symbol or icon placed before a line or block of text to visually draw attention to it and set it apart. Bullets are commonly used in multimedia presentations to set related lists apart from the rest of the image, page or slide.

The following is a bullet list:
- ♦ It visually sets a mood.
- ♦ It makes it easier for the viewer to absorb related information.
- ♦ It breaks up the printed page.

Bullet: The diamonds at the beginning of each point in this list are the bullets. But bullets can be any graphic, including a company logo, a face, a pencil, or whatever.

Bump map is a representation of **texture** that some **image editing, illustration** and **3-D** programs can use to affect the way light, paint and images lay down onto the surface. In other words, if your program allows you to use bump maps, you could possibly create the effect of a painting on burlap, or a photograph processed on burnished metal. This is done by creating "bumps" or 3-dimensional surfaces on which light or paint is reflected. The same effect may be created using some programs' **alpha channels**, which control how color and light may be applied to the **image**.

Bundling is the marketing strategy of adding free or greatly discounted software to the purchase of a piece of hardware (though it's sometimes the reverse—adding free hardware when you buy a particular program). It's an incentive to entice you to buy the company's product. For example, **image editing** and **OCR** programs are frequently bundled with **flatbed scanners**, and **communications programs** with **fax/modem** boards. Sometimes the bundled software is a **lite**, or scaled-down version of a program. In that case, there may be a special offer coupon in the box for upgrading to the full version.

Burn or **Burn in** is a photographic term carried over to **image editing**. Burning is the act of increasing **exposure** to a very light or overexposed area (such as a subject in direct sunlight) to squeeze out more detail or contrast.

The burn tool is often clustered with two other tools: its opposite, the **dodge** tool, which is used to hold back light from dark or shadowed areas to bring out details that would be otherwise lost; and the **sponge** tool, which is used to increase or decrease color saturation. These three may be **nested icons** in the program's toolbox and/or options in the same tool **dialog box**.

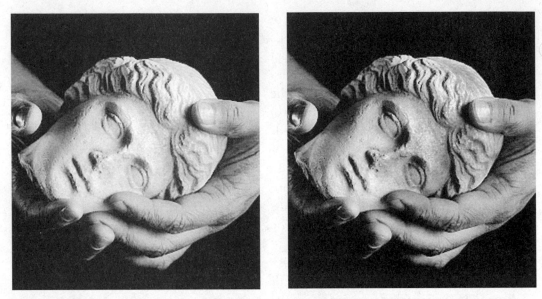

Burn: By using the Burn tool in the same manner as a brush, we were able to selectively paint areas of this overexposed picture with shadow, built up from the hidden details within the picture itself. Wherever the brush strokes, that area is darkened, while leaving the rest of the image as it was.

Burn in is also a computer term applied to the initial testing of new **hardware**. Since most electronic components either fail during their first 24–72 hours or will last for many years without problems, many manufacturers or retailers subject their products to 24-, 48- or 72-hour burn-in periods of continuous running.

Another definition of *burn-in* refers to the tendency for a bright image to become permanently etched on a monitor, if left on too long. Burn in was, until several years ago, such a serious problem that **screen savers** were developed to avoid having the same image on screen for more than a few minutes. Although most modern monitors incorporate special phosphors that resist burn in, it's still a good policy to use a screen saver, turn the brightness down, or even turn off the monitor for extended periods of inactivity.

Burst mode sets a camera for taking a rapid sequence or series of pictures, one right after another. Burst mode is usually invoked for capturing a live action subject, such as a child running or an athlete catching a ball. A camera's burst mode is rated by how many pictures it can capture in a set time—such as 4 pictures in 2 seconds, which is expressed as 2 **fps** (frames per second).

Depending on the camera, the burst mode is either fixed (such as 2.5 fps) or can be adjusted (such as between 1 shot every 30 seconds and 10 fps).

Film cameras can shoot continuously in the burst mode until the camera either runs out of film or the batteries die. With digital cameras, once the initial burst mode is shot, there is usually a wait of 5–10 seconds, or longer, before you can take another burst of shots. That wait is caused by the time it takes to convert the currently captured images from **analog** to **digital** data, and then save them to the camera's internal **storage device**. Not all cameras have a burst mode, and not all burst modes are equal.

Bus describes the **architecture** or design of a computer **board**. Its origin is, as it sounds, taken from the function of a city bus, which has a set route and picks up and drops off passengers along the way. Similarly, a computer bus moves **data** from one point to another. You'll often hear the type of computer **motherboard** described as a bus, such as an **AT** bus or **PCI** bus.

Byte is a unit of measure of computerized information or data. Eight **bits** make a byte, in the same way that 12 inches make a foot. Similarly, 1,024 bytes equal 1 **kilobyte** (k), 1,024 kilobytes equal 1 **megabyte** (MB), and 1,024 megabytes equal 1 **gigabyte** (GB). (Most people use the figure 1,000 rather than 1,024, because it is easier to say.) You'll see these units in descriptions of file or image sizes, storage capacity of drives and other situations in which a measure of data volume is involved.

Cable modem is a device that will allow cable television companies to carry **data** signals. Its advantage is speed: It can send large **image** files far faster than current analog **modems** and even **ISDN** modems. Reportedly, a 1-**megabyte** file can be transferred in under 15 seconds; by comparison, it takes about 7 minutes to upload the same file with a standard 14.4 modem. Cable modems are just being developed, and it may be some time before they are offered by most cable companies and generally accepted everywhere.

Cache is an area of **memory** that is set aside as a holding area for often accessed or last accessed **data**. Caches can be hardware (special high speed memory chips or a small board) or software (a permanent or temporary **swap file** set up by the operating system or application program). The reason for using a cache whenever possible is better performance. Everything will run faster when your computer has frequently used **data** instantly ready in a high speed caching area instead of having to find it over and over again on a much slower **hard drive**.

Cactus was a company that made a large, expensive 4-color floor model inkjet printer capable of producing large near-photoquality banners, prints and murals. Cactus prints can be up to 55 inches wide and 100 feet long; and, while the output quality is excellent, Cactus printers can't produce true continuous tone, photoquality prints like those which can be run off on an **Iris** printer.

CAD, short for Computer Assisted Design, is often expressed as **CAD/CAM** (Computer Assisted Design/Computer Assisted Manufacturing). CAD and

CAD/CAM software are usually high powered, heavy-duty design and graphics programs used primarily by engineers, scientists, architects and other design professionals for the purpose of creating highly precise schematics, blueprints, **3-D renderings** and technical drawings. CAD programs differ from standard illustration and image editing software in function, tools, higher price, and the more extensive computer resources it needs to operate.

CAD/CAM SEE **CAD**.

CalComp tablet is Lockheed's brand name for a line of **drawing tablets**, or **digitizers**. It uses either a **stylus** or a **puck**, instead of a **mouse**, to navigate around the computer screen. SEE **Wacom**.

Calculations is a command option in some

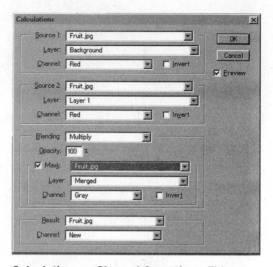

Calculations or **Channel Operations:** This Calculations dialog (from Adobe Photoshop) shows how you can control the way channels will combine or otherwise interact.

image editing programs in which a variety of different types of mathematical calculations or **channel operations** are performed on the **pixels** in two or more **channels** or pictures. For example, Calculations may be used to duplicate exactly all or some of the information (**masks** and **layers**) contained in one channel to the other channel, and then compare it to the original without having to invoke the **Save As** command. It may also be used to apply channel information from one document to another document. The calculations command can limit which pixels are transferred, copied or applied, by specifying mathematical or range criteria or **blend mode**s.

Calibration is the act of tweaking or fine-tuning the colors of a printer, **scanner**, monitor, **plotter** or other device so that it matches or most closely approximates an ideal, a standard or the optimum color of another device or established printed or electronic **swatch** (a color or **grayscale** graphic). For instance, one would calibrate a monitor so that the colors displayed are the same or nearly the same as the colors output by a particular desktop color printer.

Calibrations bar is a **grayscale** and/or color graphic that a user can print out along the side, top or bottom of a test. The calibration bar, or test pattern, provides information that can then be read by a **calibrator** or **densitometer** to adjust it relative to the monitor or another **output device**. Or, the user can study the visual information and use it to make color adjustments to a system, albeit in a less precise manner than when a densitometer is used.

Calibration target is the name given to a print or transparency that is used as a standard for calibrating one device relative to another, such as a scanner with a printer. It usually consists of a **calibrations bar, color wheel** or **test pattern**, and may include commonly used subjects, such as a face to judge skin tone. Calibration targets may be provided by the scanner or printer manufacturer, your **service bureau**, or it may be one that users generate themselves from a desktop printer or **film recorder**.

Calibrator is a device that measures color and light on a monitor, printer, scanner, etc. It then feeds that information back to the computer and its **graphics board** to make corrections and adjustments. Most calibrators are, in reality, **densitometers** that measure the density, wavelength and intensity of a light source. A monitor calibrator is plugged into a serial port or a dedicated port on certain graphics boards, and the sensor head is attached to the **calibration target** on the monitor with a suction cup.

Calibrators can also be handheld devices that look like **handheld scanners**, or small boxes that sit on the desktop that have fixed or movable probes that read selected areas of prints, **color swatches**, calibration targets, etc.

Callout is a notation attached to an object that identifies it or draws attention to it. It usually has a line pointing to the object with text on the other end describing it or referring the viewer to another bit of text.

Some illustration programs have callout tools that will attach a callout to an object. When the object is moved, the callout will move with it.

Camera ready is a **prepress** holdover term from the presilicon era that refers to any finished drawing, illustration, photograph or page layout that is ready to be shot by a copy camera to make a plate or plates that can then be used to print on an offset press.

The term is also used to describe top-quality printed output, such as a high resolution laser printer, i.e., a printer that produces camera ready quality. That means that the output from that desktop device is so good that it can be used as the original for a printing plate.

Canvas is the same electronically as it is physically—the area on which an image is created.

Canvas is also the name of an illustration program marketed by Deneba.

Canvas Size, as a command, could more accurately be called Canvas *Resize*, because it allows the user to change the size of the background canvas, without affecting the size of the picture that is displayed within that area.

Caption refers to the title, subtitle or line(s) of explanatory text placed under, above or near an image or illustration.

In those software **drivers** or **image databases** that display **thumbnails** (small representations of pictures that are stored on your **hard drive**, in **removable media** or on a **filmless camera**), captions are lines of information supplied by you or by your hardware that provide data about the picture and its origins.

Card SEE **Board**.

Cartridge usually refers to a **removable storage** device that contains **data**. It plugs or inserts into a **drive** and acts as a **floppy drive, hard drive** or other type of storage device. There are a number of different cartridges—**MO** (**magneto-optical**), **SyQuest, Zip, Jaz, tape**, etc.—each of which works only with the devices designed to accommodate those types of cartridges.

A cartridge may also refer to a self-contained module of ink, pigment or toner that is inserted into a printer. A cartridge may be a small module containing **read-only memory** (**ROM**) instructions that plugs into high end imaging devices, such as **film recorder**s or **imagesetter**s.

Case sensitive refers to those computer commands or searches that must be input with the correct upper- or lowercase letter to work. For instance, typing in *image file #41* may not work, whereas *Image File #41* or *IMAGE FILE #41* will.

CCD is an acronym for **Charge Coupled Device**, a photosensitive semiconductor chip that is used in **scanners, camcorders** and **filmless cameras** to capture images. It is somewhat analogous to film in that light through a lens registers **image** information on the CCD. But unlike film, CCDs have neither the ability to record or preserve image data, nor the capability to accumulate light saturation (for time exposures). All image data are immediately offloaded to an analog-to-digital convertor, a signal processor, then to some sort of storage device, such as **memory** chips or cards, or a hard or floppy drive. CCDs range in size and shape from a pea (about one-fifth of an inch) to a 2×2 inch square. Generally, the larger and denser the CCD, the better the quality of image it can capture, the greater the density of **data** and the larger the image file size. SEE **CMOS**.

CCITT is the commonly used abbreviation for the Comite Consultatif Internationale de Telegraphique et Telephonique or, in English, the International Telephone and Telegraph Consultive Committee. It's the organization that develops, adopts and promulgates communications standards, most notably, the technical specifications and protocols for **modems**.

You may encounter CCITT protocols when buying a high-speed or **ISDN** modem for sending or receiving **data** files to and from **service bureaus**, clients, associates, the **Internet** and other communication purposes.

CD, also known as compact discs or **CD-ROMs** (Compact Disc-Read Only Memory), are high density 2.5-, 3.5- or 4.75-inch plastic discs that hold up to 680 **megabytes** of **data**. Their exceptional high density makes them a popular method for storing huge amounts of data, such as photoquality **images, clip art** or **fonts**. They're also used for **installing** new programs, since making CDs in quantity is less expensive than copying software to many **floppy** diskettes (which was previously the traditional installation method). Although they're recorded and played back differently, the same CDs used in computers can also carry music, video and animation.

At present, most CDs are **read-only** discs that cannot be changed or rewritten to in any way. However, the latest generation of **CD Recorders** (**CD-R**) and CD Writers (CD-RW) can read or write to specially formatted CDs, either once or many times. While current CDs are limited to about 680 megabytes of data, or 74 minutes of playing time, the newest recording technology—DVD—makes it possible to record up to 6 gigabytes of data on the same disc.

CD-I is a **multimedia CD-ROM** format developed by Philips. It is used primarily for **interactive** participation, such as in training sessions.

CD-R   SEE **CD-Recorder**.

CD Recorder (CD-R or **CD Writer)** is a drive capable of not only reading but also writing to **compact discs** (**CDs** or **CD-ROMs**). Most CD recorders are **WORM** (Write Once, Read Many) drives that permanently burn data into the plastic disc, which cannot be erased, changed or overwritten. But CD-RWs can record over and over again, just like a **hard drive**.

CD-ROM   SEE **CD**.

CD-ROM drive is an internal or external playback device that connects to the computer's **SCSI** or **IDE** port that reads 3.5- or 4.75-inch **CD**s. Unlike a **CD Recorder**, which can both read and write to CDs, CD-ROM drives are **read-only** devices and cannot write to or in any way change the data on the CD. CD-ROM drives are rated according to speed: 2X, 16X and 24X—the larger the number, the faster the drive. Almost all drives sold today are capable of playing Kodak's **Photo CD**, music, and multimedia CD formats, though drives made before 1993 may not be compatible and therefore incapable of reading these newer formats.

CD Writer   SEE **CD-Recorder**.

Cel animation is a throwback to the Hollywood era, when animated cartoons were produced by painting individual **frames** on clear acetate, called *cels*. Sometimes, digital animators and **animation programs** will still refer to frames or, more rarely, to **layers**, as cels.

Central processing unit or **CPU** (also known as the *processor*), is the "brains" of any computer. It is the semiconductor chip that controls everything the computer does or attaches to. **Intel, Motorola** and other companies design and manufacture CPUs that often define the computer. For instance, Intel's **Pentium** CPUs are always PCs. Motorola/Apple/IBM's **PowerPC** CPU is the heart of Apple's current line of computers. **Alpha** is the name of Digital's **RISC**-type CPUs used in its high powered computers. Besides the name, CPUs are usually rated according to speed: 150 MHz, 233 MHz, 300 MHz, etc.—the larger the number, the faster the processor.

At present, most computers are powered by a single CPU, but the newest, fastest generation of systems often incorporate dual, quad or more CPUs. While that seems as if it might significantly boost speed, multiple CPUs can assist only if the software is properly **optimized** to take advantage of that configuration. And at that, the speed increase is usually incremental—doubling the number of processors will not double your speed.

Centronics is the name given to a specific type of connector, mostly for PC **parallel** printers. Sometimes, you'll see it written as Centronics parallel port or cable.

CGI, short for Computer Graphics Interface, is a graphics standard or language used by printers, monitors, etc.

CGM stands for Computer Graphics Metafile, an **image file format**. While primarily for **vector** graphics, it can contain bitmapped information.

Channel is information about an **image** that relates to specific types of **data** within that image. Depending on the program, there may be a dozen or more channels that can be used and/or saved concurrently. However, most **image editing** programs limit the number of channels that you save for any single picture. To put it more simply, channels are one of the ways in which software organize, separate and combine picture data.

For instance, the **RGB** color channels visually and digitally describe the color information that is displayed on a computer monitor, separating out the red into the red channel, the green into the green channel, the blue into the blue channel. **CMYK** color channels are often used to create **color separation** files, in which each color channel defines how color ink (Cyan,

Magenta, Yellow and BlacK) should be laid down on the paper by the printing press.

On the other hand, an **alpha channel** may be used to **mask** the picture and thereby limit the software's access to those areas of the picture that you wish to edit. An alpha channel may also be used as a **bump map**, to define how a **texture** is laid down on a picture, an **object** or an area of an **image**.

Channel operations is a method of image editing in which, by choosing specific parameters, a user may define how **pixels**, or points of data within a picture or between pictures, combine. For instance, if you have a black & white photograph on your computer screen and you paint with a red color, the normal result is that the red pixels being laid down would replace the **grayscale** pixels where you paint. But in some programs, you can set **parameters**, such as **Color Only, Darken Only, Lighten Only, Dissolve** or **Multiply**. So, if you are painting with the red color onto your black & white picture and you set the channel operation at Color Only, the red color will overlay the grayscale pixels, replacing the gray, black & white colors, but not the **contrast** or other values. The result is a red-tinted photograph. Channel operations are very creative tools that are particular to computerized art. SEE **Pixel value manipulations, Blend modes** and **Calculations**.

Channels palette is a **box** or **dialog** which displays information about the **channels** of a picture. It may also provide options for viewing, editing and manipulating those channels.

Character refers to a single letter, number or punctuation symbol. Examples of characters are A, 5, ; and ↺. All standard characters, including upper- and lowercase letters, numbers, punctuation and even some symbols, can be expressed in a common computer code called **ASCII**.

Character set refers to a family of letters, numbers or punctuation symbols. For instance, if all the letters or numbers in a document happen to be composed of Helvetica type, it is said to be a Helvetica character set.

Charge Coupled Device SEE **CCD**.

Checkerboard pattern refers to a user-selectable design of large, medium or small alternating squares that can be displayed in the background (or bottom) **layer** of a picture, when that layer is empty (has no picture data). The visual information of seeing that checkerboard is much more valuable to the user than the typical default value of displaying white when there is no data, because white emptiness can be confused with white **pixels**. The checkerboard will continue to show through other superimposed layers that have empty or translucent areas.

Chooser is the section on Apple's operating system that allows users to select a printer or other device, as well as the type of network. It is found by clicking on the Apple icon and pulling down to Chooser.

Chroma is the technical term used for **color saturation**, or a color's degree of purity.

Chromalin is the name for Du Pont's process for producing color **match prints**.

Chrome is a generic term for any color transparency film, such as **Ektachrome, Cibachrome** or **Kodachrome**.

It is also the type of film used to produce slides as opposed to prints.

CHRP, pronounced chirp.   SEE **PPCP**.

Cibachrome is the name for Ilford's high quality, silver-based photographic prints. In many photographic quarters, Cibachrome is the standard against which all other photoquality prints, especially **dye sublimation** prints, are compared.

CIE is the Commission Internationale de l'Eclairage, an international organization responsible for developing and promulgating color systems and standards.

CIE is also a **color model** occasionally used by graphics programs, which includes the color spaces of both the **RGB** and the **CMYK** color models. SEE **LAB**.

CIE L*a*b   SEE **LAB**.

Circle tool is a **vector** drawing tool with which users may create perfect circles. Typically, it is used by clicking on one point (which users may be able to select to be a point on the circumference or the center point of the circle) and dragging out. As users drag, the growing circle is displayed, so that they may judge when to release the **mouse** or **stylus** button. In some programs, the numerical and/or *x/y* size of the circle that is being drawn may be shown in a **status bar** at the top or at the bottom of the **workspace**, so that users may draw precisely sized circles.

Often, the circle tool is an option of the **ellipse tool**—usually selectable by using a **constraining** key (such as **Shift** or **Control**) with the ellipse tool.

CISC stands for Complex Instruction Set Computing and refers to those **CPU**s, or **microprocessors** (the "brain" of every computer), in which most of the code needed to run the system is built into the chip. This contrasts to **RISC**, or Reduced Instruction Set Computing, in which some or much of the code is software based. There is fierce debate over the superiority of CISC over RISC, and vice versa, and here are the points that fuel one camp or the other:

- CISC chips are inherently slower.
- RISC chips are less complex.
- CISC chips can execute more internal instructions, therefore requiring less software code.
- RISC chips are less expensive to produce.
- CISC chips may have less speed, but they have greater raw power.
- Intel's CISC chips are much more mainstream—about 80% of all computers use them.
- RISC chips, while gaining in popularity, are found in less than 10% of all computers.

IBM, Motorola and Apple's newest generation of computers use RISC chips, while Intel, NewGen and AMD use faster, high powered CISC chips. Which one you may wish to have in your computer is far less important than the software that you wish to run.

Clear is another term for **delete**, or to eliminate an image, an area of an image, a file, etc.

Clear also denotes when the user purges a **command** or commands, or resets the computer or the program to the state before any work or changes were made.

Clear mode makes the **pixels** being painted or edited transparent. The clear mode allows pixels from another **layer** to show through the top layer of transparent pixels. The level of transparency/translucency may be **customized** by the user.

Click and **double-click** are common computer commands that instruct the user to push a **mouse, puck** or **stylus** button to initiate a particular sequence or instruction. The double-click requires the user to push the same button twice in rapid succession.

Click and drag is one of the important methods by which a **mouse** or **stylus** interacts with **icons**, commands, tools and other items on the computer monitor. The user clicks the mouse or stylus button down (the left button on a PC, the only button on a Mac) when the cursor is on the item that is to be moved or on a specific point in the picture. Then, while still holding the button down, the user drags the item and/or cursor to a destination point. When the drag is finished and the item and/or cursor is in place, the button is released.   SEE **Circle** for an example of click and drag.

Clip art is any drawing, illustration, photograph, etc., that is contained in and selected from a collection of dozens, hundreds or thousands of commercially available images. Clip art is usually sold as collections contained in books, on **floppy diskettes** or on **CD-ROM**s. It saves the user time, money and energy by providing already drawn or photographed images that may be inserted as elements in a **collage**, or to graphically illustrate a point. However, be sure to read the **license** carefully, to know what you are permitted to do with the clip art; some offer a limited-use license only.

Clipboard is the name for a **RAM**-based memory **cache** that temporarily holds **data** while being copied from one part of a program to another, such as from one **image** to another or from a primary image to its **alpha channel**. Any time you use the **copy** or the **cut** command or icon, the selected data (whether they are part of an image or of a paragraph) are put into the clipboard. Then, when you use the **paste** command or icon, it takes the data from the clipboard and puts them into the currently active picture or document. Only one set of data may occupy the clipboard at any one time. Therefore, when you execute another cut or copy, the new data in the clipboard replace the previous clipboard data.

By the way, the clipboard can be used to copy data from a file in one program to a file in another program. Some programs allow you to disable the **export** clipboard ability of your computer operating system, to help save on computer **resources**. If you won't be copy/cutting and pasting between programs, you might as well allow the export clipboard to be turned off.

Clipping occurs when an **image** is larger than the screen it is being displayed on or the paper it is being printed out on. Since the computer can't always automatically downsize the image (some programs have an option for preventing clipping), a certain percentage of the image won't be seen or printed. Whenever that occurs, the image is said to be clipped, or cut off, or involuntarily **cropped**. The way to prevent clipping is to **resize** the image so that it will fit properly onto the **page**, or to **zoom** out so that it will fit onto the screen.

Clipping group is a **user-defined** group of **layers** in which the **clipping path** of the lowest layer is applied to the other layers in the group. (The background layer, generally, can't be the lowest or the clipping layer, though that depends on the program.) Therefore, the only **image data** that will be displayed from any of the layers in the clipping group would be those that are in the right position—within the clipping path of the lowest layer.

Clipping path is a mask, selection or outline around an area of an image that limits what portion of the image is visible. Clipping paths may be exported with the image, so that the picture, when it appears in another program, is not rectangular (the normal shape of any picture), but irregularly shaped according to the shape of the clipping path.

The clipping path of a **layer** may be made to affect how the **image data** from other layers will be displayed or output, when a **clipping group** is defined.

Think of a clipping path as a stencil or cut-out through which you can view a picture or portions of a picture. In other words, if you cut a hole in the middle of a piece of paper and, then, lay the paper over a picture, the only portion of the picture you would be able to see would be what is visible through the hole. A clipping path is similar to the edge of that hole.

Clockwise spectrum is a command option used to create **gradients**, or continuous color transitions, which use the colors from a standard **color wheel**. When the gradient is defined, rather than making a direct transition from the starting color (say red) to the ending color (such as yellow), the gradient would progress through the spectrum of colors that are intermediate between red and yellow. Since the colors are defined, in this case, as positions on the color wheel, the direction of the gradient is important. That's because different colors exist in the clockwise transition between red and yellow than exist in the **counterclockwise**.

Incidentally, the starting, ending and transition colors may come from any position in the color wheel, which means they may be chosen from lighter or darker **hues**, or more or less **saturations**.

Clone is a tool that allows the user to duplicate exactly one portion of an **image** somewhere else. It is also called the **rubberstamp** tool, since it has the effect of rubber-stamping one area into another. The user sets a source point for the clone tool by clicking with the tool and a modifying key (such as the Shift or the Control key). Then, the next click with the clone tool (with no modifying key) sets the destination. After that, when the user strokes with the clone tool, he or she will actually be painting with the colors, contrast and other elements from the source area.

A clone may be aligned (the source point and the destination point are always the same distance and direction from each other) or unaligned (the initial source point remains the same, at the beginning of each stroke with the clone tool). Incidentally, the source and destination points need not be in the same picture, which means that the clone tool can be used to paint elements of one image onto another.

In some **image editing programs**, the clone tool may also be used with transparency levels, **blend modes, special effects** (such as cloning with the same picture but using something like an **impressionist** stroke), etc.

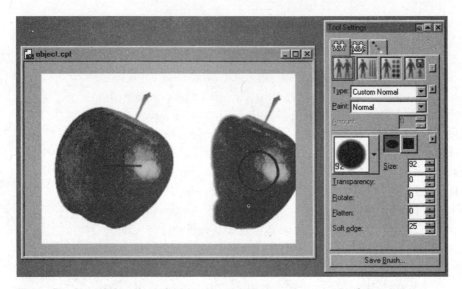

Clone: The X-mark (on the left-side cherry) indicates the source of the clone, and the circle (on the partially painted cherry on the right) shows where the tool is applying the paint it picks up from the source. Some programs offer different options for artistic variations on the clone, as is shown by the pictured dialog from Corel PhotoPAINT.

In the context of a computer system, a clone is a 100% compatible version of a PC or Apple computer.

Cloning is the process of replicating or duplicating a portion of an image in another place or on another image. It is done by using the **clone tool** or the **rubberstamp**.

Closed path refers to a type of line or curve that is formed between **anchor points**, in which there is no fixed beginning or end-points. In other words, the figure being drawn is continuous, i.e., a circle or some other shape that has no beginning or end. Conversely, an **open path** has fixed anchor points, or endpoints; it has a beginning and an end.   SEE **Bezier** and **Spline**.

Clouds filter is a special effect filter in some programs that generates random clouds made up of two colors. Often, it can be adjusted to change the type of cloud pattern.

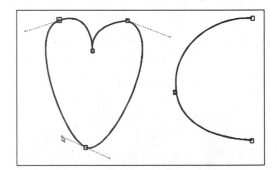

Closed path: The heart is a closed path; the C is an open path. A closed path can be filled with colors, gradients, pictures, etc. But, in most cases, you can't fill an open path.

CLUT, or Color Look-Up Table, is a color reference index used by some graphics programs to convert **24-bit** color files (16.7 million colors) into a lesser number of colors. The reason for this is so that the colors may be represented as accurately as possible on computer systems (such as most color laptops) not physically capable of displaying 24-bit color. SEE **Adaptive Color table, Black body** and **System color table**.

CMOS (Complementary Metal Oxide Semiconductor) is a chip used in a number of computer applications, notably in storing information about a system needed to **bootup** the computer, and as a photosensitive sensor used in entry-level digital cameras. SEE **CCD**.

CMS is Kodak's file format for **Photo CDs**.

CMY SEE **CMYK**.

CMYK stands for the four primary colors of Cyan, Magenta, Yellow and blacK. (*K* is used instead of *B* for black, so as not to confuse it with the Blue of the **RGB color model**.) CMYK are **reflected** or **additive** colors, which are used for inks, pigments, dyes, etc., that are printed onto paper. In contrast, RGB are transmitted, or **subtractive**, colors that are viewed on computer monitors, film slides, etc.

One of the major problems in computer imaging is that CMYK and RGB are not directly translatable to each other. So, when you are working on your monitor, the colors you see are RGB (even if the software says you are working in CMYK **color space**). Then, when you go to print out your picture onto paper (or any other opaque material), the colors are created using the CMYK color model. That's why the colors you see on your computer are quite often not the colors you get when you print out. Billions of dollars are riding on which corporation (or group of corporations) will come up with the reliable answer—the perfect **color management** system. So far, all solutions that are being sold are still just approximations. The majority of digital artists use their common sense, experience and reference printouts to try to control color, rather than depend on the many high-tech schemes. SEE **Color calibration**.

CMYK composites are the four primary printing colors—Cyan, Magenta, Yellow and blacK—layered together to create the entire spectrum of colors.

Coated paper, or coated stock, refers to paper that contains clay to produce a smooth, shiny surface. That's the kind of paper used by slick magazines and expensive coffee table books. Coated paper (instead of common paper) is often used in **inkjet** and **bubblejet** printers when the user wants optimum print quality. However, coated stock paper doesn't feel the same as regular photocopy paper, and some may find it objectionable for regular business use. **Glossy paper** is a highly polished coated paper designed for highest quality photographic reproduction.

Collage is the process by which various **objects**, photographs, **type** and/or other **image elements** are combined into a single picture. The word has roots in the traditional arts, when artists would use knives or scissors to cut up items and glue them together into a composition.

Collage is also the name for the end result—the final picture—that was created by the process of collaging.   SEE **Composite**.

Color balance is a **dialog box** in **image editing programs** that allows the user to control picture colors, according to continuums that range between the complementary colors of cyan and red, magenta and green, and yellow and blue. Usually, depending on which program you are using, these color corrections can be limited to the highlights, shadows or midtones of a picture or a selected area of a picture. If the dialog has a preview button or check mark, it is possible to view the effect of the color-balancing edits as they are done.

Color bar is a long rectangular box filled with a **gradient** of continuous tone colors from which the user may select **background** or **foreground** colors. The Color bar **palette**, or the range of color **hues** on the bar, may be defined or selected by the user.

Color calibration is the method by which the user attempts to coordinate displayed, **scanned** and/or **output** color to each other or to some established standard. The problem is that color is not a universal absolute but changes according to the device being used, whether it is being viewed as **reflected light** or **transmitted light**, the environment in which it is viewed, and even the individual viewer's eyes. The idea behind color calibration is to fine-tune the colors displayed or printed out so that they closely match. Calibration is an important procedure for users who need to closely match computer colors with the colors that will ultimately be output.

There are various calibration methods and devices used. The most precise method is a device called a **densitometer**, which "reads" colors by measuring their density or color wavelength, and then feeds back that

Color balance: The primary colors of red, green, blue (RGB) are the direct opposites (or complements) of cyan, magenta and yellow (CMY). Therefore, increasing the amount of one complementary color decreases the amount of its opposite. That's the idea behind color balance dialogs.

information to the computer monitor, **graphics board**, printer, etc. Another method uses test control strips which the user tries to visually match with what is displayed on the computer monitor or printed out by a desktop printer, **imagesetter** or printing press.

Color casts are usually unwanted, nonrealistic color hues that can appear on a computer monitor or a **halftone** print, which look as if the entire monitor or page has been shot through a very light green, red, magenta, or other color, color filter. Color casts are usually caused by poor **calibration** of the monitor, or nonuniform (random) **dot gain** on a printed page. Most color casts may be removed by calibrating the monitor, or changing the halftone **screen angle**, the printing order of the inks, or the inks themselves.

On the other hand, digital artists sometimes want to introduce a color cast to their images. **Image editing programs** have several tools (such as **color balance** and **hue** control) for adding and controlling picture color casts.

Color channels refer to the individual primary color components of red, green and blue that make up every color image displayed on a computer monitor. Given that every **pixel** (point) in a color image is created by combining varying percentages of red, green and blue, it is possible to isolate each primary color into a separate channel. In many image editing programs, those channels may be altered or combined in precise increments.

Color channels are also very useful in preparing what are called **color separations**, or the color **negatives** that are used to create **impression plates** for a printing press. However, then, the primary colors are cyan, magenta, yellow and black (**CMYK**). Even though some image editing programs may display channels in CMYK, you are still viewing it in an RGB color space for the simple reason that is how monitors display color.

Color conversion is the process of translating the colors that live in the computer (which are based on the **RGB color model**) into the correct colors for ink, paint or pigment (the **CMYK** color model). The latter colors are output by desktop printers, **imagesetters** and printing presses. Many graphics programs have a conversion **applet** built in, but graphics professionals often use more expensive and robust **stand-alone** programs for producing CMYK files and **color separations**.

Color correction is the process of fine-tuning the colors on a computer monitor, desktop printer, **imagesetter, slide printer** or printing press. Unlike **color calibration**, which adjusts the colors according to a standard or a **profile**, color correction is performed on a specific image or image file.

Most graphics programs have numerous tools for correcting color by individually adjusting the specific amounts of red, green and blue (**RGB**), working on the **color balance**, using the **hue, saturation, brightness (HSB)** controls, as well as the **brightness** and **contrast, levels** and **curves**, etc. Often, this can be done automatically, though there is more control by doing it selectively with **sliders** or adjusting the **histogram**.

Color gamut is a system or a **model** (graphic display) of the range of printable colors. Color gamut becomes important because, while the human eye can discern approximately 14 million different colors, the number that realistically can be displayed on an **RGB** computer monitor at any given time is only about 5,000 colors (but out of a **palette** of about 16.7 million different colors). Worse yet, the practical range of colors that can actually be printed by most desktop printers, **imagesetters** or printing presses is between 256 and 1,024. Those figures vary according to the specific inks or pigments, and the type of device being used. For instance, the color gamut of a **Tektronix** Phaser 480 printer will be different than that of an **Apple** StyleWriter 2400, which in turn would be different than if **Pantone** or **Trumatch** color **swatch** is selected. So, the problem is the colors that you see with your eyes will be far more varied than those displayed on a computer monitor, which in turn will be richer than those output onto paper or some other reflective media.   SEE **Gamut, Out of gamut**.

This is where color gamut comes in. It's a method used by many graphics programs to show which colors on the computer monitor can actually be printed by a selected printer or other **output device**. When a color that you see can't be printed, it's said to be **out of gamut**. The color gamut works by automatically highlighting unprintable colors with a **marquee, dancing ants** or a highlight color. The user then has the option of using the color palette to change unprintable colors to printable colors, or to tell the software to make automatic adjustments.

Color halftone filter is an effect that simulates a **halftone** print or a print broken into thousands or millions of tiny colored dots. It works by dividing each **color channel** into tiny rectangles and then replacing those rectangles with circles. To simulate the halftone effect, the size of each circle is proportional to the brightness of each rectangle. However, in some programs the user may adjust the halftone effect by entering a value, in **pixels**, to determine how large each circle may be. It may be further enhanced or fine-tuned by adjusting the **screen angle** of each color channel.

Color list is a reference of all the colors used in a **vector program.** It helps maintain color continuity throughout the production process, providing precise, nonsubjective information (data and names). This may include **spot color** names and numbers, or primary color percentages and numbers. SEE **Color mixing, Pantone, Trumatch, Process color, Spot color**.

Color lookup table SEE **Color palette** and **CLUT**.

Color management refers to schemes, programs, devices, etc., designed to attempt to control and standardize computer color. Essentially, the experience of color is subjective—there is no absolute definition of what, for instance, constitutes red. Is the color you are describing fire engine red, apple cherry red or sunset red? Is the sunset red you see on the computer monitor the same sunset red output on a desktop printer, or the copies that come off a high speed printing press? Various companies have tried to create universal color standards. Kodak, Adobe, Apple, IBM and others formed the Colorsync Consortium, an entity whose sole purpose is to produce a universal color standard. SEE **Color calibration, CMYK, RGB, Color gamut, Color correction** and **Color conversion**.

Color map SEE **Color table**.

Color mixing is done in two different ways.

In some programs, it is the process by which the user selects a color by choosing specific percentages or amounts of each primary color. For instance, in an **RGB** system that measures red, green and blue components in increments between 0 and 255, a particular purple is made up of 140 parts of red, 68 of green and 195 of blue. (That's written as R140, G68, B195.) In a **CMYK** system, in which the mixtures are described as percentages, a similar purple may be made up of 62% cyan, 72% magenta, 0% yellow and 1% black (or C62, M72, Y0, K1).

Other programs have a mixing window, in which the user actually paints with various colors, mixing them together as a painter might mix pigments on a real world palette. Then, using an **eyedropper** tool, the user picks up color from the mixing window by clicking on it. That makes it the current foreground color, which in turn is used by any painting tool, such as a paintbrush.

Color mode is a **blend mode** that takes the **hue** and **saturation** of the upper **layer** or color and combines it with the **luminance** of the lower. By keeping the **luminance** the same, the created **composite** will then retain the same **grayscale** value of the original **image**. For instance, suppose you paint with your brush set at color mode, using red, onto a grayscale picture of a flower. The result would be a flower that is colored red, with all its original shadows and highlights intact. If the paintbrush had been set at **normal mode**, the red pixels would have replaced all those of the flower that they touched, resulting in a red blotch with no hint of the flower underneath. Color mode is useful for tinting monochrome photographs, or washing out or dramatically changing certain colors in color photographs. In some programs, color mode is called **color** or **color only**.   SEE **Channel operations, Pixel value manipulations, color plate 1**.

Color models are scientific attempts to delineate how colors are created, described and viewed. Graphics programs use various color models for different purposes. For instance, the **RGB** (Red/Green/Blue) is used for displaying color on the computer monitor, while **CMYK** (Cyan/Magenta/Yellow/blacK) is applied to images that are to be printed with ink or some other pigment onto paper. There are other color models that are also used, such as **HSB** (Hue/Saturation/Brightness), **PMS** (Pantone Matching System) and **CIE** (Commission Internationale d'Eclairage). CIE is also known as the **L*A*B** mode or model.

Color negative is a photographic term where the cyan, magenta and yellow emulsion layers are reversed during the film processing. When the negative is put into an enlarger and projected onto photosensitive paper, the colors revert to positive, i.e., the original colors. Some **scanner** programs allow users to scan color negatives directly—the software will automatically reverse the negative color to positive color.

Color only   SEE **Color mode**.

Color palette is a dialog box in which the user can choose and edit the current **foreground** and/or **background** colors.

In some programs, it may also be where the colors for **gradient fills** may be chosen, or it may be **nested** with other palettes for editing and choosing gradients, **patterns, textures** and other fills.   SEE color plate 1.

Color picker is either a command or a tool in graphics programs that allows the user to select colors.

In those programs in which the color picker is an **eyedropper**-type tool, it is used to click on specific colors on the screen, in the image, or from a **color palette**, to set that color as either your **foreground** or **background** color.

In those programs in which color picker is a command or **dialog box**, it may or may not be restricted to choosing your colors from the palette(s) within the box.

However the program allows you to select color, the process is usually available by double clicking on the current foreground or background color box, and/or within tools or painting **dialog boxes**, such as the **gradient fill** and/or in the **toolbar** as an **icon** tool.

Color probe is the term that some programs use for their **eyedropper** or **color picker** tool, which the user positions over a selected part of an image or anything else on the monitor. It then samples the color and displays its numerical primary color values, and/or it uses that color as the current **foreground** or **background** color, with which tools will paint.

Color probe also refers to the device used by a **color calibrator** to sample the colors on a computer monitor, print, transparency, etc. It may resemble a pencil or a suction cup, though some probes, such as the **Colortron,** have unique shapes.

Color proof is a color print used as a point of reference to check or confirm how the colors in the final version of the print will appear. It is also used as an aid to correctly **calibrate** the color of the computer monitor or printing device being used, or to color correct the **image file**.

Color range is a command that allows the user to select a particular color in either a specified area of an image, or the entire image. This means that a user may, for example, select everything that is blue within an image.

A user may also build a color range by sampling colors from various areas of an image, as well as **midtones, highlights** and **out-of-gamut** options.

Or, he or she may choose a range of colors based on specific numerical **color model** values.

The selected color range is useful for **filling** selected areas or in changing or editing the selected colors.

Color separations are either electronic files or photographic film that separates the colors in a photograph, illustration or image to their primary components of Cyan, Magenta, Yellow and blacK (**CMYK**) or to whatever colors are being used for the printing inks. The purpose is to make printing plates that will then be attached to a press. Some advanced **image editing, desktop publishing** and **illustration** programs come with built-in color separation capability, but most professional computer-generated color separations are done with powerful **stand-alone** programs. Most professional color separation files are output to an **imagesetter**, and the imagesetter's negatives are used to prepare the metal or paper plates that will be put onto the offset printing press.

Color separation tables are profiles of how color images are specifically separated, relative to a **calibrated** device (such as a printer), as well as the inks and paper being used. Most programs that have color separation capability will allow the user to build and save color separation tables. Saving them to a file is very useful when a specific setup—color monitor, printer, inks, paper, etc.—is used more than once, since another color separation table does not have to be built anew.

Color sequence refers to the specific order that Cyan, Magenta, Yellow and blacK (**CMYK**) inks are used on a four-color printing press run. Printers may vary the sequence to produce a certain effect, maximize use of the printing press, or squeeze out as much quality as possible.

Color shift is a physical and chemical phenomenon that occurs to film when the emulsion is old or improperly stored, the temperature of the developing chemicals is too hot or cold, or a time exposure lasts longer than normal.

In image editing, a color shift is an unwanted change in **hues**, which may occur because of an uncalibrated or miscalibrated computer monitor, or old or improperly stored **consumables**. Color shifts can usually be minimized or eliminated within a graphics program by adjusting the **color balance** or **hue**, or by recalibrating the monitor.   SEE **Color cast**.

Color space is the environment in which a specific color or image has been defined or can be described. Scientists and engineers have created numerous **color models**, such as **RGB, CMY, HSB** and **CIE**, to try to gain some level of control and repeatability in the chaos that is color. Similarly, different graphics software will allow the artist to create images, using one or another of these color models. But each color model is only a portion of the entire spectrum of many millions of colors that are possible in the natural world. While we cannot use all the colors of the natural world in the computer, we can chose which portion of the spectrum (which is often represented as a three-dimensional space) from which we wish to pull our much smaller menu of color possibilities. That portion of the full spectrum which you choose is referred to as the *color space* in which you are working. Therefore, if you use, for instance, the RGB color model in your image creation, you can also say that you are working in the RGB color space.   SEE **Color management**.

Color swatch is a color or series of colors printed on paper or displayed on a computer monitor and used as a visual point of reference. The color usually correlates to a specific ink or pigment created by a manufacturer, called **spot colors** or **SWOP colors** (**Standard Web Offset Publication**). **Pantone** and **Trumatch** are among the best-known color swatches, which may be in the form of electronic color samples displayed on a computer screen, included as **palettes** in **graphics programs**, or in the form of printed palm-size fan books called *swatchbooks.*

Color tables are profiles, or collections of colors, that may be used as points of reference when converting **24-bit color** (which can show up to **16.7 million** colors) into **8-** or **16-bit color**. The color tables determine how the original colors will be **mapped** into (or replaced by) the fewer colors. SEE **CLUT, Black body, Adaptive** and **System color**.

Color temperature, in physics, is the degree on the Kelvin scale that a particular light source emits. Color temperature is said to be warm (which gives the light a tendency toward yellow) or cold (which produces a blue cast). Tungsten lights (photo floods) have a color temperature of about 3,200°K, while sunlight is about 5,000°K to 10,000°K. The preferred color temperature for viewing **transparencies** or **chromes** is about 5,000°K.

Color trap   SEE **trapping**.

Color wand   SEE **Magic wand**.

Color wheel is the circular representation of the color spectrum, with a continuous gradient going from red to magenta to blue to cyan to green to yellow. The color wheel is a graphic display of the relation of colors to each other.

In some programs the user may select any color on the wheel simply by clicking on it with a **mouse** or **stylus**. There is usually also a **color bar**, in which the selected color is displayed in a continuum from bright (starting at white) to dark (ending in black). The color wheel may also be known as the **Color picker**.

Colorize is an option that allows a user to tint all or part of an image a particular color, by selecting a color or its numerical value from the **Hue/ Saturation dialog box**. It is often used to give a black & white photo the look of an antique sepia-toned picture. The same effect can be generated more precisely by painting specific areas of a picture using a **color only blend mode**.

Also, colorization is a process of converting black & white movies to color movies. Made popular by CNN's Ted Turner when he owned MGM Studios, the colorizing process uses computers to assign, create and track colors in black & white movie frames. Everything in a single frame is colored completely, and as the individual elements move about in subsequent frames, the computer automatically tracks and maintains the color with the boundaries of each element. For instance, if an actor is wearing a bandana that is colorized red, even if the actor moves, fills the frame, or moves off to a corner, the bandana will continue to be filled with the assigned red color. Of course, as with any creative process that is handed over to computers, there is usually quite a bit of manual labor involved in fine-tuning and tweaking.

Colortron is a brand-name **densitometer** or **color probe**, which reads color values on your monitor and aids in **color calibration**. The company belongs to **X-Rite**, the primary manufacturer of computer and printing industry calibration devices.

Column inch is a typographer's term that refers to a single inch of typeset material in column form, such as is commonly used in newspapers. It's the way that the length of an article or story is measured, so that it will fit in exactly the required space. For example, a story 17 column inches long will extend the width of the column and will be 17 inches long, even if it is carried over to another column or page. Typographers, as well as desktop publishers, will often adjust the size or the **leading** of the type to fit it into a specific column inch space.

Column width, sometimes referred to as column wide, refers to the width that text, an image or the combination of the two, extends within a printed column. It comes from the publishing industry, in which material is laid out in columns, as in a newsletter or newspaper. It may be measured in inches, centimeters or **points**.

Combine is a command in many illustration programs that takes two different objects and merges them into one object. Sometimes the method of combining can create new shapes, using the way the objects meet. For instance, when two objects are combined using an **intersect** command, then the new object consists only of that area where the two objects meet. A **trim** command would cut away one object from the other.   SEE **Punch, Union**.

Command is a specific instruction given to the computer, either by typing or clicking on the name of a **program** file, clicking on an **icon** or **pulldown menu** option or using a **hot key**.

Command box is a pop-up **dialog** box in graphics programs that allows the user to enter **commands**, change **parameters**, select **brushes**, choose colors, etc. It differs from a **pulldown menu** in that it is shaped like a box that appears somewhere on the computer monitor, either inside or abutting an image, or below or to the side of the image. Command boxes can be made to appear or disappear, and usually may be moved anywhere on the screen by simply dragging them to the desired spot.   SEE **Dialog box, Palette**.

Command file is a PC file that loads in an application, utility, driver or some other function. In the **DOS** world, a command file always has the three-letter extension COM, such as MOUSE.COM.

In addition, Command.COM is a DOS file that must always be present when the computer **boots up**.

Command key is an important key on the Mac keyboard. Also known as (and illustrated as) the **Apple key**, it is often used in conjunction with commands, tools or other keys, to extend their functionality. For instance, if you hold down the Command key while using a drawing tool, the object being drawn may be **constrained** to specific proportions or shapes.

Commands palette is a **dialog box** that gives the user direct access to the most commonly used commands. Depending on the program, it may be user-**customizable**. That is, the user may determine which commands are listed in the palette.

Common Hardware Reference Platform   SEE **PPCP**.

Communications program is **software** that allow **computers** to talk to each other, either over **modems** or through **networks**.

COM port is short for communications port, or a computer's **serial port**. It's generally used for **pointing devices** (like a **mouse** or a **drawing tablet**), or a **modem** (for communicating with another computer or an electronic service like the **Internet**). On a PC, each communications port is assigned a number, such as COM1 or COM2.

Comp is short for composition art, or a printed proof that is used to roughly show what the final printed version will probably look like. It is often provided as a point of reference or a guideline for those who are working on a project. Comps are most often produced for graphics professionals whose work will ultimately be output on a commercial printing press. Comp is also short for **composite**.

Compatible refers to software or hardware that work with other hardware or software without any problems. When buying a **modem**, printer, **graphics board**, or any other device, make certain that the manufacturer or vendor guarantees that it is compatible with your computer.   SEE **Incompatible**.

Compel is a brand-name business **presentation** program.

Composite is the blending or combining of two or more **images**, or **image elements**, into a single image. For example, putting the head of a wolf on the body of a lion is a type of composite. **Image editing** programs provide superb tools for compositing.   SEE **Collage**.

Composite path, or **compound path**, is a number of **objects** or **paths** that are **grouped** together so that they may be edited, manipulated or moved together. For instance, several letters grouped together into a composite path will move as a whole, and a **gradient** fill applied to the entire word will usually fill all the letters as a whole single gradient, rather than with individual gradients for each letter.

Compositor is an obsolete word for **typesetter**, whose profession has been made obsolete by the computer.

Compound path   SEE **Composite path**.

Compression is the process of shrinking or condensing data to reduce the file size. Compression is often desirable as a means to save space on the **hard drive**, or to fit an image file onto a **floppy diskette** or to transmit images faster over the Internet. It is also used to store Image files on a digital camera. Compression can be accomplished by software **utilities**, by hardware (compression chips or boards), or a combination of the two. Once compression is achieved, the data must be saved in a special file format, such as **GIF, JPEG** or **LZW**.

However, there's good news and bad news about compression. The good news is it can save significant space (some compression schemes can shrink a file to one-fiftieth of its original size, though more common methods typically shrink a file by 50–90%). The bad news is that compression can be very slow (saving and opening a file can take 2–10 times longer than normal), and depending on the method used and the degree of compression specified, there may be slight to significant loss of quality.

Generally, there are two types of compression: **lossless** and **lossy**. The lossless method shrinks a file in such a way that when the file is **decompressed** (which is necessary to be able to read the file), the **image** will appear exactly as it was in its original state. The lossy method will discard some of the data during the compression process, so that when the image is decompressed, it will not have the same values as the original image. Most digital cameras use a lossy compression scheme, such as JPEG. Lossless compression is faster and will produce better-quality images, while lossy compression can shrink files much smaller. The image quality loss may or may not be significant, depending on its intended use. On the other hand, the ability to shrink files to manageable, transportable sizes may be more important than overall image quality.

CompuServe Graphics Interchange   SEE **CGI**.

Configuration in the computer world means the specific arrangement, setup, makeup or design of a **program**, computer, **peripherals** or **operating system**. When you call **technical support** because of a problem with your computer, usually, the first thing the technician will ask is "what is your configuration?" He or she wants to know what kind of computer you have, how much **RAM**, the size of your **hard drive**, what sort of **graphics board** is installed, and so forth. That configuration information will give the technician a better idea of what sort of system (or software or peripheral) you have and how it is set up.

Constrain is a type of command or key combination which locks changes made to the dimensions of an **image** so that the original proportions or **file size** remain constant. For instance, if you have an image that is 2×4 inches, and if constrain proportions (or constrain **aspect ratio**) is activated, no matter what size the user increases or decreases one dimension, the other will always change proportionately so that the 1 to 2 ratio is always maintained.

Similarly, if the file size is checked in the image size **dialog**, it is constrained to remain the same. Therefore, if you increase the resolution, then the width and length will proportionately decrease, and vice versa. Constraining file size also means that no **pixels**, or image data, will be lost or gained when resizing.

Constrain Aspect Ratio SEE **Constrain** or **Aspect Ratio**.

Constraining key is **Command, Apple, Alternate, Option, Shift** and **Control** keys, when they are used to control, limit or change how a command or tool will act. For instance, pressing the Control key on your keyboard while drawing with the rectangle tool may constrain the shape to a perfect square.

Consumables are printer supplies—inks, ribbons, paper, toner, etc.—that are used or consumed as prints are made, and must be replenished to continue printing. When a salesperson talks about consumables, he or she is usually referring to the per print cost.

Context sensitive means that a command, tool or whatever will provide the **data** and options required for whatever file is open at the time that it is called up. The phrase is most often used in relation to context sensitive **help**, which provides the user with information about whatever window, tool, **palette**, etc., is open and active. For instance, if the user presses the help button when the printing **dialog box** is open, the help information that will be displayed will be about printing.

Continuous tone color refers to the visually imperceptible transition, or **gradient**, from one color to another. In other words, there are no breaks, bands or other obvious or subtle demarcations among the colors. The ability to display continuous tone color is a characteristic of **photorealistic color**, which is also called **true color** or **24-bit color**.

Contract is a command that shrinks the **selected** area of an image by a user-specified number of **pixels**. It is the opposite of the **Expand** command.

Contrast is the ratio, or difference, between the **highlight** and the **shadow** of any image. A very high contrast image consists of stark blacks and whites only (or any other solid light and dark color), with virtually no gray shades in between. A low contrast image has no strong blacks or whites, but an ethereal, nearly uniform gray fog where the subject appears indistinct. An image with a good contrast has a visually pleasing blend of lights, darks and midtones.

The computer's ability to see areas where there is strong contrast is what strengthens focus, because strong contrast at edges within a composition is what the human eye (and the computer) looks for in a well-focused picture.

All image editing programs have tools for adjusting contrast. Contrast is usually evaluated and adjusted relative to **brightness**, which is the amount or intensity of light in an image.

Control (CTRL) is a keyboard key that is often used in conjunction with another key or with a command or tool to activate a command or action. For instance, if you see CTRL + S in a program's **documentation**, it is telling you to hold down the Control key while you press the S key.

Control points are any points in an image, **object** or a **selection** within an image, on which the user can **click and drag** to **interactively** change the shape, size or orientation of the image or selection. For instance, the interactive rotation of an object or selection involves pulling on a control point until the item is turned to the extent wanted.

In addition, control points are the **nodes** or defining points of a **Bezier** or **spline** curve, where the user defines the angle, direction and length of that segment of the curve.

Controller in computers refers to a device, either built into a **peripheral, board** or even the **motherboard**, that literally controls another device. A **hard drive** controller runs your hard drive, a **SCSI** controller may operate your **scanner, digital camera**, and so forth.

Corel Corporation is a Canadian **software** company that specializes in graphics programs, such as **CorelDRAW**. They also market WordPerfect word processor software.

CONTRAST A

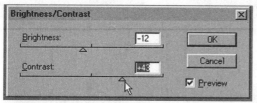

CONTRAST B

Contrast: Contrast increases the difference between the darkest and brightest areas of an image. For instance, **(A)** looks dull, but when we use the Contrast/Brightness command **(B)** to increase the contrast (as well as diminish the brightness), the result **(C)** looks much crisper. But be careful with contrast—what looks good on your monitor can be too dramatic and unrealistic in print. *(Original image from Corel Stock Photo Library)*

CONTRAST C

Convert images is the process of taking one file format, such as **TIFF** (**Tagged Image File Format**), and saving it in another format, such as **EPS** (**Encapsulated PostScript**).

It also refers to converting an image using one **color model**, such as **RGB** (red/green/blue), into another color model, such as **CMYK** (Cyan/Magenta/Yellow/blacK). Or changing a 24-bit color picture into one of 256 colors or grayscale or whatever other color or lack of it.

The last definition is translating a photographic, or **bitmapped**, image to or from a **vector** image.

All graphics programs have convert images capability to varying degrees.

Convert to Curves, or **convert to paths**, is a command often applied to text, in which the letters are converted to **spline** or **Bezier** curves, so that their outlines and shapes may be **interactively** edited.

The same or a similar command may be used to turn a primitive shape (i.e., one that is defined mathematically, such as a circle or a rectangle) into a curve.

Coprocessor is an auxiliary **CPU**, or **Central Processing Unit** (the brains of any computer), which is dedicated to a specific task. Its purpose is to perform a single function, such as speeding up **screen redraws** or mathematical calculations. Many state-of-the-art CPUs, such as the **Pentium**, have a math coprocessor built into the chip itself (which is very useful for significantly speeding up some **image editing** functions), and many **graphics boards** incorporate coprocessor chips soldered to or plugged into the board.

Copy is a command (found in the Edit **pulldown menu**) that places the selected **object**, image area, text or other element into the **clipboard**. It may then be **pasted** into another image or **document** or elsewhere in the same image or document.

The difference between copy and **cut** is that the cut command removes (**deletes**) the selected element from its current document or image. Copy leaves the original selected element where it was and puts a duplicate of it into the clipboard.

Copyright is a legal term that defines who has the legal right to copy or reproduce documents, books, photographs, pictures and other printed or printable material. Automatically, without any registration, the creator owns the copyright, unless he or she sells it or gives it away and signs an agreement to that effect. However, formal registration (with the government Office of Copyright), as well as other previously written statements regarding ownership of the image or document, assists in proving any legal case which you might wish to pursue.

Instead of selling or giving away copyright, an owner of documents and pictures will often license an individual or organization to use the document or picture. When you buy a **CD** of **clip art**, there is usually a license attached to the package that tells you what reproduction rights the owners of those pictures are allowing you. Read the license carefully to be sure you can use the clip art as you were planning. For instance, a clip art license may permit you to include the pictures or elements in presentations, internal reports and such, but not in books, magazines, on the Web, etc.

It is not only illegal to violate another person's copyright, it's considered tacky, selfish and infantile.

CorelDRAW is probably the best-known and most widely used professional-quality illustration program for the PC, although it is also available for the Mac. It is generally marketed as part of the rather large and powerful Corel **graphics suite**, which includes **PhotoPAINT** (an **image editing program**), **Ventura** (a **desktop publishing program**), **WordPerfect** (a **word processor**) and several other **applications** and **applets**. It is manufactured by the Canadian Company Corel Graphics, and is noted in the industry for its annual upgrade.

Counterclockwise Spectrum is the opposite of a **Clockwise Spectrum**, or when a color **gradient** changes or makes a transition between two colors as it moves counterclockwise around a **color wheel**. It can be used as one way to pick the colors of a color **gradient** that will be used as a **fill** in a selected area of an **image** or an **object**.   SEE color plate 4.

C-Print is a photographic term that refers to a particular type of **continuous tone** color print manufactured by Kodak. C-Prints are made in a darkroom by projecting a **color negative** image onto photosensitive paper and then immersing it in a series of chemicals to develop and fix the image.

CPU   SEE **Central processing unit**.

Crash is a disaster of enormous proportions to those of us who run our lives and businesses using computers. It occurs when the platters of a **hard drive**, which ride on cushions of air, literally crash or fall, because the air is no longer cushioning them. **Data** are inevitably lost, unless you have a **backup** system. While some hard drives can be resuscitated using various utilities, such as **Norton Utilities**, other crashes are fatal and require that the hard drive be replaced.

Create publisher, or **Publish and Subscribe**, is a Mac command that permits the user to link a file created in an image editing or other kind of program with another file in a separate program, such as a **page layout** or **desktop publishing** program like **PageMaker**. The file can be changed or updated, and, when it is saved, these changes will be reflected both in the original file and in the document in which it is embedded. It is similar to **OLE** in Windows.

Crop or **crop tool** is a command that allows the user to select a portion of an image. The portion of the image not selected is then discarded. Cropping has four purposes: (1) to better frame the image, (2) to eliminate unwanted portions of the image, (3) to decrease the file size, or (4) to make it easier to fit the image into another or onto a printed page. When cropping, the user may specify the **size** and/or **resolution** of the cropped portion.

Crops are usually done by clicking the **mouse** or **stylus** either on the horizontal and vertical image **window** or the **marquee**, and pulling or pushing its corners until it is in the desired position. Users usually may define or lock in the **aspect ratio**, or the horizontal and vertical dimensions.

The crop tool is sometimes also called the **Trim** tool.

Crop marks is an option that may be selected in the **Page setup**. It allows the entire image to be printed, with visible corner or center crop marks (or both)—usually dotted lines—to indicate where a cut or trim will be made on the printed page.

Crop tool   SEE **Crop**.

Cross-platform indicates that software, hardware or a **file format** may be used on vari-

CROP A

CROP B

Crop: Cropping this Photoshop tutorial image **(A)** can create a pretty vertical image **(B)** that has a whole different feel to it from the original.

ous computer platforms (PC, Mac, etc.) with no difference in capabilities. Usually, hardware and software are platform-specific. That means they will work with only one kind of computer system. But it is becoming more and more common for them to be compatible with more than one type of computer. On the other hand, some file formats are and always have been cross-platform, while others never will be.

CRT, which stands for Cathode Ray Tube, is the screen or monitor on which all your computer-based **data** and work are displayed. It's the eye of the computer, or the TV screen–like device that you look at while you work, and without it you couldn't see what you are doing or what the computer is "thinking." Typical sizes are 14, 15, 19, 20 and 21 inches, which are all diagonal measurements. Larger screens are typically used for **graphics** to help users see **images** in better detail. Smaller CRTs, which are less expensive, are usually better suited for business applications, such as **word processing**.

Crystallize is a filter that breaks up an image into impressionistic-like solid color polygon shapes. It can be a beautiful effect, since the polygons may be more or less random shapes and may take on the appearance of a painting. The crystallize filter may be changed by the user to create small crystals that

CRYSTALLIZE A

CRYSTALLIZE B

Crystallize: A Crystallize filter can convert a photograph into an abstraction or something resembling an oil painting. (Original photo from the Color Stock Photo Library.)

show the picture as having recognizable form and shape, or large abstract crystals that look like random splotches of color.

Crystallize differs from **Pixellize** in that the shapes are random-size polygons, whereas pixellization changes everything into a pointillist abstraction in which each point of color is the same size and shape.

CTRL   SEE **Control**.

Cursor is the **pointer**, arrow, vertical line or underline that denotes where the next character, line or paintbrush that you intend typing or drawing will begin. It's the position where your **mouse** or **stylus** is relative to your monitor. For better recognition, the cursor often flashes. When working in most programs, the **documentation** or **on-screen help** will ask the user to move the cursor to a particular position, which is usually done by pushing a **mouse, stylus** or **puck**, while watching the corresponding movement of the cursor on the computer screen.

Curve dialog box refers to a **command box** in which the tonal range of a **bitmapped image** may be adjusted. Whenever it is opened up, it is a straight diagonal line in which the pixels that are in the shadows are represented at one end, those in the highlights are at the other end, and the midtones are along the line between those two extremes. Moving the curve at different points along that line adjusts the relative brightness and darkness of those midtones, highlights and shadows. In most programs, it is possible to adjust the curve of the overall picture or of each of the **color channels** of red, green or blue. For those that are mathematically inclined, the curve is actually the graph of the original **histogram** of a picture before you edit it plotted against whatever changes you make to the histogram each time this dialog is open. Since *gamma* is the mathematical term for change, it is often also called a **gamma** or **gamma curve**.

Cusp node is that point on a **path** at which the curve changes direction. On a **Bezier** or **spline** curve, it is a point where the **directional lines** or **handles** no longer act like a seesaw but, instead, can fold into an acute angle.

Custom, or **customize,** is the term used by many programs when the user is allowed to create or modify a **filter, dialog box, palette, toolbar**, etc.

Cut is a command that deletes a **selected** object, area, text, **image** or other element from its current location and places it into the **clipboard**. Then, it can be **pasted** elsewhere, into the same image or document, or into another image or document.   SEE **Copy**.

Cut/Copy/Paste is a series of commands that uses the computer's memory, or **clipboard**, as a temporary holding area for data that you will want to use again very soon. It allows you to delete or copy all or part of an **image** or

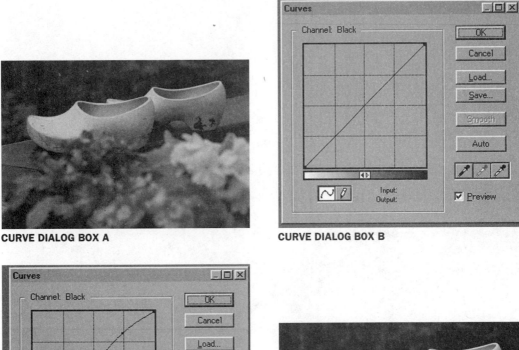

CURVE DIALOG BOX A

CURVE DIALOG BOX B

CURVE DIALOG BOX C

CURVE DIALOG BOX D

Curve dialog box: The original Photoshop tutorial image **(A)** has a straight gamma curve **(B)**, as would any image when you open the curve dialog. But pulling various points on the line **(C)** can adjust the tones of the image **(D)** with greater precision than just using the brightness/contrast command.

document and then move that information to another part of the image, to an entirely different image or document, or to one of the **layers**.

Cylinder anamorphosis is an effect in which the image is deliberately reversed and can be viewed properly only through a mirror. Cylinder anamorphosis was a popular art form in the 18th century, and any images using this effect create an old-fashioned or anachronistic mood.

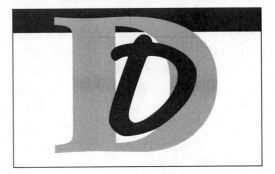

Dad   SEE **Digital Audio Disk**.

Daisy chain describes linking two or more devices—usually **SCSI** drives, such as a **scanner, removable drive** or **film recorder**—one after the other, to the computer by cable. To denote which device is last on the chain (and prevent tying up the computer in an endless search for it, thereby rendering the computer useless for any constructive purpose), the last device must be **terminated**, either by plugging in a small block called a **terminator**, or by flicking a switch on those devices that come equipped with built-in termination.

Under optimum conditions, most computer systems with SCSI capability allow up to seven separate devices to be daisy chained together. Practically speaking, usually only four or five SCSI devices can be daisy chained together, because the total length of the cable connecting the devices can be no more than 18 feet (longer than that, and the electrical signals are too weak to carry an error-free signal). However, more advanced SCSI controllers allow up to 15 devices to be daisy chained, or can extend the total length of the cables beyond 18 feet without fatally weakening the signal. When a daisy chain fails, the cause may be faulty cables, too long a chain or conflicting SCSI IDs.

Other kinds of devices may be daisy chained.

Dancing ants is the colloquial term used to describe what is known as a **marquee**, or a series of active, blinking, advancing dots (like the marquee lights above a movie theater) that appear around a **selected** area of an **image**. This indicates that the active, selected area may be edited, deleted, moved or changed. The lack of dancing ants indicates that an area or image is not currently selected or active, and therefore no changes made will be applied to it (or any changes made will affect the entire picture and not just that small area). However, some programs allow a marquee to be temporarily hidden, even though it is still active, to make viewing the image easier and unobstructed.

Darken is a user-made adjustment that reduces the brightness of all or a selected part of an image. Increasing **contrast** will darken those already dark parts of an image, while brightening the light areas.

Darken is also the abbreviated term that some **image editing** programs use for **darken mode**.

Darken mode, or **darken only,** is a **blend mode** command that samples all the **pixels** in the **selected** part of an **image** or in the

Dancing ants: Using the magic wand tool on this Photoshop tutorial image created a selection that is defined by a pattern of moving dots. Those dots are called *dancing ants* or *marquee*. Further refinement of the selection is possible, so that the dancing ants surround only the head or only the hands, or any specific area of the image.

color being applied by a **painting tool**, relative to the underlying **layer** or image. It then chooses to apply the darkest of each pixel (whether from the new image or color, or from the underlying one) and applies it. It is a special effects technique that will darken, or tone down, an image. SEE **Channel operations** and **Color mode**. See also color plate 3.

DAT is short for **Digital Audio Tape**. While conventional tape recorders, **camcorders** and other devices record **analog data**, DAT records data **digitally**. This means that it doesn't have to be converted from analog to digital to be recognized by the computer, and that in turn means more speed, greater accuracy, and the ability to pack far more data onto DAT tape than conventional tape. DAT drives are often used as backup devices, since a single 6-dollar, 4-mm tape can store up to 4, 8 or more **gigabytes** of data.

Data are information that can be all or part of an image, a letter, a spreadsheet, address list, or whatever. Technically, data is the plural of the Latin word *datum,* which is an experience, fact or principle that one accepts as a given or an established fact. It used to be that its correct English usage was as a plural noun, such as data *are,* but common usage has transformed it into a collective singular noun, so that it is now becoming common to say *data is,* though we still prefer the more grammatical and traditional plural treatment.

Database is an **application** program that organizes, stores and displays any sort of information, organized into **fields** or categories. Therefore, a contact list of art buyers could be turned into a database, in which you could search the various fields to see which ones live in a certain geographical range, or buy a type of image, etc. It is the categorization of information that makes databases most useful in this manner. A **visual database** also stores images with text information.

Data compression   SEE **Compression**.

Data density refers to the ratio or percentage of an image relative to the white space (i.e., nonimage area) of a page. It's used to estimate the file size an image will produce when **scanned**, minus the white around it.

Data density also refers to the amount of information, or **pixels**, in an image. The denser the data, the sharper and more detailed an image.

And data density is analogous to the old theological argument of how many angels can fit on the head of a pin. It's the amount of data that can be physically packed into a specific space. On storage devices such as **hard drives** or **CD-ROMs**, it refers to the proximity of zeros and ones, the components of the computer's **binary** language, that can be jammed together. The closer they can be physically recorded, the more data can fit in that space and, also, the faster the device will be able to read and write data.

Data flow is, simply, the flow of data through a device or as part of a program.

Data transfer rate refers to the speed that data (be it images, text or whatever) can be transmitted or shared across cables or other connections. As such, it is used as a rating or spec for various devices, such as hard drives and removable storage drives. The higher the data transfer rate, the faster the device can move, save or open data.

Db   SEE **Decibel**.

DC stands for direct current, which is a continuous current—the stream of electricity used to power computer peripherals, such as **modems**, drives, and many other devices. Most homes and businesses do not have DC power outlets; instead, they use AC (alternating current) power. DC current is produced by taking standard household AC current and converting it to DC current via an external transformer.

DC also stands for Digital Camera, and it is the prefix for Kodak's entry-level **filmless cameras**. The DC120 is a current model capable of capturing images at a maximum resolution of 1280×960 **dpi**, with an autofocus 3X zoom lens and the ability to accommodate interchangeable memory cards and other refinements.

DCS   SEE **Desktop Color Separations**.

DCS cameras are professional filmless cameras manufactured by Kodak and built around Nikon camera bodies that use Nikon lenses and accessories. The DCS-200, now discontinued, has as its front end a Nikon 8008 body. It's an **8-bit** device with a **CCD** that has a maximum **resolution** of 1524 × 1012. The DCS-420 and 410 both use Nikon N90 bodies, are **12-bit** devices, and also have a maximum resolution of 1524 × 1012.

The difference between the 420 and the 410 is that the 410 doesn't have a burst mode, or the ability to shoot continuously, and its ISO equivalency is fixed at 100. Kodak's top-of-the-line camera has two versions: the DCS-460, which is built around a Nikon N90 body, and the DCS-465, which can be used as a Hasselblad back. Both are 12-bit devices that feature a maximum resolution of 3060 × 2036.

The EOS-DCS series is similar to DCS cameras, the main difference being that they are built around Canon's EOS camera bodies.

DCSEPS format is an **Encapsulated PostScript file format** that contains information about **color separations**. It is used almost exclusively for **pre-press** purposes.

DCS format is Kodak's **native (compressed)** file format that the company's **filmless cameras** save to when they capture an **image**. With the proper software, it may be viewed as a **thumbnail** and in compressed form. The advantage of saving the original image file in the DCS format is the space savings: It is about one-third the size of an uncompressed file. But opening (expanding or **decompressing**) the file to edit it takes appreciably longer. In addition, many **graphics programs** cannot read DCS files, so they must be decompressed with a program that does recognize the DCS format and saved in a standard file format (such as **TIFF** or **PICT**) before they can be used. The **software driver** that comes with the cameras can read the DCS format and convert it to more standard file formats.

DDE stands for **Dynamic Data Exchange**, a feature built into **Microsoft's Windows** that transfers data from one application to another. It's analogous to the **clipboard** used in many **applications** programs. DDE can be very useful in moving data created in one program, such as part of a **spreadsheet** or **word processing** file, and pasting it directly into an **image** or other **document**.

DDS stands for Digital Data Storage, a commonly used **format** for **DAT** tapes. Although the DDS format may be used on the DAT drive making an **archival backup**, because of different **compression** levels and other factors, it may not be readable by a second drive on another computer system (though, of course, it will be easily readable by the system that created the backup).

Decibel (Db) is the unit of measurement of how soft or how loud a particular sound is. Average background noise is 65 Db, while anything over 90 Db is considered loud. Over 100 Db can be painful, and can even cause permanent damage to your eardrums.

Decompression is the process of expanding a **compressed** file to its original size, so that it may be read, opened and edited. Compressed files usually take a little to a lot longer to open, because of the time involved to decode and expand the **data** to normal size.

Dedicated describes a piece of software or hardware that works with only one brand name or design. Theoretically, a dedicated device or program assures compatibility and trouble-free operation, but all too often, it's a way to gouge the user because it eliminates the competition. For instance, if you buy a printer that uses a dedicated ink **cartridge**, you must buy that company's cartridge and no others and pay whatever price they ask. Generally, it's better to buy products that use common standards, although there are exceptions, especially if you need a particular product.

Default is the normal, standard condition or setting of a program, tool or device, either as it came from the factory or the manufacturer, or was established by the user either in software, or by toggling **dipswitches**, setting **jumpers**, etc. Often, programs allow the user to revert to default settings (such as **scanner parameters**), which can be very useful if the current settings are screwed up, or the user is lost or confused about which settings to apply.

Definition is another word for **image quality**. An image said to have good definition is generally thought to be clear, sharp, detailed and well exposed. A picture with poor definition may be muddy, soft, indistinct, dark, etc.

Defloat is, to state the obvious, the opposite of the command **float**. In some bitmapped image editing programs, it is possible to define a selected area as an **object**. The new object, once floated, can be edited or moved independently from the rest of the picture, as it would be in **vector** or **object-oriented** programs. In effect, it floats above the rest of the picture, as a

layer would. Use the defloat command to merge the floated object back into the pixels of the picture.

Defragging   SEE **Defragment**.

Defragment is a routine procedure that helps speed up your computer's **hard drive**. It's a **utility** that's either part of your **operating system** or a separate program that finds all the bits of **data** that are randomly scattered on a drive, and then organizes them into contiguous files. That way, instead of having to access 2, 10 or 50 different places on the hard drive where the data were randomly squirreled away—which can be a time-consuming search— it's all in one place and therefore can be read from or saved to the computer faster. You should always defrag your hard drive at least once a week, or after completing any large or involved image editing project.

Defringe is a command that removes the **pixels** along the edge of a **selected** area in a **bitmapped** image. It can be set to specific pixel depth, such as one, two, three, etc., pixels. The purpose of this command is to remove extraneous color that was once part of the background out of which the area was pulled.

For instance, suppose you draw a **selection** or **mask** around a banana that was sitting on a red tablecloth. A perfectly drawn selection wouldn't contain any red pixels from the tablecloth. But few selections are absolutely perfect. So, if there is a tiny border (or fringe) of red pixels around the edge of the selected banana, you can use the defringe command to remove them. The problem with this command is that it is color blind. It doesn't seek out the red pixels of the tablecloth. Instead, it simply removes the pixels that make up the edge of the selected area.

Degaussing is the act or process of removing or defusing a built-up magnetic charge on a computer monitor, tape recorder, VCR, camcorder, etc. Most high quality color monitors have a built-in degaussing button that the user pushes whenever wavy lines, strange colors or other magnetic effects appear. Note: Degaussing is effective only when a charge has built up, and it will take the monitor about a half-hour to reset after degaussing. So, don't try to degauss more than once during a half-hour period.

De-interlace is a video term for a filter that removes either the odd or even scan lines of a television signal, for a clearer image. An **interlaced** signal on a television set or computer refreshes, or displays, every other scan line on each pass. It's less expensive to build than a **noninterlaced** monitor or TV set—which displays every line on each pass—but the image is not as sharp and may exhibit an annoying flicker.

Delete means to erase, zap, do away with, end, get rid of, eliminate, etc. It generally applies to files and images that the user wishes to remove, either because they are no longer needed or wanted, duplicates or backups exist elsewhere, and/or because the user wants to free up disk drive space.

Demand publishing, also called *on-demand publishing,* is, as it sounds, publishing on demand, or the ability to publish a single work (book, portfolio, image, annual report, etc.), or a small **press run** at short notice. Because **laser printers** and other printer technologies are fast and relatively inexpensive, and can print double-sided (usually by manually flipping the paper), it may be very economical and eminently practical to print and bind single or small numbers of works, rather than paying a printer to run off hundreds or thousands at a time.

Densitometer is a device that measures the density (tonal quality, or light and darkness) of an image, computer monitor, **film, negative** or **transparency**, print, etc. It is the piece of **hardware** that is applied to a monitor and held there with a suction cup, when the monitor is being **calibrated**. But it may also be used to read the colors of any other item, including a piece of color, a **swatch book** or whatever. In that case, its software will then provide the percentages of **primary colors** that would recreate that color. For this reason, densitometers are useful in attempting to develop precise **color management**.

Density is how much data are packed in a particular space. In imaging, it usually refers to how many **pixels**, or picture elements, are contained in a particular **bitmapped image**. A low density image has relatively little data, so while the **file size** is smaller, the image itself will contain little detail or **definition**. On the other hand, a high density image may contain many **megabytes** of data (i.e., be a large-size file), as well as great depth and detail.

Density also refers to how much data can be stored on a **diskette**, a **hard disk drive**, etc. A low density diskette or drive may be less expensive and marginally safer (that is, have less chance of the data being scrambled or corrupted) than high density **media**. But high density media can pack, or store, from 50 to 500% more data in the same space. In addition, because the **bits** are physically packed closer together, high density media can often **read** and **write** data faster, which translates into a faster **data transfer rate** and shorter delays. Most media are of the high density variety.

Depth is the distance an effect or an object extends into the background, or along the *z*-**axis**.

It is also the amount of information associated with each **pixel** in a **bitmapped image**. SEE **Resolution, Bit depth**.

Depth of field is a photographic term that denotes what range in a picture will be in focus. According to the physics of optics, a lens must be curved to collect and reverse an image onto light-sensitive film or, in the case of a **digital camera**, onto the **CCD** or the **CMOS** chip. Being curved means that part of the image will be distorted, i.e., out of focus. The more curvature, the less will be in focus. Most camera lenses have built into them a device called a *diaphragm*, which reduces the curvature, as well as controls the amount of light falling on the film or chip. The smaller the opening, the smaller the curvature, and consequently, more of the foreground and background will be in focus. Most lenses have engraved marks that accurately indicate what range will be in focus at any particular diaphragm setting. For instance, a wide-angle lens with a small opening may have a depth of field ranging from a foot to infinity, whereas a telephoto lens wide open may only have a half-foot depth of field. The closer one gets to the subject—which is called a **macro** shot—the less the depth of field. The farther away from the subject—such as shooting a panorama of a mountain or seascape—the greater the depth of field.

Depth resolution SEE **Bit depth, Resolution**.

Desaturate is a command in **image editing** programs that removes color density. Use it enough and it will remove all color and change the picture to a **grayscale**.

Descender refers to any letter that has a "tail" that dips below an actual or imaginary line of type. Letters with descenders are *g, j, p, q* and *y*. SEE **Ascender**.

Deselect is the act of eliminating the **marquee** or **marching ants** around all or part of a **selected** image, **object**, text or other picture element. This removes any mask that was drawn around the area, unless it was previously saved. It is usually achieved by clicking the **mouse** or **stylus** anywhere outside the selected area, when a **selection tool** is active, or by choosing the deselect or none command from a selection **pulldown menu** or a **selection palette**.

Deskewing corrects a problem common to most **handheld scanners** and many **flatbed** or **sheet-fed scanners**, when the original is not scanned absolutely straight. When a scan is crooked, it is said to be **skewed**. Depending on the software, deskewing may be done automatically or manually. If possible, it is usually better to just rescan the picture.

Desktop refers to any computer or device—such as a printer, **scanner**, or **film recorder**—that is small and light enough to fit on the top of a desk. Larger devices—**imagesetters, drum scanner, large printers** and the like—are said to be professional models.

But size doesn't seem to be the only determining factor anymore. Larger printers or other devices that are designed to attach to a Mac or PC may be called *desktop devices,* even though they wouldn't fit on the top of any typical desk.

Desktop also refers to standard PC and Mac computers that work under **Windows, System 8** and other common operating systems. This is to distinguish them from souped-up, high-powered computers called **workstations** (though with the introduction of **Pentium Pro** and **PowerPC microprocessors**, the difference and distinction is becoming practically nil).

The last definition of desktop is a system background screen, in Windows and on Macs, on which the **icons, dialog boxes** and **pulldown menus** appear.

Desktop Color Separations, or **DCS,** is a format created by **QuarkXpress desktop publishing** program) that extends the **PostScript EPS** (**Encapsulated PostScript**) color format. EPS files save **CMYK** color information in four separate files: Cyan, Magenta, Yellow and blacK. DCS saves CMYK images in five files: Cyan, Magenta, Yellow, blacK and a master file. While DCS files are appreciably larger than EPS files, they provide more information for checking **proofs**, or examining the accuracy of the color. While EPS files may be printed by any desktop device equipped with PostScript capability, DCS files are almost exclusively used in **prepress** for making **color separations** that will be used on printing presses.

Desktop publishing, or **DTP**, is the phrase that covers any and all **typesetting, page composition, layout** and other skills and procedures associated with formatting, preparing and printing documents done by **desktop** computer. **Adobe PageMaker, Corel Ventura** and **QuarkXpress** are the most widely used **stand-alone** desktop publishing programs, though most **word processing** programs now include many desktop publishing tools and capabilities. DTP is used by newsletter publishers, report writers and anyone who wants a document to have a professional look.

Despeckle is a special type of **filter** in some bitmapped programs that diminishes **noise**, or stray **speckles** (unwanted **artifacts** or dots of dirt), in a picture. It does this by blurring all but the visual edges (or areas of high contrast) in an image. However, it does soften the picture, rather than truly remove the noise.

Destination point is the **pixel** where a **clone** tool or **brush** is painting.

A clone tool (aka **rubberstamp** tool) picks up picture information from a **source** point and the area around it, and uses that information as a **paintbrush** might use color. Therefore, suppose the source point is in the middle of the nose in a portrait of a child. As the user paints with the clone, a new nose will appear in the area of the destination point. How the source area is used in the destination area, and the location of the destination area, have a lot to do with whether the tool is set at **aligned** or **nonaligned**, and what other options are chosen.

Device in computerese refers to a piece of hardware attached to the computer, usually external to the computer itself, such as a printer, **scanner, modem, removable drive**, or **mouse**.

Device driver is a software utility that tells the computer that a particular **device**, or piece of hardware, is attached to the computer. Most computer **peripherals** ship with drivers, though several companies, such as **SyQuest**, sell collections of drivers that work with a variety of devices.

Device drivers for the Mac are usually installed in the Init folder, while on the PC, a line is usually added to the **Config.sys** file that reads: DEVICE=(the name and location of the device driver file).

Dialog SEE **Dialog box**.

Dialog box, or **dialog,** is a box, square, menu or **window** that allows the user to select, use and/or customize a **command, tool**, or **filter**, or to input information. When it is available, the user is actually able to maintain a "dialog" with the software, telling it what to do or keeping track of what is happening. For instance, when the print command is activated, a print dialog box appears on the monitor, in which the user may choose how many copies should be printed of which pages and other **printing parameters**.

A dialog box may **pop up** when a condition occurs that requires a decision or action (such as running out of disk space or memory, or asking if you want to **save** by **overwriting** an existing file), or it may be a box that the user can make appear on or disappear from the computer monitor. Most dialog boxes **float**, which means they may be moved anywhere on the screen by dragging on their tops with the **mouse** or **stylus**.

A special type of dialog box is a **palette**, in which the user can make creative choices about tools and commands.

Dialog box: This Lighting Effects filter dialog from Corel PhotoPAINT gives the user control over the many aspects that will affect how, where, and how many lights will be placed to change the image. The better dialogs (such as this one) have previews, so you can see the results of your choices on your picture. *(From the Corel Stock Photo Library.)*

Diazo is, in nontechnical terms, a photographic process that stains a transparency so that it appears as a blue and white **negative** rather than a **monochrome**. It is generally used in architecture and drafting. Some graphics programs allow a user to produce Diazo-like effects.

Difference is a **blend mode** option in some **image editing** programs that subtracts the numerical **pixel** values of the upper layer or color from the one below to create a special effect. For instance, suppose the underlying color is made up of Red 214, Green 100 and Blue 70 (which is a tangerine-like color), and the color being used by the paintbrush (which is set at difference mode) is Red 150, Green 75 and Blue 25 (a darker orange). The resulting color (a very dark purple) would be one that subtracts the values of the first from the other to produce Red 64, Green 25 and Blue 45.   SEE **Channel operations, Color mode** and **Darken only**.

Difference mode   SEE **Difference**.

Diffuse is a **special effects bitmap filter** that softens the focus of a picture by shifting pixels. It is similar in results to a photographic diffusion filter, which is used to create soft-focus, ethereal portraits.

Diffusion is a **conversion** option related to converting **grayscale** or color pictures to **1-bit** pictures. **One-bit** pictures (also called *single bit* or, sometimes, *bitmap*) are made up of only white and black pixels. To emulate the gradual gradients between colors that grayscale and color pictures have, the black dots are **dithered**, or organized in various ways to trick the human eye into seeing more subtlety than really exists in the black and white. One type of dithering is diffusion, in which the probability of conversion error is applied to all surrounding pixels in a decreasing radius, depending on how far from pure black or pure white each original pixel is.

Digital is what lives inside a computer. Digital information is expressed using a binary system that consists solely of two states: zeros and ones (or ons and offs, positives and negatives, pluses and minuses, etc.). In contrast, **analog** is everything else in the universe: what we see, hear, taste, touch or smell. Photographs, TV shows, live concerts, the wide outdoors, etc., are all analog information. The trick is to convert analog information into digital data. **Digital cameras, scanners** and **modems** are among the better-known devices that translate information (including pictures, words and other material) from analog to digital data.

Digital is often used as an adjective to indicate something related to using a computer, or as part of the name of a device to indicate that it can process or otherwise handle digital data.

Digital artist is a person who uses computer technology to aid in creating works of art.

DIFFUSION A

DIFFUSION B

Diffusion: Using a diffusion option when we converted this Corel picture from grayscale **(A)** to black & white **(B)**, the dots of the new image create the illusion of a grayscale image. The result is also a type of *dithering*.

Digital Audio Disc, or **DAD**, is a type of **CD-ROM**.

Digital camera is a filmless, or electronic, camera that captures an image (**analog data**) onto a photosensitive semiconductor chip (a CCD or CMOS chip) then immediately converts it to **digital data** and saves it to a digital file inside the camera. The device that converts the analog information into digital data is a built-in **ADC** (Analog-to-Digital Conversion) chip. The conversion is done automatically and takes between 2 and 12 seconds, depending on the camera, the image size, etc.

A digital camera is similar to a **still video camera**, in that they both capture electronic still images. The difference is that a still video camera converts its analog information at a later time, using an external ADC (either a box between the camera and the computer, or a **peripheral** board inside the computer). Although still video images are usually inferior in quality and **definition**, they can be directly displayed on any standard **NTSC** feed, such as a television set, camcorder, VCR or broadcast signal. Still video cameras are almost obsolete, however.

Digital imaging is the generic term for creating and/or manipulating pictures using a computer. By extension, then, it includes the processes of **inputting** picture **data**, saving and opening it, **outputting** it, and everything else that enables and assists the creative efforts of the **digital artist**.

Digital picture is an image that can be displayed, edited, saved and output on a computer. It is composed of **digital data**—the zeros and ones that computers can understand. An **analog**, or real world picture—such as a photographic print—becomes digital by being **scanned** (or **digitized**). Obviously, **digital cameras** produce digital pictures and not analog images.

Digital Video Disc, or **DVD**, refers to the current generation of ultra-high density CD-ROMs that are just now coming on the market. DVDs will hold either 5 **gigabytes** of **data** per side, or 7.4 gigabytes on a single-sided 5.25-inch **CD** and 2.3 gigabytes on a single 3-inch CD. Besides far greater storage capacity, DVDs will read data up to 30 times faster than current CD-ROM drives. This means that they will play higher **resolution video** in **real time**, making them a possible replacement for VCRs and commercial movies recorded on one-half-inch videotape cassettes.

Digitize is the process or the act of converting **analog** signals to **digital** data. **Scanners** and **digital cameras** are devices that digitize analog, or real world, **continuous tone** visual information into the zeros and ones that a computer recognizes. Music and other sounds are digitized when they are recorded to **CDs**.

Digitizer, also called a *digitizing tablet* or *drawing tablet*, is a **pointing device** that attaches to a computer and is used instead of, or in addition to, a **mouse** to move the **cursor**. It consists of a flat plastic pad with an active area of 4 × 5, 6 × 8, or 12 × 12 inches, or some other dimension, a **stylus** (or drawing pen), and/or a **puck** (which looks very similar to a mouse, but has crosshairs for more precise positioning). The active area of the pad or tablet can be made **relative** (it will behave like a mouse in that your position on the pad is relative to your previous position) or **absolute** (where every point on the pad always relates directly to a specific position on the computer monitor). Digitizers are much better suited for drawing, tracing, painting, handwriting, and other activities that require precise positioning and manipulation of your cursor on the computer monitor. In addition, the stylus feels more natural to artists, because it is shaped like a pencil or pen. Some tablets have a **pressure-sensitive** stylus that reacts to the artist's hand, as a natural brush would.

Digitizing board SEE **Digitizer**.

Digitizing tablet SEE **Digitizer**.

Dimension lines are lines that measure the distance that they cover. They are used in illustration and drafting programs for measuring objects, spaces and other elements in blueprints and other designs. For instance, a dimension line might be drawn to measure the width and height of a wall.

Dingbat is a printer's term for decorative symbols that are usually interspliced with normal text. **Zapf Dingbat** is the best-known set of computer dingbats.

Dip is a temporary drop in electrical power. If severe enough, it can cause a computer freeze, and the user will lose all unsaved data. If dips are frequent and severe (i.e., if the source of electricity is **dirty power**), it can cause serious and permanent damage to the computer and significantly shorten the life of its **components**. Users will often attach a **UPS** (Uninterruptable Power Supply) to their computers to help maintain a constant level of power. SEE **Brownout**.

Dipswitch is a tiny rocker-type switch, usually on a **motherboard, peripheral** board or the rear of a device like a **modem** or a **scanner**, that the user may toggle on or off to get a desired setting. Whether it is changed depends on the computer's hardware or software **configuration**. Usually, there are 4, 6 or 8 dipswitches in a line, and the **default** positions are preset at the factory. Once very common, especially on **PCs, Windows 95's and 98's Plug and Play** capability is rapidly rendering them obsolete.

Direction lines are the controls that define the direction and angle a **Bezier** or **spline** curve will turn. The user drags the lines out of the control **nodes** (the defining points where the curve changes) in the curve, using his or her mouse in a click and drag. Once the direction line exists on the monitor, the angle from which it takes off defines the angle of the curve at that point, and the line's length defines the depth and severity of that angle.

Directional light is a special effect that allows the user to **illuminate** an image or illustration as if it were being lit by professional studio lights, sunlight, moonlight, or any other source. It is called *directional light* because the user may control the direction from which the light(s) come. Depending on the program, there are other controls that allow the user to specify the intensity, color and quality of the light or lights.

Directory, or DIR, is a **DOS** command that lists all files in a particular **subdirectory**.

In DOS and **Windows** versions prior to **Windows 95**, a directory is a designated divider where specific programs and files are stored. Since most **hard drives** are designed with the letter *C* or a letter lower down on the alphabet (*A* and *B* are usually reserved for **floppy drives**), the **default**, or main directory, will appear like this: C:\. Nestled below the main directory are **subdirectories**, or additional directories into which **application programs, utilities**, data files, images, etc., are stored. Directories on PCs are the equivalent of **folders** on Mac machines and on PCs running under Windows 95 or **Windows NT**.

Dirty power is electricity that exhibits frequent or periodic **spikes, surges, dips** or other electrical anomalies that may affect a computer. At the very least, dirty power may cause a computer **freeze** or render the computer inoperable until it is **rebooted**. A strong surge or a prolonged period of dirty power may result in serious, permanent damage to computer **components**, such as **memory chips, hard disk drives**, and even **CPUs**. It may also greatly shorten their useful life spans. There are various controls and cures for dirty power, such as a **surge suppressor, line stabilizer, UPS (Uninterruptable Power Supply)**, **SPS (Standby Power Supply)**, and **lightning arrestor**. It has been estimated that up to 90% of computer **glitches**, or problems, can be attributed to dirty power.

Disc with a *c* usually denotes any storage media that cannot be changed once the data is written on it. **CD-ROMs** are probably the best-known types of discs.

Disk with a *k* refers to any media that can be read, written to or changed many times. **Hard drives, floppies, SyQuest** and **Jaz** cartridges are examples of disks.

Disk array   SEE **RAID**.

Disk cache is a scheme for speeding up disk **I/Os** or **read/writes** (data being read or written to the drive). It works by placing frequently accessed or last used **data** (such as an image file or part of an **applications** program) in a high speed memory area built onto the drive. When and if the computer requires such previously accessed data (which, statistically, is about 90% of the time), rather than accessing the much slower drive, it will take that information from the much faster disk cache. Most computers and disk drives incorporate hardware and software disk caches to boost performance, since drives are about the slowest part of a computer system.

Disk drive is a device that incorporates a rapidly spinning platter or **disk** with a magnetic coating, and is used to permanently store both programs and data. Almost all computers incorporate at least one disk drive, usually a **hard disk drive** or hard drive, as part of their systems. **Floppy disk** drives are also a type of disk drive.

Diskette, or **disk**, is a portable, removable medium, usually a **floppy disk**, that inserts into a **disk drive**. It is designed for a variety of purposes: to **install** new software, to **backup** files and programs, or to exchange **data** with another computer. Because diskettes are small, light and inexpensive, they are popular for storing relatively compact files of 1.44 **megabytes** or less. Some high density diskettes, such as the diskettes made by **Iomega** for its popular **Zip** drive, can hold 100 MB or more. The chief disadvantage of a diskette is speed: They access data far slower than a **hard disk drive**.

Displace is a type of distortion filter that pushes the pixels of a picture in accordance with a selected **displacement map**. Where the pixels in the displacement map (which can be a grayscale picture or texture) are pure black or pure white, the pixels are shifted the most. Where the displacement map pixels are less than pure black or pure white, the shift is proportionately less. And, where the displacement map pixels are pure gray (exactly halfway between black and white), there is no shift in the picture's pixels. Some interesting special effects and textures are based on this filter.

Displacement map is a grayscale image that is used as a reference for the distortion that is applied to another picture when using the **Displace** filter.

Display refers to a computer monitor, screen or **CRT**.

It is also a command in which the user opens up a **dialog box, palette** or other portion of a software interface, so that it is visible on the monitor.

And, display is a verb which is used when an item (**image**, file, **palette, icon, interface**, etc.) is shown (displayed) on a computer monitor.

Display colors is a **command** or **option** in which a computer monitor or **graphics board** capable of showing only 256 colors can be used to simulate **24-bit color**.

Dissolve is a **blend mode** that applies the foreground color or the upper layer as fine dots of color. SEE **Color mode, Channel operations** and **Difference**.

Distort is a group of filters and/or tools that change the relation and position of the components or the pixels of a picture. For instance, a **ripple** filter applies a distortion that makes it look as though a pebble has been dropped into the picture and, like a lake, has formed concentric ripples around that point. Or, pulling on the corners of a rectangle with the **skew** tool in a vector program will distort that rectangle's shape.

Dithering is a technique used to simulate **halftone** printing on a **desktop** printer. It works by altering the size, shape or position of the dots that a printer produces. Dithering is used primarily to print **continuous tone** photographs or images on printers capable of producing only black and white dots. The human eye will see gradients of color and grays though there are only dots, if the dots are placed well. Many programs feature various dithering options to allow the user to select the best quality, fastest printing time, etc.

DLL stands for **Dynamic Link Library**, a **Windows subroutine** that provides information to the computer that allows an **application program** to operate properly. Sometimes, a software manufacturer will **update** the DLLs instead of the entire program.

Document is computerese for a letter, message, note, manifesto, list, or any other data that contain text, numbers, or a combination of both. Because documents are generally **character**-based, the files in which they are contained are generally much more compact than image files. However, it is possible to insert images into documents, and vice versa. A document may be created by a variety of programs, including **word processor, desktop publishing, database, spreadsheet** and others.

Document imaging is the copying and storing of records on computer, **microfiche, microfilm** or other storage media. Although it uses the same or similar hardware (**scanners, film recorders, CD-R drives**, etc.), it differs from **image editing** in that the information is document- or text/numbers-based, not graphics-based. Corporations and institutions use document imaging instead of filing cabinets to archive invoices, correspondence, accounts and other company records.

Documentation is the instruction or operating manual(s) that comes with software or hardware to aid in installing, using and troubleshooting that software or hardware. It may be a book, booklet, folder, brochure, video tape, **CD-ROM, Acrobat** or a text file read on the computer monitor. Most programs complement documentation with **on-line help**, or assistance accessed from the computer. **Third-party documentation** refers to books, tapes, **discs** and other aids prepared and sold by companies other than the product manufacturer. Users often resort to third-party documentation when they need to know more than the manufacturer's documentation provides.

Dodge and burn is a photographic term that has its origins in a darkroom technique for holding back or letting light shine on photosensitive paper. Where light is withheld—dodging—that section will be lighter or even white. Where light is allowed to fall through—burning—that portion of the image will appear darker.

Dodging and burning are commands in **image editing programs** to improve a photographic image with less than perfect **exposure**. It is also used to selectively increase or decrease areas of contrast, shadows and highlights.

Some **digital artists** will use dodge and burn tools to "sculpt" shapes and areas of pictures with light and shadow, as well as to increase or decrease detail.

Dongle is a small hardware device on a cord that attaches to a **serial, parallel** or **ADB** port, and into which the printer, **mouse, digitizing tablet** or other device may be plugged. Its purpose is to function as a lock against unauthorized use of an **application program**, usually expensive **image editing** or **CAD/CAM** software: one program, one dongle. Dongles work in one of several ways. In one scheme, the program periodically and automatically commands the computer to send an electrical signal. If the dongle responds correctly, the program continues, but if it doesn't, it will **freeze** or exit the program. Another method is to scramble and descramble electrical signals going to the printer, so that the program will function normally but may not be able to print unless the dongle is present. Dongles are annoying devices that the computer industry has periodically forced manufacturers to abandon, but you may still encounter them with some programs.

DOS is the acronym for Disk Operating System, the software that is "God" to your computer. DOS keeps track of everything that happens on a computer and its drives.

While a disk operating system is necessary for any computer, the term *DOS* usually applies to IBM compatibles, or **PCs**. *Operating System,* or **OS**, is the term most often used in regard to Apple Computer Company's **Macs** and **PowerMacs**, though it also applies to other non-Apple operating systems, such as IBM's **OS/2**.

Dot is a point of ink, color or black displayed on a screen or output to a printer. It is usually expressed in **dpi**, or dots per inch, the number of dots that a particular device can display or output per square inch. The more dots, the higher the **resolution** (i.e., the more detailed and better looking the image). While 300- and 600-dpi **laser** printers are common office devices, 720-dpi **inkjet** printers are common low end color printers. Some dots are immutable, with fixed size, shape and position. Other devices have the ability to vary the size, shape and position of the dots, to further enhance resolution and image quality.

Although frequently used as interchangeable terms, dots per inch is not the same thing as **pixels per inch** (**ppi**) or **lines per inch** (**lpi**). Technically, ppi is used to measure resolution of pictures that exist inside the computer or are about to be scanned into the computer, while **lpi** measures **halftone**, or printing press resolution. Dots per inch measures desktop printer output.

Dot gain is a printer's term that measures the amount of ink bleed, spread or smear that occurs when **halftone dots** increase in size during the **proofing, platemaking** or **printing** process. Dot gain will darken a printed image if not adjusted properly. However, it can be predicted relative to the ink and paper being used and must be compensated for to produce the best, smear-free images. Programs that include **prepress** tools and capabilities usually have a set of commands for adjusting dot gain.

Dot leader refers to a series of dots used to fill up all or part of a line, so that the reader's eyes may more easily follow items in a list. For instance, there may be a dot leader between the name of a chapter and the number of the page on which it starts in a book's table of contents.

Dot matrix printer is a nearly extinct technology in which 9, 24 or more tiny electrically driven needles that form a **character** hit a ribbon and leave an impression on paper. Dot matrix printers can be noisy and, relative to newer technologies, slow and inferior. They have been largely superseded by **inkjet** printers, which are faster, quieter, and generally produce better image quality.

Dot shape refers to the shape and configuration of **halftone** dots. To increase print quality, halftone dots vary in shape. The size of the dots depends on the angle of the **screen**, or mask, used for transforming a **continuous tone** image into a series of dots that can be run off on a printing press. Screening and dot shape must be coordinated correctly to avoid producing an undesirable effect called a **moiré pattern**.

Double-click is a command that requires the user to quickly depress a button twice on the **mouse** or **stylus** to make something happen. A single-click and a double-click on the same **icon**, button or command may produce different results. For instance, a single-click on a **paintbrush** icon will select that tool to be used in painting. But a double-click on the same icon may open up the options **palette** associated with that tool.

Download is the process of transferring **data** from another computer or from an **electronic mail** system to your computer, via a **modem**, through a cable, or over a **network**. It is the opposite of **upload**, when a user transfers data from his or her computer to another computer or an electronic mail address.

DPI stands for Dots Per Inch, or the number of dots or points that a printer or a computer monitor can output or display in a square inch. Dpi is often written as an equation of length versus height, such as 300×300 dpi or 600×1200 dpi.   SEE **Dot**.

Draft quality is what a printer outputs at top speed. It is not as dense as (that is, it doesn't have as many **dots per inch**), and therefore of inferior quality to, an image or document printed in the **output** or **high quality mode**. Draft quality prints are useful for file copies, to send over a **facsimile machine**, or as an **FPO** (**For Position Only**) to check visual information like lighting or model placement.

Drag is a very commonly used action in which the user clicks his or her **mouse** or **stylus** on an **image, dialog box, window** or **block** of data, holds the button down, and moves or drags it to another location.

In graphics programs, drag is often used for changing the dimensions or shape of a **selected** area or **object**.

Drag and drop is the ability to move data from one program and literally drop it into another program. For instance, a user might drag and drop an image created in an **illustration** program directly into a **layout** in a **desktop pub-**

lishing program. Of course, both programs must be open at the time, and a portion of each must be displayed on the screen.

It is also the ability to move data between **windows** in a single program, such as dragging a selected part of a picture into another picture. As such, it is an alternative to the **cut** and **paste** commands.

DRAM, also called **RAM**, stands for Dynamic Random Access Memory, the most common form of short-term electronic memory in a computer. DRAM comes on **chips** and chewing gum–size plug-in boards called **SIMMs** (Single In-Line Memory Modules) or DIMMs (Dual In-Line Memory Modules). It differs from the faster, more expensive **VRAM** (Video Random Access Memory) used in some graphics boards, and very expensive **SRAM** (Static Random Access Memory) that is rarely used in **desktop** systems. DRAM is usually configured in 4, 16, 64 and 128 **megabyte** SIMMs or DIMMs, and it's almost axiomatic that the more DRAM your system has, the better and faster it will run. A typical **PC** running under **Windows 95** will have between 32 and 64**MB** of DRAM, though one running **Windows NT** usually needs at least 64 to 128MB, and a high end **PowerMac** or PC being used for professional imaging may have anywhere from 128MB to 1024GB, or even more of RAM.   SEE **RAM**.

Draw   SEE **Drawing programs, Illustration**.

Drawing programs are graphics programs that use **vector tools** to create pictures. They are also called **illustration** programs and are a type of **object-oriented** software. Popular drawing programs include **illustrator, CorelDRAW** and **FreeHand**.

Drawing tablet   SEE **Digitizer**.

Drivers are software **applets** or **utilities** designed to connect a piece of equipment or a **peripheral**, such as a printer, **CD-ROM** drive, or **scanner**, to the computer. Drivers are usually provided by the manufacturer of the device and are typically installed after the hardware has been attached.

Drop cap is the first capital letter of a paragraph, which is larger than the rest of the letters and dropped down so that it fits squarely, aligning to the tops of the other, smaller letters in the first line. Popular in

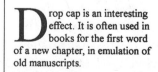

D rop cap is an interesting effect. It is often used in books for the first word of a new chapter, in emulation of old manuscripts.

Drop cap

medieval manuscripts, it is now used to interesting effect in book and magazine printing. All **desktop publishing** and most **word processing** programs provide tools and commands for creating drop caps.

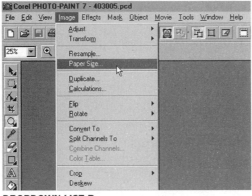

DROPDOWN LIST A

DROPDOWN LIST B

Dropdown list: In just about every program, the names at the top of the screen **(A)** are the headers for dropdown lists. Click on any of the words and other commands drop down **(B)**. Also called *pulldown menus,* dropdown lists may be found in numerous other places in your software. When uncertain, just click on a name to see what happens.

Dropdown list is a group of commands, tools or options that scrolls out into full display when the user clicks on a button, arrow or command. It is also called a **pulldown menu**.

Dropouts, or data dropouts, are **bits** or **character**s that, for a variety of reasons, are deleted from an image or file. Literally, there are tiny holes in the image where information no longer exists.

In **scanning** and with **digital cameras**, dropouts are those data bits that fail to be transferred and saved to a file.

Drop shadow is a special effect that creates the appearance of a shadow behind portions of a picture, **text** or **objects**. The result is that the object, text or image area looks as though it is floating above the rest of the picture and casting a shadow.

Some programs have an automatic drop-shadow effect, others require that the user

DROP SHADOW A

DROP SHADOW B

Drop shadow: While drop shadows are popular for setting type apart from an image, they can be used on any object or masked portion of an image.

do some **copying, pasting, moving, feathering, filling**, etc., to a **mask** or object **silhouette** to create the effect.

Drum scanner refers to an expensive, high quality, professional **service bureau**–type device for scanning **transparencies, negatives** and reflective art. They're called *drum scanners* because the original film or art being scanned is taped onto a rapidly rotating clear glass cylinder. Unlike conventional **flatbed scanners**, which incorporate a **linear CCD** to recognize and translate scanned material into **digital data**, drum scanners use a more expensive and precise technology, called a **photomultiplier tube**, or **PMT**, to do the same thing.

However, there are now **desktop** drum scanners that also use CCDs and are less expensive than their service bureau cousins.

Dry processing is a chemical-based photographic technology in which the developer and fixer (the chemical that makes the image stable and permanent) is incorporated in the printing paper and is usually activated thermally. The Fujix Pictography 3000 **continuous tone** color printer is an example of a computer printer that uses dry processing.

DS-505, DS-505a and **DS-515** are Fujix's **digital cameras**, identical to the **Nikon E2, E2n** and **E2s**, that capture images onto a **CCD** and store them on a **Type I** or **Type II** solid state **PC memory card**. Both the Fujix and the Nikon digital cameras are 8-bit devices built onto altered Nikon camera bodies and can take Nikon lenses.

DSP chip stands for Digital Signal Processor chip, a souped-up, high speed **coprocessor** that manufacturers use to accelerate a variety of different functions. Most DSPs are used to speed up **screen redraws**, which will be boosted from 40 to 1500% faster. DSPs were very popular for graphics applications, but more extensive use has been eclipsed by faster, more sophisticated **CPUs**, which largely eliminated their need.

DTP SEE **Desktop publishing**.

Dummy is a printer's term for a mock layout in which text is represented by nonsense characters (also called **greeking**) and the space for pictures is blocked out by any graphic that happens to be at hand. It is used to show the overall design of a page.

Duotone is a two-tone print. Technically, it is a black & white photograph that has been reproduced as a two-color (green & white, red & white, etc.) **halftone**. Some graphics programs feature the capability to transform a black & white or color image into a duotone.

Duplex applies to both scanning and desktop printing—it's the ability of a device (a scanner or a printer) to read or print to or from both sides of the page, usually by flipping the paper.

Duplicate is another word for copy, but it usually refers to a selected image, layer, object or area of an image.

In many illustration or 3-D programs, a selected object or image may be duplicated by simply using the **hot keys** Control+D (on a PC) or Command+D (on a Mac).

In other situations, software may have an icon for the purpose, such as one that is often in a **layers palette**, which automatically duplicates the currently active layer.

Dust and Scratches is a filter that, like the **despeckle** filter, attempts to remove unwanted dirt and other **artifacts** by applying a special **blur** filter. If the dust and/or scratches that you are trying to eliminate came from faulty or dirty scanning, it would be best to rescan. That way, you won't have to lose any sharpness or focus for the sake of removing the dirt.

DVD   SEE **Digital Video Disc**.

Dye sub   SEE **Dye sublimation printers**.

Dye sublimation printers, also called gaseous diffusion or thermal diffusion printers, are **output devices** that produce true **continuous tone**, photographic-like prints. They work by heating the primary colors of Cyan, Magenta, Yellow, and blacK (some printers use only three primary colors and produce black by blending all three colors) until they turn into a gas, and then spraying the gas onto specially **coated glossy paper** stock. Unlike most color desktop printers, where the three or four colors are laid down as tiny but separate dots that appear to the eye to blend, dye sublimation printers actually do blend the colors.

Dynamic Data Exchange   SEE **DDE**.

Dynamic Link Library   SEE **DLL**.

Dynamic range is the measurement of highlights and shadows in a picture. The wider the range between highlights and shadows, the larger or wider the dynamic range. Contrasty pictures have a wide dynamic range, whereas dull, foggy pictures have narrow ones.

In bitmapped or image editing programs, the dynamic range of a picture may be directly viewed and edited in the **histogram** or **levels** dialog. The **brightness/contrast** commands and tools also affect dynamic range.

The human eye can distinguish a much wider dynamic range than can film. Transparencies can capture more than prints; monitors more than desktop printers; film more than scanners or digital cameras. Therefore, some device manufacturers will rate their scanners or filmless cameras according to a dynamic range scale in which that of film (4.0) is optimum.

Dynamic sliders, or **dynamic scrollbars,** look like horizontal or vertical calibrated sticks with an arrow or marker that can be pushed or pulled in either direction by **clicking and dragging** with a **mouse** or **stylus**.

Or, they may be bars with arrows on either end and a box in the middle. When the user clicks on the end arrows the box in the middle moves toward that end, or the user may drag the box in either direction.

Dynamic sliders and scrollbars are used to quickly change a particular value, such as **brightness, color** or **saturation**. Depending on the program and the function, the user may see a corresponding, instantaneous change to the picture, or the effect may take place only after a command is given. Usually, the immediate change occurs when a **preview** option is checked. Most programs also permit changes to be input by typing in a **numerical value**, which is more precise than using a dynamic slider.

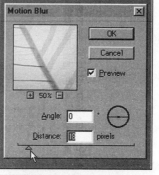

DYNAMIC SLIDERS A

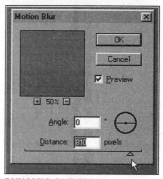

DYNAMIC SLIDERS B

Dynamic sliders: The slider at the bottom of this Photoshop Motion Blur dialog is dynamic. To change the value in the box just above the slider, all you have to do is click and drag on the slider's arrow.

Edge connector refers to a type of port that is used primarily by **floppy drives** and **hard drives**. It's a thin (about ¹⁄₁₆″) board with gold plated or tin "fingers" that are in essence **male connectors**, and into which a **header** (a cable with a plastic **female connector** on the end) is plugged. Edge connectors sometimes become tarnished, which can interrupt or even impede electrical signals from making the proper connection. Whenever that happens, most edge connectors can be renewed by going over them lightly with a pencil eraser (but making certain that the pieces of erasure that flake off are properly dusted off).

Edges are those areas in a **bitmapped** picture where there are strong lines of demarcation between differences in **contrast** (light and dark). The software recognizes these areas as edges. For instance, suppose you have a photograph of a white picket fence. Unlike in **vector** or **illustration** programs, in which objects are defined mathematically by their shapes, outlines and fills, the pixels that make up the posts in that white fence are no different from the pixels that make up the darker background—except that they are lighter than the background. Therefore, that line where the dark pixels of the background meet the white pixels of the fence is recognized by the software as an edge. It's actually the way the human eye sees edges.

The ability of bitmapped software to identify (or detect) edges within the composition of a picture is important so that many of the filters and other commands that act on those edges (such as the **unsharpen mask** or **find edges** filter) can work.

Incidentally, contrast is such an important aspect of how the human eye sees edges that such contrast is integral to the concept of picture sharpness. That's why a slight increase in contrast may improve an out-of-focus photograph.

Edit is the process of changing, refining, enhancing, deleting, condensing or consolidating text and/or images. It is not an automatic process, but one that requires the user to make and execute decisions or choices.

It is also a very common **pulldown** menu in nearly all programs (usually the second menu from the left at the top of the screen), where, typically, the **cut, copy, paste** and other commands are **nested**.

Editor is an **applet**, or program within a program, that allows a user to change, refine, enhance, delete, alter, condense or consolidate text or images. A text editor works with text, and an **image editing** program with **bitmapped images**.

In some programs, an editor is also a portion of the software (sometimes represented as a **palette** or **dialog box**) where the user may edit, customize or create **special effects, fills**, colors, **layers, animations**, etc.

EDO is short for Extended Data Out, a relatively new type of high speed **RAM**, or memory chips.

Effects are changes that can be made to a picture, such as those caused by using **filters** and other special commands. Usually, these changes involve a series of computations, which may or may not be customized by the user. For instance, some programs have lighting effects in which the user may **interactively** place a light into a picture or **scene** and define its direction, intensity, type, color, etc. After the user has made all those choices, the software then computes how the introduction of that specific light will affect the rest of the picture, and changes the picture accordingly. Effects can be much more simple, or even more complex.

Effects is also a **pulldown menu** at the top of the screen of some programs, where filters and other available effects are **nested**.

EFI (Electronics for Imaging) is a hardware and software manufacturer that specializes in color solutions. You'll see their EFI color tables incorporated in various imaging programs. Other products include Fiery color servers and Fiery XJe controls for desktop color printers.

EGA is the abbreviation for Enhanced Graphics Adapter, a now obsolete video standard used on IBM-AT–type computers in the 1980s. It has long been superseded by **VGA, SVGA** and XVGA graphics standards.

EIDE stands for Enhanced IDE, an updated, souped-up version of **IDE** that has become the most common type of interface for **hard drives** and **CD-ROM** drives. Its main improvement over IDE is that it allows the computer to attach four, rather than two hard drives and/or CD-ROM drives. It also permits faster **data transfer rates**.

EISA is the abbreviation for Extended Industry Standard Architecture, the first practical **32-bit** interface for **PCs**. It fell out of popularity when **VESA** and more recently, **PCI peripherals** and boards entered the marketplace.

Elastic Reality is a high powered, **cross-platform morphing** and **animation** program that has been used by Hollywood and Madison Avenue for some very famous and visually exciting **special effects**—such as the malleable evil robot in the movie *Terminator 2*.

Electrostatic process uses magnetism, iron filings and heat to print text or **images** onto a piece of paper. Most laser printers (including color **laser printers**) and photocopiers are electrostatic machines.

Ellipsis is a **vector tool** used by **illustration** or **draw** programs to make 2-D circular shapes that may or may not be longer in one dimension than in another. An ellipsis that is perfectly even in all directions is a **circle**. The ellipsis tool is used by clicking and dragging until the ellipsis is the size that you want and, then, releasing the **mouse** or **stylus** button. To make a perfect circle with an ellipsis tool, most programs use a **constraining key**, such as **Shift** or **Command**, which is pressed while the tool is being used. The ellipsis or circle that is thus created is defined by its underlying mathematics, which is what makes it a vector shape as opposed to a conglomerate of **pixels**, which would make it a **bitmapped** shape or **image** area.

Em dash is a printer's term for a long dash or line used to separate words or letters. It's

Ellipse: The Ellipse tool is found in the toolboxes of most imaging programs, and it is one of a number of *primitive* shape tools, which also include rectangles and polygons.

An em dash — which was originally meant to be the width of a capital M — is used in this manner in sentences.

Em dash: An em dash is often used to break up long sentences, to insert a supplementary thought related to the rest of the sentence, or to replace commas or parentheses.

called an *em dash* because it's supposed to be the width of a capital *M*—one of the largest **proportionately spaced** letters in the alphabet.   SEE **Proportional type**.

E-mail is the same as electronic mail, or data delivered electronically over a **network** or via a **modem**. E-mail is quickly replacing normal postal delivery (now called *snail mail*) for sending memos back and forth between colleagues, friends and clients. Image files can be sent to remote computers through some sort of e-mail system, though because of the size of some image files and relatively slow transmission rates, it may not be the most practical or economical means.

Embed is a command or process by which an item from one program (such as a picture from **Photoshop**) is placed into an item in another program (such as a document in **PageMaker**). A truly embedded item continues to be editable in its native program, and any editing done to it is reflected in its display in the other program. This is part of **Windows Object Embedding** and **Linking** or **OLE**. The equivalent on the Mac is **Publish and Subscribe**.

Also, **firmware**—software instructions on a chip—are often embedded, or attached or inserted into hardware devices, such as **scanners** or **drives**.

Emboss is an **edge**-detecting filter that seeks out areas of contrast in a bitmapped picture. Then, it turns the picture into an embossed or sculpted version of that image. Often it is a **monochrome** (usually of a user-selected color), with the edges a darker version of that color. But some emboss filters use the original colors of the picture.

Emergency boot diskette is a **self-booting** 3.5- or 5.25-inch diskette or a custom-made CD-Rom disc, that you create while installing an **operating system** or **utility**. It

EMBOSS A

EMBOSS B

Emboss: Emboss is an edge-detecting filter that makes an image look like a bas-relief.

allows you to **boot up** when your computer won't start normally, and it usually contains files that will diagnose and correct problems and even **fatal errors** that cause your computer to **freeze**.

Emittive color is another name for **Additive** color.

EMS stands for Expanded Memory Specification, which was a method used to get around the **DOS** memory limitation of being able to access only 640 **kilobytes** (**K**) of **RAM**, or electronic memory. When DOS was first developed, few computers had more than 64K of RAM. That's because RAM was very expensive, and neither computer nor software design had been developed to the point that they could even access, much less utilize, more than 64K of memory. In what was thought at the time to be very progressive and far reaching, DOS greatly extended the frontiers of RAM, to 640K of user-accessible memory, plus another 384K of nonaccessible memory that could be used for a variety of system functions. It soon became apparent that 640K was not enough memory to run certain programs (**Windows 95** requires a minimum of 8 **megabytes** of RAM—that's more than 12 times 640K—and some software require 64 megabytes to operate properly).

EMS was developed by **Intel, Lotus** and **Microsoft** to access memory higher than 1 megabyte (640K plus the extra 384K). EMS is transparent to the user and, once set up, requires no maintenance. It is largely a moot issue, since Windows 95 and **Windows NT** are no longer crippled by the DOS 640K limitation.

Emulation is the process of imitating. In imaging, it most often refers to a tool, command or program that is capable of imitating something from the non-computer real world. For instance, a **paintbrush** tool in a **bitmapped image editing program** may be set up to emulate a real world watercolor brush.

Emulation is also the process or act of mimicking or imitating other software or hardware. For instance, there are several programs and **peripheral boards** that will allow a **PowerPC** computer to run **Windows**, a **PC operating environment**, in emulation. Usually, there's a trade-off to running in an emulation **mode**, either in slower speed, or in certain problems and incompatibilities that prohibit 100% compatibility. But it's a relatively inexpensive way to run programs designed for a different computer system that wouldn't otherwise be possible.

Emulsion is the photosensitive material that coats the plastic, which is film. There can be significant differences in emulsions made by various manufacturers. (In other words, Agfa film and Kodak film capture light differently.)

And because of the inherent instability of color dyes and pigments, there are even slight differences among emulsion batches from the same manufacturer, depending on when the film was made. These differences can affect the **color balance** of the photograph, which is the reason professional photographers will test shoot an emulsion batch before doing an important job. Then, they'll make certain that the entire job is shot with film that comes from the same batch (i.e., from the same manufacturer, with the same emulsion ID number). There are no emulsion problems or considerations with **digital cameras**.

> An en dash is shorter than an em dash, and it is used to separate letters or numbers in a series, such as in the reference to chapters 1–4.

En dash: Typographers and desktop publishers use en dashes to separate letters and numbers.

En dash is a printer's term for a short dash, or line, used to separate words or letters. It's called an *en dash* because it's supposed to be the width of a capital *N*—a midsize **proportionately spaced** letter.   SEE **Em dash**.

Encapsulated PostScript, or **EPS,** is a **file format** that is used primarily for exporting graphics into **documents** and **layouts**. As a **PostScript** file, it is **resolution-independent**, which means that it will output at the resolution of the printer or **output device**.

When you place an EPS graphic into a **desktop publishing program**, it may display as only a gray box or placeholder. That doesn't mean that the picture hasn't been imported correctly, just that the **DTP** program can't display it. The picture will still print out properly. If you want to display the picture in the layout, then, when you export it, be sure to click on the option for including a **bitmap preview** with the EPS file. That will provide a low resolution preview, which the DTP program will be able to use for display.

End node is the last point on a **Bezier** or **spline** curve. It defines where the curve will end. In an **open path** or curve, there are two end nodes. In a **closed path**, there are no end nodes, because the curve goes around in a continuous loop.

Endpoint   SEE **End node**.

Engine is the computer term for a **dedicated** or purpose-built processor or mechanism. In graphics, an engine is usually any hardware device designed to speed up operations, such as an **accelerator** or a **coprocessor**.

Another example of an engine is when one manufacturer uses another company's product as the heart of its own product, i.e., a **Canon** engine powers the **Hewlett-Packard** Laser Jet Series II printer.

And then, there are the technocrats who call any **application** a software engine. For instance, they would call an **illustration** program a **vector** engine, because it is meant to take vectors and do something with them.

Enhanced IDE   SEE **EIDE**.

Entry level describes software or hardware that is less expensive and less powerful than the latest, best, **state-of-the-art** product. An entry level is often the best choice for novices or people on a limited budget. Many (but not all) entry level programs and machines may be **upgraded** to a higher level of productivity, power and expense, when the user becomes more sophisticated and/or has more money available.

For instance, an entry level **digital camera** is an under-$500, **point-and-shoot** device with virtually no user-changeable controls, few features and relatively limited **resolution**. But, when you are ready for a more powerful, higher quality camera, you'll have to buy another one.

Envelop is a type of **bounding box** that tools or commands (such as **perspective** or **skew**) which reshape objects or areas may place around that object or area. To change the shape of the object or area, the user pushes on the corners of the envelop. As the envelop changes, so does the object or area inside it.

Environment describes the combination of computer and **operating system**, such as a **PC** running under **Windows** or a **Macintosh** operating under **System 8**. Technically speaking, **Microsoft**'s Windows 3.0, 3.1, 3.11 and 95 are not self-contained operating systems, but operating environments that function under **DOS**. However, **Windows NT** is a full operating environment in that it isn't built on, or designed to run under, DOS.

EPS   SEE **Encapsulated PostScript**.

Envelop: Using a *perspective tool*, we placed an envelop of dotted lines around the bottom word, which we were then able to reshape. The reshaped envelop in turn reshapes the word (which originally looked like the top word).

Equalize is a command that evens out the percentage of bright and dark pixels in a bitmapped image. It is usually an automatic command that requires no **interactive input** from the user. To see what it does, look at the **histogram** (or **levels** dialog) of the picture before applying equalize. Then, look at the histogram again, after using equalize.

Erasable optical   SEE **CD-R drive**.

Erase is a command that deletes (removes) a selected or active area, object, layer, text or other element in a picture or document.

Eraser is a tool that acts like a real world pencil's eraser, in that it rubs out whatever it presses on, in effect removing color. However, the eraser in a bitmapped program is much more versatile, acting like a paintbrush that either paints with the **background** color instead of the **foreground** color, or with levels of transparency. In either case, depending on the program, the eraser may be **pressure sensitive**, which means that it will react to the user's pressure on a **digitizing stylus**, and it may be customizable, as to shape, size, transparency, etc.

ESDI stands for Enhanced Small Device Interface, a type of **hard drive interface** that once rivaled **SCSI** in speed and popularity, but is now all but obsolete.

Ethernet is the most popular type of **LAN**, or **Local Area Network interface**, a method of linking computers and other devices. In most IBM-type PCs, Ethernet is implemented by installing an Ethernet **peripheral** board in any empty **expansion**

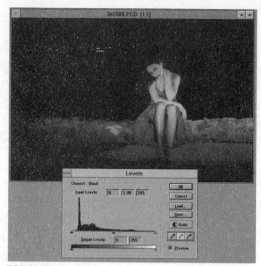

EQUALIZE A

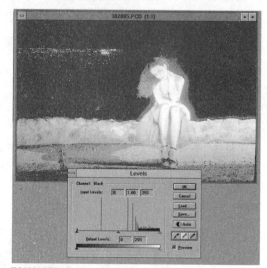

EQUALIZE B

Equalize: In these before **(A)** and after **(B)** pictures, you can see how destructive the Equalize command can be. Notice in the *histograms* how pixels have actually been destroyed. (That's the areas of the graph where there are now less dense or shorter spikes.) *(Photo from Corel Stock Photo Library.)*

E

slot. On most Macs (except for the least-expensive **entry level** systems), an Ethernet port is built into the computer.

Ethertalk is Apple Computer Company's software that operates and controls its **Ethernet** port or card.

Exabyte is the name of the corporation that produces **8mm DAT drives** and other **tape backup** devices.

Excel is the name of **Microsoft**'s best-selling **spreadsheet** software, available for both the PC and the Mac.

Exception word dictionary is a user-defined dictionary in **desktop publishing** and **word processing** programs that overrides or supersedes the program's automatic **hyphenation dictionary** to break a word at the end of a line at a specific point or points. For instance, if you prefer that the word *bachelor*, whenever it appears at the end of a line, be hyphenated as bache-lor rather than bach-elor, that's how you would input it in your program's exception word dictionary.

.EXE, or Execute, is the **file extension** in **DOS** that indicates that the file is a program, i.e., it can be executed by typing in the name of the file at the **DOS prompt**, or at the **RUN . . .** command on Windows 95, or by **double clicking** a **mouse** or **stylus** on it or its icon.

Exit is a command to terminate or end a program (usually on PCs). On Mac computers, the Exit command is **Quit**. In either case, it is usually the last option on the left-hand **pulldown menu**, under File.

Expand is a command that allows the user to enlarge or spread out the **border** or **marquee** around an image by selecting a specific number of **pixels**. The larger the number of pixels, the greater the border expansion. Its opposite is the **Contract** command.

Expansion board   SEE **Peripheral board**.

Expansion slot is an **interface** built into a computer's **motherboard** into which **peripheral boards**, such as a **modem, graphics board** or **network card**, may be plugged. There are a variety of expansion slots: **ISA, EISA, PCI**, VESA, etc., according to the type of computer system. Keep in mind that the peripheral board interface must be compatible with the expansion slot, i.e., a Macintosh-based NuBus board cannot fit into PC-based ISA or EISA slots. Better-equipped systems may have six, eight or more slots.

Export refers to translating and transferring data from one form to another, to a file, another computer, a device like a printer, etc. It is often a **menu option** that allows the user to select the file format and the destination to which the exported image will be sent. Export sometimes is a faster print option than the Print command. Its opposite is the **Import** command.

Exposure is the act of allowing light to fall onto a **photosensitive** film or chip to capture an image. In other words, it is the essence of photography. An overexposed photograph is too light, washing out details and tone. An underexposed photograph is too dark, so that you can't see enough of the subject. Exposure problems can be corrected in the darkroom or in the computer, though there can be trade-offs in image quality. The best answer is to take a well-exposed picture in the first place, but that can be difficult in less than ideal lighting situations. On-camera exposure controls include f-stops, shutter speeds and exposure compensation, all of which work to increase or decrease the amount of light the lens allows to fall onto the film or the chip. Of course, professional cameras provide even more controls with f-stops and shutter speeds.

Extension is the three-letter abbreviation that comes after the dot in a PC file. It often indicates what **file format** is being used. For instance, in the file name *face.tif, face* is the name of the file, while the *.tif* is the extension that indicates that the file format is **TIFF**.

On the Macintosh, an extension (formerly called an *INIT*) is a small program or **driver** that loads into the computer on start-up. These small programs do all kinds of things, from attaching a digitizing tablet to running a color matching system. When installing a new program, it is often necessary or helpful to turn off the Mac's extensions. This is done by holding down the Shift key when you turn on the computer. When you see the message *Extensions Off,* release the Shift key.

External storage device is any **drive** (**hard drive, DAT drive, MO drive, SyQuest, Bernoulli, CD-ROM**, etc.) that is attached externally by cable to the computer's **SCSI, USB** or **parallel** port. (Internal devices fit inside the box that is your computer.) Unlike similar drives that are internal to the computer, external storage devices are self-contained in that they almost always come in a separate case and have their own power supply. In addition, SCSI devices may also require a **terminator**, or terminating plug, though some devices come equipped with built-in terminator switches.

Extrude is a filter that transforms a 2-dimensional object into what appears to be a 3-dimensional one. It's a special effect that is often used by Madison Avenue to make text snap off the page.

Extrude: The Extrude command or filter is often used on *2-D* text to make it appear *3-D*.

Eye icon is generally used as a quick on/off visibility button. For instance, if the eye icon on a **layer** in a **layers palette** is shown as open, then that layer is visible. To make the layer invisible, click on the eye icon, which closes the eye. To make the layer visible again, click on the eye icon once more, which opens the eye.

Eyedropper is a tool (also called a **color probe**) that is shaped like a medicine eyedropper and is used to sample color. In many programs, it reads the color and interprets it in terms of its component **primary colors**. That way, the user has the data necessary to accurately repeat that color precisely, to determine if it is a printable (within the **output** device's **color gamut**), or a number of other tasks and decisions that require precise color information.

The eyedropper is also used by some bitmapped programs to set **white point, black point** and the midtone point of a picture. Users click the white point eyedropper on the pixel that they want to set as the brightest in the picture. Similarly, they can use the black point eyedropper to set the darkest pixel. Then, the software realigns the **dynamic range** of the picture accordingly. To see the results, view the **histogram** of a picture before and after using a white point or black point tool. In many cases, the white point/black point

Eye icon: Whenever you see an icon that looks like an eye, you can make the object (or layer, channel, or whatever it is associated with) temporarily invisible by just clicking on the eye. In some programs, that will cause the eye icon to close. In other programs, the icon will also become invisible. To make the object, channel, layer, etc., visible again, just click on the closed eye or on the space where the eye icon was.

tools are very good for fixing a poorly exposed photograph. But, sometimes, they can destroy very subtle or effective coloring. For instance, they have been known to turn a beautiful sunset photograph into one that looks as if it were taken at midday. That's because there may be no pure white in a sunset photo, but the white point tool will force the color range to create white where the tool is clicked.

F keys refer to the Function keys, along the top or the side of the keyboard, which are generally numbered F1 through F12 (though some keyboards go up to F15). They are used in different ways by various programs to initiate commands or functions, such as bringing up a **Help menu**, executing a file **save**, and displaying a **palette** or **toolbox**. Sometimes, F keys are used in conjunction with other key combinations, such as with the **Shift, Command, Control, Option** or **Alternate** key.

Facet is a geologic term that refers to one side, surface or face of a crystal, such as the facets of a diamond. In graphics, it refers to each side of an object, or **polygon**, which may be selected, colored, given a texture, etc.

Facet filter is an effect in which clumps of similar, adjacent **pixels** are automatically selected and then colored or treated as geometric solids. The result is often the appearance of a hand-painted picture.

Facsimile   SEE **Fax**.

Fade-out is a user-controllable effect in which brush, pencil, pen or airbrush strokes are laid down so that the end of the strokes fade. Its intent is to imitate how real media tools lose paint at the end of a stroke as they are applied. Fade-out can be adjusted so that the fade is gradual or abrupt, it loses color, or it becomes transparent at the end of the stroke.

Another definition of Fade-out, taken from the movies, is to create a cinematic effect in which a scene ends by fading to

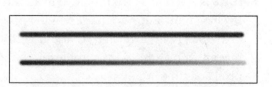

Fade-out: The top stroke was painted with no fade-out. The bottom stroke was set to fade to transparent after 200 steps.

black or to another picture. Not surprisingly, it's used in multimedia as a transition from one scene or slide to another.

Faster is an option in many graphics programs that allows the user to control the rate of speed at which an effect or a command is executed. For instance, faster applied to a **mouse** or **stylus** will move the **cursor** across the screen more rapidly.

Fast SCSI is one variety of **SCSI**, or a high speed **interface** between the computer and a **peripheral** or peripherals. It can transfer data at speeds up to 30 **megabits** per second, which is 2 to 4 times faster than plain SCSI. Fast SCSI cables can be physically discerned from **SCSI** and **SCSI-2** by their slim connectors.

FAT stands for File Allocation Table, or the section of the hard disk that holds information about the location of all stored files. FATs occasionally become corrupted, which is the reason most disk **utilities** have a mini-program for making a "snapshot" or duplicate of the FAT each time the computer **boots** up and stores it in a safe area on the hard drive. Then, if the FAT becomes corrupted, the user may use the utility to restore from the duplicate FAT file.

Fatal error is, alas, just as it says: an error committed by the computer or the software from which the user cannot recover. When it occurs, it may be impossible to save data, properly exit the program, or even get any response from the keyboard or **mouse**. The best way to get beyond a fatal error is to turn the computer off for about 10 seconds, and then start it up again. Depending on what caused the error, you may be able to resume normal start up in the **Safe Mode**, or you may have to reinstall part or all of the program in which the error occurred. The worst-case scenario is that you can't start your computer normally, which may require you to find the **emergency boot diskette** that you prepared while installing the **operating system** or use a **utility** like **Norton Utilities**, and follow the directions for repairing the error.

FatBits is the Mac's own primitive image editing program that allows the user to change **bitmapped** images on the **pixel** level.

Fatbits (with a small *b*) is also used to describe using the **zoom tool** to magnify a picture to the pixel level, so that tiny details may be edited, one pixel at a time.

Fax is short for Facsimile machine, a device which transmits exact images (pictures, text or whatever) stored on paper or as a computer file to another facsimile machine or computer via a telephone line. Faxes that handle paper are stand-alone machines that attach directly to the phone line and need no other device to operate. Those that handle computer files are usually **fax/modem boards**, which plug into the computer and require that the computer be turned on and the fax software be active to send and receive faxes. Once received, a fax will reproduce the image, on paper or as a computer file, depending on the receiving fax. The received image will look exactly like the sent one. Most faxes are Type III devices, though more advanced faxes that send color may be newer, faster, more-expensive Type IV devices.

Faxback is a type of service often offered by **software** and **hardware** companies' **tech support**. The way it works is you fax your questions or problems to the company's fax number, and they will respond to your fax machine or board within 24 hours with the answer. It is far cheaper for the company to maintain than live tech support and, supposedly, a good deal for users because faxback is usually free. (Increasingly, companies charge by the minute or the call for live tech support.) The main problem with faxback is you may not get the correct or complete answer to your question.

Fax/modem specifically refers to a board or device that may be used either to send or receive faxes from a computer, or as a **modem** for transmitting or receiving computer files via a telephone line. Most modems now come equipped with fax capability.   SEE **Fax**.

Feathering is the process of softening or blurring edges of a **selected** part of an image (by blending the **pixels** on the edge with adjacent or surrounding pixels). Feathering is often used to remove the hard, unnatural edge that is associated with cutting and pasting selected or **masked** areas.

Another definition of feathering relates to the kind of **brush** you are using. One that does not have a hard edge, but, instead, has an area of **transparency** around it, is said to be feathered.

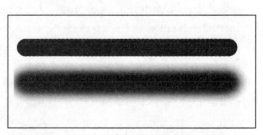

Feathering: This is the process of softening an edge by applying an increasing amount of transparency from the inner part of the edge to the outer. The amount of feathering is usually expressed in terms of a radius of pixels. The line on the bottom is feathered; the one on top has a hard, nonfeathered edge. Similar feathering may be applied to masked image areas and objects.

Female connector is a coupling device in which the part that plugs into the computer or cable consists of small round holes. A **male connector** is the opposite—it consists of small round pins that fit into the female's round holes. The trick is to make certain that you have the right sex connector. Fortunately, there's a small device called a **gender changer** that consists of either female-to-female or male-to-male connectors that will allow you to attach the same sex connectors.

Field hails from database nomenclature and describes a category into which a specific type of data are entered. For instance, there may be separate fields for first name, last name, street address, city, state, phone number, etc. In many programs, the user moves between fields by pressing the Tab key or clicking on a **mouse** button. Sometimes, imaging programs' **dialog boxes** will describe options, in which the user types preferences, as fields.

FIFO is short for First In/First Out. It is commonly used with hardware and software **queues** or multiple tasks scheduled to be executed, such as a dozen images that the user wants to print out at one time. These tasks are assigned and executed one at a time, based on the order in which they were placed in the queue. Usually, the first one in a FIFO queue is the first task executed. In other words, the first in is the first out.

File is the computer term for a cohesive, related collection of data—an image, a letter, a spreadsheet or whatever—that can be given a unique name and therefore may be saved or retrieved at will. Files can be any size and can come in a variety of different **formats**. Usually, an **applications program**, such as **Photoshop** or **Microsoft Word**, will generate files. This is why the same, or a similar, application program will be required to properly access or **open** that file.

File Allocation Table SEE **FAT**.

File conversion is the process of changing the **file format** in which **data** are saved. For a variety of reasons, a user may wish to save a file in a particular format. Usually, it has to do with **compatibility** with other computers or programs. File conversion is also used to exchange data with clients, **service bureaus**, etc., that have specific requirements that may be different from yours or your machine's. Many application programs allow files to be automatically converted when they are saved. All you have to do is click on the appropriate file format; sometimes, you also have to add or change the extension in the file name. In addition, there are specific file conversion programs.

File extensions are identifying letters or codes—usually three spaces long—manually or automatically placed at the end of the file to identify the type of data in the file. For instance, **TIFF** (aka TIF) is a type of image file, as are **BMP, GIF** and **EPS**. On **PCs**, any file with an EXE, COM or BAT extension is a program file or will launch a program file. The extension is written after the file name and is separated from the file name by a period. For instance, in the file george.bmp, *george* is the name of the file, and *bmp* is the extension. File extensions are used primarily in **DOS** and **Windows** environments.

File formats refer to the structure or the way data are stored. For many technical and marketing reasons (both logical and frivolous), there are literally hundreds of different file formats. It's important to use a file format compatible with the program, equipment and ultimate destination (client, **service bureau, print shop**, etc.) that you are using.

Because file formats are not created equal, users should choose their file format not only based on compatibility, but also on the kind of information the format will save. For instance, some bitmap image formats will save **masks** (**alpha channels**) and some will not. If you need to retain a mask, you'll want a format that will save it for you. Many major graphics programs include a **utility** for converting one file format to another, though there are also heavy duty **third-party** utilities better equipped for faster and more accurate file conversions. However, if your graphics program supports (opens and saves) both formats, conversion can be as simple as opening the file and then saving it under another name to the new format.

File Manager is a **Windows** 3.x **subprogram** that displays and controls all the files on the computer's **storage devices**. It allows the user to perform a number of file-related functions, such as **format, view, delete** or **copy**. In **Windows 95** or **NT**, the file manager has been replaced by **Windows Explorer**, which functions similarly to file manager.

File server is the computer that runs a **network**. It's like a traffic cop, determining where files are stored, how each computer communicates with the other computers on the network, managing **e-mail** or electronic messages, etc. Often, it will have **gigabytes** of data on its hard drives as a central repository that can be quickly accessed by attached computers. It may also double as the **print server**, or the computer that controls which files are output on which devices.

In addition, some network managers consider it simpler and more efficient to store all **data** for the network on a server. However, others prefer redundancy (saving the same data on the server and on the individual **workstation**) for the purposes of security and convenience.

Fill is a command, tool or process that puts color, a **gradient**, a **texture** or other material into a selected area or object. For instance, in a drawing of a fruit basket, the user might select the apple to fill it with red, or he or she might select the basket to fill it with a wicker texture.

F

The fill tool is usually represented by a tilted bucket **icon**, and it is sometimes also referred to as a paint bucket tool.

Fill bucket   SEE **Fill**.

Filler, in newspaper jargon, refers to any piece of **text**—a definition, factoid, snippet of history, one-sentence biography on a famous person, statistic, etc.—placed to fill up a blank space in a **layout**. It doesn't much matter what kind of material is used as filler. Sometimes, a small graphic (cartoon, photo, illustration, etc.) may be used as a filler.

Film generally refers to any photosensitive material (slide, negative, roll or sheet) exposed in a conventional camera or **film recorder** that produces a realistic image of a subject.

In **prepress**, film is the shortened term that refers to the **color separated** files that have been individually recorded onto photosensitive material and processed.   SEE **Color separation**.

Except for Polaroid instant film, other types of film must be developed in a series of environmentally hazardous chemical baths, which usually take at least an hour or so to process. Those are two reasons **filmless cameras** are growing in popularity.

Film camera, or conventional camera, is a light-proof box consisting of a lens, aperature, shutter and a **film** holder. The shutter and aperature are used to regulate the amount and duration that light falls on the film. Often when there is insufficient light, an auxiliary source, such as a built-in flash or a set of studio strobelights, is used for proper illumination. Except for Polaroid cameras, which use instant film that is developed and printed in the camera, the exposed film must be removed and processed through a series of chemical baths. Film cameras are generally less expensive, more versatile, and produce higher quality images than **filmless cameras**. However, before a film camera's image is suitable for use in a computer, it must either be **scanned** or burned onto a **Photo CD**.

Filmless camera is an electronic device that uses a photosensitive **CCD** or CMOS chip instead of **film** to capture images.

Generally, there are two kinds of filmless cameras. In a **digital camera**, the just-captured image is immediately passed to a built-in **ADC** (**Analog-**to-**Digital** Convertor) chip that translates the analog image into a digital file consisting solely of zeros and ones. A **still video camera** captures and stores its images as analog data (just like videotape), and the analog-to-digital conversion is executed later, either externally through an ADC box, or with a **video capture board** or **frame grabber** board.

Filmless cameras are further subdivided into a variety of categories: real-time cameras, studio cameras and backs, scanner cameras and backs, and entry level, midlevel and high end devices.

Real-time cameras, also called **array cameras**, are portable handheld devices capable of capturing live action, such as sports, activity scenes and live models.

Studio and scanner cameras and backs, of which many are **linear** devices, take three separate exposures (one exposure each through a red, blue and green filter) to create a color image. Therefore, they must be stationary devices mounted on a tripod. Although they cannot capture real-time action in color, which limits their applications, studio cameras and backs are capable of producing much higher **resolution** (more detailed) pictures. Most studio devices do not contain internal memory, but must be tethered to a **desktop** or **laptop** computer.

There is a wide range of filmless cameras, from comparatively inexpensive (a couple hundred dollars) **entry level** to midrange and on to high end (for tens of thousands of dollars).

Film recorder is a device that **outputs** a computer graphics file onto conventional photosensitive film (usually transparency film). On its most basic level, a film recorder works by displaying the image, line by line, on a small, very high resolution black & white television monitor inside a sealed cabinet (which can range in size from a breadbox to a refrigerator). Then it is photographed with a camera, lens and film that are inside the same light-proof box as the screen. To capture color, the red, blue and green color channels are scanned and displayed separately, and photographed through corresponding red, blue and green filters. Because the scanning can take anywhere from seconds to minutes (depending on the **resolution** and **file size** of the image), the camera shutter is left open in the bulb position (time exposure) during the entire exposure.

Film recorders are rated according to how many lines' resolution they are capable of outputting. A business film recorder may output 2K images, or images with a total resolution of 2,000 lines. Better 35mm slides usually require a film recorder capable of outputting a minimum of 4K. Larger film sizes and better film recorders may output 8K, 16K or even as high as 64K. Generally, the higher the resolution, the more expensive the film recorders.

Film recorders are used primarily by businesses and service bureaus that need to output to film for highest quality printing, slide shows and multimedia presentations. As art and photo buyers become more computer savvy, the necessity to translate computer images onto film, and hence the need for film recorders, becomes less important and significant.

Film scanner is an **input** device specifically designed to **scan** or "read" an image from film negatives and/or slides. It then **digitizes** the picture and sends it to the computer, where it may be edited, enhanced, output, saved, etc. A film scanner works similarly to a **flatbed scanner** but with a much higher resolution, superior optics and a smaller field of coverage. However, the biggest difference between them is that they scan different kinds of material—film as opposed to reflective media (such as paper). Because of greater precision and the ability to produce higher **resolutions**, film scanners are generally much more expensive than flatbed scanners.

There is a hybrid device that slips on top of many flatbed scanners, called a **transparency module**, that allows the flatbed scanner to scan film (which requires a direct light source) as well as flat art (which needs a reflected light source). While it may do a servicable job with film formats larger than 4×5 inches, most are not suited to produce high quality scans with 35mm or 120mm film.

Filters are **macros** that contain a series of commands that will change the appearance of an image. A filter may be accessed through a **dialog box**, in which the user makes choices among options. Or, a filter may require nothing more from a user than to choose it from a **pulldown menu** or elsewhere in the program; then, it runs on its own.

Among the popular filters are those that **sharpen, render**, create **special effects**, change a picture's color and/or quality, etc.

While most image editing and illustration programs contain some filters, there are also **third-party** filters, which are purchased from other **vendors** and then **plugged into** the main program. Xaos and Kai's Power Tools are examples of third-party filters.   SEE **Plug-in**.

Another (and older) definition of filters are optical devices that fit over camera lenses to affect how the light from a scene is captured on to film, a **CCD** or CMOS.

Find is a command that allows the user to locate specific files, words or sentences stored in the computer or a document. A related command is Find/Replace, which will find the specified file, word, sentence or whatever, and replace it with another specific word, sentence, etc.

Find edges is a **special effects filter** that turns a bitmapped picture into something that looks like a hand-drawn sketch. It does this by seeking out

FIND EDGES A

FIND EDGES B

Find Edges: There are a number of different Find Edges filters, but they all act on the same principle (as do the Sharpen filters)—seeking out areas of high contrast (which software defines as an edge) and then heightening them. *(Photo from the Corel Stock Photo Library.)*

areas of high contrast, which it turns into lines (based on colors in the picture), while changing all other areas of the picture to either white or the current **background** color (depending on the program, the specific find edges filter and how the preferences—if there are any—are set up).

Finder or **multifinder** is a part of the **Macintosh operating system** (**System 7.x**) that keeps track of icons, files, extensions, etc.

Fine art emulation uses digital imaging tools to make pictures look as if they were drawn or painted using real world fine art techniques, such as impressionism and cubism. Most fine art emulators also create effects that are meant to look like the brush strokes of famous artists, such as Van Gogh and Seurat. Fine art emulation is often offered in conjunction with other tools and effects that provide **natural media emulation**. A pioneer program in fine art emulation is **Fractal Design Painter**, but now many image editing programs have some brushes, filters or other tools that emulate the traditional arts and artists.

Finger Painting can be emulated in bit-mapped programs by using the **smear tool**, which pushes pixels around. It is usually represented by a pointing finger **icon**. If you are using a **digitizing tablet**, and if the program is **pressure sensitive**, then the smears can even emulate the pressure of your fingers by reacting to how much or how little you press on the **stylus**.

Firewall is the term used to describe a device or strategy designed to keep a **network** running smoothly without any intrusions from the outside or from within the network.

FireWire is a high speed interface that may eventually equal, or even replace, **SCSI** as the interface of choice for image editing drives and **peripherals**, especially because it can be **daisy chained**. Technically, Fire-Wire is known as the **1394 serial bus**. It can operate at speeds of 50 **megabits** per second, about 5 times the speed of normal **Ethernet** and between 2 and 5 times faster than SCSI.

FINE ART A

FINE ART B

Fine Art Emulation: While there are many filters that can convert a photograph into something that looks like it is painted, most of the best digital fine art emulations are achieved by using the software tools available, rather than a simple filter.

Firmware is any instruction set (or programming) built into a device or placed on a chip or cartridge that acts as a **driver** (software directions) to provide the information necessary for properly operating the device. Firmware is generally not user changeable or programmable, though some devices put their firmware on accessible chips that can be easily removed and replaced when an **upgrade** is desired.

FITS is the French company that developed **Live Picture**, a **resolution**-independent image editing program designed for very large image files (typically 100 **megabytes** or more).

It's also the name of the Live Picture file format that retains the image data—the file format that contains editing information is called **IVUE**. FITS and IVUE work in conjunction to allow the user to edit large image files in **real time**. This system is the basis for **Flashpix** format and technology.

Fit Text to Path, or **Fit Text to Curve,** is a command that aligns text to a **path, curve** or other object. In this way, you can have your name laid out in the shape of a star or a rollercoaster (when the star or rollercoaster is the previously drawn path or curve).

Fixed disk is another word for **hard disk,** or a high speed internal or external storage device on which the **operating system, application programs, utilities** and **data files** may be found. It's also called a **Winchester disk** or **Winchester drive.** Most computers have one or more internal fixed disks as part of their standard system (or configuration). However, hard disks can also be of the removable type, such as **SyQuests** and **PCMCIA Type III.**

At the beginning of the microcomputer era, the largest hard drives held 5 or 10 **megabytes** and cost hundreds of dollars per megabyte. Today's state-of-the-art hard drives typically hold 1 **gigabyte** or more and cost as low as 10 cents per megabyte.

Fixed spacing, or **monospacing,** in typography refers to giving equal space to every character. For example, the letter i would be given the same space as the letter w, even though the w is actually several times as wide as the i. In **proportional spacing,** each character is accorded a variable space, based on its physical width, so that capital W would take up 5 times the amount of space as the small i.

Flashpix is a multiresolution or tiled-image file format developed by **Live Picture** and popularized by Kodak that is becoming increasingly important with **digital cameras** and storing and exchanging pictures on the **Internet.** Because it is more versatile and can produce better quality images, it is being groomed as a replacement for the popular **JPEG** picture format.

Fit Text to Path: This text was set to fit to a circle, then the line defining the circle was turned off. Similarly, text can be fit to a path, drawn using a Bezier or spline tool.

Flatbed scanner is a desktop device designed to **scan** or **input** any flat art or text, such as a sheet of paper or a book page. Resembling small photocopy machines, most flatbed scanners are capable of scanning color originals. However, older or less-expensive flatbed scanners may be capable of scanning only **grayscale** or **black & white** originals. Generally, desktop flatbed scanners can accommodate originals up to 8.5 × 12.7 or 8.5 × 14 inches, though some can scan tabloid-size originals 11 × 17 or 12 × 18 inches.

Depending on the make or model, a flatbed scanner may accept attachments like an automatic document feeder, or sheet feeder, and/or a **transparency head** or module. The automatic document feeder can take a stack of papers and automatically scan them in without user intervention, while a transparency module has a built-in light source (usually fluorescent or cold cathode) for transparent material, such as slides or negatives. It used to be that flatbed scanners were used only for documents and low quality, low resolution picture scans, but as the technology continues to improve and prices drop, they are now being used professionally for many midquality image scans.

They are also used for OCR, or Optical Character Recognition, which scans documents into the computer not as images that look like the letters and numbers, but as characters, words, sentences and paragraphs that may be inserted and edited by a word processing program.

Flatten image is a command that **merges** the **layers** of a picture, so that all the **image** elements that were in those layers are in one layer only. It is usually possible to select which layers will be merged without touching any of the other layers. But in a flattened image, all the layers are collapsed into one.

Flicker SEE **Jitter**.

Flip is a command that turns a picture or a selected portion of an image upside down (vertical flip) or over (horizontal flip).

Float is a command that lifts an object, area of an image, text, selection or whatever, up off the image or layer in which it resides. Then, it may be edited, manipulated, moved, etc., independent of any other element in the picture.

Palettes, toolboxes and dialog boxes may also be said to be floating, if they can be moved by **clicking and dragging** on the top bar, and/or if they can appear over an image.

Floating point calculation, or FPC, refers to any math-intensive function that directly accesses the computer's built-in or separate math **coprocessor**, to speed up the calculation. In some graphics programs, there are various **fil-**

ters and **special effects** that use floating point calculations instead of raw **CPU** speed. However, their widespread use is limited by the extra programming sophistication it takes to access FPC instead of normal CPU activity.

FLOPS stands for Floating point Operations Per Second, a unit of measurement for **floating point calculation** speed and performance. The figure is often expressed in megaflops, when the number of calculations performed exceed 1 million per second. Obviously, the higher the number, the better the performance.

Floppy SEE **Floppy disk**.

Floppy disk is an inexpensive removable diskette—usually either 3.5 or 5.25 inches in size—capable of storing a limited amount of data. Floppies are most commonly used to install new programs, to make **backups** and **archival** copies of small-size files, and as a transfer medium between computers. But because files now tend to be larger than a floppy's capacity (typically, 1.2 or 1.44 **megabytes**), their use is waning. Many new programs are now installed from **CD-ROM**s, not floppies, and most backups and data transfers are made to other, higher capacity media, such as **SyQuests, MOs, CD-Rs** and **Zip cartridges**.

Floptical is a storage medium (from Insite Peripherals, Inc.) that combines the size, convenience and relatively low cost of a **floppy diskette** with the accuracy of a laser beam. Because of greater precision, a Floptical features a significantly larger storage capacity than a simple floppy diskette. But competition from a number of other removable storage media has kept Flopticals from achieving a great market success. Therefore, they are relatively rare.

Flyout menu holds a list of selections or options that are found by clicking on an arrow or some other icon or button in a pulldown menu, dialog box, palette or elsewhere. After the click, the menu opens up in such as way that it looks like it is scrolling out or flying out—hence, the name.

FLYOUT A

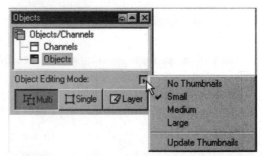

FLYOUT B

Flyout: (A) Anytime you see an arrow pointing sideways in any dialog or palette, as in this Corel PhotoPaint Objects Palette, click on it. **(B)** A list of additional options, commands or features will flyout (be displayed).

FM screening   SEE **Stochastic printing**.

FOCOLTONE colors is a brand-name electronic color palette that matches a printed swatch for **process** inks. Like **Trumatch, Toyo, Pantone** and other swatch/palette systems, it attempts to more precisely define and match **digital** design colors to printed colors.

Focus is the mechanical or electronic process of assuring optimum sharpness of a subject being photographed through a lens. It's when the lines surrounding the subject are darkest and thinnest. Soft-focus and out-of-focus subjects display blurry, soft lines. The various **Sharpen** filters and commands in image editing programs attempt to improve the focus of pictures by increasing contrast in various ways.

Folder refers to the method used to organize **files** on the Mac and in **Windows 95** and **Windows NT operating systems**. Using the file cabinet metaphor, each group of files is collected and stored in a folder; several folders may be nested in a folder, and so on. In earlier versions of Windows and **DOS**, files are collected and organized in **directories** and **subdirectories** rather than folders. It's strictly a matter of nomenclature, since folders and directories are virtually the same thing.

Font is the name given to a family or collection of **typefaces** of a similar design. For instance, a single typeface, such as Courier, may be normal, italic, bold or bold italic; all those typefaces collected together are described as a particular font.

Computer fonts generally come in two different formats: as **bitmaps** and as **scalable** (or **outline**) fonts. Bitmapped fonts are premade to a specific size and style and stored as individual files. They're made up of a set number of tiny dots and cannot be changed. Scalable fonts are stored as **vector** information, so while the shape remains the same, the size may be varied. Most modern fonts are scalable rather than bitmapped because they look better (that is, they don't exhibit the "**jaggies**") and can be stored as smaller files. Most printers have at least 4 different fonts built into them, while others come with 70 or more fonts. Most graphics and **desktop publishing** programs also come with fonts. In addition, many software companies sell collections of fonts. In fact, one big problem is that a user may have too many fonts available, which can hog **hard disk** space and which, in turn, can appreciably slow up computer operations.

Font generator is a program that creates **bitmapped font**s from an outline. As the size of the font increases, its characteristics change to retain its optimum appearance. Unlike the **font scaler**, which generally makes **on-the-**

fly fonts, a font generator creates the requested fonts and then saves them to a file for future use.

Font scaler is a **subprogram**, often built into printers or included as part of graphics, **desktop publishing** and **word processing** programs that generate on-the-fly **vector**, or **scalable fonts**. Each font is defined mathmatically as an **outline** and can be enlarged to any requested size.

Footprint is the amount of space (also called *desktop real estate*) that a particular device (printer, monitor, scanner, etc.) occupies. The smaller the footprint, the less area it requires.

Foreground is literally that which stands or is in front or is the primary action. Therefore, the foreground **layer** or **window** is the one that is on top (i.e., in front) of all the others. And the foreground program is the one that takes precedence in **multitasking**. SEE **Background**.

Foreground color is the color that will be used by drawing and painting tools and by various commands. For instance, if the foreground color is red, then, when you used a **paintbrush tool**, you will be painting with that color red. In graphics programs, the foreground color can be chosen from a **color palette**. Some software also allow users to create new colors in a mixing palette, where they combine colors that already exist—much as an oil painter combines pigment from tubes of oil paint to create just the right color.

Format is the structure of a file, page layout, image or whatever. For instance, the format for the first page of a monthly newsletter may involve two columns of text, a company logo in the upper left corner, and a picture in the middle.

Format is also the structure of a **disk**—be it a **floppy disk, hard drive** or any other **storage device**—that divides or sections the drives to receive and store data in such a way that they can be identified and retrieved whenever necessary.

The command format is invoked to prepare, or **prep**, fresh, unused disks and drives. There are literally scores of different formats, so it's important to know the exact type needed for your application or device, as well as the correct command nomenclature for creating the correct format. SEE **File format**.

For position only, or **FPO,** is a graphics arts term that describes a photograph or print generated to check that the subject is correctly positioned and the composition laid out as expected. Unlike a **comp**, an FPO is strictly to ensure that the subject is framed properly, and not to make sure that the lighting is correct, the exposure accurate, the colors true, etc.

Forum is an electronic meeting place where users connecting to the **Internet, America Online** (**AOL**), and other **on-line** services can share ideas and information. Sometimes it is conducted in **real time**, where anywhere from two to hundreds of participants can log on simultaneously and interact with each other with no delays. Other forums are conducted over a period of time, and the participants never directly communicate with each other—they leave questions, answers or comments, leave, and log on at another time to see who responded to them. Forums can be useful venues for obtaining ideas, information, tips, tricks, or whatever, on programs, techniques, hardware or software problems, buying advice, and so forth. The only caveat is that there's no guarantee that the information you obtain on a forum is accurate or complete.

Fountain fill is the same thing as a **gradient fill**, which is a smooth transition between colors.

Four-Color Process, also called *full color,* refers to the use of the **process colors** of Cyan, Magenta, Yellow and blacK (**CMYK**) on a printing press. When these four fundamental printers' inks are combined, they create all the other colors possible from that kind of printing press. They do a rather good job, printing images that look like **true color** or **photorealistic** color images.

FPO   SEE **For position only**.

fps is an abbreviation for *frames per second,* or how many images or **frames** a camera can capture in a second. It's used to describe the speed of a film or video camera, with 30 fps being the normal full-motion speed used for television and computer video. Film cameras usually operate at 24 or 25 fps, depending on whether they're going to be shown on American or European television. Web video speed ranges from 1 frame every minute to 1 fps up to 30 fps, depending on the **color depth, resolution** and dimensions of each **frame**.

Fractal Design Painter is a popular **paint** program for both the **PC** and the **Mac** that emulates **fine art** and **natural media**, thereby providing the tools for creating paintings in the computer that look as if they were made with oils, watercolors, charcoals, etc., on textured canvas. It can also transmutate a normal photograph into what looks like a work of art.

Fractals come from the world of mathematics and the attempt to quantify and predict chaos. In the world of graphs, these mathematical formulae generate fantastic geometric patterns, in which colors and shapes are compressed, twisted and turned into themselves, like strange surrealistic swirls of color. **MetaCreations' Kai Power Tools** provide filters that give digital artists easy (nonmathematical) access to fractals.

Fragmentation occurs when a file is saved at two or more physical locations on a **disk** or **hard drive**. One of the most important innovations in computer storage was the development of what is known as **Random Access**. This allows data to be saved, not as a contiguous block in which all the **bits** and **bytes** from a single **file** are physically next to each other, but are saved randomly, as fragments, anywhere there is free space on the disk or drive. The **operating system**'s **file allocation table** (**FAT**) keeps track of where all the fragments are stored. Random access significantly increases the amount of storage space on a disk or drive.

Fractals: Despite their mathematical origins, fractals are visually exquisite, and you don't have to be a mathematician to use them in your art.

But there's a penalty for random access storage, and that's performance degradation. As more and more files are split apart and stored randomly, it takes the computer an increasingly longer time to find all the fragments and stitch them together. Fragmentation can gradually slow disk **I/O** performance by 5 to 25%. The solution to fragmentation is a process called **defragging** or **optimizing**. That's when a utility is run to physically move related data (by writing and rewriting them) to a contiguous, or continuous, file which occupies a single block. This allows the operating system to find, load and save the file much faster, since it does not have to take the time to search out and either stitch together (load) or fragment (save) it.

Frame is the box or **window** on the monitor that holds an image. Many programs allow a user to have more than one frame open simultaneously, although only one (the frame on top) can be active at a time.

In **illustration** and **desktop publishing programs**, a frame is also the outline of the **page**, which may or may not be made a printable border, depending on the program.

F

Frames that look like picture frames from the real world can be made in graphics programs. Some software have a command for this (sometimes called **border**) and/or **clip art** frames that can be added to the current picture.

Frame buffer is the part of **RAM**, or electronic memory, used to hold an image, the editing processing that is being done to it and the related **undos** (or information about the appearance of the image before it was edited). The more memory specifically apportioned to a frame buffer, the greater the number of or the larger the images, or the greater the number of image edits (and undos) that can be held in memory. Otherwise, they must be held in **virtual memory** (part of the **hard disk** used as a substitute for much faster, but much more expensive RAM). SEE **Scratch disk**.

Frame grabber is a **board**, box or device that intercepts and freezes a single still image from video (broadcast) signals. The video signals could originate from almost any video source, such as a camcorder, VCR, network or cable television feed, etc. Once captured, the image is converted to **digital data** via an **ADC** (Analog-to-Digital Convertor) **chip** and can be saved in almost any standard **bitmap file format**, such as **TIFF** and **PICT**. Frame grabbers are useful for capturing or intercepting relatively low resolution images, but generally, the image quality is inferior to pictures that originate as digital files (such as from a **digital camera**). **Snappy** is the name of a popular frame grabber device for **PCs** that attaches to the computer's **parallel port**.

Free is the amount of **RAM** (electronic memory) or **disk** space available to the user. When checking out your computer's **resources**, you'll often see information regarding what is free and what is used.

Freehand is a **selection** or **tracing tool** that is used to draw lines by hand (well, by **mouse** or **stylus**), as you would with any pen or pencil when you have no ruler, compass or any other aid for steadying your hand or your stroke. In some programs, the freehand tool is called the **lasso tool**, because the icon often looks like a rodeo lasso.

FreeHand is also the name of a popular high-powered **drawing** program by Macromedia, available on both the **PC** and the **Macintosh**.

Freeze refers to a computer failure. Generally, it means that something has happened in the computer, so that it stops working. You can't get the cursor on the screen to move, and it doesn't recognize input from the keyboard. Usually, the only answer is to reboot or turn off the computer. Hopefully, when you start up again, everything will work normally. However, in drastic situations, a freeze can be an indication of a hard drive crash or other catastrophe. Then, you may need to use a utility like **Norton Utilities,** or even resort to replacing some computer components to get up and running again.

Freeze-frame video is the term for slowing down motion picture animation (30 **fps**, or frames per second) to single frames displayed either one at a time, or changing once every second or half-second.

French spacing harks back to typewriter days, when all characters were **monospaced**. That is, all characters were assigned the same size, whether they were a small *i* or a capital *W*. To help the eye easily distinguish between the end of one sentence and the beginning of another, an extra space, called a *French space,* was added after the period. Modern word processing programs and **proportional spacing** have made French spacing obsolete.

Frequency is a graphics arts term that refers to the number of lines per inch (**lpi**) in a **halftone screen**.

It is also a unit of measurement for vibrations, or cycles per second (**cps**) of any electrical device or appliance. It's usually expressed in **hertz (Hz)**, **kilohertz (KHz)** or **megahertz (MHz)**.

Fringe is made up of the extra pixels that surround the edge of an imperfectly drawn **selection**. It consists of color from the original background out of which the selected area was lifted. To picture it, remember cutting out someone's face from a magazine—say, Marilyn Monroe or Elvis. When you didn't use the scissors precisely, you ended up with what looked like a halo around the head. Some **image editing** programs have a **defringe** command for removing these extra pixels. The problem is that the fringe may also contain stray pixels that belong in the selection, such as strands of hair. That's why many digital artists simply go back to the original selection and refine it, so that the extra pixels are left behind, while important parts of the selection aren't lost. (That's like carefully using the scissors again on the cut out of Marilyn, to remove her halo.)

Frisket is a graphics arts term that refers to the board or paper that was used to mask out areas of a picture. In the early days of digital imaging, programs often used the word to describe that portion of a picture which hadn't been selected. However, we have found no references to frisket in software recently, though digital artists will still use the word.

From saved is an **image editing** tool option that allows a user to paint (usually using the **clone tool**) with elements of a picture as it was when it was last saved. It is a very useful local **undo**, but it can also create **special**

effects when used in combination with **blend modes** and other options. SEE **From snapshot**.

From snapshot is similar to the **from saved** tool option, except that it takes advantage of the **snapshot** command that is found in some **image editing programs**. While editing an **image**, using the snapshot command saves, into memory, a copy of the picture as it is at that very moment. An interesting use of this option is to apply an effect to a picture, take a snapshot, then **undo** the effect. Then, when you paint from snapshot, you can apply that effect in precise locations in the image.

F-stop is a photographic term for the speed or aperature of a lens, or the amount of light that passes through the lens to the camera's **film** or chip. A smaller number (f2, f1.4, etc.) means that either the diaphram is opened wide or the lens itself is designed and constructed for capturing and passing more light to the film or chip (a "fast" lens). Curiously, the smaller the number, the faster the f-stop. A larger number (f16, f22, etc.) means that the diaphram has been reduced ("stopped down") in diameter to admit less light, or the lens is "slow" or designed to capture and pass on less light. A fast f-stop is useful in shooting available light or low light situations. A slow f-stop is used to increase **depth of field**, or the area (range of distance) in which the photograph is sharp and in **focus**.

Full bleed occurs when an image is printed onto paper without any margins or border. A few high end color printers offer full bleed as an option or as the default mode for printing. The other way to get a full bleed picture is just to cut the white margins off the print.

Full duplex in communications refers to simultaneous two-way transmission, i.e., the ability to send and receive data at the same time.

Full flush is a printer's term that refers to columns that align on both the left and the right. It's also called **full justified, left justified** and **right justified**, or **left and right justified**.

Function keys   SEE **F keys**.

Fuzziness in graphics means indistinct, hazy, vague, unsharp, unclear or blurry.

Gallery Effects are special effects filters that use the **Adobe open plug-in architecture** so they can be used in just about every **image editing program**, including those marketed by companies other than Adobe.

Galley is a typesetting term that refers to a **proof** or page proof that is produced before the page is printed in its final form. Galleys are most frequently used for final **proofreading**, or checking for typographical or grammatical errors in text, or unwanted lines or stray **artifacts** in images.

Gamma, when mentioned in relation to a monitor, refers to the brightness level of the computer screen and other aspects of the way it displays color and light. When **calibrating** the monitor, one of the aspects that is usually adjusted is the monitor gamma.

Gamma is also the highlight, shadow and midtone values that are changed in an image editing program's **curve dialog box**.

Gamut is a range. In **imaging**, it most often refers to a range of colors that fits certain criteria, such as being reproducible on a specific printer or some other **output device**. In some programs, you can set a color gamut alarm, so that you will be warned when a color you have chosen won't be printable on the chosen output device. In other programs, when you choose a color that is outside the gamut, the software will automatically substitute another printable color that will, hopefully, be close to the one you picked. Or, the program may allow the user to select between the two options.

The reason a color gamut alarm may be important is that the number of colors that can be displayed on a computer monitor is far greater than the

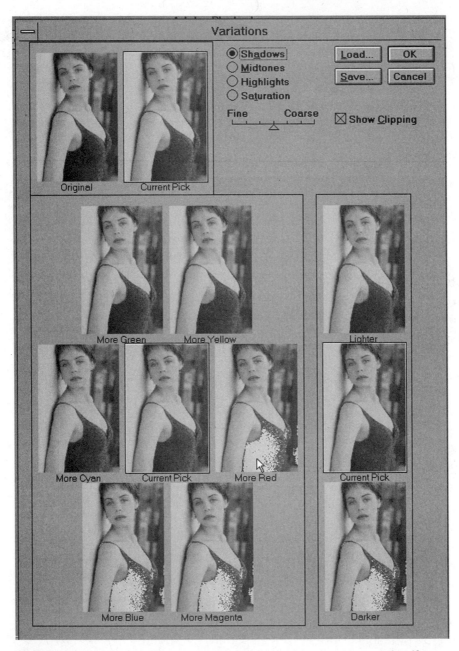

Gamut: In this Photoshop Variations dialog, off-color blotches warn us that if we add more red, more blue, more magenta or make the picture darker, we may produce a picture that is out of gamut (i.e., unprintable). This is also called *clipping*. *(Photo from Corel Stock Photo Library.)*

number that a desktop or prepress printer can output. Therefore, the colors you see on your monitor will often not be the colors that you get from your printer.

Gang is grouping or collecting two or more photographs or other art in a **queue** for automatic **scanning**.

Gateway refers to any device, usually a computer, that translates or **converts** data from one computer to another. Gateways are commonly used in **LANs**, or *Local Area Networks*.

Gateway is also the name of a large mail-order PC clone manufacturer headquartered in Souix City, South Dakota.

Gaussian blur is a **filter** that softens an

Gaussian blur: The Gaussian blur dialog gives the user a bit more control over how and where a picture will be softened, than other blur commands or filters give.

image, making the **edges** appear less sharp and distinct. Blurs are useful for blending two or more visual elements; reducing or eliminating scratches, dust and other unwanted **artifacts**; or creating an ethereal or hazy special effect. The Gaussian blur filter allows the user to select the precise degree of blur, as opposed to other blur filters that apply their effect at a preselected strength.

Gb or **GB**   SEE **Gigabyte**.

GCR   SEE **Gray component replacement**.

Gender changer is a plug that allows two connectors of the same type (**male** or **female**) to attach to each other. We always have a shoebox filled with gender changers, because inevitably, the cord on the new device that we are trying to attach to our system has the wrong gender plug at the end.

Geek   SEE **Nerd**.

General Preferences or **Preferences** is the series of **dialog boxes** that some programs have, which allow users to set various options for their personal default working environment. These options include how the **interface** looks: display or hide **dialog boxes, palettes, menu bars, exports**, etc.; what units of measure to use for any **rulers** or wherever users must make choices about size and dimensions; the **tolerance** level of the **color wand** and **fill bucket**; the look of the **background layer**; the distance that a **duplicate** will be placed in relation to the original **object**; and numerous other options that relate to that specific program. Once set up, users may choose to save the general preferences so that the selected options will appear as the **default startup** screen. But users can change them at will.

General Protection Fault, or GPF, is a **Windows 3.x** error message that tells you that the program you're in has ceased working. Alas, it's a fatal, unrecoverable error that forces you to close your program—you'll lose all the data that you haven't saved—and may force you to close Windows as well.

Generation is one step removed from the original. In photography, a copy of an original transparency, or a print from a black & white negative, is said to be *second generation*. A copy of a copy is *third generation,* and so on. Although using an enlarger to produce photographs from an original negative will always create second-generation prints, making copies from copies of slides may produce a 3rd-, 10th- or 50th-generation image. Generally, the further a generation is from the original, the more degraded the photograph will be. However, when an **image** is created digitally, each generation or successive copy, if it isn't altered or edited, will be identical to the original, with no quality degradation whatever.

Get Info is a Macintosh command that allows the user to display information on any file or program, such as its time and date of creation; in which **folder** it is stored; when it was last modified; and if it's a program, text or image file. It also allows the user to change the memory allotment for a specific program.

Ghost is a barely visible artifact, usually a line or lines that parallel solid edges in an image. Ghost images are generally annoying and unwanted, and are created by such things as a mistimed signal on a computer monitor or ink smears on a printout. Ghosts may often be eliminated by cleaning the **print head** or adjusting the cable from the monitor to the computer.

GIF is an acronym for **Graphics Interchange Format**, a popular **format** for color **images** displayed on and downloaded from **on-line services** and the **Internet**. Originally developed by **CompuServe**, GIF is an **8-bit** color file (that's a maximum of 256 colors). Although originally thought to be a **public domain** format and hence usable by anyone without paying royalties,

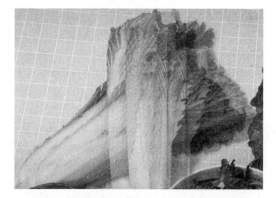

Ghost: A ghost image often looks like a faint double exposure.

CompuServe recently asserted its right to license and control the format. That, in turn, may force many companies sending graphics files to abandon the GIF format for one less expensive.

Gigabyte (**GB** or **Gb**) is, literally, 1,073,741,824 bytes of **data**. It's also expressed as 1,000 **megabytes**. That may sound like a huge amount of data, but most modern computer systems used for **imaging** have a minimum **hard drive** storage capacity of at least 4 gigabytes.

GIGO is computerese for **Garbage In/Garbage Out**. In other words, if you type the wrong **data** into a computer, you're certain to get the wrong results. GIGO is frequently used to describe human errors that cause computer errors. It was also the name of our first and most lovable computer.

Glitch is any computer error, problem, freeze or bug in which the computer, device or program being used doesn't work as intended.

Global describes setting a command or tool that affects an entire image, document or file. For instance, a Global Replace would replace all occurrences of a specified word, **object** or **image** element with another specified word, object or image element.

Gourand shading is one of the methods by which color, textures and illumination are applied to **3-D objects** and **scenes**. It is not as complex (and, therefore, not as realistic) as **Phong** shading. But it requires less processing power and fewer **resources**.

GPIB, the acronym for General Purpose Interface Board, is a **board** (for the **Mac** or **PC**) designed to transfer **data** at a high speed from the computer to or from a device such as a **film scanner** or a **film recorder**. GPIB boards and devices are mostly used for high volume professional applications, though they have been, in large part, replaced by **SCSI** boards and devices.

Grabber or **frame grabber** refers to a board or **peripheral** that captures **video images** from a variety of sources—camcorder, VCR, broadcast signal, or **still video camera**. Then, it converts the **analog** video signal to the **digital data** that a computer can read and use. It is also called a **digitizing board** or **capture board**.

Frame grabbers can be very inexpensive, such as the **Snappy** that plugs into a PC's **parallel port**, or expensive, like the **Targa** line of boards for **Macintosh, PowerMac** and **PC** computers. Some are designed to capture single, still images, while others are **multimedia** devices that will capture and convert animated sequences. As a rule of thumb, the image files captured by frame grabbers are of inferior quality to images that were originally captured as digital data. This may not matter with multimedia presenta-

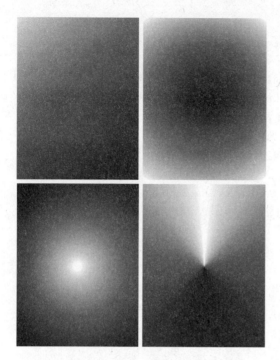

Gradient fill: Here are four rectangles filled with a linear fill (top left), a radial fill (top right and bottom left) and a conical fill (bottom right). Depending on the program, you may have quite a few options in how the gradient fill will be defined. For instance, the two radial fills pictured here are opposites of each other: one starting at white and going to black and the other starting at black and going to white. And the linear fill is set at a 45-degree angle to go from one corner to the other.

tions, but it can be a factor when those video-to-digital images are printed as a single, sizable photograph.

Gradient is a continuum of color with transitions between at least two or more colors.   SEE **Gradient fill**.

Gradient fill is a command or tool that colors an object or an area of a picture with a smooth transition of colors. The **gradient** is a transition between two colors or a series of colors. The direction and shape of the gradient may be defined as options of the fill.   SEE **Linear gradient fill, Radial gradient fill, Rectangular gradient fill**.

Graduated fill   SEE **Gradient fill**.

Grain, in photographic parlance, is the pattern formed by the coating of tiny photosensitive **silver halide** crystals on a clear Mylar film or opaque paper. Like atoms, granules are the smallest building blocks of a photographic image—a single photo may contain literally millions of granules that make up the grain. (It's similar to a **pixel** being the smallest element in a **bitmapped** image.) The more a photograph is enlarged, the more visible and pronounced the grain pattern. Extreme enlargement will transform a coherent, recognizable photograph into a pointillistic mosaic of grain—this can either be aesthetic or objec-

GRAIN A

GRAIN B

Grain: Adobe has been using this lovely little girl's picture in their tutorials for so long, we wonder if she might be a grandmother by now—or at least a CEO of some major corporation. Whatever, we used Gallery Effects' Film Grain filter on the portrait, to create the grainy appearance of a newspaper photo. Adding a smaller amount of grain sometimes assists in making disparate components of a collage look as though they belong together.

GRAIN C

tionable, depending on whether the viewer needs direct visual information or wants an artistic expression.

Because grain creates an effect and an impact upon the viewer, it is often included as a **filter** in many graphics programs.

Graphical User Interface, or GUI, is an **icon** and pictorial method of allowing a user to access a computer by using the **operating system**. Instead of typing in letters, numbers and names of commands and files, the user pushes a **mouse** which in turn moves the **cursor** on the monitor, then uses the mouse button to select an icon (by clicking) or to activate (by **double-clicking**) the icon's program or other purpose.

Graphics is the term used to describe or identify **images**, pictures, drawings, photos, illustrations, or any other nonverbal representation. On the computer, there are generally two types of graphics: **bitmapped** (or **pixel-based**, which is what photorealistic images are) and **vector** (which is mathematically defined, **object-oriented**).

Graphics is also an adjective that identifies items as being related to the display, manipulation, **output** or whatever of pictures, as they relate to and are used by computers.

Graphics board is a **peripheral** that plugs into a **motherboard** and provides the **interface** between the computer and the monitor. Most graphics boards consist of **memory** (either **RAM** or higher speed **VRAM**), one or more **coprocessors**, and electronic circuitry that will interpret the signals generated by the computer and translate them into the dots that will be visually displayed on a computer monitor. There are literally dozens of different types of graphics boards: **monochrome**, color, **true color, VGA, XGA, SVGA, high resolution**, etc. Users may buy a graphics board best suited for their needs and budgets from a wide variety of manufacturers and models.

Graphics suite is a group of graphics programs (such as **image editing, illustration, 3-D** and **animation**) that are packaged together and sold as an **integrated** whole. That means that the manufacturer usually claims that the programs will communicate with each other easily, sharing files and providing a wider range of tools and features than any single program could offer.

Sometimes, the suites are superb buys, offering power at a price that would normally cover only one program. But some suites are just thrown together as a marketing ploy rather than as an advantage or bonus for the user. In either case, graphics suites are getting bigger and bigger, requiring hundreds of **megabytes** for a full installation.

Graphics tablet   SEE **Digitizer**.

Gray balance is the process by which a program or a **calibration** system attempts to set a standard for neutral colors (white, gray and black), which will display no color tendencies at all. If the neutral colors are set correctly, there is a greater likelihood that other colors will also be displayed and **output** accurately. But, when it comes to computer color, nothing is 100% guaranteed.

Gray Component Replacement, or **GCR,** is a process that is used in preparing **color separation** files for **prepress**. When the **RGB** (red, green, blue) colors that are displayed on the computer monitor are translated into the **CMY** (cyan, magenta, yellow) **color model** that is used for printing inks, some black ink must be added. That's because in the real world of printing inks, the only way to get true blacks and good contrast is to add some black ink. The trick is to know how much black ink should be added, and to remove an equivalent amount of cyan, magenta and yellow inks. (Remember, cyan, magenta and yellow, when mixed together in equal amounts, theoretically make black, but in reality make a grayish muck.) The GCR setup for the **color separations** determines how much cyan, magenta and yellow to remove and how much black to add. This is similar to the **undercolor removal** (UCR) setup,

Gray Component Replacement: Setting up the GCR or *UCR* preferences for your printed images requires a certain level of expertise in *prepress*, or a considerable amount of trial and error. However, professional level *image editing programs* offer the tools for doing it. Pictured here is Picture Publisher's ink setup dialog.

though GCR usually adds more black and is considered to be more drastic and less subtle.

Grayed out refers to any commands, tools or options in a **menu, dialog box, palette, toolbox**, etc., that are not available to the user, either because the commands are not appropriate or applicable, a related or needed file is not open or available, or the needed hardware is not installed. For instance, an

Grayed out: Depending on how you have your system colors set up, grayed out commands may be some other light color. For instance, on one of our systems, the grayed out commands are actually white. Notice that the save commands (and others) are "grayed out," because we don't have an image open at the present. Therefore, those commands are irrelevant and unavailable.

image window must be open to use a **filter** on it. So, if no image window is open, the filters commands will be grayed out.

Fonts, programs and **drivers** may also be grayed out and hence not available under a particular **application**.

Grayscale is a picture that consists of up to 256 or 1,024 levels of gray, ranging from white to black. A black & white photograph is a grayscale picture.

Since a grayscale image contains **8** or **10 bits** of **image** information, it is the equivalent of a single-**channel** picture. In fact, three grayscale images, combined, using **channel operations**, can create a **24-bit RGB** color picture, even when the original image is 30 bits.

Greek, or Greeking, is a printer's term that refers to random or nonsense **type** that is set to show how the text will be laid out on a **page**.

Greeking is also the display of two or three continuous or broken horizontal lines as a substitute for the actual letters or numbers, because they are too small to be seen on the computer monitor. The lines are usually the same height as the characters, letters or numbers would have been.

Grid, or **guides,** relate to the precise position of the **cursor** according to what is known as an ***x/y* axis** or **matrix**. The grid consists of very fine lines or dots (which may or may not be displayed) along the horizontal and vertical axes of an image or the entire computer monitor. As the cursor moves, a displayed number denoting its exact position is correspondingly changed, using a **status line** at the bottom of the screen or the bot-

Grayscale: This color (RGB) photograph was turned into a grayscale, using Photoshop's mode conversion. *(Photo from Corel Stock Photo Library.)*

Greek: Page layout programs (such as Page-Maker or Quark) will often "greek" text that is below a certain size or is on a page that is being viewed at a reduced magnification. The purpose is to see where the text will be laid out and how, so it isn't necessary to read the words (which could increase the *screen redraw* time).

tom of the picture. Or, the numbers, or coordinates, may be entered as numbers, and the cursor will snap to that position.

Grids are useful when exact dimensions, boundaries or spatial relationships between **objects** are required, such as in architectural renderings and draftsperson's drawings. Most programs that use grids have a grid setup that allows the user to determine what increments and units of measure will be used to define the grid.

Group, or grouping, is a collection of programs, files, fonts, images, etc, that are grouped together for convenience.

In **Windows**, a group is any collection of **icons** that have something in common. Most **application programs** generate their own groups, but a user may easily create or change groups.

Group is also a command in **vector** or **illustration** programs that **combines** two or more **objects** into one. Sometimes the method by which they are grouped will create an entirely new object. For instance, the new object may be made up of the **intersection** of the two original objects. Or, the shape of one object may be subtracted from the shape of another.

A group of objects will react to edits, fills and other manipulations as a single object. If users wish to edit a component of a group, they may use an **ungroup** command.

Group III is the current **protocol** for most office **facsimile** machines. It is ubiquitous: Anyone with a Group III machine may fax, over standard telephone lines, any text or **graphics** to another Group III machine owner, regardless of the make or model, or where in the world it may be located, and be assured that it will print out virtually the same as the original input. SEE **Group IV**.

Group IV is the newest **fax** protocol. It can fax **data** at a much higher speed than **Group III** machines, and with a far higher degree of accuracy and fidelity. However, it will not work over standard telephone lines, but requires both the sender and receiver to have an **ISDN** telephone line

Grid: In CorelDRAW, we laid out a grid of nonprintable dots that are exactly 1 inch from each other. That way, we were able to precisely line up our rectangles and circle to each other, as well as draw them at just the size we wanted. Grids and guides can usually be set up at any increment that you want. And you can arrange to have your shapes "snap to" the closest point in the grid, which helps diminish human error in drawing.

installed. Group IV machines are still relatively uncommon and are used primarily by corporations needing high speed fax capability, as well as design studios, **service bureaus** and **printing plants** for sending annotated or approved **proofs, comps** and **FPOs**.

Grow/similar is a command that increases a **selection** based on a user-input number of **pixels** (grow) or on a similarity of color (similar).

GUI, short for **Graphical User Interface**, is a picture- and **icon**-based means of giving the user access to **operating system** commands and files. Apple's **System 8, Windows 98** and **Windows NT** are just three examples of GUIs.

Guidelines are nonprinting lines that the user or the program may place on an **image** window to assist in **aligning** and/or precisely placing **objects**, text and other **image** elements.

Guides SEE **Grid**.

Gutter is a typesetting term that refers to the space in between two adjacent pages where the binding is. Most **desktop publishing** programs have a command for shrinking or enlarging the size of the gutter.

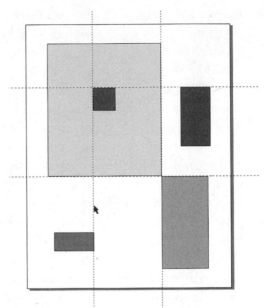

Guidelines: By placing guidelines along the edges of our first two rectangles, we were able to accurately line up the other rectangles in relation to each other and the first two. The dotted guidelines don't print out and are visible only on the computer monitor.

Hairline is a very thin line, about one-half-**point** thick, used to underline text or as a box around an **image** or **object**. Sometimes, several hairlines are placed closely together (or with thicker lines) to form double or triple lines.

Hairline also refers to a very thin line defect in an image **scan, transparency** or **negative**, usually the result of a scratch or an actual strand of hair that falls on the original during the copying or scanning process.

The last definition of hairline comes from typography and refers to the thinnest part of a character, such as the line that makes up the *l, d, p,* etc.

Hairline: All lines (straight, curved, looped, or whatever) are said to have different "weights"—that is, they are different widths. The very thinnest of lines is called a *hairline,* because it is as thin and weightless as a strand of human hair.

Half duplex is a computer communications term which describes **data** that can be sent in two directions (from the sender to the receiver, or the receiver to the sender), but in only one direction at a time. Contrast this with **full duplex**, which describes data that may be sent simultaneously in both directions. What is important to know about half duplex and full duplex is the settings your **modem** and **communications program** require. For instance, if you see two characters on the screen for each one that you type, change the duplex to full or half. Keep in mind that you must set the duplex to match that of the receiver, or else you won't be able to communicate successfully.

Halftone is the most commonly used method to print **continuous tone images** (such as photographs) onto paper or some other **hardcopy** medium. Halftones are made up of hundreds, thousands or millions of tiny dots, which appear to be a single, coherent, continuous tone image. The greater the number of dots, the more detailed the image. The size and shape of the dots may vary according to the halftone method being used. Those dots may also be made up of 2, 4, 6 or more colors, or they may simply be black (for black & white photographs).

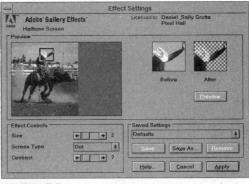

HALFTONE B

There are other methods for reproducing continuous tone images, such as **stochastic** or FM (*frequency modulation*) printing. Most inexpensive desktop printers

HALFTONE A

HALFTONE C

Halftone: Converting a *continuous tone* photograph into something that a printing press can reproduce usually involves breaking it up into dots or lines, using a halftone screen, because the printing press applies points of color, rather than continuous areas of ink. *(Photo from Corel Stock Photo Library.)*

that mimic continuous tone printing do not use true halftones, but a method called **dithering**, which produces erzatz halftone prints.

Halftone screens are used to produce **halftone images**. Traditional graphics arts halftone screens are etched dots on glass or film, which are placed over the **continuous tone** (i.e., photograph) material. Increasingly, **image editing, illustration** and **desktop publishing programs** include software to create the electronic equivalent of halftone screens. In addition, there are specialized programs designed specifically for generating electronic halftones.

Halftone screens are defined by **dpi** or the number of *dots per inch;* however, when applied to halftoning an actual image, it is expressed in **lpi**, or *lines per inch.* The finer the screen, the higher the **resolution**

Halftone screens: When defining the halftone screens that will be used on the *color separated* files of a picture, you can usually choose the shape of the dots, their frequency, and the angle along which they will lay. These settings require a knowledge of *prepress* and, specifically, an understanding of the specific printing press and inks that will be used for that particular job. Discuss the job with your press-man before setting up your color separation files.

and, hence, the better the quality of the image produced. For example, 85 lpi is a typical halftone screen used for producing newspaper-quality images on newsprint. Many magazines use 133-lpi screens, and fine art reproductions on **coated paper** may use 200-lpi screens, or even higher.

Halftone **negatives** or **plates** are produced by sandwiching the halftone screen over an image, and photographing them with a large copy camera to produce a **negative** or plate. Negatives are used to produce printing plates, although it is becoming more common to bypass them altogether and photograph directly onto aluminum or paper printing plates. The latest technology is to produce plates directly from computers, from special printers that output offset plates. Continuous tone color prints require four or more halftones (the primary colors of Cyan, Magenta, Yellow, plus black), which are superimposed one atop another, to build the illusion of continuous tone colors. For higher quality printing, five, six or more colors are separated, screened and put on individual printing plates. SEE **Color separation**.

Halo or **fringe** is an unwanted effect in which stray **pixels** are accidentally included in a **selected** part of an image when it is moved or **pasted** into a new location. The halo or fringe is actually parts of the old background that moved over with the selection. Many programs provide tools to edit or eliminate halos.   SEE **Defringe**.

HAM is short for Amiga's Hold And Modify format, a fairly low **resolution** color **file format**.

Handheld scanner, or hand scanner, is a small, relatively inexpensive device that looks like a cheese cutter or a miniature paint roller, which the user holds in his or her hand and rolls over an original photograph, **image** or page of text. The image or text is instantly converted into **digital data** and saved as a **bitmapped** file. Most hand scanners are **serial** devices with relatively limited **resolution** and a small scanning swathe of 4 inches or less, which makes them unsuitable for most professional purposes. They are useful mostly for "**quick and dirty**" scans, low resolution scans, and scans of small originals that will be used as image elements in a **collage**.

Handles are the 4, 6 or 8 small square boxes that appear around a **selected object** in **vector** programs. Or, they are the tiny squares that appear on the **marquee** of a

Halo: When we cut this truck out of its original photograph (in a tree-lined lane), we purposely did not create a perfect, tight-fitting selection. The result is a halo or fringe of extra pixels around the edges of the truck. That halo is made up of parts of the old background. *(Photo from Corel Stock Photo Library.)*

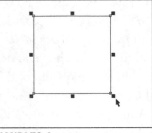

HANDLES A

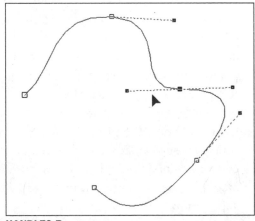

HANDLES B

Handles: (A) A selected object in CorelDRAW displays these eight boxes, which you can pull on with your mouse cursor to change the shape and size of the object. **(B)** The dotted lines that can be pulled out of the nodes of a Bezier curve are handles, by which you can affect the shape and angle of the curve.

selected area of a bitmapped image, when certain tools or commands are invoked. In both cases, the handles are provided so that the user may **click and drag** on them to change the shape, orientation or perspective of the object or area, **interactively**. The handles are not part of the picture and disappear when the area or object is **deselected** and/or when the tool or command is finished.

Handles are also the lines that the user can pull out from the **nodes** of a **Bezier** or **spline curve**. The angle and length of those handles determine how the **path** or curve will behave as it leaves one node and moves onto the next.

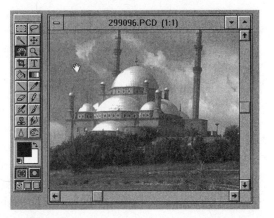

Hand tool: Using the hand tool (which is shown here in the Photoshop toolbox as the selected tool), we are able to click and drag to see other portions of this picture. *(Photo from Corel Stock Photo Library.)*

Handshake indicates that two computers or devices (usually **modems**) are successfully communicating with each other.

Hand tool, so named because it looks like a cartoon hand, is used to **scroll** any image that is larger than the display area on the computer screen. By **clicking and dragging** on the picture, the user is able to push it about within its viewing window.

Hanging indent is a typesetter's term for positioning the first line of a paragraph to the left of the rest of the paragraph. It's the opposite of an **indent**, which shifts the first line to the right of the rest of the paragraph. Hanging indents and indents have little practical purpose, but they are stylish and help to quickly focus the eye on the beginning of the paragraph. So, they are used frequently in **desktop publishing** and **word processing**.

Hard copy refers to a printed **page** of text or an **image**, as opposed to the same **data** displayed on a computer screen or saved to a **hard drive, floppy diskette** or some other electronic storage media. It's a copy of the image or text that can be held in your hand.

This is a hanging indent. It is often used in legal briefs and other documents to set off the beginning of a thought or concept. It is also used similarly to bullets, to delineate points in a discussion.

A hanging indent sets the beginning of a paragraph to the left of the margin. That is in opposition to a tabbed line, which starts a paragraph by pushing the first word a few spaces to the right of the margin.

Once a document has a hanging indent, it usually continues to use the same formatting for all paragraphs.

Hanging indent: Hanging indents give a clean and strong appearance to a document.

H

Hard copy is often preferred for permanent records, legal documents, and **FPO** (*For Position Only*) prints, or **proofs**, to double check that the image being created or edited on the computer is being done correctly.

Hard disk   SEE **Hard Drive**.

Hard Drive, also known as a **hard disk, fixed drive, Winchester drive** or **hard disk drive**, is a device for storing large amounts of **data**. The computer's primary hard drive is usually configured with the **bootup** information and contains the **operating system**—the basic instructions needed to run the computer. Ordinarily, the computer's primary hard drive is installed within the computer case. Additional hard drives (for more storage of programs or data) may be installed **internally**, or by putting the drive within a self-contained case and power supply, added **externally** via a cable to the computer's **drive controller** board or **port**.

Hard drives typically spin at high speeds—3,600 to 7,200 rpms—and may hold anywhere from 10 **megabytes** to 23 **gigabytes** of data. While hard drives can read and write data much faster than any other permanent storage device, such as a **CD-R** (Compact Disc Recorder), **MO** (magneto-optical) or **floppy** drives, they are many times slower than **RAM**, or electronic memory. However, while whatever is stored in RAM disappears the instant the computer is turned off, hard drives retain the data whether or not there is any power. Hard drives are often used as rather slow substitutes for RAM (in what is known as **virtual memory**), since hard drives are far cheaper than electronic memory.

Hard hyphen in a **word processing** or **desktop publishing program** refers to any hyphen that remains with a particular word or in between words, regardless of how it is subsequently formatted. For instance, if the word *hazard* occurs at the end of a line and is automatically formatted to fit, it will be hyphenated as *haz-ard*. But if you wish to use a word that should remain hyphenated regardless of where it appears in the line, such as *fast-forward*, you must type in the hyphen instead of allowing the program to insert it as an end-of-line break.

Hard Light is a mode in which an **image** is electronically illuminated as if it were lit up by a bright spotlight. When the Hard Light **mode** is applied to an **object**, it will cast shadows relative to the angle of the light, its intensity, and its proximity to the object.

Hardware is the ubiquitous term for anything physical that relates to computers. This is in opposition to the **software** (**programs** and other code) that exists only as code and data. Hardware includes the box that holds the computer, the components inside that box (such as the **hard drive** and **peripheral boards**) and anything that plugs into and interacts with the computer (**monitor, printer, scanner**, etc.). If you can hold it in your hand or touch it (and we don't mean floppies or CDs of software), and it relates to a computer, then it is hardware.

Harvard Graphics is a brand-name business **presentation** program.

HCI is short for **Host Controller Interface**, a new standard for a device designed to convey **USB**, or **Universal Serial Bus data**, to the **CPU** at high speeds. In other words, the HCI may become the next generation of **serial ports** capable of transferring data far faster than existing serial ports. It's not only faster, but like **SCSI**, it will allow serial devices to be linked on the same cable and operated from a single controller built into the **motherboard**.

HDTV stands for High Definition Television, a new (and as yet unadopted) broadcast standard with twice the **resolution** (1,050 lines, as opposed to regular TV's 525 lines) of current televisions. It is generally believed that HDTV and computer monitors will eventually merge into one standard, so that the same device may be used for viewing commercial television programs or displaying computer data.

Head, also known as a read/write head, is a magnetic component of a **storage device** (such as a **hard drive**) that reads or writes **digital data**. The head either floats above or touches the magnetic media (such as a platter or tape), and as the media pass by, the head either detects (reads) magnetically encoded zeros or ones and passes them onto the computer, or is instructed by the computer to produce an electrical charge (write) that leaves a magnetic charge on the media.

Head crash occurs when a drive **head** accidentally falls, or crashes, onto the magnetic media it is passing over, often as the result of vibration, being knocked, or a malfunction of the drive mechanism. A head crash physically gouges (damages) part of the media. Depending on its severity (i.e., how many milliseconds it touched the media), a head crash can either destroy a small amount of **data**, or virtually all the data on the drive. Mini-head crashes are common occurrences, and there are **utilities** that allow the user to recover damaged data and prevent further destruction by "locking out" the damaged area (preventing data from being written to the area where the head touched the surface). Serious, or catastrophic, head crashes can wipe out most or all data and may render them unrecoverable or unusable. The possibility of head crashes is the best argument for backing up your **hard drive** often.

Header is the title or information at the top of a **page**.

It is also basic information about an **image**, text or **database** file, and may even establish the **format** that the **data** are stored in.

Help is, we hope, self-explanatory. Whenever you are stuck in a program, you usually press F1 or click on the pulldown menu to open up that program's **on-line** Help menu. That will bring up information, often **context sensitive** (which means it will give help on the particular function or tool you are currently accessing), that will assist you in understanding or solving a particular problem.

Hertz, usually expressed as **Hz**, is the unit of measure that describes the number of waves or cycles per second. For instance, American AC (*alternating current*) power pulses at 60 Hz, or 60 cycles per second, while European power pulses at 50 Hz. This makes American AC electrical devices incompatible with European devices. (Most computer-related electrical devices use DC, or *direct current*, which is a continuous flow of electricity. It can be boosted or stepped down with a convertor or transformer, which is the reason many computer power supplies, **disk drives, scanners**, etc., have a switch that allows them to be operated in America as well as in most other countries.)

A larger unit of measure is **kilohertz**, or **kHz**, which measures pulses in thousands of cycles per second. Audio equipment falls within the kHz range. For instance, a **Sound Board** may be able to reproduce sounds as low as 50 kHz or as high as 20 kHz.

Then there is **MHz**, or **megahertz**, which measures pulses in the millions of seconds. For instance, computer **CPU** speeds are often expressed in MHz, such as 133 or 266 MHz. The larger the number, the faster the device.

Hex, or **hexadecimal,** is a computer term for a 16-digit numbering system. Computers often digest and process information in chunks of 16 digits. Because computers are **binary** systems that recognize only zeros and ones, number and letter combinations are formed by writing out sequences, such as 0010 1110 0101 0001. However, working with and recognizing long sequences of zeros and ones is difficult for human beings. It is easier to assign a number for each digit. The problem is, our numeric system has only ten, 1-digit numbers (0–9), and 2 digits cannot be used efficiently to replace a zero or a one. But hex numbers substitute a letter for the six (hex) numbers of 10 through 15—the sequence is 0,1,2,3,4,5,6,7,8,9,A,B,C,D,E,F. For instance, the letter *B* is a substitute for *11, F* for *15,* and so on. What each hex combination stands for, however, is best left to engineers and developers.

Hidden line is the side or the line in a 2-dimensional representation of a 3-dimensional object that is obscured or hidden. It is often shown as a dotted line.

Hidden Line Removal is a method of removing the dotted lines that represent the third dimension in a 2-dimensional graphic. The reason it is useful to remove such unneeded lines (or even hidden surfaces) is that a saved file requires less storage space. Also, removing the **hidden line** allows the user to better visualize the graphic as a solid object.

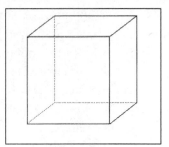

Hidden lines: The rear edges that are, actually, invisible, because the more forward edges cover them up, are represented here as dotted lines. Those dotted lines are known as *hidden lines*.

Hide Edges is a command that allows the user to temporarily hide, or remove, the border or **marquee** surrounding a **selected** area of an **image**. However, the selection area is still active; and even though the edges are not visible, changes may be made to the image only within the area selected. The reason for a Hide Edges command is to assist in viewing an image unencumbered with marquee lines.

High Definition Television   SEE **HDTV**.

High density refers to high capacity storage media, in which more **data** can be packed into the same space. For instance, the first **magneto-optical** (**MO**) 3.5-inch **discs** held 128 **megabytes** of data. But with better technology, manufacturers were able to increase that capacity to 230 and 520 megabytes on the same size disc. Thus, it is said to be a high density disc. Of course, today's high density may be tomorrow's dead technology, as new and denser storage devices become available.

Highlight is the brightest or lightest part of a picture. Its opposite is **shadow**, and in between is the **midtone. Image editing** programs have numerous tools for editing and augmenting highlights, shadows and midtones.

High Pass is a **filter** in some **image editing** programs that increases the apparent sharpness in a **bitmapped image** by improving highlights and brightness and cutting down on shadows.

High resolution refers to an **image** or device (such as a computer monitor or printer) that contains, displays or produces much detail or **data**. A high resolution **bitmapped** image has a high density of pixels.   SEE **Resolution**.

High Sierra is, like **ISO 9660** and **XA**, a technical standard for **CD-ROM discs**. When CD-ROMs first appeared in the early 1980s, compatibility was an important consideration, not only between Mac and PCs, but between drives and **discs**. You were out of luck if your drive were not capable of reading a particular **format**. High Sierra was one of the first common standards that became universally adopted by drive manufacturers and disc publishers. Almost all modern CD-ROM drives are capable of reading High Sierra discs, so you probably won't have to check on compatibility, if you see in the technical specifications that a particular disc has a High Sierra format.

Hi res   SEE **High resolution**.

Histogram is a statistical graph that displays a representation of an image's **dynamic range**, or its light-to-dark ratio. The histogram, which is sometimes displayed in a **levels dialog**, is usually interactively editable, which means that the user can change the dynamic range of a picture, as well as particular light and shadow values, by clicking and dragging on the histogram's **dynamic sliders** or by using the dialog's other controls and options. Users will often refer to a picture's histogram to read how a filter, tool or other command has affected its dynamic range.

Histogram: The original version of this picture **(A)** has a limited *dynamic range*. We see that in the photograph itself, where there are no dramatic highlights or shadows, and also in the histogram, where there are no pixels in the edges of the graph—only in the midtones. That is known as a *flat photograph*. In the second version **(B)**, we moved the highlight and shadow pointers from the empty far edges of the graph to the edge where pixels are evident in the histogram. The preview of the photograph now shows more snap, greater depth of shadow and brightness in the highlights. So, we applied the new histogram (levels in Photoshop) settings to the picture. And when we open the histogram up again, to view the edited picture's dynamic range **(C)**, we see a graph in which the pixels are spread throughout the entire range of highlights to shadows. *(A Corel stock photo.)*

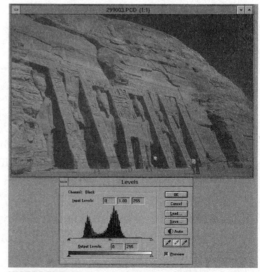

HISTOGRAM A

HLS   SEE **HSL**.

Home key on a **PC** and some **Macintosh** keyboards returns the **cursor** to the beginning of a line.

Horizon scanner is a brand-name desktop color **flatbed** scanner manufactured by Agfa, that is used primarily by design studios and **service bureaus** for scanning in drawings, illustrations and other paper-based originals.

Host Controller Interface, a new high speed **serial port** built into **motherboards,** allows serial devices like **filmless cameras, pointing devices, modems**, etc., to be daisy chained from a single port.   SEE **HCI**.

Hot key refers to a key or a combination of keys that, when pressed, will perform a specific function, such as initiate a **screen capture**, save a file, apply a particular **filter**, and create a new **window**. Depending on the program, hot keys may (or may not) be customized by the user. When creating your own hot keys, it is important to make certain that the new hot key combination does not conflict with another function triggered by the same key sequence. Hot keys are also called **keyboard shortcuts**.

Hot spot is the precise location of the tip or point of the **cursor**, when it is in a position. When the user clicks on the **mouse** or **stylus** button, the click strikes the hot spot, which will initiate a command, tool or whatever. Recognizing the hot spot is important when doing precise drawing or painting.

HISTOGRAM B

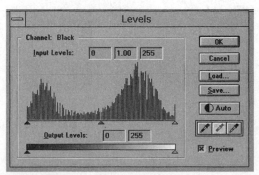

HISTOGRAM C

Hotspot (usually spelled as one word) can be defined more narrowly as a clickable area of an image or a **Web** page that will automatically access another **Web** page or another area in a document.   SEE **Mapping, URL**.

Hot swap is the process of removing and/or replacing a device that is attached to the computer, without turning the power off. If it is a **firewire** or **USB** device, then it is quite okay to hot swap it. In fact, that is what their design specs state. If it is **parallel** or **serial**, then, officially, it is dangerous to hot swap it. Their manufacturers will discourage it, for fear of damaging the device. However, we have never heard of any physical or data damage related to hot swapping a parallel or serial device. We have experienced drivers not loading in those circumstances, which, then, requires a reboot. Under no circumstances should you attempt to hot swap a **SCSI** device. If you do, you can permanently damage the SCSI device, your **motherboard** and/or your SCSI interface, as well as lose your data.

Hourglass cursor is the iconic symbol that a program may display when it is busy doing something. It tells the user to wait a moment or longer, until the current computational activity is concluded. Then, it releases the cursor to the user. Some programs use a clock face instead of an hourglass for this purpose.

Howtek is a manufacturer of high end **drum scanners**.

HPGL stands for *Hewlett-Packard Graphics Language,* or the commands that control Hewlett-Packard's line of **plotters**. HPGL language **drivers** are frequently used by large floor model color printers capable of generating long strips of photorealistic output.

HSB stands for the **Hue/Saturation/Brightness color model**, in which all colors are generated by a combination of their positions within the spectrum (hue), their depths of color (saturation) and the amount of light or dark (brightness).

HSL (Hue/Saturation/Luminance) and **HSV** (Hue/Saturation/Value) **color models** are, for all practical imaging purposes, the same as **HSB**.

Hub is a device that **links networked** computers. It also refers to the device that connects **USB** peripherals, like **drawing tablets, digital cameras,** and so forth.

Hue describes and defines color, i.e., a red truck, a green ball, a yellow banana, according to its position on the continuum that is the full spectrum of colors. Officially and technically, hue is the wavelength of any color of the spectrum. In imaging programs, hue is often expressed as a component of

Hue/Saturation/Brightness (**HSB**), or, less often, as part of the **Hue/ Saturation/Luminance** (**HSL**) **color model**.

When a user wants to adjust a picture's color or give it a color tint or **color shift**, he or she will use the **Hue/Saturation dialog** or command.

Hue/Saturation is a **dialog box** in which the user may adjust the overall color of a picture, or a portion of a picture, by pushing on **dynamic sliders** that change its hue, saturation and/or lightness.   SEE color plate 4.

Hue Shift is a **color shift** that is applied to a picture or a portion of a picture when the user pushes the **hue dynamic slider** in the **Hue/Saturation dialog** box. Pushing back and forth on the slider is like pulling the picture behind a transparent rainbow of colors or looking at it through a series of tinted glasses. Where the slider is stopped determines the color that will be applied to the picture.

Hybrid is any combination of technologies. For instance, many **filmless cameras** are hybrids: Kodak's **DCS-460** uses a standard, off-the-shelf Nikon N90s film camera as its front end, and Kodak's **CCD** and electronics for its back end.

The result is a camera that captures and records its images digitally, but provides front-end controls similar to traditional film cameras. The new **Advanced Photo System** (**APS**) is a pure film technology (which records its pictures using silver halide film), but it is designed to interface with various digital products, such as a **film scanner;** therefore, it, too, may be considered a hybrid technology.

Hypertext is the name Apple gave to an early Macintosh application capable of linking any word or phrase with any other words, phrases or **data**. It still survives as part of various commercial programs as a way to input and order random notes.

Hyperware is fictitious software. That is, a manufacturer will announce its intention to produce a particular program to determine if, or how much, demand or interest exists for actually producing such a program. Therefore, all that exists is the hype and not the software. Hyperware is similar to **vaporware**, or software that actually exists in one form or another but hasn't been perfected or released (and may never be) to the public.

Hyphenation is a **desktop publishing** or **word processing** option that allows the user to automatically or manually hyphenate words. Automatic hyphenation compares a text file against a standard or customized hyphenation dictionary, or a set of grammatical rules, that indicates when a word should be broken and carried over to the following line. The user can select various options, such as the shape and size of the hyphen, whether four- or five-letter words should be hyphenated, and if words to be hyphenated should be done automatically or approved or changed when the text is being prepared for printing or saving. Hyphenation is an important aspect of **page layout**, because it helps to make the text look cleaner and aids in **proportional spacing**.

Hz   SEE **Hertz**.

I-beam is a **cursor** that looks like a capital *I*, sometimes with curved extensions on top and bottom. The I-beam appears whenever text is to be inserted in a program, and it indicates the point at which the next typed letter will appear.

IBM is, of course, the trade name of the International Business Machines Corporation, one of the largest computer manufacturers in the world.

Icon is a small picture, image or representation of a program, file, command, function, process, utility, font or tool. It is selected by

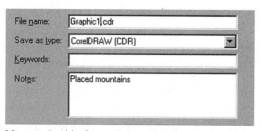

I-beam: In this Save dialog, the I-beam is the line between the *1* and the *.cdr* extension. You'll always want to be aware of the location of the I-beam before you begin to type, because that is where the typed letters will be placed.

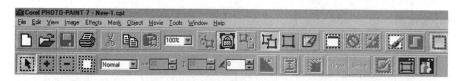

Icon: Icons are pictographs that represent commands or programs. Clicking on them with your mouse or stylus activates the related command or program. Luckily, most programs use similar icons, so that, for instance, those shown here in a Corel PhotoPAINT screen are easy to recognize. For example, the print icon is usually a picture of a printer, and the cut icon is usually a scissors. Of course, there are exceptions which can sometimes make understanding icons something of a challenge.

clicking a **mouse** or **stylus** anywhere on the icon; when selected, it changes color (or is **highlighted**). When double-clicked, it launches the program, file, function, etc. Icons may be **dragged, trashed** or copied by **dropping and dragging** an icon into a **folder, subdirectory** or **trash can**.

Icons are placed on the **desktop** when a program is **installed**, so that the program can be started by a double-click. In addition, many desktop **interfaces** allow the user to **customize** and choose icons.

Icons are an integral part of **GUI, Graphical User Interface**, which replaces the old way of interacting with a computer, by typing commands in, with pictographs and commands that are implemented by a mouse click.

IDE is an acronym for *Integrated Drive Electronics,* an **interface** for **hard drives, CD-ROM drives** and other devices. Originally developed and made popular on PCs, IDE has recently been installed in **PowerMacs,** notably, in **PowerBook** notebook computers.

Instead of placing all the **intelligence** on the **drive controller**, IDE places it on the hard drive itself—it's more efficient, cost effective, and simpler. Most PCs use an IDE or its faster cousins, EIDE or IDE-2, as their primary drive interface. However, it does have some limitations, which is why the **SCSI** interface is the choice of graphics professionals and other **power users**.

IEEE (eye-triple-E) is the abbreviation for the Institute of Electrical and Electronics Engineers. Often, computers and **peripherals** receive an IEEE certification number, which means that a particular piece of hardware conforms to a specified standard.

IFF format   SEE **Amiga IFF**.

Illustration is the process of drawing objects, pictures or scenes, using **vector** tools as opposed to **bitmapped** tools. These vector tools describe, define and manipulate **objects** and other picture elements by mathematical formula, which takes up less time and less space than handling all the many individual **pixels** of information that bitmaps require.

Illustration programs are those draw programs that have such vector tools. **CorelDRAW, FreeHand** and **Illustrator** are just a few of the many illustration programs that are available.

Illustration: Illustrations are composed of vector shapes and fills, all of which are defined mathematically by the software. This rectangle (filled with a gradient), circle and star are typical illustration components.

Illustrator is an **illustration** program from **Adobe Systems**.

Image is a picture that exists in the computer. It may have originated in the real world as a photograph, a **scanned** item or anything else. Or, it may have been completely created within the computer. But, it is now a **digitized** picture that may be edited, manipulated, saved and **output** from a computer program.

Image database is a database program that can keep track of **images**. Usually, the information that it contains can include: when the picture was originally created, where it is stored, what kind of file it is, and other useful data. A **thumbnail** (a tiny, low **resolution** representation of the image) is usually attached to the file, so that the user can tell at a glance to which picture the information relates. Image databases are important **utilities** for digital artists, because it is easy to lose track of how and where your pictures are stored.

Image editing program is software that can **acquire**, edit, manipulate, save and output **bitmapped** pictures, including photographs. They work on the individual **pixels** that make up the pictures, as opposed to the **vector** editing of **illustration** programs. Therefore, they are more detail oriented. **Photoshop, PhotoDeluxe, Picture Publisher, Corel PhotoPAINT** and others are examples of image editing programs.

Image element is anything that can be put into a **digital picture**, including **objects, brush** strokes, lights and their effects, **layers**, type, **scanned photos**, etc. In a **bitmapped image**, a **pixel** is the most primitive, or smallest, element. In a **vector** image, the smallest element is a simple object, with no fill, **texture** or other manipulation.

Image processing is the computing involved in editing and manipulating **digitized** pictures, or **images**. Whenever a **filter** is applied, a **brush** stroked, a **color balanced**, or anything is done to a **bitmapped image** that changes that picture, the computer must do some work, in **memory** or on the **hard drive**, and in **redrawing** what is on the screen. That is image processing, which occurs within **image editing programs**.

Image resolution is the measure of the amount of **data** that exist within a **bitmapped image**. Usually described as **ppi** (**pixels per inch**), the more data there are, the larger the file and the more detail in the pictures. But larger files also require greater computing power, more **RAM**, bigger **hard drives**, etc. On the other hand, if there isn't enough data (if the image resolution is too low), then the picture will break up, be blurry or **pixelate**, when it is magnified on the screen or printed at too large a size. Therefore, the user must correlate his or her need for **output** or display resolution to the picture's image resolution—preferably at the time the picture is created. The trick is to be sure that the image has enough data for its final display or output, but not too much for the computer system to handle.

Sometimes resolution is described as the full number of **pixels** in each dimension, such as 640×480. Other times, it is expressed as **pixels per inch** (ppi) over the length and width of the image, such as 72 ppi and 8 by 6 inches.

Often, ppi and **dpi** (**dots** per inch) are confused. Technically, pixels exist in the computer display, dots on the printed **page**. But you'll often see the two terms used interchangeably. It hasn't quite reached the point of common usage (in which words' meanings are changed), but everyone expects everyone else to understand what they mean, so such slips of the tongue (or pen) are generally overlooked.

Imagesetter is a **high resolution** professional **graphics** printer designed to **output** black & white, **monochrome** and/or color **camera-ready page layout**, type or pictures. Unlike most desktop computer printers, which are pure **digital** devices that output to normal paper, most imagesetters use **photosensitive** (photographic) paper or **film**, which produces sharper, higher resolution images and type.

Image Size, expressed in **megabytes** (**MB**) or **kilobytes** (**K**) is directly related to **image resolution** and refers to the amount of space that a **bitmapped image** file takes up (on the **hard drive** or other storage devices, and in **memory**, when it is displayed). The higher the resolution, the more **data** an image file must hold, and the larger the image size. Therefore, an **RGB** picture that is 4″×5″ and 300 **ppi** is 5.15 MB in size. (**CMYK** images are slightly larger than RGB, because they hold more color information—four primary colors and **channels** as opposed to three.) The easiest way to find out an image size is to look in a program's **resize dialog**, or in the **new file** dialog.

Vector images tend to be much smaller, because they are **resolution-independent**. That means that they don't deal with the individual **pixels** that make up a picture, but with the mathematical formulae that describe the **objects** in the picture. Therefore, an empty 4″×5″ vector picture can be as small as 4K, but can move up into the hundreds of **kilobytes** (and more), as objects, **gradients**, text, **layers**, etc., are added. Still, hundreds of kilobytes is considerably smaller than the megabytes of typical bitmapped images.

Imaging is the process of creating, manipulating, **inputting, outputting**, opening and saving pictures on a computer. It is generally used as an overall generic term for just about anything that can be done to or with pictures, **digitally**, which is the reason it is used interchangeably with the phrase *digital imaging*.

Impact printer is a device that transfers ink to paper by physically making an impression on the paper through a ribbon. **Dot matrix** and daisywheel printers are the best-known impact devices. With the advent of **laser, inkjet** and other technologies, impact printers have become virtually obsolete.

Import is the process by which a file is brought into a program, when the file is in a **format** other than those that are **native** to the program. By contrast, a native file format is one that can be opened directly by the program. In other words, if you can't **open** a file in a program, try importing it. While that won't always work, it might. Import, like open, is usually found in the File **pulldown menu** at the top of any program's screen.

Import is also a command that is used to bring color **palettes, databases**, libraries of symbols and other items into a program or one of its **dialog boxes**.

A third definition of import is the process of opening a file, such as an **image** or a table, and inserting it into the currently opened document or image. In this manner, you can **place** a photograph that is saved on, say, your **hard drive** into a page **layout** that you are working on in your **desktop publishing** program.

Impressionist is a **filter, special effect** or **paintbrush** option that creates a **fine art emulation** that makes an **image** look like a French impressionist painting. It does this

IMPRESSIONIST A

IMPRESSIONIST B

Impressionist: An Impressionist filter will diffuse the colors in a bitmap image (such as this photograph of a flower), so that it emulates the appearance of an impressionist painting.

by breaking up each individual color into small dots of several component colors. When the picture is viewed from a distance (or through squinting eyes), the component colors meld into very rich **hues**, in which the picture details become very obvious. But when seen close up, it produces a soft sense of color in which the details of the composition may or may not be as easy to see.

Imprinting, or overprinting, is the process of printing over a sheet of paper that has already been printed, such as printing a letter on letterhead stationery. Some color printers do not permit imprinting, either because they use a **thermal** process to place an image or type on a page, or the original ink may smear when overprinted.

Incompatible is when hardware or software does not work or interact correctly with a device, program or file. Sometimes, incompatibilities can be overcome with a device such as a **gender changer,** or by changing the **file format**.

Indeo is a file format for transmitting medium-quality video files.

Indexed color image is one that has only **8 bits** of color, or **256 colors**. That is much more limited than **24-bit color**, which has **16.7 million colors**. However, in certain situations, indexed color is preferable or necessary. For instance, image files on the **Internet** are generally only 8 bits or less.

Info button is a small box, usually found in a **dialog box** or **palette**, that, when clicked on, will provide information about that dialog, palette or its options.

INI is the **extension** that **Windows** uses for files containing information about what programs, **devices** and **peripherals** are installed on your **PC**.

INIT   SEE **Extensions**.

Initialize is the act or process of preparing, **formatting, installing** or starting a program, **driver** or **device** for the first time. Or, it is resetting or starting anew after a device or a program has failed or the **parameters** must be changed. Usually, initialization requires clearing the **memory** or resetting the **defaults** so that the reset is "clean."

Inkjet printer is a high speed printing device that shoots tiny droplets of black or colored ink out of a series of nozzles onto paper. Most inkjet printers are capable of producing medium or high **resolution** images by using more nozzles and making multiple passes over the same area. Depending on the manufacturer and model, an inkjet may spray cold or hot inks (hot ink dries faster), or may heat a crayonlike wax pigment (solid ink) until it is a liquid, and then spray it.

Inkjet printers presently dominate the low, midrange and business color printer market because of their relatively low initial cost, ease of use, speed, etc. They are less popular for professional graphics because of one not-as-yet-solved problem: permanency. Alas, the pigments used in most inkjets deteriorate rapidly, causing **color shifts**, fading and image degradation.

Input is entering **data** into or sending **data** to a computer. It's the process of creating or transferring any data, whether text, graphics, or information. Input applies to data keyed in or transferred from any storage device, such as a **floppy diskette**, or other sources.

Input device is any piece of equipment that provides a physical means of **inputting** or entering **data** into a computer. This may be, but is not restricted to, a keyboard, **digital camera, scanner, Photo CD, frame grabber board, modem**, etc.

Insert is a command that places a file (consisting of text, a picture or some other information) into a document or **image**.

The insert **mode** is an option (usually in **word processing programs**, but also in others) that automatically makes room (at the **cursor** point) for whatever is being typed or added. For instance, suppose you have the sentence: *The dog likes bones.* If the insert mode is active, then you could put the cursor in front of the word *bones* and type *crunchy.* The result would be: *The dog likes crunchy bones.* The opposite of insert mode is **typeover**, in which whatever you type or **input** replaces what is at the cursor point. So, if you put the cursor in front of the word *dog* in the previous sentence, and type *cat* in the typeover mode, the result would be: *The cat likes crunchy bones.*

Insert is also a keyboard key that some programs use to toggle between typeover mode and insert mode.

Install is adding hardware or software to a computer. There are full installs, in which every **program, subprogram, font, image, utility, etc.**, are copied to the **hard drive**. Since some full installs can take 200 or more **megabytes**, most software gives the user the option to do a partial or custom install, or to select only those components that are needed. Later, the user may opt to install additional components.

De-install is removing part or all of the program, images, utilities, fonts, etc. While there are commercial de-installers available, **Windows 95**–compliant programs have the ability to de-install themselves.

Integrated is an adjective buzzword in the computer industry, which denotes that a piece of software fits well with another piece, or that hardware will seamlessly install and work with another. One popular type of integrated software is the **suite**, which packages together two or more programs that complement each other, like an **image editing, desktop publishing** and **illustration** suite.

Intel is the name of the world's largest manufacturer of **microprocessors** and **motherboards**. The **CPUs** that power the majority of **IBM compatibles** or **PCs**—the **8088, 80286, 80386, 80486, Pentium, Pentium Pro** and **Pentium II** CPUs—are all designed and manufactured by Intel.

Intelligence is a much maligned term that indicates when a piece of **software** or a **hardware** device has built-in capabilities that automatically analyze the context, system or configuration and adjusts accordingly. In other words, it's computer "smarts." All other things being equal, intelligent products are usually better and easier to use than "dumb" products.

Interactive refers to a command, tool, process, **dialog box** or whatever, in which the user is involved in controlling or choosing controls over the action or purpose. For instance, an interactive **tutorial** is a computer-based lesson in which the user actually participates by **inputting** keystrokes, mouse clicks, drawing pictures, etc., while the lesson progresses. The opposite of interactive is passive, in which the user just sits back and watches while the computer does whatever it is supposed to do. Since you learn better by doing than by watching, passive tutorials are not as effective as interactive ones.

Interface is any connection between or among the user, hardware and/or software. It often describes the physical connection between a device and a computer, via a **port**, i.e., the mouse connecting through a **serial** interface. But it also refers to the physical display and appearance of a program and how the user interacts with it.

Interlaced is the display of every other line in one scan on a monitor. Therefore, it takes two scans to display an entire **image** on the screen. Interlaced monitors are less complicated and less expensive than **noninterlaced** monitors, which display every line. However, they are not as sharp, nor can they display as high a **resolution**, as noninterlaced monitors. In addition, there may be an annoying flicker with interlaced monitors. Some Digital Video Camcorders record in the interlace mode, for better, sharper, more detailed frames.

Internet is said to be the most important innovation since the invention of movable type. It's a loose, worldwide collection of over 40 million computers (at last count) that allows an individual to connect to any other computer

Ruby Mask or **Quick Mask:** When editing a mask, it is useful to view it in Ruby Mask or Quick Mask format. That shows the image through a red (or other user-defined color) silhouette. The red area is equivalent to the black in the alpha channel mode, in that it defines those areas not included in the mask. Where there is no red (which is the same as the white of the alpha channel), those areas are inside the mask. When you paint on the mask in this mode, you paint in black or white (or gray for levels of transparency). To see both the marquee (or marching ants) and the alpha channel view of this mask, look at the illustrations for the Mask definition. (Photo from the Corel Stock Photo Library.)

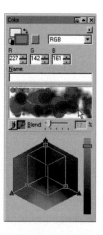

Color Palette: At first glance, most programs have very different Color palettes, but they all work along similar lines, with the key option relating to the color model with which you want to work. Pictured here is Corel PhotoPAINT's Color palette, which also includes a doodling area for creating and saving custom colors.

Blend Modes (also channel operations and calculations): Remember that every *pixel* (or point of color) in a *raster* image can be described mathematically, according to whatever *color model* is being used. Therefore, a pixel in an *RGB* image can be said to have red of 25, green of 120 and blue of 35. So, when you put two images together or paint on an image, you can use mathematical processes to combine those values. Here are some examples.

Normal: When two pictures or layers are combined, the normal result is that the pixels of the upper layer replace those in the lower layer.

Add: When the Add or Additive command is used, the values of the overlapping pixels from the two images are added to create a new pixel value that is (in the RBG model) lighter than the two originals.

Subtractive: The Subractive mode ends up with pixels that are equal to the value of the underlying pixels minus the value of the upper layer's (or image's) pixels.

Lighten: The Lighter or Lighten Only mode selects and uses the lightest pixels from either image. Therefore, if a pixel on the upper image is darker than the corresponding pixel on the lower image, the composite image will use the lighter pixel from the lower image. Each individual pixel is chosen in this manner, to create the composite picture.

Darken: The darker pixels of the two overlapping images are used to create the composite.

Luminance: The grayscale values that define the shadows, highlights and midtones of the overlapping image are applied to the lower image. The result is a picture that has laid the underlying colors onto the upper image.

Color Only: The Color Only command applies the colors of the upper image to the grayscale values of the underlying image. (The Hue Only command works similarly.)

A   **B**

Counterclockwise spectrum: These two CorelDRAW dialogs are exactly the same in how they define a gradient from red to yellow. The one difference is that **(A)** is set for clockwise around the hue wheel between the two colors, and **(B)** is set for counterclockwise. In this case, counterclockwise produces a direct gradient between red and yellow, since they are adjacent colors on the wheel.

Hue/saturation: The original photograph of this flower was a bright pink. By changing only its hue, we can alter all of the colors in the picture. Think of the sliding scale that represents hue as pulling the picture through the *color wheel* that represents all of the colors of the rainbow.

also on the Internet. **The Net**, as it is colloquially called, allows for inexpensive high speed access to literally any and all information, including that found at universities, libraries, research facilities, corporations, businesses, etc. It's also the most important conduit for **e-mail**, or electronic messages, and file transfers, including graphics files (**images**), through a part of the Net called the **World Wide Web** (**WWW**).   SEE **Page**.

Interpolation is the process by which software creates new **data** to make an **image** bigger (such as using the **resize** command to enlarge a picture's dimensions). The new data (or **pixels**) are based on the program's interpretation of existing pixels. As a rule, interpolated data are not as accurate as original image data, which can result in a less-sharp or less-well-defined picture. But there are different kinds of interpolation, some of which are less destructive than others, and a small amount of interpolation may involve no noticeable image degradation.   SEE **Bicubic interpolation, Bipolar interpolation, Nearest Neighbor interpolation.**

Intersect is a **vector** command that **combines** two **objects**, and the result of that combination is a new object that is the shape and size of the area that the two objects have in common (or, where they intersect each other).

Inverse is a **selection** command. It reverses the current selection (**mask**), so that everything in the picture that wasn't selected becomes selected, and anything that was within the mask is no longer selected. For instance, suppose there is a picture of a park, and the statue in the middle of the park is selected. If the selection were inverted, then everything but the statue would become selected.

Inverse video   SEE **Reverse Video.**

Invert is a command that turns all colors in a picture to the opposite color in the spectrum. It's like seeing the film negative of a photograph.

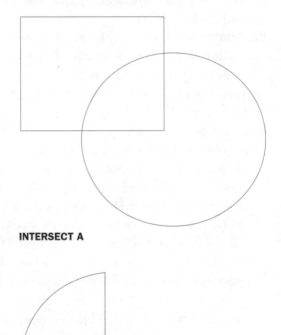

INTERSECT A

INTERSECT B

Intersect: The intersection of this rectangle and ellipse **(A)** is that area where the two of them overlap—i.e., the arc **(B)**. This and other combining commands are useful for creating complex or unusual vector shapes.

Invisible layer or **invisible object** is a command that hides a layer or object, so that the user can see and work on what is "underneath." **Layers** or **objects palettes** often have an icon for making a layer or object visible or invisible. Many programs also have a command to "Show All" and "Hide All." It is important to keep track of what is invisible and what isn't. Make sure everything that is relevant in the picture is visible, and that **guidelines** and other production elements are invisible, before the image is **output**. SEE **Eye icon**.

I/O, short for In/Out, describes **data** flowing to and from the computer. An I/O **board** on a **PC** usually consists of two **serial ports** (for a **mouse, modem**, etc.) and one **parallel**/printer port. Most I/O boards are **8-bit ISA** boards, because printers, modems and **pointing devices** usually do not need the higher operating speeds that **16-bit** boards allow. **Macs** do not have I/O boards.

Iris printer is a high quality **inkjet** device manufactured by Ilford and capable of outputting gorgeous **continuous tone** prints. These are professional, floor-model devices that cost from $40,000 to over $100,000, and individual prints can cost hundreds of dollars. Iris printers are often used for fine art digital prints.

IRQ is **DOS** nomenclature for **Interrupt ReQuest**, that part of the **operating system** for **PCs** that manages communications with **devices** attached to the computer, such as a **mouse, modem, scanner, network card** and **hard drive**. Most PCs have a total of 16 IRQs, some of which are permanently assigned to certain devices, such as the keyboard and **serial ports**. Others are automatically reserved when a device is added to the system. Problems may occur when two devices are assigned the same IRQ, or when the system runs out of available IRQ numbers. Usually, these problems can be resolved by assigning another number or sharing IRQs (but never at the same time). One of the advantages that the **Mac** system has over PCs is that it doesn't use IRQs and, therefore, does not suffer from some of the problems that they can create.

ISA is the abbreviation for *Industry Standard Architecture*, a design developed by **IBM** for communicating with **16-bit peripheral boards** or **expansion slots**. It's also known as the **IBM-AT**, which was first introduced in 1984. ISA **slots** are still commonly used for **modems, I/O boards** and other **8-bit** or 16-bit peripherals, but it has been largely superceded by faster, more modern designs, notably, **PCI**.

ISDN is an acronym for *Integrated Services Digital Network*, a high speed communications telephone line for sending and receiving large amounts of **data**, such as **high resolution image** files. ISDN requires a special ISDN **modem** and a dedicated telephone line (which is not available in all areas). ISDN is useful only when the sender and the receiver have the same ISDN equipment and telephone line. It has had slow acceptance, is plagued by high telephone rates and certain technical limitations, and may be made obsolete by other technologies, such as the coming generation of **cable modems** that will use cable television wire to transmit and receive data.

ISO is the abbreviation of the *International Standards Organization*, which approves standards for a variety of **devices** and **formats**.

ISO 9660 is the standard **format** that most **CD-ROMs** use. Other CD-ROM formats include **High Sierra** (now almost obsolete), **Photo CD** (Kodak's system for storing images) and **XA** (for **multimedia** files).

Isometric perspective displays three-dimensional **objects** in two-dimensional programs with none of the **linear perspective** corrections that would make those portions that are further away appear smaller. In other words, if a real world object is evenly shaped, with the back and front the same size, then a drawing of that object, if done with isometric perspective, would show the front and back as measurably the same (i.e., you could measure it with a ruler held up to the monitor or the

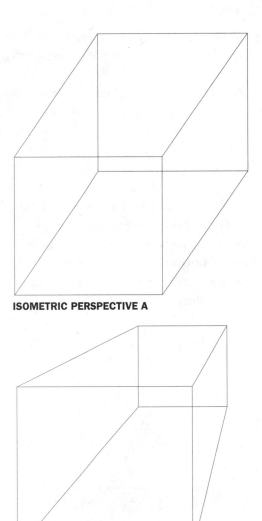

ISOMETRIC PERSPECTIVE A

ISOMETRIC PERSPECTIVE B

Isometric perspective: (A) Isometric perspective does not correct for the way the human eye sees distant objects as smaller than near ones. Therefore, the back end of this box is measurably the same size as the front end, though we see it as apparently larger. **(B)** Contrast that to this box which uses linear perspective to make it obvious which end of the box is farther away from the viewer.

printed page). In a linear perspective drawing, the back would be drawn smaller than the front.

Italic is a style of **typeface** that slants forward. It is usually used to emphasize a word or phrase, though italicizing some **fonts** can make them look more like handwriting (albeit very regular and mechanical).

Ivue is a file format used by Live Picture software. Live Picture has two file formats. **FITS** retains all original **image data** (the picture), and Ivue holds all of the information about the editing that is done to the picture. Before the picture can be **output**, it must be **rendered**, which applies the editing (Ivue) to the picture (FITS) and creates another more common file format with the combined information (such as TIFF).

Normal
Italic

Italic: By just slanting a typeface, italics can create a heightened emphasis, as well as an artistic statement.

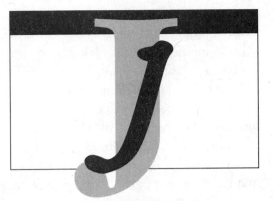

Jaggies is the popular description for the staircase-like appearance of **pixels** along an angular or curved edge of an **object** or an area in an **image** or a text-based **character**. (The official term for this effect is **aliasing**.) Most pixels are represented on a computer monitor and output on a printer as square blocks. Therefore, when displayed on an angle, the lines will not be smooth, but more like a staircase or building block effect. Jaggies are an unwanted, unattractive byproduct of the **digital**, as opposed to the **analog**, world.

There are various ways of minimizing or eliminating the jaggies effect. One is to bump up the **resolution**, which reduces the size of the blocks (compared to the overall image size) and, thereby, makes the curves or angles appear smoother. The other method is a software scheme called **anti-aliasing** or **feathering**. The program or printer automatically applies an **algorithm** (specifically created software **utility**) designed to smooth out the jaggies by blurring the line with the background. The effect is to soften the angular or curved lines so that they appear to the eye as smooth and unbroken.

Java is an operating environment (some say only a programming language) that allows users to run a variety of applications on a **Web page**. Depending on when and if

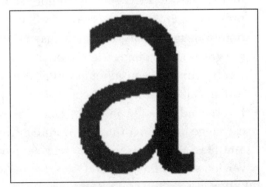

Jaggies: Slanted lines, curves and text tend to show a staircase-like edging, which is called *jaggies*.

Microsoft and **Sun** (the inventors of Java) ever settle their differences, Java may become an important component of graphics on the Internet.

Jitter is another word for **flicker**, or the rapid pulsing or flickering of a computer monitor. It's an annoying result of a slow, **interlaced** or malfunctioning monitor, and can cause headaches and fatigue. The only cure for screen jitter is to repair or replace the monitor.

Job refers to a batch or collection of items to be processed together, such as photographs to be **scanned** or **images** to be printed. In graphics arts, a job is a specific project that is to be prepared and printed.

Join is a **vector** command used in some **illustration** programs to freeze the current spatial relationship between two **objects**. If one is moved, the other moves, too, in the same direction. They don't have to be touching or adjoining to be joined and, in fact, can be on opposite ends of an **image**.

Another kind of Join command connects the two **end nodes** of an **open curve** or **path**. The result is a **closed path**.

JPEG stands for *Joint Photographic Experts Group*, a popular, industry-standard **file format** that **compresses** a photographic image to a fraction of its original size. (Compression is an often desirable and useful state for recording images on a digital camera, when an image file is too large to fit on a single **floppy diskette** or some other **removable storage**, to transmit over the Web or when space on a **hard drive** is limited.) There are many variations of JPEG, as well as compression levels. JPEG can shrink a file anywhere from 50% to 2% of its original size. However, JPEG is a **lossy compression**, which means that when the image is compressed and **decompressed, data bits** will be lost, or literally thrown away. Also, the more times a JPEG's file is compressed (saved and closed) and decompressed (opened), the more **data** will be lost. This may result in a degradation of image quality, though it may be slight and unnoticeable. However, the greater the compression level, the more apparent the image-quality loss can be. Another consideration: JPEG, as well as any other compression file format, takes extra time to compress and decompress—anywhere from a few seconds to a few minutes. That's the reason JPEG is used mostly as an exchange medium format, or to store infrequently used, relatively unimportant files. When it is used to exchange pictures, an original, uncompressed version should be **archived** (saved elsewhere).

Jukebox is a multiple **CD-ROM** drive that can change **CD**s within seconds. A jukebox-like mechanical arm selects and moves the requested CD in and out of its storage slot into the active playing area. Depending on the manufacturer and model, jukebox drives can hold from 3 to 100 CDs.

Their chief advantages over a single drive are the ability (1) to quickly swap CDs with a single command without having to physically remove the old CD and insert the new one; (2) to avoid the necessity of having to buy and connect multiple drives.

This	This	This
is	text	is
left	aligned	right
aligned	on	aligned
text	center	text

Justified: Justify is a desktop publishing and word processing command that *aligns* text in relation to the paper and/or margins.

On the minus side, jukeboxes are much slower than an **array** of individual **CD-ROM** drives or a single DVD drive, and because they are much more mechanically complex, may be more prone to breakdowns.

Other multiple storage devices may also be set up in a jukebox arrangement, but it is most common with CD drives.

Jumper is a tiny block of two rows of pins that are left open or shorted out with a tiny metal-lined plastic hood. Usually found on a **motherboard, peripheral** board or the rear of a device like a **modem**, the user may toggle the jumper on or off (by putting on or removing the hood) to get a desired setting. Whether they need to be changed depends on the computer's hardware or software **configuration**. Usually, there are 2, 4, 6 or 8 jumpers in a line, and the **default** positions are preset at the factory. Once very common, especially on **PCs, Windows 98's Plug and Play** capability is rapidly rendering them obsolete.

Justified is a typesetting term that refers to a block of text that is lined up to the same margin to make text more readable and visually appealing.

Most printed works and computer-generated printouts are left-justified, which means that on every line the letters always begin at the same point on the paper (except if the first word of a paragraph is indented).

Right-justified margins always end at the same point on a line.

Center justification aligns each line to a center point in the page.

Full justify will align type to both the right and the left margins. If there are not enough words or letters, the computer will automatically adjust the **proportional spacing** so that it will fit correctly. Or, if it is **monotype**, the spaces between the words will be adjusted. Many printed works are full justified. The opposite of proportional spacing is **fixed spacing**.

K or **Kb**   SEE **Kilobyte**.

Kai's Power Tools (KPT) is a group of **third-party special effects filters** from MetaCreations, which use the **Adobe open plug-in architecture**. That means they can be used from within just about all **image editing (bitmapped) programs**.

KPT has been such a successful product for MetaCreations that they use the same three initials in front of other products, such as KPT Bryce, which is a landscape **modeling** program.

Kanji is a set of Japanese characters. Because of its importance, many desktop printers, **word processors** and **desktop publishing** programs include a kanji **subset** of characters.

Kbps   SEE **Kilobits per second**.

Keep away is a graphics arts term for printing two colors, one on top of the other, with the darker one on top and the lower, lighter one not jutting out and showing outside the edges of the upper color. **Prepress** experts will surround the lower, lighter color with a border of the darker color, to keep the lighter color away from the edges.

The opposite of keep away is **trapping**, in which two colors are printed next to each other, and each one is allowed to spread a bit, to avoid showing slivers of white (paper color) between them.

Both keep away and trapping are necessary in prepress, because the printing presses work by running the paper through different color inks. (The most common is the four-color process which consists of cyan, magenta, yellow and black inks.) Because each color is applied to the same paper, individually, even the most precise presses can have difficulty with **registration** (the accurate aligning of the paper, so that it enters the press and receives the ink in the exact same manner for each run and color). Keep away and trapping attempt to make up for imprecise registration.

Kelvin is a unit of measurement of temperature, expressed in degrees K. It is germane to **imaging** in that the quality of light—and, therefore, how it is balanced for the best possible image—is expressed in kelvin. For example, tungsten light is 3200°K, fluorescent is 5500° and sunlight is 6000–10,000°. Some **image editing programs** allow the user to specify what kind of light, in degrees kelvin, will illuminate the subject.

Kermit is a communications program for transferring **data** over a **modem**. It's mainly used for communications between a **desktop computer** and a **mainframe computer**. Reportedly, it is named after Jim Henson's beloved little green frog.

Kerning is the special positioning, or adjustment of the closeness, of certain letters when they appear next to each other, to create a better, more natural look. For instance, when the capital letters *A* and *V* are adjacent, such as in the word *AVERY,* or a *T* and an *a* as in *Table* (these combinations are known as *kern pairs*), the word will look awkward unless the letters are kerned, or put closer together, instead of given their normal individual spacing. Many **word processing** and most **desktop publishing** programs will automatically kern specific

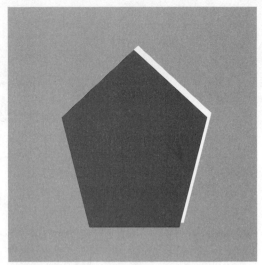

ABOUT A

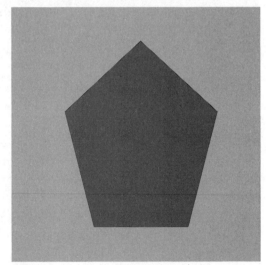

ABOUT B

Keep away: Because printing presses apply one color at a time to paper, you can often end up with misregistration **(A)**, with the color of the paper showing through where it shouldn't. Keep away and trapping are two methods used to make sure that color shapes fit each other correctly, with no paper showing through where it shouldn't **(B)**.

combinations of letters; some programs allow the user to manually kern letters and/or to create libraries (custom references) for defining new kerning rules for the program to follow.

kerning: The bottom *Trick* has the *r* kerned to move closer to the *T*.

Keyboard shortcut, or **hot key,** is a combination of keys and/or of key(s) with a mouse click, which will invoke a command or tool. For instance, CTRL+S (hold down the **control key** while pressing the S) is a hot key in many programs, which will save the active file or window under its current name. Keyboard shortcuts are often shown next to a command in its **pulldown menu**.

Keyframe is the **frame** where the user places animation information (such as a change in position or lighting).

Keyline is a viewing option in some 2-D illustration programs that displays only the outlines of objects and none of the fills. Using the keyline view may

KEYLINE A

KEYLINE B

Keyline: A Keyline illustration **(B)** uses fewer resources and, therefore, takes less time to redraw and edit than a view that shows you all your fills **(A)**.

help to speed up **redraw** and editing times. It is similar to the **wireframe** option of 3-D programs.

Keyword or key is a phrase, word or **alphanumeric** that the user defines as a kind of shortcut to aid in searches, browses and other otherwise complex commands or functions that can be made easier by having a single word or phrase to seek out.

KHz   SEE **Kilohertz**.

Kilobits per second, or **kbps,** is a unit of measurement applied to the speed of a **transmission** signal—including sending and receiving **image** files—sent from one computer to another, usually via a **modem**. The larger the number, the faster the transmission. Most modern modems are capable of transmitting and receiving at 28.8 or 56 Kbps, though some more advanced modems, such as **ISDN** modems, can carry a signal at speeds of 128 Kbps. Informally, those numbers are sometimes referred to as 33.6, 28.8, 128 k, etc.

Kilobyte, often written as **K** and sometimes as **Kb**, stands for 1,024 **bytes**. (Actually, among nontechnocrats, you'll often hear it said that a kilobyte is 1,000 bytes. That doesn't change the mathematical relationship of the two units of measure. It's just easier to say.) It's a way of expressing how much **data** or **RAM** a file or a program requires. For example, an **image** file may contain 650K of image data. Or a computer may have 640K of RAM, or electronic memory.

Kilohertz, often abbreviated as **KHz**, is the engineering term for thousands of cycles per second. It's a unit of measurement that is, among other purposes, applied to sound. **Hertz** (a smaller unit of measure) is the lower register (speech, voices and some musical instruments like drums and trombones, traffic noise, etc.), and kilohertz are sounds in the upper register (sopranos, flutes, songbirds, the whine of electronic circuitry, etc.). **Multimedia** programs that have audio editing capabilities will display sounds in either hertz or kilohertz.

Kludge is the word computerists use to describe an awkward, inelegant, poorly engineered, and sometimes Rube Goldberg-type device or software **interface** that, despite it all, works. For example, kludging occurs when you do not have the proper cable to connect a **scanner** to a computer, so you use a **gender changer** attached to a **SCSI-1** to **SCSI-2 adapter**. Or, it could be **JPEG**ing an image file created on a **PowerMac** computer onto a **DOS**-formatted **floppy disk** to transfer it to an **IBM-compatible PC**.

Knife is a tool found in some **vector** or **illustration** programs, which can be used to actually cut lines or objects, **interactively**. For instance, you can use the knife tool to cut a circle into two uneven halves, by drawing a squiggly line from one side through to the other side.

Kodak (Eastman Kodak, officially) is the world's largest **imaging** company. Based in Rochester, New York, the century-old corporation manufactures film, cameras, and both amateur and professional photographic supplies. It is also a leader in **digital imaging** products, and in manufacturing and marketing **digital cameras, film scanners**, printers, **CCDs**, and many other items.

KPCMS is the acronym for Kodak Precision **Color Management** System, the system used to control colors in **Photo CDs**. KPCMS is often supplied as part of many **image editing** and **desktop publishing** programs.

Kurta is the name of a defunct **digitizer tablet** company that ceased manufacturing in 1996.

L*a*b (aka *Lab* or **CIE**) is a **color model** based on standards established by the Commission Internationale de l'Eclairage, the French organization responsible for developing and promulgating color systems and standards. The L°A°B color model was defined in an attempt to create a device-independent color system, in which the colors would remain true to the original design regardless of the stage of production or how they are viewed (monitor, **output device, scanner**, etc.). L°a°b is a 3-D model in which any color can be located within a 3-D space in which one axis is luminance or lightness (measured from 0 to 100), another is the green-to-red axis and the third is the blue-to-yellow axis. The L°A°B color model contains both the **RGB** and the **CMYK** color spaces, so that it can be used as a translator between the two.   SEE **Color management**.

LAN is short for **Local Area Network**, a hardware/software method of linking computers together. LANs are the most common means of permitting computers to **link**, or share resources, such as **hard drives, scanners, CD-ROM drives, printers**, etc. LAN hardware consists of a high speed **interface**, usually contained on a **plug-in peripheral board** or built into the **motherboard**. The peripheral board or motherboard is connected by cable to a device (a **bridge, router, mau, gateway** or **hub**) that functions as the computer equivalent of an automated telephone switchboard. The software may be part of the **operating system** or a supplementary program that interacts, or works in conjunction, with the operating system.

Landscape mode, or **orientation**, is any displayed or printed text or image (or combination of the two) in which the horizontal dimension is greater than

LANDSCAPE A

LANDSCAPE B

Landscape: (A) Landscape orientation is wider than it is tall, and it is often (though not always) used for pictures of landscapes. **(B)** The opposite of Landscape is Portrait, which is taller than it is wide. *(A Corel stock photo.)*

the vertical dimension. Its opposite is the **portrait mode**. Most magazines, books, letters, documents and photographic portraits are printed or displayed in the portrait mode, but most group shots and panoramas are displayed or printed in the landscape mode.

In almost all **application programs**, users may select either the landscape or portrait mode when setting up printed page **preferences** and/or creating a new file.

The **Rotate** command can also change a picture's orientation from landscape to portrait or vice versa. (The two modes are a 90° rotation to each other.)

Language is how the information that tells the computer what to do is organized and presented. Like human languages (English, French, Chinese, Swahili), computer languages are created, developed and used to codify instructions. The application or use of computer language is called *programming*. Basic, C+++, Cobal and Pascal are all types of computer languages. So, too, are **page description languages** like **PCL** and **PostScript**. Fortunately for most users, it is entirely unnecessary to know anything about languages, except that they exist and that they may define how your computer functions and relates to its **peripherals** and software.

Laptop is a small portable computer that can fit into a briefcase and be used, literally, on your lap. It usually has a battery, so it doesn't need to be connected to any power source, which means that it may be used anywhere (as long as the battery power holds out). Laptops are useful for portable presentations and for **imaging** demos, but current models tend to have limited resources (**RAM, hard drive** space, etc.). Therefore, they are, generally, not yet powerful enough for serious, **high resolution** imaging.

Laser disc, also known as a **video disc**, is an **analog optical** disc, usually 12 inches in diameter, that is most often used for viewing high quality, full motion videos, such as Hollywood movies. Although most laser discs and laser disc players are designed to play on television sets, they may also be viewed on a computer. Because they have a capacity that far exceeds that of a **CD-ROM**, laser discs are sometimes used for lengthy or complicated **interactive** training or games. Creating a laser disc requires expensive **mastering** hardware; therefore, it is rarely a technology that **desktop** users would or could **write to**. Video discs are considered obsolete technology and are currently being superceded by **DVD**s, or **digital video** discs, which are high capacity storage media the same size and shape as CD-ROMs, but with the ability to store 4 or more gigabytes on a single disc.

LaserJet is the name of **Hewlett-Packard**'s popular **monochrome** and color **laser printers**.

Laser printer, also called an **electrostatic printer**, is a widely used technology that employs a laser beam to rapidly "paint" a **digital image** on a photosensitive surface (usually a cylindrical drum). Those areas where the laser light strikes the drum become electrically charged and, like a magnet, attract and pick up a fine iron powder, called *toner*. The toner—which is black in a **monochrome** printer and cyan, magenta, yellow and black in a color laser printer—is then transferred from the drum to paper and "fixed" by passing the paper through a hot roller. All this happens in a matter of seconds, and except for the laser **imaging**, is virtually identical to photocopier technology. Most laser printers output onto plain, inexpensive photocopy paper, which makes the cost per print among the lowest of any printer technology. Laser printer **output**, especially text and **line art**, is of such a high quality that it exhibits near-typeset quality.

Depending on the make and model, laser printers have the capability of producing text and images at a resolution of 300 to 1200 **dpi** (and higher); outputting 8.5×11- to 12×18-inch pages; speeds between 3 and 16 prints per minute; **halftone** or **camera ready** prints; **near-photographic** color prints.

Images and text output by laser printers are fairly stable, which means that they will fade or change colors more slowly than prints output by most other types of printers.

L

LaserWriter is the name of **Apple's** line of **PostScript**–equipped **laser printers**.

Lasso is a **selection** tool that allows a user to draw **freehand masks** or selections around a part of a **bitmapped image**.

Launching is the act of opening or starting a program. This is usually done by **double-clicking** on the program's icon on your computer's **desktop** or **program manager**, or by using the **Run . . .** command in **Windows 98** or **Windows NT**.

Layers are similar to the acetate sheets of old-fashioned cartoons, in that they are **image** components that may be laid one on top of the other. For instance, suppose you have a photograph of clouds and another of a dog. When you **cut** out the dog from its original picture, it can be **pasted** onto a layer that rests above the layer of the clouds. Each layer may be edited independently, without **merging** into the other layers. So, you can return to each layer and re-edit it without having to maintain **selections** or **masks**. In other words, the dog sits on its own layer and doesn't have to be remasked to change its color, sharpen it, enlarge it or whatever. Layers are also very useful for keeping track of **image** objects and sections.

Layers palette is a **dialog box** that maintains a list of all the **layers** in a picture, as well as provides access to commands that control or manipulate layers.

Layout is the process of putting text and/or pictures onto a **page** in preparation for printing. It is generally a **desktop publishing** term that refers to laying out the elements of a **page** attractively and effectively.

Some programs will use the term *layout* to refer to the original page setup for a new **image** or **document**. In that setup, the user will define the size and **orientation** of a page, **image** or **document**.   SEE **Page setup box**.

LCD   SEE **LED**.

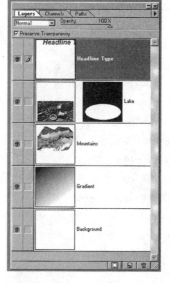

Layers palette: In this Photoshop Layers palette, the user has control over the order, the blend mode, mask, transparency level and other properties of an image's layers.

Leader is a typesetter's term that has carried over to **desktop publishing**. It describes the dots or dashes that lead up to a word, phrase or, even, a graphic. The purpose is to direct the viewer's eyes to a specific point on the **page**, usually from another specific point.

Leading (pronounced like the metal *lead*, and not the verb to *lead*) is a typesetter's term that continues to be used by **desktop publishing** programs. It refers to the space between lines of text. Its origin harks back to the days when type was set by hand and thin strips of lead were physically inserted between lines—the more lead used, the further apart the lines.

The digital command for controlling leading is often called **line spacing**.

In this sample of text, the leading is rather tight.

This leading is normal. With the space between lines set to be equivalent to the size of the font.

And, this is looser leading,

which is usually not used for

a paragraph, but for spaces

between paragraphs and

other text that you want to set

apart.

Leading: Leading, like line spacing, controls the amount of space between lines of text.

Leaf, or Leaf Systems, is the name of a company that produces **digital camera backs**. The Leaf Digital Camera Back currently outsells all other high end filmless cameras put together. Leaf is a division of **Scitex**. (Leaf no longer manufactures scanners, but it does make the Digital Camera Back.)

LED, or light-emitting diode, is the bright red or green alphanumeric readout that you see on computer **peripherals**, alarm clocks, stereos and other electronic equipment. It is much brighter and, therefore, uses more electricity than an **LCD** (*liquid crystal diode*), which displays in nonilluminating gray (or, sometimes, a color). You can see an LED in the dark, but not the LCD. Most filmless cameras use LCDs rather than LEDs, to conserve battery life.

Left mouse button, or **left mouse click,** activates or chooses commands, tools and other things on the **PC** monitor. The **PC mouse, trackball** or **stylus** has at least two buttons—a right and a left. (The **Mac** has only one.) Therefore, most **PC** software take advantage of this, using the left button for all traditional mouse activities and the right button for other options.

Lens flare, in photography, is usually an unwanted effect that occurs when bright light strikes a camera's lens at an oblique angle and produces an internal reflection that radiates or flares out in a circle. However, because it has become associated with a camera shooting into the sun or any other bright light, which is sometimes a creative element in imaging, flare is often included as a **filter** in **image editing** programs.

Letterhead is the type and, sometimes, picture and/or logo that are placed on business and personal stationery. It says to the receiver of a letter or memo: This came from me, here's my name, address, phone numbers and/or **e-mail** address. With the advent of **desktop publishing** and sophisticated **word processing** programs, most correspondence has some kind of letterhead. Letterheads are a great opportunity for **digital** artists to show who they are and what they do, because they can include **images**.

Levels is a **dialog**-based tool for reading and adjusting a picture's **dynamic range** (its contrast and lightness). It usually has a **histogram** displayed, which is a statistical graph that shows how many and where pixels are in the range from absolute dark to full white light.

License is a legal document and/or agreement

Lens flare: Lens flare filters add a bright light that emulates what was once considered a photographic no-no in most situations. Now, it's an artistic element. We prefer using the greater control of Lighting Effects filters to add light to most images, though a flare can sometimes be interesting, if used judiciously. *(A Corel stock photo.)*

in which the owner of intellectual property (such as software, photographs, **digital** art, etc.) grants the right to use that property to another individual or group. The terms of that license limit or define how you may use the property.

When you buy software, its license is usually a sticker that must be broken to open the package where the **install disks** or **CD-ROMs** are. By breaking that seal, you are agreeing to the terms.

When you purchase a library of **clip art**, it may be license-free, which means you can use it however you want. Or, it may have a limited license, in which case you may not be able to use the pictures for publication or other named purposes.

Many artists no longer sell their photographs and/or digital **images** to clients. Instead, they sell licenses to use the art in specified ways, for a certain length of time.   SEE **Copyright**.

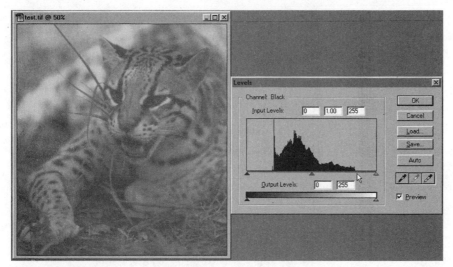

LEVELS DIALOG A

LEVELS DIALOG B

Levels dialog: The graph in the Levels dialog (which is called a *histogram*) shows the distribution of highlights, shadows and midtones in a picture. Therefore, the histogram of the overexposed picture in **A** displays no data in the outer reaches of the graph. You can click and drag on the triangles at the bottom of the graph to adjust the tonal range of the picture. By comparison, look at the histogram of the well-exposed picture in **B**. It shows data in all areas of the graph—from the deep shadows into the bright highlights. *(A Corel stock photo.)*

LIFO stands for *Last In/First Out,* as opposed to **FIFO** (*First In/First Out*). When users want to send a half-dozen **images** to the printer at one time, many programs allow them to **queue** up the projects or specify the order in which they are to be printed. If users want the last image worked on to be printed first, they will use LIFO order.

Ligature is a single **character** that is formed from common two-letter combinations, such as the *ae* in æroplane. Some **word processing** and **desktop publishing programs** have libraries or customizable options for creating ligatures. However, they are not very popular, and within a generation they will probably be the electronic equivalent of the dodo bird.   SEE **Custom/ customize**.

Lighten is a command, **filter** or tool that increases the brightness of a picture, object or area of an image. It may also be written as Brighten.

Lighting effects are **special effects filters** that allow the user to place localized **brightness** in an **image**, so that it appears as though a light is shining on the picture. Depending on the software, the user may define the inten-

Lighting Effects: Lighting Effects provides the tools for placing different kinds of lights into bitmapped pictures. These lights can then be manipulated and edited, changing numerous properties (such as color, focus and direction).

sity, color, direction, size, angle and source of the light(s) and how they will affect and illuminate the picture.

Lightning arrestor is an electrical or electronic device that is placed between the power source from the electric company (the cable that comes into your house or office) and the circuit breaker box. Its sole purpose is to melt or disintegrate when struck by lightning, thereby severing the connection to your electrical system and preventing a fatal overload from destroying your equipment.

While every computer-intensive business or profession should have a lightning arrestor, it should be noted that not even NASA or the U.S. military has been able to develop protection from a direct lightning hit. However, a lightning arrestor may save you thousands of dollars in damages from a nearby lightning strike. We not only have one on our box, but we also turn off all our computers during violent electrical storms.

Light source is, quite literally, where the light is coming from that illuminates a picture or **scene**. Because the quality, intensity, color, angle, direction and type of a light source directly affects the appearance of the picture, some programs have filters and tools for defining light(s).

In animation programs, a **rendered** scene will be completely black, unless at least one light source has been defined.

Light Source is also the name of a company that manufactures the Colortron, a device for **PCs** and **Macs** for measuring color quality and intensity.

Linear cameras (or backs) are top professional-quality, **high resolution** studio **digital cameras**, which use a **scanning** linear **CCD** to capture images. A linear CCD differs from an **array** CCD in that instead of being shaped like a circle or square, the linear CCD is a thin strip that must be moved, or scanned, across the film plane. To capture a color image, a linear camera must take three separate scans, or exposures, shot through red, green and, then, blue **filters**. This means that linear cameras capture only still color images and not **real-time** subjects (such as people, animals and sports). Depending on the make, model and type of technology used, a linear camera may require anywhere from 10 seconds to 15 minutes to scan an entire image. Therefore, it must be stationary on a tripod and tethered at all times to a computer.

Linear gradient fill is a smooth transition between colors that follows a direct line of gradation. For instance, to fill a square, the gradation may start in one corner (with the first color) and end in the opposite corner (with the last color in the gradient). Or, it might go from the top of the rectangle to the bottom. SEE **Gradient fill, Rectangle gradient fill** and **Continuous tone**.

Linear perspective displays three-dimensional **scenes** or **objects** so that objects or areas that are farther back look smaller. This is how things look in the real world, to the human eye. In fact, you could make a far-away skyscraper appear smaller than a child standing in the **foreground**. No, the child isn't a giant, that's just how linear perspective works. SEE **Isometric perspective**.

Line art shows pictures or illustrations as black and white, with no gray or other colors. This is also known as **1-bit** art or color, because the image is defined by one piece of information: Is the **pixel** black or is it white?

Confusingly enough, some programs also call this kind of picture *bitmap,* which is not the same as a **bitmapped** picture. The 1-bit bitmap is only a black and white. But a bitmapped picture is any kind of picture (including a **24-bit** or **index color** picture) that is made up of **pixels**.

Line screen was, originally, a very fine mesh

LINE ART A

LINE ART B

Line art: Converting this Corel Stock photo to a one-bit black and white line art image emulates old woodcuts and is also a feasible option when you want a stylish picture in a piece that uses only one-color ink.

grid or screen that was placed over **continuous tone** pictures to create the **halftones** that could be used by printing presses. The finer the mesh—that is, the higher the number of lines per inch (lpi)—the better the picture looked, with greater detail and a better approximation of the original continuous tone. Generally speaking, pictures in newspapers are 85 lpi, whereas magazine illustrations are generally 133 lpi, and glossy fine art books will use a 200-lpi screen. The screening of pictures is now done by computers; however, the terminology and the measurements have remained the same.

If you are creating **digital images** that will be **output** onto a printing press, you need to know what line screen will be used, so that you provide enough image **data** or **resolution** for the intended screen. As a flexible rule of thumb, your image's **pixel** density, or **ppi** (pixels per inch), should be about one and a half to two times the intended lpi. For instance, if your picture will be in a newspaper that uses an 85-lpi screen, you should create your image at 170 **ppi** (though at the same height and width as it will be printed).

Line spacing   SEE **Leading**.

Lines per inch   SEE **Line screen**.

Line stabilizer is an electrical device designed to smooth out the spikes, peaks and dips of ordinary current. Computers and other electronic equipment are very sensitive to voltage fluctuations ("dirty power"). Prolonged voltage fluctuations can damage or even destroy hardware and can permanently corrupt software and **data**. A line stabilizer uses various electrical and electronic components to produce an even, consistent flow of electricity ("clean power"). They are often used in conjunction with **surge suppressors, uninterruptible power supplies** or **standby power supplies**.

Link is a command that creates a connection between two objects. Then, if one object is moved, the other will follow.   SEE **Object linking**.

Linking is one-half of **Windows object linking and embedding** (OLE), in which a file or object from one **application program** can reside in another application. It is different from importing and exporting, because the linked or embedded file remains editable in its original program. For instance, suppose you have an **image** created in an **illustration program**. It can be embedded into a **word processing** program (or any other OLE-compatible program). There, in the **word processor** document, the image is displayed (and not saved), but it remains linked to its original program, where it is saved. Any changes made to the linked picture in its original program can be updated to be seen in the displaying or linking program.

Linotronic is a well-known brand-name **imagesetter**. Linotronic also produces consumer flatbed scanners and color management and calibration software, which is used in Windows operating systems.

Linotype-Hell is a brand name of high end **drum scanners** and flatbed scanners.

Lite, or LE, designates a program that is an abbreviated, less-powerful version than the full-blown software. For instance, a lite version of an **image editing program** may be included or **bundled** in the purchase of a **flatbed scanner**. The program will work well, but it won't have all of the features, tools and commands of its bigger brother. However, there is usually a coupon included in the scanner box for a comparatively inexpensive **upgrade** to the full version.

Lithium ion batteries are expensive, but desirable, rechargeable batteries for digital cameras, laptops, etc. They hold more electricity than nickel cadmium or nickel hydride batteries and are generally faster to recharge. But they may cost three to five times more.

Live Picture is a **resolution-independent image editing** program that is used to edit, manipulate, save and **output** very large, **high resolution images**, without the delays that high resolution editing often involves. This is done by using two different file formats: **Ivue** and **FITS**. The FITS file format saves the original picture **data**, and the Ivue saves all the editing information. Then, the picture must be **rendered** (the information in the Ivue and the FITS files is combined) to be output.

Load is a command that will bring additional color **palettes, typefaces, clip art** and other tools into a program.

For instance, suppose you are creating a picture in an **image editing program** and you want to conform to the **Trumatch color swatches,** so that you can be certain to get the right colors from your **output**. In the program's color controls, there will be a load command that will pull into its color palette the Trumatch swatches from elsewhere on your computer.

Local Area Network   SEE **LAN**.

Local bus (aka **VL** bus or **VESA**) is a high speed, **32-bit interface** that was briefly popular for a year on many PC **motherboards**. It has been almost completely superseded by the **PCI** bus, and practically no VL bus motherboards or peripherals are still manufactured.

Lock is a command or option that fixes an **object, layer, guideline, grid** or other **image element** in place, so that they can't be accidentally moved, edited or otherwise changed, while other parts of the picture are being created and edited. The lock can usually be removed, or **unlocked**, by the user.

Logarithmic gradient fill is a smooth transition between colors in which most of the color changes occur near the starting and ending points of the **gradient**.

Logic board is any **board, card** or **motherboard** that contains a logic chip, i.e., a **microprocessor** or **CPU**.

Log on/off/in is the process of typing in your name and, sometimes, a password, to enter a computer, program, **network** or **Internet** server, such as CompuServe or America Online.

Logitech is a manufacturer of computer **peripherals**, such as **mouses** and trackballs.

Lookup Table, or LUT, is a reference profile that gives the dimensions and specifications of a particular device, film, color table, process, etc., and directions on how to translate computer data to or from the device, etc. The computer recognizes the needed LUT and automatically configures its hardware and/or adjusts its software to accommodate the criteria of the LUT. The whole idea of lookup tables is to make a perfect match between the device, color or whatever, and the final **output**.

LUTs are critical pieces of programming for quality imaging, distributed either as **firmware** or as software. Luckily, as long as they work the way they are supposed to work, the average user doesn't have to be bothered with LUTs, after they have been installed properly.

Lo res describes an **image** or device that contains, displays or **outputs** a low volume of **data**. It is sometimes insufficient data to accurately display depth, detail and definition. In a lo-res file or device, the space between the dots that make up the image is further apart than in files or devices with mid-resolution or **high resolution**.

The level of resolution of a file is relative to output and display purposes. On a computer monitor, low resolution is usually any display showing less than 640×480 **dpi**; high resolution is anything over 1024×768 **dpi**. On a printer, any text or image printed at less than 150 **dpi** is low resolution; 300 to 600 **dpi** is midresolution; anything over 720 **dpi** is high resolution.

Lossless compression is an algorithm or software scheme for reducing the size of an **image** file without compromising its quality. Although image integrity is maintained, the file won't get as small as it can with **lossy compression**. SEE **Compression**.

Lossy compression throws away pieces of **data** that the software consider unimportant (based on a predetermined mathematical formula), when attempting to shrink files (most specifically **image** files) to make them fit onto storage devices, such as **floppies**. The result can be a file that is as much as 1/100th of its original size. Of course, there is always the potential problem that the computer might consider extraneous the **pixels** and other **image elements** that you feel are integral to your design. But with a good lossy compression program, set at a not-too-high level of compression, you may not see any difference in image quality, unless you are a **graphics** expert or the originator of the picture.

Lossy compression is becoming increasingly important for saving images for electronic display and distribution, such as with **digital cameras** or on **Web pages**. However, any compressed file will take longer to save and open than the same file uncompressed. SEE **Lossless compression** and **Compression**.

Lotus is a division of IBM that produces software products, most notably Lotus Notes.

Lowercase relates to type that is uncapitalized. For instance *a* is lowercase, but *A* is uppercase or capitalized.

LPI, or **lines per inch**   SEE **Line screen**.

LPT1 is the **PC** nomenclature for parallel printer port interface. While other parallel port positions are possible (LPT2, LPT3, etc.), for practical reasons, most stand-alone (non-networked) **PC**s use only LPT1 to connect to a printer.   SEE **Parallel interface** and **Port**.

Luminosity is the measure of light in an **image**. The greater the luminosity, the more light there is.

Luminosity is one of the three components that define a color in the **HSL color model**. The other two components are **hue** (the position of the color in the spectrum) and **saturation** (the density or amount of color).

LUT   SEE **Lookup Table**.

LZW compression (Lempel-Ziv-Welsh) is an option associated with some variants of the **TIFF file format**. However, some programs that can handle TIFF files are not equipped to compress or decompress those that have LZW encoding. Officially, LZW is **lossless compression**.

Mac is the common moniker for Apple's Macintosh computers. Usually, any **hardware, software**, etc., preceded with the word Mac, refers to something tailored for the Macintosh system, such as MacTools and MacWorld. Mac and **PowerMac** are often used interchangeably, although they don't always mean the same thing.

Macro is a shortcut in which one or several keystrokes will do the work of many keystrokes. For instance, holding down the **Control key** or **Options key** and pressing the number 6 may initiate a user-created macro that searches for any **TIFF** graphics files under 1 **megabyte** in size created on the 6th of the month, and automatically places them into a **queue** that can then be loaded into **memory** and displayed on the computer monitor. Most **application programs** come with a series of predefined macros. In addition, many will allow users to create their own simple, user-defined **program** in which the correct keystrokes are recorded and saved as a file or part of a file that can be played at will.

Magic wand, or **color wand,** is a **selection** tool that allows a user to automatically select all the **pixels** in an **image** that are adjacent to and similar in color to the pixel on which the wand is clicked.

For instance, suppose a picture has a gray sky that you want to **mask** or select, so that you can replace it with a blue sky. Click on one of the gray points in the sky with the magic wand, and (if everything works perfectly) the entire sky will be selected, as long as all the pixels are contiguous (touching another gray pixel and another . . .) to the original clicked pixel.

Magic Wand: (A) With the tolerance of the magic wand set at 18, the background mask created by clicking the magic wand in this picture includes some of the hand, too. **(B)** But with the tolerance set at 13, a nearly perfect background mask is created. (Note that the dotted lines—which are also called a *marquee* or *marching ants*—show the edges of the mask.)

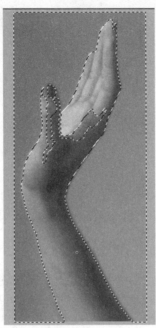

MAGIC WAND A   MAGIC WAND B

The user may adjust the **tolerance** of the magic wand, so that it will select adjacent pixels that are within a specific range of the color of the pixel on which the tool is clicked. To extend the above example, if the gray sky really has several shades of gray in it (as most real skies do), then opening up the tolerance (increasing the value in the tolerance box) of the magic wand will select more shades of gray. The trick is to find the right level of tolerance that will select all the pixels you want and nothing else.

It's called a *magic wand* because, when conditions are ideal, it works instantly and can save hours of tedious tracing around areas of a picture on the pixel level. Alas, conditions are rarely, if ever, perfect, so most of the time when it is applied, the magic wand fails to accurately and completely select the desired object. The user must fine-tune by selecting by hand (using other selection tools) all nearby pixels left out of or included in the mask that don't belong or weren't included because their color was too close (or not close enough) to the initial click color, or because they weren't in a swathe adjacent to the original click.

To make the magic wand work better, studio photographers and cinematographers often shoot a subject against a contrasting color background (often referred to in Hollywood as *chromakey* or *blue screen,* though the color may be green, red or any other solid color). This makes the magic wand's job of selecting the subject to be masked much easier.

Magneto-optical drive, or **MO drive,** is a storage device that combines two technologies: the magnetic read/write of a **floppy** or **hard drive**, with the permanency of an **optical drive**. It is relatively inexpensive and a very stable (permanent and safe) storage. Reportedly, the media (cartridges) will last 25 to 100 years without any **data** loss. Most come in a variety of sizes, from 128 **Mb** to 4.6 **Gb**.

Magnifying glass icon and **cursor** represent the **zoom tool**, which will increase (or decrease) the magnification at which you can view a picture. If you magnify a **bitmapped** picture enough, you see the square **pixels** that represent the individual **bits** of information that make up that picture. That's when you can edit the picture on the pixel level.

Using the zoom tool with a modifying key, such as the **Option** or the **Alt** key, may toggle the tool between zooming in and zooming out. But that depends on the kind of software you are using.

Also, the magnifying cursor or zoom tool can be used with a **click and drag** that draws a rectangle around the area that the user wants magnified to fill the entire picture **window**.

Mainframe computer, also referred to as *Big Iron,* is a very large, very expensive high speed computer system designed for large corporations with lots of **terminals**. Mainframes usually occupy a special chilled room and are attended to by an army of skilled technicians. They are the antithesis of small, inexpensive **desktop** computers used by individuals. Mainframes are rarely used in imaging. In fact, they're considered technological dinosaurs and fewer and fewer are being built.

Male connector, or **header,** is a plug with prongs or a strip of pins, that inserts into a **female connector**. The cables and ports that they plug into, which connect computers and their **peripherals**, are male or female. If you have one, you must use the other. When you have two male or two female connectors, you can use a contraption called a *gender changer* to bridge the connection.

Mapping is the process by which the **16.7 million** possible colors in a **24-bit color** image are associated with and converted into the **256 colors** of an **indexed** or **8-bit color** image. 8-bit color is necessary for displaying in some applications, such as on the **Web**. Because there are so many more colors in the 24-bit file than can be represented in the 8-bit image, all the colors in the original picture must be mapped or directed to change into colors that are represented among the 256 in the new picture. For instance, in a 24-bit color picture, a pink dress may actually be made up of numerous hues of red and pink, but when they are remapped down to an 8-bit picture, all of the different reds and pinks may be translated into a single pink that might be an average of the original colors.

How the colors are mapped depends on the **color table** used. This may be chosen by the user, or it may be selected by the software, depending on the program. Strange and, sometimes, creative effects can be achieved by mapping colors to a table that is not representative of an average of the original colors, but based on some other spectrum. SEE **Adaptive color, Black body, System color**.

Bitmapping is another issue, in that it defines a **pixel**-based picture by keeping track of (or mapping) each and every pixel, its color and its position.

Mapping can also refer to the image mapping that defines areas of a picture which may be set as **hotspots** for a **Web page**. When users viewing the page on the **Internet** click on that hotspot, they will automatically be sent to the new place within that document or, even, to another page on the Internet. The designer of the image or page defines where the hotspot will take the viewer, and the image map saves that information within the **file format**.

Marching ants are the flashing dots that surround a **selected** or **masked** area of an **image**. Also called a **marquee** because it looks like the flashing lights that surround the marquee of a movie theatre, it is the border or outline that defines a selection.

Margin is a nonprinting area along the border of an **image** or a **document** that sets the text or picture away from the edge of the page. **Full bleed** printers can **output** without any margins, so that the image or the document fills the entire paper.

Marquee SEE **Marching ants**.

Mask limits any editing and manipulation to a specific area in a **bitmapped** image. It is usually created using **selection tools**, which draw a **marquee** or border around the area. Then, any special effect, manipulation or whatever editing is done will affect only those **pixels** within the mask and none of the pixels outside it.

A mask may be saved as an **alpha channel** or an additional channel that is used to modify or affect the **primary color channels**. When the alpha channel is viewed separately from the color channels, it is seen as a black and white silhouette in which white covers the area that is included in the mask, and black covers the rest of the picture.

However, a mask need not be an either/or, on/off or black/white limiting tool. A mask may be modified, using a program's **quick mask, ruby mask**

MASK A

MASK B

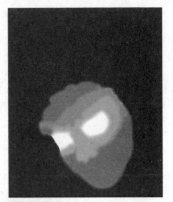

MASK C

MASK D

Mask: Masking is a powerful tool for working with bitmapped images that provides a great deal of artist control and creative potential. Here is an example. **(A)** The marquee or marching ants (the dotted line) around a portion of this woman's face delineates the masked area of this picture. **(B)** A mask may also be shown (in its alpha channel state) as a black and white silhouette, in which black covers the area not included in the mask, and the white is that area that is inside the mask. (Think of it as a cut out cardboard stencil that you place over a canvas—where the cardboard is, the paint won't get through—that's the equivalent of the black area.) **(C)** However, you can also use different levels of gray to fine tune a mask more precisely. The darker the gray, the more transparent the result. **(D)** Therefore, when we copied and pasted the face onto this background using the black and white mask of picture **B**, the result was a fully opaque face, which was the shape of the original mask (on the left side). But when we use the mask pictured in **C**, those areas in which the mask was darker gray (on the outer areas of the face) were more transparent than those where the mask was light gray. And the white areas of the mask (around the eyes) pasted as fully opaque. *(Photo from the Corel Stock Photo Library.)*

or by working directly on the alpha channel. Painting various levels of gray onto the alpha channel silhouette establishes areas in which whatever editing is done while the mask is active will be partially limited—but some editing will be allowed to get through the mask to the underlying **image**. The grays act as a translucency. The darker the gray, the less the editing will affect the color pixels. The lighter the gray, the more the editing will change the color pixels.

Match print is output generated by a special **desktop** printer that mimics the inks that will be set up when the **page** is finally reproduced on a printing press. It is far cheaper and faster to produce a match print to fine-tune an **image's** color and density, than it is to set up a short print run. Different companies (such as Kodak, Agfa and 3M) have their own brand names for match prints.   SEE **SWOP, Process color, Pantone, Spot color, Trumatch**.

Matrox is a Canadian company that manufactures high powered **graphics** and **multimedia boards**.

Mau is the hub or box that connects the various pieces of a **token-ring network** to each other.

Mavica is the name Sony Electronics gives to its line of **digital cameras**.

MB   SEE **Megabyte**.

Media is anything that can hold an **image, page, document** or **file**. It is paper, film, a **SyQuest** cartridge, **a hard drive**, etc.

There are fixed, removable and **hardcopy** media. Fixed are permanently attached to your computer, such as a hard drive. But a **floppy disk** is removable, because the disk is the media, not the drive. And, hardcopy has to do with what can be held in your hand and viewed without any electronic gadgets.

Megabyte, abbreviated MB, is a unit of measure of data or information, which is equal to 1,024 **kilobytes**. Nontechies often round it off to 1,000 **kilobytes** or 1,000,000 **bytes**. Memory and storage space are frequently expressed in megabytes.   SEE **Bit**.

Megahertz   SEE **MHz**.

Memory is an electronic medium of storage and processing in which **data** can be held or channeled. Using a computer, you can read, write and process data that are in memory.

For **imagers**, a very important type of computer memory is **RAM**, or **Random Access Memory**. RAM comprises chips that retain everything that you or your software does, instructs, creates or whatever. The more RAM your computer has, the faster you'll be able to edit pictures, **draw,**

paint, etc. RAM lasts only as long as there is electricity to power it continuously. Whatever is in RAM when the computer is switched off will disappear. That's the reason there is another type of long-term memory that will store information and instructions when the computer is turned off. The long-term memory is stored in devices such as **disk drives** and **CD-ROMs**.

Serious **graphics applications** are very memory intensive, requiring lots of RAM, big **hard drives** and various other **media**. Alas, memory can be expensive. The more you have the more it costs.   SEE **Virtual memory**.

Memory management attempts to make the most of your computer's memory. In **pixel**-based **image editing**, it seems that there is never enough memory for the task at hand—especially when working on **high resolution images**. When software can find no more available **RAM**, it stores short-term information (**data** that it expects to need again, soon) in empty spaces on the **hard drive** (which is then called **virtual memory**). Since electronic RAM is thousands of time faster than magnetic drives (such as a hard drive), using virtual memory can bog down processing and imaging considerably. So, different software and hardware memory management schemes have been developed to use RAM more efficiently.

Menu is a list of options, tools or commands. When the user chooses one, that usually causes some action to occur. Many menus have a header word, which, when clicked on or next to, opens up the entire list. Every program has menus; most have extensive **pulldown menus** whose headers sit at the top of the screen.

Merge, as the word implies, combines two or more items into one.

A **floating object** may be merged into the underlying picture or **defloated**. Then, it becomes part of the underlying picture and you may or may not be able to edit it separately afterwards.

Layers may be merged or collapsed together, so that they become one layer. Usually, the user can choose which layers will be merged, leaving other layers in an **image** separate. If all the layers in a picture are merged into one, the picture is said to be **flattened**.

Documents can be merged, with one filling in user-specified or programmed holes or **fields** in the other. For instance, a mailing list can be merged with a form letter, to create a series of personalized letters that are individually addressed.

MetaCreations (formerly HSC Software) is a company that develops and markets **special effects filters** and **applications**, such as their **Kai's Power**

Tools filters and **KPT Bryce**. Their software is marked by impressive visuals, unusual **interfaces** and the frequent use of words like "cool" (by users and by the company).

MHz is the abbreviation for **megahertz**, which is a unit of measure for frequency vibrations. It is used to gauge the speed and power of a computer **CPU**. The higher number MHz, the faster and more powerful the machine. The first IBM-PC was 1 MHz. Current **Pentium Pro** and **PowerPC** CPUs are up to 350 and will continually rise to 1,000 MHz, or 1 gigahertz. SEE **Hertz**.

Micrografx is a company that develops and markets image editing programs and business graphics such as **Picture Publisher, Designer**, the ABC **Graphics Suite**, and ABC FlowCharter.

Microprocessor   SEE **CPU**.

Microsoft is the mega-company that creates and markets software, including **Windows**, Word, Excel, etc. It's the company that made Bill Gates the richest man in the world. Virtually every desktop computer has some Microsoft software on it.

MIDI (*Musical Instrument Digital Interface*) is a **file format** that records how music is created so that it may be repeated. For instance, if an electric piano is connected to a computer through a MIDI interface, then, when the musician plays the piano, the computer annotates the music and how it is played. That annotation can be edited before it is played back on a synthesizer. The MIDI file, unlike **WAV**, does not actually contain any music, just the information about how it can be reproduced. **Multimedia** makes extensive use of MIDI files.

Millisecond (ms) is one-thousandth of a second. Often, **disk drive** performance, or **access** speed, is expressed in milliseconds. A drive may have a speed listing of 12 ms, 9 ms, etc. The lower the number, the faster the drive.

MIPS is the name of a **RISC CPU** used to power **workstation**-speed computers.

MIPS is also a measure of computer speed, in how many millions of instructions per second can be executed. Because of rapid advances, MIPS is beginning to be supplanted by **BIPS**, or billions of instructions per second.

Mirror is a command that flips an **image**, a **selected** area of an image or an **object**, so that it creates a mirror reflection of the original.

Another definition of mirror is a protection for the **FAT**, or *File Allocation Table,* to prevent it from being accidentally corrupted or destroyed. A snapshot, or mirror, of the FAT is made by a **utility** program and preserved elsewhere on the **hard drive**, and it is accessed when needed.

Mirror is also used in **RAID**, or *Redundant Array of Inexpensive Drives,* as a fail-safe system in which all **data** are backed up to two drives. If one goes down, the other kicks in instantly and automatically. RAID systems are used mostly by businesses and organizations that can't afford interruptions or data loss.

Miter is a shaped corner of lines or angled **objects** that looks like the mitering done by carpenters on wooden molding. It gives the lines and objects a more polished, stylish look.

MO drive   SEE **Magneto-Optical drive**.

Mode describes the ways or styles of using some tools or commands. For instance, a **Bezier** tool may have an elastic mode, or a default universal mode, in which the elastic mode causes the **nodes** to behave differently than they usually do.

A tool's or a command's mode can be changed by clicking in a **dialog box's** check box, by choosing the mode in a **pulldown menu**, or by using some other **toggle** in the software.

Blend modes are **layer, composite, channel operations** and **paintbrush** options that define how **pixels** will interact, **merge** or affect each other.

Models are **3-D objects** that can be viewed comparatively realistically from all angles. And regardless of the angle of the view, all the mathematical information that defines that object remains part of it (including what isn't seen). And, therefore, that information continues to be editable. The word model comes from the modeling that was originally done in clay, wood or other materials, which helped designers and manufacturers see how a design (that was initially on paper) would really look, once it was brought into the real (3-D) world. Now, most modeling is done on the computer, in 3-D programs, and it is used not only for manufacturing, but also fine art, **animation** and other purposes.   SEE **Wireframe**.

Modem is a device for transmitting and receiving **data** from another computer, usually via a telephone connection.

Modem actually stands for modulate and demodulate, because it reduces a **digital** signal to an **analog** tone that can be sent over telephone wires. The receiving modem does the opposite, translating the analog tone back into digital data. Modems have become ubiquitous with the extraordinary explosion of the **Internet**.

Modem speeds are measured in **baud** or the number of **kilobits per second** (kbps) that can be transmitted. Current high speed modems transmit at 56 kbps. The new generation of **ISDN** and **cable modems** can transmit many times faster, which is necessary for sending or receiving large **image** files.

Moiré is an undesirable pattern that becomes embedded into the display or **output** of a picture. It looks something like a wavy water stain on satin. Usually, it is caused by creating **halftone screens** inaccurately (so that the output device or printing press can't define the printing **dots** properly), by scanning in a picture that was printed using halftone screen, or by using a dirty scanner. (Try cleaning the **scanner's platen** of oils, fingerprints, etc., if you get moirés.)

Incidentally, sometimes, an **image** displayed on your computer monitor may exhibit phantom moirés, which disappear when you view the image at a different magnification. That kind probably won't print.

Monitor is the TV-like screen or **CRT** that you look at to see what is happening in your computer. When you type on the keyboard, draw with your mouse or give the computer any other command, you see the results on the monitor. The monitor is just a window into your **data**, and not the actual data. This is a relevant issue, because what you see on the monitor is often a representative rather than an exact display of the data.

In imaging, bigger is usually better. Monitors come in a variety of sizes and configurations. Those most suitable for **graphics** start at 19 inches and above. The other thing to remember about monitors is **dot pitch**, which is the distance between **pixels** or points of color. This is measured in millimeters, such as .31 and .25 mm. The smaller the number, the finer the display.

Monitor gamma   SEE **Gamma**.

Monochrome refers to a two-tone picture that is made up of white and one other color. The most common monochrome is a black and white grayscale. But monochromes can be based on any other color, such as red, green, or orange, in combination with white.

Monotype is text that is made up of letters in which every character is given exactly the same amount of space on the page, regardless of the character's relative size. For instance, a small *i* is given as much space as a capital Z. This is in opposition to **proportional type**. When page designers want to make a layout look like it was produced on an old-fashioned typewriter, they would use monotype.

Morph is the process of gradually changing one **object**, picture or area of an **image** into something entirely different. For instance, a portrait of a man could be morphed into a portrait of a woman. Halfway through the morph, the face would be a combination of the two—so that it could be said to look like a relative of both the man and woman.

Morphing programs are usually **animation** programs, which show the process in action. But it is possible to get still images from morphing software, by choosing a **frame** out of the animation. How close that frame is to the beginning or end of the morph determines how much of the initial or final picture it contains.

Morph: The center picture is a morph between the photo of the child on the left and the one of the man on the right—exhibiting elements of each. In an animated morph, you would see a more gradual staging of changes from one picture (the child, in this example) to the next (the man). And, you would be able to freeze at any intermediate frame.

Motherboard is the primary board on which the computer is built. It contains the **CPU** and a variety of specialized chips, circuits and transistors to connect all the **components** or **peripherals** together. Every computer has a motherboard, even if it has no other components or accessories. In fact, many would argue that the motherboard is the computer. **Graphics cards, SCSI** boards and other peripheral boards are plugged into specific slots on the motherboard, as are **RAM** and **DRAM**. The **ports** for your **keyboard** and **mouse** are there, too. Other peripherals that may connect through your motherboard may include **printers, networks** and **speakers**. One popular method of upgrading a computer system is to replace the motherboard and CPU with a more advanced, faster version.

Motion blur is a **special effects filter** that makes an image or an area of an image look as

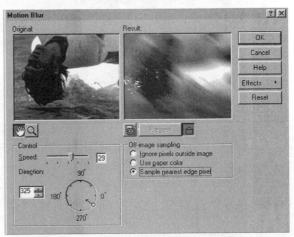

Motion blur: In this Corel PhotoPAINT Motion blur dialog, you can see the before and after results of applying a directional blur to a picture. By controlling the direction (angle) and the amount (speed) of the blur, you can create an effect very similar to photographing action that is going too fast for your camera and film. (Tip: Try pasting the original, unblurred image on top of the blurred one, at a transparency somewhat less than fully opaque, for a more recognizable photo.)

if it were moving. This is done by creating a direction blur, which is usually linear.

Mouse is the primary and most common **pointing device** used with computers. Shaped to fit neatly into the palm of the hand, it controls the **cursor** on the **monitor**.

A Mac mouse has only one button, but a PC mouse has two or more buttons. Usually, the PC's **left mouse button** corresponds to the Mac button, and the PC's **right button** or middle button is used to activate other options (as defined by the software or by the user).

A **single-click** of the mouse button is generally used to choose or anchor something on the monitor. A **double-click** usually opens up **dialog boxes, programs** and other options associated with **icons**, commands and tools.

Move to front, move to back, move forward, move backward are commands that arrange the order of **layers** and **objects** in an **image**.

For instance, suppose a picture is made up of a bottom-layer picture of a bottle of wine. The next layer (on top of the first layer) has a picture of a table. And the third layer (the uppermost) has a picture of a plate. When the top layer is active, the command move to back would put it under the table layer. But if, instead, the command move backward or move back one were used, the plate layer would end up between the table and the bottle layers.

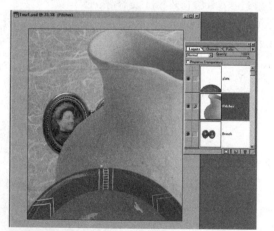

MOVE TO FRONT, MOVE TO BACK A

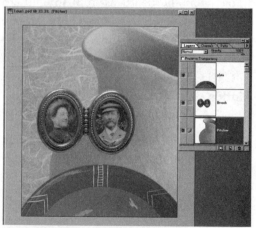

MOVE TO FRONT, MOVE TO BACK B

Move to front, move to back . . . : In **A**, the brooch is behind the pitcher. You can select the pitcher in the layers palette and use the Move Backward command, or select the brooch and use the Move Forward command. Either way, the result will be picture **B**, with the brooch on top of the pitcher.

The placement and order of layers and objects are integral to proper composition (a plate on a table is much more logical than a plate under a table).

MPEG (which stands for *Moving Pictures Experts Group*) is a **multimedia file format** used to store and play back full-motion video in **24-bit color**. MPEG-2 is a more advanced version for displaying larger frames of full-motion in 24-bit color.

MRP-2 compliant is a Swedish standard for a safe level of radiation emissions from a computer monitor. Monitors said to be MRP-2 compliant are believed to be safe and are not supposed to cause cataracts, miscarriages or other ill effects thought to be associated with frequent and constant computer use.

Multichannel image is one that, literally, has more than one **channel**. An **RGB** picture has at least three channels (red, green and blue), but it may also have other channels—to save **masks** and other information.

Multimedia has become the catch-all phrase that refers to anything created, displayed or saved on a computer, which contains music, speech, and other sounds; **animation**; video; and/or pictures. It's an update of *son et lumiere*, digitized.

Multiply is a **blend mode** or **channel operation** that mathematically multiplies the color values of a **layer**'s or **brush** color's **pixel** with the pixel value of the underlying layer or image, then divides by 255. The result of that multiplication is the value of the **composited** pixel, which is always darker than the two original pixels.

Multisession drive is a **CD-ROM format** that allows more than one **data** session to be written on to the disc. Before multisession, CD-ROMs could be written to only once (they were actually **WORM** drives—Write Once/Read Many). It was not possible to add or append data into the empty spaces on the disc after the initial burning. Multisession allows the directories that keep track of all the data to be added to, which is the reason it is an important component of **Kodak's Photo CD** format. Adaptec is the company that provides software for the PC (CD-Creator) and Mac (Toast) that creates multisession data on **CD-R** drives.

Multisync is the brand name of NEC's line of color monitors.

It's also a term that describes any color monitor capable of automatically detecting and adjusting for the correct frequency of the **video graphics boards** in the computer. But with the advent of more or less standardized **XVGA** graphics boards for the PC, multisync has become somewhat irrelevant.

Multitasking is a computer's ability to perform what appears to be more than one task simultaneously. For instance, an **image** can be **rasterizing** out to the printer in the background, while you are **color balancing** another. Very few **desktop** computers and **operating systems** can presently do true multitasking. Instead, they split the **CPU**'s time between tasks.

Nanosecond (ns) is one-billionth of a second. That sounds infinitesimally short, but to paraphrase the late Senator Dirkson, a nanosecond here, a nanosecond there, and pretty soon we're talking about real time. Actually, computer functions are often measured in nanoseconds, and because many millions of functions may be executed within a single second, the issue of speed becomes quite relevant. In fact, the speed of light is one of the limiting factors in how quickly **data** will move through your computer. A bit of information that must move 12 inches along a copper wire may take several nanoseconds longer than the same data moving just 3 inches along a copper wire. That's why you should find out how fast some **components** of your computer, such as **memory**, are in nanoseconds. Of course, the lower the number, the faster the component.   SEE **Data path.**

Native is the adjective applied to file formats that can be opened and saved by a program. If a format isn't native, and you want to edit it in that program, try **importing** it.   SEE **Proprietary format**.

Natural media emulation uses digital imaging tools to make pictures look as though they were drawn

NATURAL MEDIA EMULATION A

NATURAL MEDIA EMULATION B

Natural media emulation: Using Fractal Design Painter (or various tools in other programs), an artist can create original paintings (or convert photographs) that look as though they were drawn using oils, watercolors, charcoal or many other real world media from the traditional (nondigital) arts.

or painted using traditional real world media, such as oil paints, watercolor and charcoal. The **canvas**, or the **background**, may also be made to act like different kinds of paper, causing the paint to bleed in certain ways, or to react to a texture, etc.

A pioneer program in natural media emulation is **Fractal Design Painter**, but now many image editing programs have some brushes, filters or other tools that emulate the traditional arts.

Negative is a command or filter that reverses the shadows and highlights, as well as colors, to their complements. The result looks like a film negative.

Near-photoquality means that an **output** device is capable of printing pictures that appear to be **continuous tone**. In other words, if you don't look too closely, they resemble photographs. But if you use a magnifying glass or loupe to look at the details of what makes up the pictures, you'll be able to discern the dots of ink. True **photoquality** printers (such as **dye sublimation** printers) blend the inks together, so that no dots are seen.

NEGATIVE A

NEGATIVE B

Negative: Picture **B** is the negative (or inverse) of **A**—with all of the colors reversed to their opposite. It is a term and technique taken directly from photography. *(A Corel stock photo.)*

Near-photorealistic is another way of saying that a picture is **near-photoquality**. In other words, if you don't look too closely, it could almost be mistaken for a traditional, **continuous tone** photograph. Many color **inkjet** printers output near-photorealistic images.

Nerd   SEE **Geek**.

Nested   SEE **Nested icons**.

Nested icons are those icons that are grouped together, sometimes under one master icon. If you see an icon with what looks like a torn or cut corner (usually in a **toolbox**), click on that corner, and other icons may scroll out.

Network is a series of linked computers. It allows each computer to access other computers' **data**, programs, storage devices (such as **hard drives**) and **peripherals** (such as printers); to send and receive **e-mail**; and to access and share other resources. It also allows two or more users to simultaneously work on a single file.

In **imaging**, networked computers are useful for offloading renderings, **queueing** print jobs or, in some hardware configurations, borrowing the network's combined processing power to speed up operations.   SEE **Render**.

There are various kinds of networks and network connections. The one most frequently used in smaller companies (under 1,000 units) is called a **LAN**, or *local area network*. The type used by large companies is called a WAN, or *wide area network*.

Networks require a certain kind of connection, hardware and software. The two most common kinds of connections are **Ethernet** and **token ring**. It doesn't matter which kind is used, as long as all the computers on the network have the same kind of **interface** and operate at the same speed.

Many networks use a computer dedicated to running the network (like an electronic traffic cop), which is called a *server*. Other networks are peer-to-peer, which means that all the computers are equal and no server exists.

Network card is a **peripheral board** that plugs into the computer to allow it to communicate with other computers via a **network**.

New is the command that creates a new **image window** or **document**. The new image or document is usually blank, with no information in it, or it may contain a **background** color, depending on how the program's **preferences** are set up or what options are checked in the New **dialog box**.

NewsCamera 2000 is the Associated Press's (AP) version of the **Kodak** DCS-200 and DCS-420 **filmless cameras**. It has a larger amount of **RAM** than the Kodak cameras to boost the **burst mode**, which is the ability to shoot a number of frames one right after the other (as with a traditional motor drive). And the **resolution** is slightly reduced (with larger **pixels**), which increased the **ISO** equivalency—up to 1,600—to enable lowlight photography. The AP markets a number of specialized **peripherals** for the camera, for quick image processing and communicating from anywhere in the world.

NeXT is an early workstation designed and promoted by Steve Jobs, one of the coinventors of Apple. When it failed to penetrate the market, the company jettisoned the hardware and developed an **operating system**/operating **environment** that is now the basis of Apple's new high end operating system for **Power Macs** and **PCs**, called **Rhapsody**.

Nickel cadmium, or NiCad, are rechargeable batteries used in many **filmless cameras, laptop** computers and many other portable **peripherals**.

Nickel hydride, or NclH, are also rechargeable batteries that offer some advantages over nickel cadmium batteries and can be used interchangeably. However, they are generally more expensive.

Node is a defining or **endpoint** (or anchor point) on a **spline** or **Bezier** curve. At the node, the angle, shape and direction of the curve are established by pulling on **handles** that the user can access by clicking and dragging on the node point.

Another definition of node refers to any device (including a computer) attached to a **network**.

Noise is artifacts or misplaced **pixels** in an **image** often produced by electric interference. It can look like a dusting of fine dirt or light particles that are splashed across the picture, either uniformly or erratically.

Noise is traditionally considered undesirable, but there are **filters** that will add noise to images for various purposes: for **special effects**, to try to make a picture look older, or to make a **pasted** in **image element** or area fit in with other elements in a **composite**.

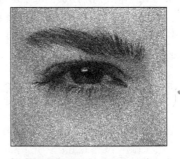

Noise: When used correctly, noise can create an interesting effect—similar to an old photo. But more often than not, it is a distracting bit of dirt.

Noninterlace   SEE **Interlace**.

Nonvolatile memory   SEE **Volatile memory**.

Normal mode is the default setting for commands, **special effects**, text, etc. For instance, while applying color with an **image paintbrush**, the normal setting would have that color replace everything it covers. Similarly, the normal mode for text is a **font** that is not bold, italics or underlined, or does not have any special attribute. Normal mode is usually the default mode of any tool, **window, program**, etc.

Norton Utilities are a collection of extremely useful and essential **subprograms** that enhance smooth operation and help in the maintenance of a **PC** or **Mac**'s **hard drive**. They also include tools for restoring or recovering from computer glitches, **crashes**, accidental **erasures**, etc. So good are the Norton Utilities that some of them have been built into **Windows 95 and 98**, but we very strongly recommend that every computer have the full version installed.

Novell is a Utah-based company that manufactures **network operating system** software.

NTSC (National Television Standards Committee) is the U.S. television broadcast signal specification. Technically, it is a composite signal of 525 lines of red, green and blue, transmitted at 60 half-frames per second, which includes an audio signal for sound and stereo.

NTSC signals can be intercepted or created by **graphics** programs to capture or create **images** and sounds used in and by **multimedia applications**. Therefore, if you have the right hardware and connectors, you can capture pictures and sound right off a video displayed on a TV, and/or create images and sound that can be broadcast over network cable or satellite TV. Also, many digital cameras have the ability to output images in NTSC form, for display on a television set or to save to a VCR.

NTSC colors are those colors that can be reproduced by a typical television set. It is a more limited number of colors than the number in a **24-bit color** image. Therefore, **graphics** programs that have NTSC color models or filters **map** the 16.7 million colors of the 24-bit file down to what can be displayed by the TV.   SEE **NTSC**.

NuBus is Apple's **expansion** slot and standard for adding **peripherals** to many of its older Macintosh computers. It has been largely superseded by **PCI** bus peripherals.

Nudge is a command that pushes an **object** or a **selected** area of an image just a little bit. It is often achieved by using the keyboard arrow keys to nudge the item in the direction of the arrow. The amount that a single nudge will push the object or area may or may not be set by the user in the program's **preferences** or elsewhere in the **interface**, depending on the program.

Numeric keypad is the rectangle of numbers from zero to nine usually placed at the right side of the computer keyboard. It is activated by pressing the numeric lock key and using the numbers as you would on a calculator.

Some **graphics** programs and **filters** will make use of the numeric keypad. For instance, in some of the **Kai's Power Tools** filters, pressing one of the corner numbers will concentrate the **special effect** into the corresponding corner of the image.

In other situations, the numbers in the keypad are redundant and may be entered, instead, using the numbered keys on the top of the keyboard. However, other keys clustered around the numeric keypad (such as the plus and minus keys) may be specifically required by certain programs.

Object is a shape, line or form that is defined mathematically and created in **vector** programs, such as **illustration, animation** or **3-D** software. Each object can be selected and edited independently of anything else in the picture, unless it has been **combined** with other objects.

An object is different from a **pixel**-based shape, in that the object is an entity that consists of its outline, fill and position. The pixel-based (**raster**) shape is made of many **bits** of information, each of which must be independently **mapped**. For instance, a vector circle is defined by its center point (for positioning), its size (πr^2), its color and its outline. But a pixel circle is made up of thousands or millions of points, each of which contains information about position, color and light. Therefore, vector-defined objects take up considerably less **memory** and **hard drive** space than equivalent pixel-defined shapes.

Object linking and embedding SEE **OLE**.

Object-oriented refers to software that works with **objects** or shapes that are mathematically defined as opposed to **bitmapped** or **raster**. All **illustration** software is object-oriented, as is **3-D modeling** and **animation**. Some **image editing** programs, though they are essentially **pixel**-based, may or may not have some objected-oriented features.

Oblique is a typographical term that describes type that is angled or slanted backward. It is the opposite of **italics**.

Oblique: Oblique text is angled backward—the opposite of italics.

OCR, or **Optical Character Recognition,** is the ability of a **scanner,** working with special software, to read text and numbers, and to input them into the computer as editable **documents**. Without OCR software, the scanner would read the text and numbers as **images** only, which would be nonsense and uneditable as far as any **word processor, database** or other document editing software might be concerned.

OEM stands for *Original Equipment Manufacturer* and refers to the fact that companies sell hardware or software that is repackaged under other companies' names. The companies that resell these OEM products are called *integrators*. OEMing is quite common with **scanners, digital cameras, printers** and other **peripherals**. The resellers may or may not add their own enhancements or **drivers**, and their selling prices may be higher or lower than the manufacturer's brand-name product.

Offload is the process of shunting **data** or processing to another device, such as a **server** or ripper. The purpose of offloading is to free up computer **resources** by assigning a resource-intensive task elsewhere. For instance, if you are working on a **3-D scene**, after you have completed the design work, you might offload the **rendering** task to another computer. That way, your computer won't be tied up for minutes or, even, hours, crunching the mathematics behind rendering.   SEE **RIP**.

Offset is the printing process that works on the principle that oil and water don't mix. Where dots are on the printing plates, ink will adhere. Where there are no dots, water will spread. When transferred to paper, only the ink will lay on the paper, not the noninked area. Because of its economy, versatility and ease of use, the vast majority of printing presses are offset presses. Where digital imaging and offset printing intersect is in preparing the **camera-ready copy** used to make the actual printing plates.

OLE and **OLE2** stand for **Object Linking and Embedding**, which is the ability of **Windows** programs to use each other's **data** and pictures. For instance, an **image** created in **Picture Publisher** or **Photoshop** can be placed into a **DTP document** in **Ventura** or **PageMaker**. The picture remains fully editable in its original **image editing program**, and the edits can be automatically updated in the document. What's more, if you are in the **desktop publishing program, double-clicking** on the image will automatically open up the original **image editing program** where the picture originated and where it really resides.

OLE 2 is more sophisticated and faster, and it will link more kinds of files than OLE.

One-point perspective stretches to a single point in the far horizon, where all vertical lines meet. There are also two-point perspectives and other kinds of perspective.

On-line help, which is also called on-screen **help**, is information provided by **software** or **hardware** about how to use that product. It is quickly replacing printed **documentation**, though on-line help never has the impact, usefulness or accessibility of good printed instruction manuals. On the other hand, on-line help is immediately available on the screen, when you need it, by just clicking on a button (which often has a question mark icon) or choosing a help command in a **pulldown** menu.

Opacity is a quality of an **object, layer**, color, etc., that does not allow any light or underlying color or shape to come through it. In many programs, the level of opacity may be varied, and it is often measured in a continuum or range between full opacity and full **transparency**.

In **masking**, the **alpha channel** controls the level of opacity or transparency of the **masked** area of an **image**. Where the alpha channel is white, the area is fully opaque; where the alpha channel is black, the area is transparent (or invisible); and the levels of grays in between those two extremes relate to levels of translucency. So, when a user edits an image that has such a variable translucent/opaque/transparent mask, where the mask is white, the edit changes the pixels; where it is black, the pixels remain unchanged; and where it is gray, they are partially changed, in proportion to the darkness or lightness of the gray.

Opacity: The leaf on the left is fully (100%) opaque. The one in the middle is set at about 60% opacity (you can see the background lines through it). And the leaf on the far right is about 20% opaque (or 80% transparent).

Open is a software command that gets a file (**image, document, scene, database**, etc.) from a **storage device** (such as an attached **hard drive, Photo CD,** and **SyQuest**) and displays it on the computer monitor. Once a file is open in a **compatible** program (that is, in a program that can work with that kind of file), it can be edited, added to, manipulated, saved, **output**, etc.

Open architecture is freely published hardware or software specifications that allow **third-party** companies to develop and sell **add-ons, plug-ins, peripherals** and devices that will work seamlessly and flawlessly with the original hardware or software.

For instance, Adobe has published the plug-in architecture for **Photoshop**, which has spawned an entire industry of **special effects filters**, hardware **drivers**, etc., that work from within Photoshop. In addition, competitors to Photoshop, such as **Corel PhotoPAINT, Picture Publisher**, and other **image editing programs** are also able to use Photoshop's plug-in architecture, which means they can use all the same filters and drivers.

The opposite of open architecture is, obviously, closed or **proprietary** architecture, which describes products that a company treats like trade secrets. This limits the number of additions, enhancements and improvements that can be used with the products, which, in turn, can limit their marketability.

Open path is a **spline** or **Bezier** curve that has **end nodes**. In other words, it doesn't loop or close in on itself, as an ellipse or other **closed path** would.

Operating system is, if you will excuse the expression, "GOD" to your computer. It is the software that literally controls and keeps track of everything: your system configuration, hardware that is attached, the **applications** that are installed, and all the files that you have created.

The most common operating systems are **System 8** for the Mac, and **Windows 95, 98** or **NT** for the PC. **DOS** is the name of the PC's system that was used for many years but has largely become irrelevant and obsolete, except as the underlying foundation for Windows.

Most operating systems are **GUIs**, or use **Graphical User Interfaces**, which allow the user to interact with the operating system via a **mouse** or other pointing device. What's more, the components of the operating system may be represented graphically by **icons**, or pictographic representations, rather than just words or abbreviations.

Operating systems can be very touchy and may require updating, fine-tuning, purging, tweaking, etc., to be kept in perfect condition. They may be corrupted, in which case you may have to re-install everything onto your computer or use tools like **Norton Utilities** to get the operating system up and running again.

Optical character recognition   SEE **OCR**.

Optical disc is any device in which the **data** are written or read by a laser beam. **WORM drives, CDs, CD-ROMs** and **DVD**s are types of optical discs. They are characterized by high **density** (the ability to record lots of data) and extreme stability (the data can last as long as 100 years, without the **media** degrading).

Optical drive is a device that attaches to a computer and can read or write **data** to an **optical disc**. The data are read and written to the **disc** by a laser beam. Optical discs are remarkably stable and, depending on the specific technology, may retain data for over a century without any degradation. **Magneto-optical discs, CD-ROMs** and **DVD**s are all types of optical discs. The reason optical drives have never and will never replace **hard drives** is speed. It's inherent in the technology that they operate at significantly slower speeds than hard drives.

Optimize   SEE **Defragment**.

Option key (OPT) is often used as a **hot key** in conjunction with other keys on the Mac keyboard, or as a modifier or **constraining** key with a program's commands or tools.

For instance, when using the **zoom tool** in **Photoshop**, if you press the option key, it turns the zoom in tool to a zoom out.

In those programs that are **cross-platform** (run on both Mac and PC), the option key and the PC's **alternate** (ALT) key are often used in similar ways.

Options are alternative ways that a tool or command can be used. For instance, a **paintbrush** might have different sizes, as well as changeable levels of **opacity**. Options may be selected or changed by the user through **dialog boxes, menus, palettes, hot keys** and in other ways.

Order relates to the arrangement of **layers** and/or **objects**, and their relation to each other. For instance, suppose there is a picture with three elements: a background, a face and a hat. The order of those three elements is very important. Otherwise, the face could be behind the background and invisible. The commands **move to front, move to back, move forward** or

move backward and their related **icons** are useful for maintaining and correcting order.

Orientation refers to the actual shape of an entire picture. If it is wider than it is tall, then it is said to have a **landscape** orientation or mode. If it is taller than it is wide, then it has a **portrait** orientation or mode.

Orientation refers also to the rotation of a picture or portion of a picture, and the angle to which it is turned.

Orphan is a typographical term that has moved over to **desktop publishing** and other computerized **layout** software and processes. An orphan occurs when the first line of a paragraph is on the last line on a page or in a column, with the rest of the paragraph falling on the next page or the next column. Orphans are often discussed in the same breath as **widows**. A **widow** is the last line or last word of a paragraph which falls all by itself on the next page or column, while the rest of the paragraph is on the previous page or column. Professionals consider both orphans and widows to be unattractive and undesirable. Some software programs have a fit-to-page command that automatically eliminates orphans and widows.

Orthogonal extrusion extends the back of an **object** or text, so that the sides are parallel to each other, and the back is equal in size to the front. Another common kind of extrusion is **perspective**, in which the back is smaller than the front, and the sides converge toward a point in the far horizon.

Orthographic perspective or **view** shows a three-dimensional object or scene as flat and undistorted—as it is, literally, without any change being introduced because of the distance or angle from which it is viewed.

OS SEE **Operating system**.

OS/2 is IBM's **32-bit operating system** used on PCs. It never really caught on because of competition from Microsoft's **Windows 95, 98** and **Windows NT**. The biggest problem was that it didn't fully support **24-bit graphics peripherals**, and not many **graphics boards** manufacturers wrote **drivers** for OS/2. However, it is still installed onto millions of current computers.

Outline is a command in **image editing** programs that draws a line or lines around the perimeter of a **selection** or area of an **image**.

In **vector** programs, such as **illustration** software, the outline is the outer edge of an **object**—the border that mathematically defines the shape of the object. Color, width and other attributes may be applied to the outline, just as the object may be **filled**.

Outline font is one in which the shapes of the individual letters are defined mathematically. When the user needs that font at a specific size, it is built, based on that outline. **PostScript** fonts are outline fonts.

Out-of-gamut refers to colors that are unreproducible by the **output** device according to criteria set by the user or the system. Many imaging programs will provide some kind of visual out-of-gamut alarm to alert the user to the situation, so that other colors may be chosen.   SEE **Gamut**.

Output is the process of taking a file (an **image, document** or whatever) from the computer and sending it elsewhere (such as to a **printer** or **film** recorder), where it can be put into a form for final display. That final display may be **hard copy** (printed on paper), screen-based **presentations, Web pages**, or other venues.

Output device is a **peripheral** that takes an **image, document, spread-sheet** or some other file from the computer and puts it into the form that is appropriate for final display. Therefore, an output device could be a **printer**, a **film recorder**, etc.

Overhead is a transparent sheet of acetate or plastic that may be fed into a **desktop** printer to create sheets that may be projected onto large screens via an overhead projector. They are most useful in business presentations.

Overhead is also the amount of resources (**RAM, hard disk** space, etc.) that a computer has available or needs for a particular **application**. A large program, like **Corel's graphics suite**, is said to require a lot of overhead.

Overlapping objects are those that have parts that cover each other. This overlap can be used to **combine** the objects into a single object and/or a new shape.

Overlay is a **blend mode** or **channel operations** option in which the shadows and highlights of the underlying **image** or **layer** remain unchanged. But the other underlying colors are changed by the new

Overlapping objects: These two objects overlap each other. It's a simple concept, but one that is useful to control accurately when combining objects.

color or layer according to their respective **hue** and **luminance** values (with light colors getting lighter and dark ones becoming darker). Those changes are governed by a **multiply** or a **screen** blend.

Then, there is the very simple definition for overlay, which involves putting one layer or **object** on top of another. The fact that the upper layer or object can be made translucent or transparent can create some interesting overlaying effects.

Overlay proof is one that is generated by putting color separated films on top of each other and then printing.   SEE **Color separation**.

Overprint is printing onto a page that has already been printed. It is used for **trapping** and for combining the colors of unscreened **color separated** files. Usually, darker colors (and black) are printed over lighter colors, in the attempt to avoid **registration** difficulties.

Padlock symbol is an **icon** that indicates something is **locked**, so that it can't be edited, moved or otherwise changed. This is useful when an **image element** is in just the right position, size, orientation, etc., and you don't want to affect it when you manipulate other elements that overlap it in some manner. Such locked **objects, layers, grids** or other elements can usually be **unlocked**—sometimes by clicking on the padlock symbol, though another tool or command may be needed.

Page is a single sheet of printed paper. But it is also the representation of that single sheet on the computer monitor. Pictures and **documents** are usually composed onto pages in **layout** and **illustration** programs. On the other hand, **image editing** programs use the established or edited **image size** as the display **canvas** for pictures. The canvas may or may not relate to the final printed page size, though it usually is the size of the picture that will be printed onto the final page.

Page is also a unit of information on the **Internet**. Corporations, publishers, TV shows, individuals, libraries and other entities maintain home pages where the user can obtain information (including software **upgrades**), enter into electronic dialogs with others who have similar interests, place orders for goods, play games, and generally explore all the possibilities that the world has to offer. Even the White House has a home page that anyone can access.

Page composition is a typesetter's phrase for the act of laying out type, **images** and other **graphics** onto a **page** that will be printed. SEE **Layout**.

Page description language (PDL) is the software code used by **desktop printers** to describe and map out where every **dot** should be placed on the paper, when they are outputting any **document, image** or whatever. **Adobe's PostScript** and Hewlett-Packard's **PCL** are types of page description language.

Page frame is the outline of the **page** as it is displayed on the computer **monitor**. It may or may not be a printable outline with editable color and line width, depending on the software.

Page layout is the process of placing text, pictures and other design elements onto a **page**, so that the result is attractive and effective. **Desktop publishing** programs are layout programs, but **illustration, word processing** and, even, **image editing** programs can also be used to design layouts.

PageMaker is **Adobe's desktop publishing program**.

Page proof   SEE **Proof**.

Page scrolling is the process of moving up or down, left or right, within a **page** or **image window**, of which only a portion is displayed on the monitor. Scrolling can be done in any of several ways. (1) When a window or page doesn't display the entire **document** or image, **scroll bars** are automatically placed

Page layout: Think of page layout as the digital equivalent of a pasteboard, where graphics artists traditionally would paste up elements onto a page in preparation for publishing that page.

Page scrolling: Notice the scroll bars on the right and bottom of this picture. That indicates that you are viewing only a portion of the image. Either click on the arrowheads or click and drag on the box between the arrowheads to move your view to other areas in the picture. Many programs also have a scrolling tool (whose icon is often a hand) with which you may push the picture about within the window.

on the side and bottom of the window. Use your **mouse** or other **pointing device** to either click on the arrows to the right, left, up or down, or to pull the **scroll boxes** in the direction you want the display to move. (2) Use the scroll tool, whose **icon** is usually shown as a hand, to pull and push the document or image about within the window. (3) Use various commands within the program, such as page up or down.

Page setup box is the **dialog** in which the user defines the size, **orientation, margins** and other attributes of the current or new **page**. The page setup can be accessed either by using the **new** command (to create a new page) or by choosing the page setup command, which is often found in the **file** or **layout pulldown menu**.

Page size is the measurement of the width and the length of a **page**. The user can define the page size in the **page setup box**.

Page setup box: As you can see in this Corel PhotoPAINT dialog, the page setup box gives you control over the properties of a page or canvas on which your picture or other image elements will be laid out or placed.

Pages per minute   SEE **PPM**.

Pagination is the command for numbering pages, so that the numbers appear on the printed page. The word is seldom used any more, with most **desktop publishing, word processing** and **illustration programs** simply calling it *page numbering*.

Pagination is sometimes also used to describe the process of **laying out** multiple-page **documents**, such as newsletters and brochures. It's in opposition to laying out single-page documents, such as posters and ads.

Paint is the same thing in the **digital** world as it is in the real world—plus more. When you paint, you lay down color using a variety of tools, including a **paintbrush**. However, in **digital imaging**, you can paint not only with color, but also with **textures, images, transparencies** and patterns. Digital painting is, generally, a function of **bitmapped** imaging, in that you are changing the characteristics of individual **pixels**. Therefore, the verb *paint* is often used to describe other processes in **image editing programs**.   SEE **Paint programs**.

Paint programs, traditionally, were any software that worked with **raster** or **bitmapped images**, i.e., **image editing software** (in opposition to **draw** or **illustration** programs that work with **vectors**). However, the definition now tends to be more narrow, including only those programs that offer **natural media** and/or **fine art emulation**. In other words, paint programs provide the tools for painting **brush** strokes onto photographs and other images, or for creating new paintings. But the circle is turning back again; many image editing programs now offer paint tools and features, so the terms may merge once more.

Paintbox SEE **Quantel Paintbox**.

Paintbrush tool is used in **image editing** and **paint** programs to apply color to an **image** (just as a real world paintbrush is used on canvas or a wall). Usually, the paintbrush has numerous options, including brush size, **bleed, opacity/ transparency** levels, and **blend modes** (**color only, darken, lighten, screen, overlay**, etc.) A **pressure-sensitive** paintbrush will also react to how the user handles a **stylus** and how much pressure he or she applies to it.

Paint bucket is a **fill** tool in both **vector-** and **pixel**-based programs.

In vector programs (**illustration, draw, animation, 3-D**, etc.) it fills **objects** and **backgrounds** with color, texture, **gradients**, etc.

In pixel programs (**image editing** or **paint**), it replaces the current color with the new color, texture or whatever. But the way it chooses where the replacement will take effect is what makes it different from the vector paint bucket. Like the **color wand** or **magic wand** tool, the paint bucket analyzes the color value of the **pixel** on which it is clicked. Then, it acts on all the pixels that are adjacent and similar in color to the clicked-on pixel. The **tolerance** level of the paint bucket tool determines just how close in color the adjacent pixels must be to the clicked-on pixel, to be changed. A higher tolerance includes a wider range of colors. A lower tolerance limits the range more.

Painter is a **paint** program developed by **Fractal Design**, which specializes in **natural media** and **fine art emulation**. It not only has fully customizable brushes that can imitate real world paints, but it can also set up the image **canvas** with textures to which the brushes may be set to react.

PAL (*Phase Alternating Line*) is a European broadcast signal that sends out 625 lines per frame, which is higher than the USA's **NTSC** signal of 525 lines. Unfortunately, with various countries and continents using different broadcast standards, signals captured from one will not be compatible with the other.

Palette is a type of **dialog box** in which the user can make creative options about the current tool or keep track of specific types of information. For

Palette: These Photoshop dialogs are examples of palettes, specifically ones that control the shape, size, color and other attributes of a paintbrush. When you see tabs at the top of the palettes, as these shown here, it means that you can nest them—i.e., click and drag them to fit into each other. When you see more than one tab in a palette, click on each to see additional pages of palettes. It's like a tabbed notebook of the type we all used in school.

instance, a **layers palette** lists all of the layers in a picture, as well as provides tools and commands for editing, manipulating, creating and deleting layers. On the other hand, a brush palette may give the user controls for changing the shape, style, **transparency** and other options related to a paintbrush tool.

Pan is the act of moving from one view of a subject or image to another view. For instance, in the movies, the cinematographer may pan from the far, right horizon to the near left foreground, in one continuous sweep. **Animation** and **video** programs often have a pan command, though it isn't always called that.

Pantone colors are brand-name **spot** and **process** inks, as well as color-matching **swatch books** and software **color palettes**. Pantone colors are industry standard and, therefore, are included in many graphics programs.

Paper color is a setting that defines the **background** color of a **page** or **image**. In other words, it defines the color of the empty picture, before any painting, drawing, pasting or whatever is done.

Paper size is an option in **page setup** and/or **print dialogs** where the user defines the size of the **page** or the paper on which the picture or **document** will be printed or laid out.

Paradigm is a word that has become so popular in computer jargon, that it has almost lost any real value or meaning. (It's something like the loss of meaning in the word *awesome*, now that it can be applied to anything and everything.) However, the original meaning of paradigm is an example or model through which one can philosophically and pragmatically attempt to under-

P

stand how the future will be shaped. Therefore, ads for hardware or software, or articles and seminars, may wax poetically about how the paradigm of "faster, cheaper, better" **CCD**s will eventually mean that everyone will carry a combination **scanner/fax**/cellular teleconference phone in their back pocket, in the near future.

Parallel   SEE **Parallel interface**.

Parallel interface (or parallel **port**) is the most common port used for single (as opposed to network) printers on the **PC**. Most PCs come equipped with only one parallel port, though it is possible to have up to four parallel interfaces. Most PCs now have a high speed, bi-directional EPP parallel port which speeds up data transfer and can work with intelligent printers, feeding information back to the computer, such as on printer status and paper tray. **Macs** do not have parallel ports. Parallel printers will gradually be replaced by the new generation of **USB** printers.

Parameter is a setting that defines how a tool, command, **filter**, program, **hardware** or whatever will be set up and used. Referred to usually in the plural—parameters—these settings cover all the possible options that could be adjusted and how the user has set them. For instance, the printing parameters for the **output** of a specific **image** would include **paper size**, number of copies, whether it is in color or black & white, etc.—or the options that are set in the **page setup** and **printer dialogs**.

Partial edit is a method of opening only a portion of an **image** to edit and/or manipulate it. Then, it is saved back into the entire picture, seamlessly, right in the spot where it was originally. Partial edit is used when the **raster**-based image is large, and its purpose is to save time and computing **resources**. Opening up the entire picture and working on it would take much longer and require more **memory** and other resources.

Partition is the command or process that separates **hard drives** and other storage devices into virtual drives. Storage devices can be very large and unmanageable, and it may be difficult to locate files in them. To make them work better and faster, the **operating system** allows the user to break them up into smaller segments (virtual drives), as if each one were a separate hard drive. Therefore, a single 10-**gigabyte** hard drive could be made to appear to be ten 1-**Gb** drives or twenty 500-**Mb** drives, etc.

Now that operating systems are more efficient, partitioning is not as necessary for speed, but it is still done to separate **programs** from **data**, or types of data from other files as well as save space.

Password is a personal word, phrase or nonsense jumble of letters and/or numbers that you define and tell to the computer, to a specific program in the computer, a **network, e-mail** service, etc. Then, when the computer is powered on, the program is launched, the e-mailbox opened, etc., it asks for the password you have defined. If the password isn't typed in (and with the correct spelling and required upper- or lowercase letters), then you (or the unauthorized person trying to get into your system) won't be able to get in. Of course, there are as many ways of getting through password protections as there are protection schemes. But it will keep honest people and/or nonhackers out.

Paste is the command that places whatever is on the **clipboard** into the current **image, document, page**, etc. It gets into the clipboard (a holding area of memory) by using either the **cut** or the **copy** command on it in its original position, document, image, etc.

For instance, suppose you have a picture of a red rose in a hedge. If you cut or copy the rose out of its original garden picture, then it will be held in the clipboard. When you use the paste command, the rose would then be put into another picture—say, of a formal dinner table. Or, it could be pasted back into the same picture, creating a **duplicate** of the rose. However, most programs also have a duplicate command that is much faster, if that is all you want to do.

Paste behind puts whatever is on the **clipboard** behind the **selected object** or area. SEE **Paste**.

Paste behind and **Paste into:** When a selection (or mask) is defined (as it is in picture **A**), you can choose to place an image from the clipboard (which was put there by a copy or cut command) either Behind the selection or Into the selection. Or, if the program doesn't have one of the two options (some don't have the Paste Behind command), just invert the selection before doing a Paste Into.

PASTE BEHIND A

PASTE BEHIND B

Paste into puts whatever is on the **clipboard** inside a **selected** area. That turns the pasted item into the new selection, which may then be moved about within the area of the old selection. In essence, the old selection becomes a stencil or **mask** through which you can see the pasted in selection. SEE **Paste**.

Paste link is a **Windows OLE** command that pastes the **clipboard** item into a **linked** file and **updates** that file wherever it resides— including in other programs. SEE **Paste**.

Paste special is an option that some programs have for controlling how the **clipboard** information will be used by the **image** or **document**. Using paste special will open up a **dialog box**, in which the user can make choices regarding the paste and its result. SEE **Paste**.

Paste Into

Pasteboard is the **workspace** area outside the **image, page** or **document window**. When working in **illustration** or **layout programs**, it is possible to paste or put elements (type, pictures, shapes, etc.) onto the pasteboard, as a kind of holding area. Then, when you want to use them, you can move them over to the page or image.

Pasteboard: In layout and illustration programs, the printable area (or page) is usually displayed as a rectangle. And the pasteboard area is that space on the screen between the page and the toolboxes and palettes. Therefore, the scene that Sally quickly designed of columns on a pentagon field with a globe on a cone set in the middle of them, is all on the page. And the extra column, cone and copyright notice, which are outside the rectangular border of the page, are sitting on the pasteboard. (Notice the floating rollups or palettes that can be opened up by clicking on the down arrowhead to display different tool options.)

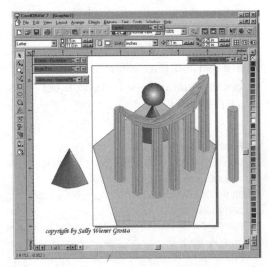

Patch is a little piece of programming or software that is added to a larger program to correct a bug or other defect. Patches are frequently issued by software manufacturers who don't want to go to the expense of sending out entire upgraded programs. This is one of the important reasons for assuring that you are a registered owner of the software, so that you can get the free and needed patches. Patches may be available **on-line**, through the manufacturer's **Web** page, as well as through the mail.   SEE **Registration**.

Path is a line or curve that forms shapes and objects, or which choreographs the movement of objects in animation. Usually, a path is defined by **nodes** and the lines that connect them. A path may be **open** or **closed**, symmetrical or irregular, straight or eccentric, etc.

A path is the basic building block for **vector**-based programs (such as **illustration, draw**, and **animation**). The curves, lines and shapes that are formed by paths define **object** outlines.

Paths are also used in those **pixel**-based **image editing programs** that have a **Bezier** or **spline** tool. In image editing programs, paths are most commonly used to trace areas of a picture, and that traced outline may or may not then be converted to a **selection marquee** or **mask**.   SEE **Bezier, Spline, Clipping path**.

Pattern is a design that is usually repeatable and repeated, such as checkers, stripes or other more complex patterns. They are often used to **fill objects** in **vector**-based (such as **illustration**) programs.

Patterns are also sometimes used in **pixel**-based (i.e., **image editing** and **paint**) programs as **alpha** channels or **masks** that, in effect, create a texture by controlling how color is applied.

PC is short for personal computer, i.e., a **desktop** computer. However, the definition has narrowed over the years to refer to those computers that use **DOS** or **Windows operating systems**. **Mac** computers are no longer considered PCs under the more narrow definition. However, with more and more Macs now able to emulate Windows **environments**, the definition of PC is beginning to change once again.

PCI (Peripheral Component **Interface**) is a 32-bit interface for both Power Macs and PCs, into which **graphics boards, SCSI** controllers, **network** boards, etc., are attached to the **motherboard. Peripherals** are then plugged into the board.

PCI is a high speed interface that is rapidly becoming a standard peripheral plug-in, replacing **NuBus** and **PDA** on the Mac, and **ISA, EISA** and **VESA** on the PC. What makes it especially appealing is the ability of PCI peripherals to work on virtually any desktop platform, when the standard is fully implemented. Unfortunately, it may be several years before that becomes a reality. So check before assuming that the PCI peripheral you are thinking of buying will truly work in your computer.

PC card, formerly called a PCMCIA card, is a tiny **memory** device the size of a credit card, that can store anywhere from 1 **megabyte** to 1 **gigabyte**, depending on the configuration. All modern PC cards are ATA-compatible, which means they can be read by any standard **IDE** PC drive.

There are three types of PC Drive: Type I, Type II and Type III. Type I and Type II are solid state devices (with no moving parts) that store **data** on low powered nonvolatile memory chips. Type III is actually a tiny **hard drive** on a card, and it requires much more electricity to operate. Type I and Type II are very fast, while Type III is relatively slow (as slow as any other hard drive). However, Type I and Type II are currently very expensive, and the highest capacity is 175 **Mb**, while Type III's range from 100 Mb to 1 **Gb**.

PC cards and adapters are popular in **digital cameras**, especially because they can be read in **laptop** computers. PC drives for reading the cards may also be added to (or come as standard) in **desktop** computers. PC cards avoid the difficulty (slow speed and inconvenience) of having to tether (or directly connect) the camera to a computer for uploading of **images**.

PCL, or *Printer Control Language,* is Hewlett-Packard's **page description language**. It translates whatever files or images you have into the dots that the printer applies to paper.

PCMCIA card   SEE **PC card**.

PDL   SEE **Page description language**.

Peer-to-peer   SEE **Network**.

Pen is usually a tool for creating **Bezier** or **Spline curves**.

Or, depending on the program, it may be a tool for painting calligraphic lines, which vary in width according to various parameters (which may or may not be set by the user).

Pencil is a **raster** tool for painting hard-edge freehand lines (similar to a real world pencil) onto photographs and other **bitmapped** images.

Pentium is Intel's latest generation of **CPU**, or *Central Processing Unit*, which is the brains behind PCs. Before the Pentium, Intel used numbers, such as **386** or **486**, to designate each generation. But since numbers could not be **copyrighted** or trademarked, and **clone** makers appropriate those numbers for their own machines, Intel switched over to a made-up word, instead of using the next number in the series—586.

The first Pentiums were only slightly faster than 486s, and their speed was measured as 60, 75 and 90 **MHz**. Later generations of Pentiums were 100, 133 and 150 MHz. The current version is named the Pentium II and is available in speeds up to 350 MHz.

Peripheral is a device that is attached to the computer to enhance the computer's functionality (increase the number of things it can do). To understand this, it is important to remember that the computer is really only the box that holds the **motherboard** with its **CPU**. A peripheral may be **external** or **internal** to the computer. Printers, keyboards, **modems, scanners, SyQuest drives, digitizing tablets**, etc., are all peripherals. SEE **Peripheral board**.

Peripheral board is a **peripheral**, or hardware add-on, that is constructed so that it is an **expansion board**, and it plugs into the computer's **motherboard's expansion slots**. A **fax/modem** board is a peripheral board.

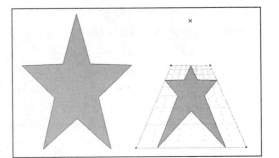

Perspective: The star on the right is a duplicate of the one on the left. However, on the right, we have applied Perspective. The perspective command places a bounding box (the dotted lines with the corner nodes) around the star. Then, we were able to move two of the corner nodes to create the illusion of the star's top disappearing to a point on the far horizon. Note also the x above the bounding box. That is the perspective's vanishing point, and you can click and drag on it, too, to manipulate the shape of the bounding box (and, therefore, the shape of the object's perspective). When you finish creating the perspective and apply it, both the bounding box and the x will disappear.

Perspective is a command or tool used by both **vector** and **bitmapped programs** to make an **object**, an **image** or a **selected** portion of an image appear as though it is stretching into the distance. With the perspective command, the user can pinch two adjacent corners of a **bounding box** rectangle (or whatever other **handles** the specific program's tool places around the object, area or image), as though they are coming together, while pulling them outward. The reshaping of the bounding box automatically reshapes the object, image or area within the box.

Phase change printers is a hybrid technology that has all the characteristics of a **wax thermal** printer (color, dot dispersion, etc.), but instead of using cellophane-like ribbons, it shoots hot wax out of nozzles like an **inkjet** printer. What makes a phase change printer useful in some professional applications, such as prepress, is its ability to print on virtually any paper, including the specific paper that will be used on the printing press. (Wax thermals usually require special paper.) This provides more accurate information about what the **output** will look like at the end of the print run. The Tektronix Phaser series are the best known of the phase change printers.

Phong shading is a method by which colors, textures and illumination are applied to **3-D objects**. Because of its mathematically intense and complex processing, it produces some of the most realistic effects. However, it also takes more time and more **resources** than other, less-detailed shading processes, such as **Gourand**.

Phong rendering is used in **3-D modeling** to create surfaces, textures and shapes. It is faster than **raytracing**, but not as detailed, working as it does by producing the graduations between the brightest and darkest points on an **object**. On the other hand, it is more detailed and accurate than **Gourand** shading, because it analyzes every **pixel** in the **scene's** objects.

Photo CD is **Kodak's** service for **scanning** photographs onto **multisession CD-ROMs**. Priced comparatively inexpensively, the quality of the scans are usually excellent, because they use high quality equipment. However, with some exceptions, the scans are automatic, with no operator intervention or tweaking.

There are two different Kodak Photo CD services: the standard and the Pro. The standard (which handles only 35mm film) records five different **resolutions** for each photo: from a small screen resolution version up to 18 **MB**. The Pro service can handle film up to 4×5 inches, and its largest file is 36 MB. This multiresolution file system makes it easier to use only the amount of **data** you need, rather than overwhelming your system with extra **pixels**.

The service is available through the mails or from some photo labs, and the pricing varies. Generally speaking, the standard Photo CD scans cost about $0.70 to $1.25 per picture, and the Pro service is about $5 to $25 per scan. Kodak also has packages that combine the processing, printing and scanning of a roll of 35mm print film; you end up with negatives, prints and a Photo CD. Since Photo CD is multisession, you can use the same CD-ROM for future scans, as long as there is empty space on it, rather than buy a new one from the lab or service everytime you bring in your film.

Photo CD is also a file **format**, which is used, almost entirely, for storing pictures on CD-ROMs. If you plan to use Photo CDs as your **input** device, be sure that your **image editing program** supports (can open or **import**) the Photo CD format.

PhotoDeluxe is an **entry level image editing program** from **Adobe Systems**. It's core programming (or code) is based on **Photoshop**, but its

interface is simpler and offers step-by-step **wizards** and other help for the novice.

Photomultiplier tube   SEE **PMT**.

PhotoPAINT is **Corel Corporation's image editing program**, which is often sold as part of a **graphics suite**, that also includes the best-selling **CorelDRAW illustration program**.

Photorealistic refers to lifelike colors, lighting, **continuous tone** and smooth transitions, of the type that is indicative of **24-bit color** (or better). A photorealistic **image** looks like a photograph. A photorealistic printer **outputs** pictures that look like photographs.   SEE **Near-photorealistic**.

Photoshop is Adobe's **image editing program**, which has been credited with bringing professional **digital imaging** to the **desktop** computer. It started out on the **Mac** and didn't move over to the **PC** for a few years. That's what opened up the field on the **PC** to competitors, while keeping away serious contenders on the **Mac**. Now that it is on both **platforms**, it is recognized as the premier image editing program, against which others are compared.

Photoshop accelerator is an **expansion board** that is designed to speed up certain **Photoshop filters**, tools and processes. Most accelerator boards use single or multiple **DSP**s (digital signal processors), which are purpose-designed chips that take the particular task (for which it was designed) from the massive load of processing that keeps the **CPU** (central processor unit) busy. In addition, accelerator boards tend to have a lot of memory, so that they will do the task in high speed RAM. This extra memory, plus the offloading of the task to the DSP chip, literally accelerates, or speeds up, the filter, tool or other process.

Photoshop plug-in, or **Adobe plug-in**, is a phrase that indicates that a **third-party filter** or other add-on **subprogram** conforms to Adobe's published **open architecture** for **plug-ins**. Therefore, it will work from within any number of **image editing programs**, including **Photoshop, PhotoDeluxe, Picture Publisher, Painter** and just about every other mainstream **pixel**-based program. Many **scanners** and **digital cameras**, as well as filter programs (such as **Kai's Power Tools**) conform to the Adobe open architecture for plug-ins.

PhotoStyler was once a contender. It was Aldus Corporations' **PC**-based response to **Adobe's Photoshop**, which had many of the same tools, features, commands, etc. However, when Adobe swallowed Aldus in a merger/takeover, PhotoStyler was killed off as a perceived unnecessary piece of **software**.

PIC is the file **extension** for Lotus 1-2-3's **proprietary file format**. The extension is also used for an entirely different (and comparatively rare) slide-output file format.

Pica is a typesetting unit of measure that **desktop publishing programs** tend to define as about ⅙th of an inch. A pica is also ½th of a **point**, which is another typesetting unit of measure. Most **fonts** are measured in points.

Pick tool has an **icon** that is shaped like an arrow, and, in **vector**-based programs, it is used to pick or choose **objects** that are on the screen. Once the object is picked or **selected**, the pick tool can then be used to push or pull on it or on parts of it, which can cause changes in its position, size or **orientation**.

PICT (an acronym for *Picture File Format*) is a complex **Mac** file format. The PICT 1 type is suited for **vector** and black & white **raster** images. But PICT 2 can also handle **24-bit raster** color. Just about all Mac **imaging** programs can handle (open and save) PICT files, and many **PC/Windows** programs can open and save or **import** and **export** them.

There are various options associated with saving an image file in PICT. **Image depth** (or **resolution**) may be from 2 up to 32 bits per **pixel**, and there are various levels of **JPEG compression** available.

Picture Publisher is Micrografx's **image editing program**, which is often bundled with several other **graphics** programs in the ABC graphics suite. While it is marketed for the business user, Picture Publisher is a high end program that has a full set of editing tools, brushes, commands, etc.

Pinch is a **pixel**-based **special effects filter** that squeezes the center of a picture in onto itself. Usually, the user can define how much of a pinch will be generated.

Pincushion is a monitor distortion in which the screen pushes all the pixels inward into a trapezoid-like shape. **Barrel** distortion is the opposite.

Piracy is theft on the electronic highway. Most frequently, it refers to using **software** for which you don't have a **license**, aren't a **registered** owner and haven't paid. But it also relates to the taking and using of **images** that were created by and belong to someone else, and for which you don't have a license.

Pitch is a measure of the number of characters a printer can **output** per linear inch. If the type is proportionately spaced, then pitch is the measure of the average number of characters per inch, because the amount of space that a character will take up is variable according to the shape of the letter.   SEE **Proportional leading**.

Pitch is also the angle of **3-D** rotation around the **x-axis**.

Pinch: In this Corel PhotoPAINT dialog, you can see the before and after effect of using Pinch on a picture. It pulls all the pixels of the image from the edges toward the center. In some programs, the opposite of Pinch is Punch, which produces a globular or spherical distortion. (Turn to the Punch definition to see what that looks like on the same portrait. *Photo from the Corel Stock Photo Library.*)

Pixel, which stands for *picture element,* is the smallest point or **dot** of information in a **raster** (or **bitmapped**) image. Each pixel contains color **data,** and when hundreds, thousands or even millions of them are put together, they add up to the information needed to describe or display a picture.

Pixels are a loose analog to the grains of silver halide that create a photograph on film. They are also taken to be equivalent to the dots that a **desktop** printer **outputs.**

Pixelate is the effect of seeing the **pixels** that make up a picture on the monitor or in a print, when that picture is blown up, or enlarged, too much. It is the result of not having enough **data** (or **resolution**) in that picture at that larger size. To avoid pixelation, you need to make sure that your **images** have enough data for their **output** purposes.

Pixelate: You'll probably recognize the pixelating special effect from TV news shows, where they use it to disguise the face of an "informer." (*Photo from the Corel Stock Photo Library.*)

Pixelate is also a **special effects filter** that creates small blocks of colors in a **selected** area of an **image**, making it look as though you are seeing the pixels that make up that image.

Pixel per inch, or **ppi,** is the measure of **data** density, or **resolution**, in a **bitmapped image**. The higher the ppi, the greater the resolution of the image, and the larger the image file.

Both ppi and **dpi** (*dots per inch*) are informally used interchangeably, though they are really two different measurements. ppi is the unit of measure for resolution in the computer, where the image is defined by the number of pixels it holds. dpi exist in the real world of printers and **hardcopy**, where pictures are defined by the number of dots it takes to reproduce them on paper. **lpi** (*lines per inch*) is an entirely different animal that relates to the printing press and **line screens**. While dpi and ppi can be used with the same numbers without affecting the quality of resolution, lpi requires a conversion formula which specifies that you should have one and a half to two times the number of ppi as you will need in lpi, for quality output.

Pixel value manipulations are **blend modes** and **channel operations**, which compare the color and light values of two sources (**layers, channels**, or an original picture and a color applied by a **brush**, etc.). Then, they combine the two sources based on the **parameters**, or choices, set up by the user, such as **color only, multiply, darken** and **lighten**. In effect, the resulting pixels that make up the new (combined) **image** are defined by these pixel value manipulations and controls.   SEE Color pages.

Pkzip is a shareware program (that is, it is freely distributed, and users are expected to pay a fee to the developer), which compresses files (including **images**) and allows them to span several **floppy disks**. Pkunzip then expands the file onto a **hard drive** (or other large **storage device**) and reassembles it from the numerous floppies. This is useful for sharing images with associates who don't have access to larger and better storage devices than floppies. However, it is a **lossy** compression that can be destructive to image **data**.   SEE **Compression**.

Place is a command that will insert a file, **document, graphic** or **image** into the current open document, image, etc. For instance, if you are working on a drawing in an **illustration program** using the place command (which is usually found in the File **pulldown menu**), you can insert another drawing (or other kind of image, a bit of text, etc.) into that picture. If you use the open command, however, a new window would be opened to hold the contents of the file, instead.

Planar is a 3-D term for the 2-D plane or surface on any **object** within a **scene**.

Platen is the glass surface of a **flatbed scanner** (or on a photocopy machine) on which you place the **page** or **image** that you want to **scan** (or copy). If your scanned **image** has bits of **noise** in it, check the platen. It may need cleaning with a Windex-like solution. An antistatic brush may help you clear dust away from the platen.

Platform is the generic term that refers to the kind of computer or **operating system** that is being used. **Mac** is a platform, as is the **PC**. But to be more precise, **Power Macs, Pentiums, PRePs**, etc., as well as **UNIX-based, OS/2, Windows NT**, etc., are all specific platforms. Most **hardware** and **software** will work on only one platform.

However, there are also **cross-platform peripherals, applications**, etc., that are compatible with more than one kind of computer and/or operating system. Cross-platform standards are becoming more and more common. In **imaging**, cross-platform applications are quite useful, as are cross-platform **file formats**, because they allow you to share **images** with associates, regardless of the kind of computer they are using.

Platemaking is the process of creating the plates (which are often now made of paper) which a printing press uses to apply inks in a press run. Some **prepress** programs have a command to make plates, and some **desktop printers** can be used to **output** them.

Playback is a command that will run an **animation** or **video**, so that the user can see how it will appear and/or how an edit has changed it from the last time it was played.

Plotter is a large pen-based or **inkjet** printer that was traditionally used for blueprints and other large-format **vector**-based schematics. It is now used to make banner-size near-photoquality prints of **images**. The **media** (paper, transparency material, etc.) is fed from a roll through a carriage width that ranges from a couple to several feet. Therefore, the **output** can be quite large—limited only by the width of the carriage and the length of the media roll. Because of their size and expense, they have tended to be used only in service bureaus. But now that their prices have come down, some **imaging** studios and other companies that need to make a volume of large prints are buying them, too.

Plug-and-Play (PnP) is the greatly touted ability of **Windows 95**, **98** and **NT** to connect easily with **peripherals** and **software**. Supposedly, Windows automatically detects what you are attaching to the computer, invokes a standard **wizard** that requires simple yes and no answers, and automatically installs the proper drivers. It sometimes works.

While it is not called *plug-and-play,* **Macs** have long had the ability to add **hardware** or **software** directly and easily, without any or much interaction from the user.

Plug-in is a **subprogram** that connects, or plugs into, a large **application** and works from within that application.

Many **special effects filters** are plug-ins, quite a few of which take advantage of the **Photoshop (Adobe) open architecture**. That means that they can work on pictures in any **image editing program** that conforms to that architecture (such as **Picture Publisher, Painter, Photo-Deluxe** and **Photoshop**) There are also filter plug-ins for **vector** programs (**illustration, 3-D**, etc.).

The software **drivers** for many **scanners** and **digital cameras** operate as plug-ins, which means that their captured **images** can be brought into the application directly from the hardware, usually through an **acquire** command.

Plug-in is also the method by which **peripheral boards** are connected to the **motherboard**. They are plugged into the **expansion slots**.

PMS (*Pantone Matching System*) is the combination **software, color palettes** and printed **swatch books** that are used in preparing **images** for **prepress**. It attempts to coordinate the computer-displayed colors with the **Pantone** inks that will be used for the final print run, to maintain a consistency of color.

PMT, or *photomultiplier tube,* is an exotic device used in high end drum scanners. It reads the color, light, shadows, etc., of a printed picture, negative or transparency with a high degree of accuracy and feeds it to an **analog-to-digital convertor** (ADC), so that it may be **digitized** and used by the computer.

PMT is based on a technology created by the military during the Vietnam War and was used by snipers to pick out targets in total darkness. These so-called starscopes achieved this by reading and magnifying starlight.

PMTs are too expensive for desktop scanners, which rely on less-precise **CCD** technology.

Point is a typesetting unit of measure (roughly equivalent to $\frac{1}{72}$ of an inch) that is used to measure characters and spaces on a line of a printed **page**, as well as the spaces (**leading**) between lines. When selecting a **font**'s size for any type that you place into a **document** or **image**, you will be asked to specify what point size you want the type to be. This is true, regardless of the kind of program with which you are working: **image editing, illustration, animation, presentation, desktop publishing, word processing**, etc.

Point-and-shoot describes any camera (film or **digital**) which has so few user controls that all you have to do is point the lens at your subject and click (shoot) on the shutter button. But it also applies to those cameras that require one or two other steps, such as turning the flash on or off. Point-and-shoot cameras are the simplest cameras to use and should be, but not always are, the least expensive to buy.

Pointillize is a **raster**-based special **effect** that breaks up colors into dots of their composite colors. In most pointillizing **filters** or commands, the user can specify the size of the dots. The result is an impressionistic-like **image**, similar to a Seurat or Monet painting.

Pointing device is an instrument that is used to interact with the computer's monitor, selecting or activating **icons** or commands, drawing or painting, moving the **cursor** to another location, etc. A **mouse** is a pointing device, as are the **stylus** or **puck** of a **digitizing tablet**.

Polar coordinates are **special effects filters** that fold a **raster**-based **image** (or a selected area of an image) in on itself. This is done by substituting the linear coordinates (the x- and y-axes) and organization of the **pixels**, with coordinates and organization similar to a reflection on a mirrored globe or in a mirrored cylinder. It's an esoteric con-

POINTILLIZE A

POINTILLIZE B

Pointillize: Pointillize converts photographs and other bitmapped images into points of color, using a process similar to Pixelate, Crystallize and other commands. However, the result is less abstract and more painterly with Pointillize. *(Photo from the Corel Stock Photo Library.)*

cept that is better seen than understood, and it is based on an even more obscure 18th-century art style, called *anamorphosis.*

Polygon is a closed shape or **object** that has three or more sides, which are usually flat or straight.

In **vector**-based programs (such as **illustration** or **draw** programs), it is also a tool that can draw such shapes, with all the sides set at equal lengths and angles. Usually, the user can define the number of sides the tool will draw, and, after the shape is drawn, it can be edited. The polygon tool is considered one of the more basic drawing tools in such programs, along with tools for creating ellipses, rectangles, lines, etc.

Pop-up menu is a list of options that appears, or pops up, onto the screen, when you click your **mouse** or other **pointing device** onto a bar, arrow, button or other specific point in a **dialog, palette**, etc.

There is a very fine point of difference between a **pulldown menu** and a pop-up menu. When you click on the header or button that opens up a pulldown menu, the menu unfolds or opens up downward from the point of your mouse click. When you open up a pop-up menu, it can appear above and below, as well as on top of, the click point or item.

Port is like an electrical outlet in your wall. Several ports are usually on the back of your computer, and that's where you plug in the cables that attach **peripherals** to the computer.

The ports are either part of the **motherboard** or are the ends of **expansion boards** that are plugged into the motherboard. Each kind of port—**parallel, serial, SCSI, USB, game**, etc.—requires its own kind of cable, and some ports are specialists—**input** only, **output** only, or input and out-

POLAR COORDINATES A

POLAR COORDINATES B

Polar coordinates: Polar special effects create strange views of the world.

put. All sorts of problems can occur when a user tries to plug a peripheral and its cable into the wrong port.

Portrait mode   SEE **Orientation**.

Positive, which is the opposite of **negative**, is the state of a picture that shows or exhibits the colors, shadows and highlights of the actual image, as it will be printed or displayed.

POST (*Power-On Self-Test*) are the series of diagnostics that the computer performs when it is turned on. These can include (but are not limited to) checking out the amount of **RAM** that is installed and recognized, what **peripherals** are attached, etc. POST is one of the reasons there is a delay (of seconds or minutes) between flicking the switch to power on the computer and being able to use it. When POST fails, turn your computer off and try again. That sometimes solves the simplest problems. More complex failures may require a technician.

Postproduction is a **multimedia** term that refers to putting together and perfecting a finished presentation. It's the act of editing, clipping and putting together disparate elements, such as sound, animation and titles, with the aid of a computer.

Posterize is a **filter** or command that converts the colors in **raster images**, so that there are fewer steps between graduations and more severe differences between adjacent **hues** or shades and, therefore, far fewer colors. It can make a photograph look like an illustration. In the **dialog box** that controls posterization, the user can set the number of steps, with the lower number resulting in a more pronounced effect.

PostScript is **Adobe's page description language**, which was created to be device-independent. That means that the **page** (consisting of text, **graphics** and/or **images**)

POSTERIZE A

POSTERIZE B

Posterize: Posterizing can turn a photograph into something that looks like an illustration. *(Photo from the Corel Stock Library.)*

will print out on any of a number of PostScript-compliant **output devices**, at the highest **resolution** that the device is capable of producing.

Many desktop printers are PostScript compliant, a feature that used to add several hundred dollars to the cost of the device. The difference between PostScript and non-PostScript printers can be negligible, if you are printing simple text and graphics, or it can be like night and day, if you are outputting more complex color images.

PostScript 2 and 3 are more up-to-date and sophisticated versions of the original, which contains advanced features for improved color **halftones, memory management** and other refinements to improve speed and output quality.

There are PostScript **clones**, which are devices that mimic PostScript capabilities, but without Adobe's official coding. Generally, their function and output is indistinguishable from PostScript; however, some exhibit minor variations and eccentricities.

You may also hear of screen PostScript, which uses the same **algorithms** and outputs them to the screen rather than to the printer. But because of the expense and complexity, screen PostScript is not generally used in most desktop computers.

PostScript fonts are **outline** fonts. That is, they are defined mathematically and generated as they are needed for **output**. Therefore, they take up less storage space and can be generated at the appropriate **resolution** for the intended **output device**.

PowerBook is an **Apple laptop** computer. Some PowerBooks are fast and powerful enough to do serious **imaging** assignments.

Power dip   SEE **Brownout**.

PowerMac   SEE **Power Macintosh**.

Power Macintosh is Apple's current generation of computers, all of which use the **PowerPC CPU**. PowerPC is the name of Motorola's CPU that is used in Apple PowerMacs and IBM workstations.

PowerPC   SEE **PowerPC Platform**.

PowerPC Platform was originally called **CHRP**, or **Common Hardware Reference Platform**.   SEE **PReP**.

PowerPC Reference Platform (PReP), formerly known as CHRP, is a system that uses similar or identical components, but not the same operating system. PReP was supposed to become the Holy Grail of operating system compatibility, but, because of philosophical and financial differences among Apple, IBM and Motorola, PReP machines are unable to be configured to run under a variety of operating systems.

PowerPoint is **Microsoft's** business **presentation program**.

Power surge   SEE **Surge**.

Power user is someone who works with computers so often and so intensively, that they have learned all the shortcuts, tricks and commands for getting the most from their system. Power users tend to work on the most powerful state-of-the-art machines. If you make your living in graphics and work at a computer all day, you are probably, ipso facto, a power user.

PPCP   SEE **PowerPC Platform**.

ppi   SEE **Pixels per inch**.

PPM, or **pages per minute,** is the speed rating for printers, which states how many pages can be printed in a minute.

Preferences are user-chosen options that relate to how a program or **peripheral driver** will function. It is an entirely personal customization that can be saved so that the program or **driver** will always look the same every time you open it—until you change your mind, at which time you can change the preferences.

For instance, you may choose how the **cursor** will look, your favorite units of measure, the level of **tolerance** for a **color wand** tool, the **prepress UCR** or **GCR** ink setups, the **default** printer, where an **object's duplicate** will be placed in relation to the original, the color of your **workspace**, the pictures for your **screen saver**, etc.

PReP   SEE **PowerPC Reference Platform**.

Prepress is the preparation of a picture, **page**, document or whatever, which will be duplicated (usually in volume) on a printing press. To many of those who are experienced in prepress, it is recognized as a black art, rather than a science, in which the small details of **color management, layout, line screens, scanning parameters**, ink setups, etc., must be handled with skill, knowledge and talent, if you want a quality end result. Many of the more important aspects of prepress, such as converting design colors to ink colors, setting the type, creating the **color separated** files and making the plates, are now done using **desktop** computers. It all used to be done by hand (sleight of hand?) and/or mechanically.

Prescan is the process of previewing what the **scanner** will see and capture. In fact, in some scanner **drivers**, the prescan button is marked, instead, preview. Depending on the **interface**, after a prescan, the user may be able to **crop** the image, edit its brightness and/or contrast, and perform other manipulations on it, before it is finally **digitized** and **uploaded** to the computer.

Presentation is a type of software that creates slides and/or **animations** that may be **output** to **overhead** transparencies or paper on a printer, to film on a **film recorder**, to the computer screen and/or to a monitor projector. The result is a slide show that graphically demonstrates and illustrates (or replaces) a lecture, demonstration, verbal presentation, etc.

Computer-based presentations borrow quite a few interesting **animation** effects from video, including **special effects** transitions between slides, moving titles, sound effects coordinated with animated **bullet lists**, etc.

Popular presentation programs include **PowerPoint**, Compel and others.

Presets are generally the **default** settings for tools, **fills, textures, lights**, colors and other visual elements. For instance, a **3-D program** may have a couple of dozen preset fills that emulate metals, glass, plastic and other surfaces. Based on those presets, the user may or may not be able to define or customize other fills.

Pressman is the person who runs the printing press, and, yes, he is still usually a man. This is the person who knows and understands ink, paper, color, plates and all the other details that must be tweaked to end up with a nice printed **page**. His hands are usually covered in ink; he yells a lot (to be heard over the clanking and banging of the presses), and he is probably the most knowledgeable person in the entire prepress team. Get to know him and discuss how you plan to set up your **images** before you begin work on a project—the result will be far superior if you take his concerns into account throughout the **prepress** process.

Press proof is a printed **page** run through the printing press, using the inks and papers that will be used for the final **press run**. It is the ultimate test to see if the page, paper, color conversions, **layout, line screens, color separations**, etc., have been set up correctly. A less-expensive and less time-consuming way is to create a **match print** or other **desktop output** that mimics a press proof.

Press run is the number of copies of the **document, page, image** or whatever, that will be coming off of the printing press. Often, a press run is just a little bit higher than the client's requirements (an overrun), just in case. . . . When the client needs more copies, another press run must be scheduled and set up.

Pressure-sensitive refers to the ability of the **stylus** of some **digitizing tablets** to impart information about how hard you press on it to **image editing programs**. That, in turn, affects how the **brush** tool will lay color onto your picture. The result will depend on the program, what brush is being used and how the options for both the brush and the program have been set. In some cases, pressing hard will mush the brush, as though the bristles were spread by the pressure. In other cases, pressing lightly on the stylus, as you draw, will result in a lighter color, while pressing harder will create a greater color **saturation**.

In **natural media emulation**, pressure-sensitivity is the necessary link between your hand and the electronic canvas.

For pressure-sensitivity to work, the stylus and tablet must be pressure-sensitive, the program must be able to react to it, and the **plug-in** and **preferences** must be set up correctly.

Preview is the picture that is shown in various situations, to give the user a better idea of the appearance of the final picture.

Many **filter dialogs** have tiny **thumbnail** previews of the current **image**. When the user changes filter **parameters** or options, the thumbnail will change according to how those changes will affect the picture.

Other dialogs have a preview button, which, when clicked, applies the various options of the current dialog to the full-size picture. If you like the appearance of those changes, just click on the OK button in the dialog, and they will be applied permanently. If you don't like the look of the preview, then clicking on the Cancel button will remove all the changes.

In **scanner** software (called **drivers**), a preview scan (or **prescan**) is done at low resolution, so that the user can crop and otherwise adjust the picture before the final scan.

Similarly, some **digital cameras** will show thumbnail previews of all the pictures in their memory. If you want to see the entire, full-size picture, you click or **double-click** on the preview, and that uploads the photograph.

3-D software usually has different preview **modes**. Since 3-D **models** can be very complex, the user will work on simple versions of them. Traditionally, that meant working on **wireframes** that exhibit no color, fill, light, shadows or anything—they are just shapes formed from see-through **polygons**. Even those more modern 3-D programs that use some rendering engine while the user works don't necessarily show all the attributes of the final **scene**. However, final rendering can be *very* time-consuming. Therefore, to see all the colors, shadows, light, textures, etc., of the final picture, without going through the entire final render, it is possible to go into preview mode. The amount of detail that is visible in the preview depends on the software, the type of preview and, often, the options that the user has chosen.   SEE **Render**.

In other words, previews are available in many places in **imaging**. They are useful and can save time, as well as creative energy. So, whenever a preview picture, button or mode is available, try it out.

Primary colors are those colors that, when combined, will create all other colors. However, primary colors will change, depending on which **color model** the software or hardware is using.

For instance, in the **RGB** color model, the primary colors are red, green and blue. But the **CMY**(K) color model has cyan, magenta, yellow (and sometimes black) as the primaries.

Primitive shapes are those shapes that are considered the bare minimum necessary in **vector**-based programs, and for which there are **icons** or tools that will draw them. Almost all other shapes can be drawn using primitives, plus various line and/or **Bezier** or **spline** tools.

For instance, in **illustration programs**, there are usually a **rectangle**, an **ellipse** and a **polygon** tool. The tool works by anchoring an initial point in the shape with a **mouse click**; then, as the user drags with the mouse, the shape opens up. Most programs will allow the user to choose to draw from the center of the shape or from a point in the perimeter. Using options associated with those tools, the user can also draw, with a simple **click and drag**, squares, circles and any number-sided shape (such as a triangle and a pentagon).

Similarly, **3-D** programs will have tools for drawing spheres, cubes and other primitive 3-D shapes.

Print dialog box appears when the user clicks on the print **icon** or chooses the print command. That's where the user sets the printing **parameters**, such as how many copies should be output, which **pages**, in color or black & white and using which printer.

Printer driver is the **software** that connects the **desktop** printer to the computer. Through it, the user can send commands, files, **images, documents**, etc., to the printer. When the user clicks on the print command or **icon**, the **dialog box** that opens up is associated with the printer driver software.

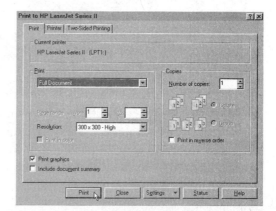

Print dialog: The options in the print dialog can vary, depending on what printer you have attached to your computer. When you have set your printing parameters, click the Print or OK button to print your file (which can be an image, document or whatever).

Printer resolution is a measure of the number of dots that a printer can **output**, and it is usually measured in **dots per inch**, or **dpi**. The higher the dpi of a printer, the finer the quality it can produce. Three hundred dpi is generally considered the minimum level for a **grayscale** printer. However, color printers will often be 600, 1,200 or even 1,400 dpi.

Another way of measuring a printer's density of dots is by the number of dots per inch in both horizontal and vertical directions. Therefore, a printer can be said to have a resolution of 600 × 600, 1,200 × 1,200 or, even, 600 × 1,200.

Printing parameters are those options that the user sets in the **printer dialog box** and the **page setup**. The parameters define the kind of **output**, as well as its volume, **resolution** and any other option that can be changed by the user.

Printing plant is a place of business dedicated to high volume output using large **printing presses**.

Print server is a **networked** computer that is dedicated to working the printer and handling files sent to the printer—and nothing else. By offloading print jobs and responsibilities to the print server, other computers in the network are freed to do other tasks sooner. It is another method for speeding up and making more efficient the printing process.   SEE **Queue, Print spooler**.

Print setup is a **dialog box** that defines which printer will be handling the **output** from an **application** or for a specific file (**image, document**, etc.). It differs from the **print dialog** in that it can be accessed at any time, while the user is working on the file. On the other hand, the print dialog is accessed only when the user is ready to send the file to the printer.

Print spooler is a **software** scheme or a **hardware** device that can accumulate and hold some or all the files or **data** that have been sent to the printer by the **application**. It then hands the files, one by one, off to the printer, when it is ready. Spoolers are useful, because software is much faster than hardware. Therefore, the application and the **printer driver** can send print jobs much faster than the printer can handle them.   SEE **Queue**.

Print to disk is a command that **outputs** a file exactly as it would to a printer, with all the codes, **outline fonts, layout**, etc. However, no **hard copy** is produced. Instead, a new file is created that looks like the printed **page**. It's useful if you have to print a file from another, non-networked computer.

Process is the act of having the computer do something, anything. Whenever you edit or create a picture, **acquire** a picture from a **scanner** or **digital**

camera, send a file to a **printer, download** to the **Internet**, etc., the computer must process that information, which takes up **resources**, such as **RAM** and **virtual memory**. Processing is the reason computers exist—because they can go through the many millions of zeros and ones that make up **digital data** much faster than any human being could.

Process colors are those that are defined by combining various portions of cyan, magenta, yellow and black (**CMYK**) inks. This is in opposition to **spot** colors, which are defined by the ink manufacturers (such as **Pantone, Trumatch** and **Toyo**) by names and/or numbers that refer to a specific dye or ink. Both process and spot colors are inks that are used on printing presses, though some **desktop** printers will emulate or mimic them.

Processor SEE **CPU**.

Prodigy is the name of a commercial **on-line service**.

Profile is a description that is saved and referred to by the computer and **peripherals**. It is then used by the computer and its **software** to generate files that conform to or use those profiles.

That description may be the color profile or characteristics of a printer or **scanner**, or the display **gamma** of a monitor. Because every device in an **imaging** system can affect how color is seen, displayed or **output**, accurate **image** color depends on the ability to correct for any color influences that may be introduced by a device. Therefore, knowing all the profiles of the various devices helps to correct an **image's** color so that it is accurate.

Program is an **application**, or **software**, that allows the user to create, organize or otherwise do something on the computer. For instance, programs include those that enable **image editing, desktop publishing, word processing, spreadsheet** development and maintenance, etc.

Program manager is the shell or **interface** that displays on your screen when you first bring up Windows 3.x, and it is the gatekeeper for entering all the other programs on your computer. That's where all the **icons** for various programs are available. In the Windows.ini (the file that sets up your Windows configuration), it is called shell=progman.exe. There is no Program Manager in Windows 95 or 98.

Prompt is a message that asks the user to type in or do something. Often, it is represented simply by a blinking **cursor**. Other times, the blinking cursor is preceded by a small greater than symbol (>).

Proof is a **hard copy** or print that shows how a picture or **layout** will look when it is sent to its final **output**. Proofs can vary in the accuracy of information that they provide about color, **resolution**, quality, etc., depending on the **output device** used to generate it. The most accurate proof is a **press proof**, which comes off the printing press and is created using the final paper and inks. But there are also **match proofs**, and even less-accurate ones, that can be generated by **desktop** printers.

Be careful how you create a contract proof. That's the hardcopy that you give to a client, promising that the final print or **print run** will look like it.

Proofreading is the process of checking a manuscript, document or **page layout** for mistakes. If you find any typos or misspellings in this book, please blame our proofreader and not the authors. (As Shoe would say, authors know how to write, not spell.)

Proportional leading is space between typeset lines that changes in size depending on the size of the type being used and the space available for it.

Proportional type gives variable weight and space to characters, depending on the relative size of the characters. For instance, a capital *M* is wider and taller than a small *i*. Therefore, in proportional type, the *M* would be given more space than the *i*. This is in opposition to **monospacing**, which would give both (and all characters) the same space (weight).

Proprietary refers to something that pertains to and is owned by a specific entity.

For instance, a proprietary **file format** is one that is owned by and relevant to a certain program—as the .cdw format belongs to **CorelDRAW**. While some other programs may recognize the .cdw format, it is very unusual to be able to open, edit and save it in any other **software** than **Corel**'s.

Proprietary **hardware** or architecture are devices or software with closed standards, special technologies or nonlicenced patents that no one else can use. We suggest staying away from proprietary hardware because, although it may be very advanced and could be the next standard, it could also turn out to be an orphan, with no support.

Protocol is a formula or way of doing things that must be rigidly observed. For instance, there may be set protocols to **log on** to a **network** or an **Internet** address. And, if you make any mistakes, including substituting lowercase characters for uppercase ones, you might not get on. Some protocols are more forgiving than others.

Proxy editing is a scheme for manipulating and changing large **pixel**-based **images** that has the user working on a **low resolution** version of the image, to speed up all the edits. Then, when the user is finished, the edits (which have been stored as a separate file of information, keystrokes, brush strokes and other **data**) are applied to (or **rendered** onto) the full-size **high resolution** image. The rendering can be time-consuming, but the user doesn't have to be there while it is happening. **Live Picture** and Macromedia's Xres are two programs that use proxy editing, though Live Picture doesn't like the expression.

Public domain refers to **software** that is available free and isn't really owned by anyone. Nor is it backed by any company, should something go wrong. Often vendors will sell collections of public domain software, for the price of the **floppy disks** or **CD-ROM**s that hold it. **Shareware** is not public domain.

Publish and subscribe is the **Mac**'s version of **Window's OLE**, in which **data**, text, **graphics** and **images** may be shared by two different programs. The first program creates the file and then publishes it. The second program subscribes to that file, embedding it into its **document, image** or whatever. When the first program changes the file, those changes are automatically made in the subscribed version, too.

Puck is a palm-size **pointing device** that is used with **digitizing tablets**. It has a crosshair for more accurate positioning than a mouse, and often has as many as 16 buttons to access additional options and commands.

Pulldown menu is a group of options that are located by the user, when he or she clicks on a button, header word, arrow, etc. The most prominent pull-

PULLDOWN MENU A

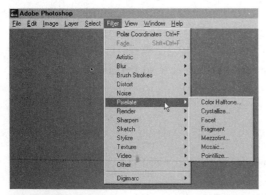

PULLDOWN MENU B

Pulldown menu: At the top of the screen of just about every program are a series of words. Click on those words to display the pulldown menu related to that word (such as File), and various commands will be revealed. If there are arrows next to the command names in the pulldown menu, as there are in this Photoshop example, click on each arrow to see another menu of related commands.

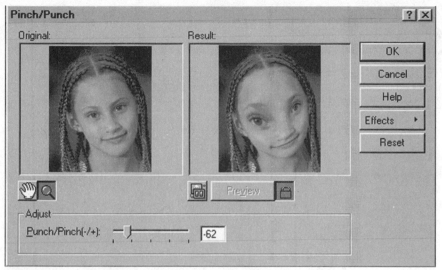

PUNCH A

PUNCH B

Punch: (A) In some bitmapped image programs, punch creates the same kind of effect as spherize—pushing the pixels of the image outward from the center. Pinch is the opposite. To see the result of a Pinch command on the same portrait turn to that definition. By the way, the reason that one eye is affected more than the other is that the portrait isn't perfectly centered in the picture. Therefore, the eye that is closer to the center of the image frame is affected more fully. **(B)** In vector programs, the Punch command creates a hole in an object the shape and size of another object. Therefore, the circle in the center of the rectangle (on the left) becomes like a cookie cutter, punching out a circular hole in the middle of the rectangle (on the right).

down menus exist at the top of the screen of every program. They are the words—such as File, Edit, Filter and Window—under which all the other commands that the program offers hide. SEE **Pop-up menu**.

Punch is a **vector** command that creates a hole in an **object** by subtracting another object from it. For instance, if you have two circles, with one inside the other, a punch command would create a donutlike shape by turning the inner circle into a hole in the outer circle.

In raster or bitmapped-based image editing programs, **Punch** is sometimes the name given to the **Spherize** command (or a variation of it), which pushes the pixels of the image outward from the center toward the edges. SEE **Pinch**.

QIC stands for Quarter-Inch Cartridge, so named for the width of the tape inside the cartridges used as **backups** for **archival storage** of computer data. Because QIC cartridges are **descrete** devices with limited capacity, they are not particularly useful for digital images that frequently require **gigabytes** of storage space. QIC drives and tapes are relatively inexpensive, however, so they are mostly used for nongraphics business and home/office backups.

Quantel paintbox is a high end and very expensive **image editing program** (sort of an industrial-strength **Photoshop**), that is designed to run on **UNIX**-based **workstations**.

QuarkXpress is considered the top **desktop publishing program**, and for that reason there are many **plug-ins** written for it. Also, just about all **output hardware**, as well as **service bureaus** and other organizations, support QuarkXpress files.

Queue is a line. If you've ever been to England, then you queued up to buy theatre tickets or to get on a bus.

Computer processing, most notably printing, can be made to queue up, too. If you want to print out several pictures, they can be sent out to a piece of **software**, which keeps track of them and of the printer's status. And, as the printer becomes available, it causes the next picture to be printed. This works on individual computers, as well as on ones that are **networked** and sharing a printer. Some printing queues provide tools that allow you to prioritize printing jobs.   SEE **Print spooler, Print server**.

QuickDraw is the programming that teaches **Macs** how to display or draw text, **icons, images**, etc., onto the computer monitor.

Quick mask (or **ruby mask**) is a view of an **alpha channel** (the black & white silhouette of a **mask**) that shows as a colored translucency over the **raster** image that it is masking. In this view, it is easier to edit the alpha channel by painting on it in blacks, whites and grays, because you can see exactly how and where these masks' edits will relate to the picture.   SEE Color pages.

QuickTake 100, 150 and **200** are **Apple Computer's** brand of **digital cameras**.

QuickTime is a **Mac subprogram** that coordinates, records and plays back video, **animation** and sound.

Radial blur is a **special effects filter** that softens a **raster image** by dispersing **pixels** in a circular pattern. The amount and extent of the blur is usually user-definable.

Radial fill is a command or tool that fills an area or an **object** with a **gradient** or **fountain fill** that follows a circular path, starting with one color in the center and ending with the last color at the circumference.

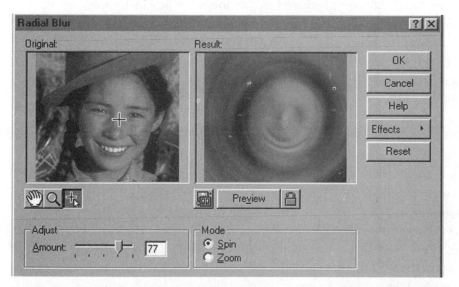

Radial blur: This filter dialog shows the result of an extreme radial blur. Used with a lighter touch (less of a blur), the effect can be quite subtle, even poetic. *(Photo from the Corel Stock Photo Library.)*

Usually, the gradient is defined by only two colors—the starting and ending colors. But if the program allows, and the user takes advantage of the feature, any gradient may be generated using a **clockwise** or **counterclockwise** spectrum of the various **hues** that exist between the two colors on the standard **color wheel**. Or the user may be able to define a gradient made up of any number and any sequence of colors.

Radio button is a circular check box. When the user clicks his or her **mouse** in the center of the radio button, that option is chosen and a mark is put into it. To unchoose the option, click in the radio button again.

RAID (*Redundant Array of Inexpensive Drives*) is a failsafe system that saves **data** simultaneously to two or more **hard drives**. So, if one of them gets corrupted, blows up, melts down or fails in any way, the computer automatically switches to the second drive without missing a beat. In this way, you'll almost never lose data. RAIDs are typically used in **applications** and by businesses that absolutely, positively must protect data and avoid costly and time-consuming shutdowns.

Rainbow fill is a **gradient** or **fountain fill** that is created by moving through the spectrum from the user-selected first color to the last color. This is in opposition to a direct fill that uses a gradient that graduates between the two colors.   SEE **Clockwise spectrum, Counterclockwise spectrum**.

RAM, or *Random Access Memory,* is the electronic **memory** in which most things you do in the computer happens. (When the computer runs out of memory, it substitutes empty areas of the **hard drive**, which is then called **virtual memory**.) RAM is volatile and ephemeral, which means that it lasts only as long as there is electric current running through it. When you turn off your computer, or if you have a dip in power, whatever is in RAM disappears, forever.

In early computers, RAM was hideously expensive and difficult to manufacture. So, most computers were limited to 48 or 64K of RAM. Early IBM PCs could be expanded up to 256K of RAM, and later models up to 640K. With the introduction of the IBM-AT, RAM jumped to 1 **megabyte**. Today, **desktop imaging** systems typically start with a 64 MB, and can go as high as 1 gigabyte. **Workstations** can have even more RAM.

The more RAM your system has, theoretically, the faster it will process **images** and everything else. That's because the speed of RAM is measured in **nanoseconds** (billionths of a second). Virtual memory, which is borrowed from the hard disk (the speed of which is measured in milliseconds or thousandths of a second), is much slower. However, because of computer configurations, **operating systems** and operating **environments**, your computer may not be able to make full use of all its RAM. For instance, Windows 95 runs most applications faster with 64 MB than 96 MB of RAM. Because of its different architecture, the **Mac** can make full use of any RAM that it has.

RAM comes packaged in three formats: chips, **SIMMs** and DIMMs. SIMMs are single, in-line memory modules, in which three to nine memory **chips** are soldered onto a tiny board (about the size of a stick of chewing gum). They are available in densities ranging from 256K to 64 MB. DIMMs are higher density boards in which 6 to 18 memory chips are soldered, and they range from 16 to 128 MB. The next generation of DIMM will be half a gigabyte.

There are other types of RAM, such as SRAM (static RAM), VRAM (video RAM) and DRAM (dynamic RAM). Static RAM is both slow and expensive, but it doesn't need to be **refreshed** 60 times a second to hold information. In fact, you can turn off the computer and then turn it on, and whatever was in memory remains intact. Static RAM is typically used in **peripherals**, to hold **user-defined** configurations and **preferences**. VRAM is high speed memory used in **video boards**; however, with other types of RAM (such as EDO memory) coming down in price, while boosting speed, VRAM is being used less and less. And DRAM is simply another name for the common form of RAM.

Random Access Memory   SEE **RAM**.

Raster is a synonym for **bitmap** and the opposite to **vector**. In other words, a raster **image** is one that is made up of **pixels** rather than defined by mathematical formulae.

Raster image is the same thing as a **bitmapped image**. That is, it is a **digitized** picture that is defined by the position and color of the many **pixels** that describe it. This is in opposition to a **vector** image, which is defined by mathematical formulae. Raster images generate much larger files than vector, because it takes more memory to describe all of the many thousands or millions of pixels that make them.

All **scanned** images, and all those **acquired** from **digital cameras**, are raster.

Resolution is an issue that is specifically related to raster images. That's because resolution is the measure of how much **data** or how many pixels an image has. On the other hand, vector images are said to be **resolution-independent**, which means that their output resolution is dependent not on their own file structure, but on the resolution capabilities of the output device.

Raster image processing is the process of **acquiring**, editing, manipulating, **painting** on, **outputting**, etc., a **raster image**, or any picture that is generated by pixels. It is done in **image editing programs**, such as **Photoshop, Picture Publisher, PhotoDeluxe** and **Fractal Design Painter**.

A more specific definition relates to how an image that exists in a computer is output to a printer or other device.   SEE **RIPping**.

Rasterize is the process of converting an image or document into representative **pixels** or dots. For instance, if you have created a **3-D** scene or a **2-D** illustration, the file is **vector**-based (or mathematically defined). To be output it to a desktop printer, those vectors must first be re-interpreted into a **raster** file, which represent the dots that the printer will place on the paper.

Raster-to-vector is a translation of the **pixel**-based information in **raster** (or **bitmapped**) images, to the mathematical information that forms **vector** images. This is usually done by tracing a raster image using a **Bezier** or **spline** tool.   SEE **Trace**.

Raytracing is a method of **rendering 3-D models** and **scenes**. It is recognized as being complex, detailed and highly realistic, incorporating information about **highlights, shadows, textures**, etc. Therefore, it can, if the file is prepared correctly, resemble photorealism. Quite a bit of computing power and programming is required for good raytracing.   SEE **Photorealistic**.

Read-only designates a file that users may open, but may not change or save it. When submitting an **image** file to an associate, especially across a **network**, or anytime it isn't possible to retain a protected original, it is sensible to make the image file read-only. Then, that associate can't change your picture.

Read-only memory   SEE **ROM**.

Read/write is the process of inputting and outputting data to or from a **storage device**, such as a **hard drive**. Actually, reading and writing are separate functions and, depending on the technology, may involve separate **hardware** within the drive and may work at different speeds. The most dramatic read/write performance differences occur with **MO**, or magneto-optical devices, where reading is simply passing over the data and transferring it to the computer. Writing on an MO, however, requires physically burning zeros and ones beneath the plastic surface of the disc, which can take 2 to 5 times longer than reading data.

Real-time is any event that either occurs live or displays as continuous live action. It's frequently used in **multimedia** applications to indicate when a feed or display from a video camera is coming in live (as opposed to recorded data from a VCR).

Rectangle tool creates an even four-sided **object** by clicking on a point (to set one corner), then dragging diagonally and releasing the **mouse** button at the opposite corner. Often, it is possible to create a perfect square with the rectangle tool by holding down a **constraining** key, such as the **Control** key, while drawing. Just don't release the constraining key without releasing the mouse button first.

A rectangle **selection tool** works in a similar manner, but it is used in **image editing programs** to **mask** or select an area in a **raster image**.

Rectangular fill is a tool or command for filling an **object** or an area of an **image** with a **gradient** that takes the shape of a rectangle.

Redo is a command that **repeats** the previous command or action. It is usually found in the **Edit pulldown menu**.

Redraw is the process that changes what is on the computer monitor. For instance, say you have an **image** on the screen, and you then apply a **perspective** correction to it. First, the changes are **processed** within the computer (in **RAM** and/or **virtual memory**). Then, the picture on the screen adjusts itself, according to the edit. That adjustment of the picture on the screen is the redraw.

Redraw also applies to the screen changes that occur when **windowing** between programs, **scrolling** through a **document**, editing text, moving or adding **objects**, or any other situation in which the dots in the screen must alter the information that they show you.

When the change to what is displayed on the screen is intricate and/or memory-intensive, there can be a noticeable delay between applying it and seeing it on the monitor; that time is called *redraw time*. With a **high resolution** file, the redraw time can be quite significant. One way to reduce redraw time is to shrink the window in which the document, image or whatever is displayed. There are several methods to shrink a window: click on the box in the upper right corner, click and drag on the lower right corner or, if the program has the option, choose a lower resolution display.

Redundant Array of Inexpensive Drives   SEE **RAID**.

Reflective color is that color which is visible because light is reflected off (sent to the eye from) a surface, such as paper, cloth and plastic. The **color model** that is used to attempt to define and describe reflective color is **CMY** (cyan, magenta and yellow), though printers add black to it to make it **CMYK**.

In opposition to reflective color is **transmitted color**, which is created by light that is sent through or created by the item, such as a computer monitor and transparency film.   SEE **Color management, Absorptive color, Subtractive color**.

Refresh is a command that tells the software to determine if the information being displayed is the exact same information that is available. In effect, it **redraws** the current window, based on what **data** are in **RAM**, on the **hard drive** and elsewhere in the computer.

Suppose you are viewing the **directory**, or list of files, of a **floppy disk**. When you change floppies, the display of the directory will remain the same, until it is refreshed to show the list of files in the new disk.

Registration is an important aspect of working with printing presses, which, by their nature, will print only one color at a time. Therefore, the paper must go through the presses again, to receive the next color, and the next, until all the necessary colors and combinations of color have been applied. But, if the paper isn't fed into the printing press in exactly the same way, then the colors might not fit on top of each other quite correctly. One color may be **skewed** a bit. It is the responsibility of the **pressman** who runs the presses and the **prepress** experts who prepare the printing plates to assure that all the colors fit together well. This proper fit is called *registration*.

Two methods that the creator of the **image** or **document** can use to help avoid some of the ugliness associated with misregistration are **trapping** and **keep away**. Both methods take for granted that there will be some misregistration, and they attempt to force the inks to look good anyway.

Another definition of *registration* is informing the manufacturers of hardware or software that you have purchased their product. In other words, you send in the registration card that is in the box, via mail, fax or e-mail. The manufacturer then, usually, provides some level of **technical support**, information about **patches**, discounts on **upgrades** and other useful material. Some even have free monthly magazines that offer articles and other tips for using their product and others. They do this to give software users a reason to be legal owners of the software, as well as to maintain a loyal customer base. The value of registration differs among manufacturers, but the support and information that comes when you register many **imaging** programs is among the best.

Relative position is a **clone** tool (**rubberstamp**) option that refers to the relation between the location of the **source point** (where the tool is picking up **color, luminance**, etc.) and the destination point (where the tool is painting with that information). When the relative position option is chosen, then the source and destination points are always at the same distance from and in the same direction to each other. Therefore, if they are separated by 2 inches, with the source point at 45 degrees to the destination point, then that is their relative position when the user starts using the tool, and as he or she continues to use it. In other words, the source point moves about within the image, as the user pushes about the destination point.

This is in opposition to **absolute positioning**, in which the source point is defined by the initial click and stays there, regardless of where the destination point is clicked. However, absolute positioning can be somewhat confusing, because it can act like relative positioning during a brush stroke. At the beginning of each brush stroke, with the clone tool set at absolute position, the source point will return to its original site, regardless of the location of the destination point in the image.

Removable drive is a storage device in which the **media** is a cartridge, **disk**, diskette, etc., that can be separated and pulled out from the drive itself. This allows the media to be exchanged and shared. It is also useful for archival (or long-term) storage.

For instance, **SyQuest** and **Jaz** drives are removable; therefore, their cartridges are commonly used to deliver images to clients, associates and **service bureaus**. When one cartridge is filled up, another is inserted into the drive. Because of their cost and, sometimes, lack of speed, they are generally not used as primary storage devices (to replace the fixed hard drive).

The big problem with removables is that there are so many technologies, brands and **formats** on the market, that you must make certain that the system that the removable drive storage media is being delivered to can read it (i.e., that it has a compatible drive).

Render is the process of applying a series of edits to an **image** or **scene**, when the edits were designed by the user on an interim version of the picture. Rendering is most often associated with **3-D software** and **high resolution proxy editing** software.

With 3-D, the user creates a **scene** made up of various **objects, textures**, lighting effects, reflections, **animations**, etc., using **views** that display minimal detail, to save **redraw** time. The most minimal views are **wireframes** that display shapes and nothing more. Other views will show basic colors but no **highlights, shadows, textures**, etc. So, while the user is editing, the software records all the ways that the user wants to create those details. When the user is finished defining the scene and/or animation, the file that contains all those edits is applied to the file that contains the objects that have been drawn.

Similarly, some **image editing software** (such as **Live Picture** and **Xres**) allow the user to work on a version of a high resolution **image**, so that only those **pixels** that he or she needs are displayed on the screen and held in **memory**. In other words, the user edits and paints on a low resolution version of the picture. This saves **processing** time. Then, at the end of the editing and painting, again, the file that contains all the user's edits, brush strokes, filter choices, etc., is applied to the full-size high resolution file. SEE **Lo res** and **Proxy editing**.

In both cases, rendering takes time—often quite a bit of time, the length of which depends on how much information is held in the editing file, which program is being used and the speed and power of the computer. (Yes, some rendering engines are faster than others.) It's like a mortgage balloon payment. You save time while you are doing the actual editing, but you have to pay for it at the end, by waiting for the final result. However, rendering can be done when you are not there, so it doesn't try your patience the way working on high resolution full-size files or on 3-D scenes that need to constantly redraw full detail can.

By the way, in **networked** imaging systems, rendering is often **off-loaded** to (sent to and done on) a separate, dedicated computer, freeing up the user's computer.

Repeat   SEE **Redo**.

Replace is a command that substitutes an **object**, word or other element with another specified by the user. Replace All searches out all the objects, words or elements in the **image** or **document** that match the user's **search parameters**, and does a **global** substitution.

Resize is a command or an **interactive** tool that changes the size of the current **object, image** or **selected** area. The command opens up a resize **dialog box**, in which the user types in numbers to resize to an absolute and specific size. Or, it can be done interactively, by **clicking and dragging** on the handles or corners of a **bounding box** that surrounds a selected object or area.

Resolution measures **data** density in a picture, or the ability of a device to capture,

RESIZE A

display or **output** that data. This translates into a definable and measurable level of sharpness and detail. However, resolution isn't the only measure of image quality, which can differ among technologies, brands and individual devices.

Inside the computer, image resolution of **raster**-based pictures is measured in **pixels** or in **pixels per inch** (**ppi**).

Monitor resolution is measured in the number of lines that the screen can display, with typical **VGA** being 640×480 and even higher. Most **imagers** will work with monitors that display XGA, or 1024×768, as well as 1280×1024 or 1600×1200.

Printer resolution is defined by **dots** or **dots per inch** (**dpi**). Most **desktop** printers have resolutions of 360, 720, 1,200 or even 1,400 dpi. But monochromes can measure 600×600. Higher resolution desktop monochrome **laser printers** are sometimes sold as inexpensive **imagesetters**,

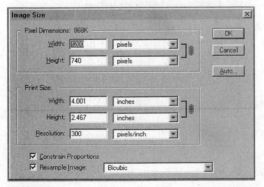

RESIZE B

RESIZE C

Resize: Resizing can be applied to whole images or selected portions of an image, in both vector and raster programs. **(A)** When you want to resize a selected portion of an image, you may be able to choose between interactive resizing or resizing through a dialog. In this picture, we have selected the ball and used Photoshop's Transform command to place a bounding box around that circle. Notice the small squares on the bounding box rectangle. **(B)** When you pull on the squares or nodes of a bounding box (by clicking and dragging with your mouse or stylus), you can interactively resize the selection. And that is what we did here. **(C)** This Photoshop Image Size dialog is quite similar to other program's Resize or Resample dialogs. It is used to change the size of an entire image. When you use a dialog to resize a selection, the dialog that pops up usually looks like this, too.

but they don't give the same kind of quality as the real thing. While most **dye sublimation** printers are 300 dpi devices, it is a somewhat irrelevant measurement of quality for that technology, because these printers melt the dots together.

The resolution of desktop **scanners** and **digital cameras** is usually measured in dpi, though what they produce (for the computer to read) are pixels not dots. On the other hand, **drum** and other high end scanners are often measured in pixels or ppi.

Resolution-independent describes some **images, fonts** or **software** that do not depend on a **high resolution** or density of **pixels** for image quality. For instance, **vector** images (such as those produced by **illustration** or **3-D** programs) and **outline fonts** (such as PostScript or TrueType) are defined mathematically by shape, fill, etc., but not by size. Only when the images, **scenes** or fonts are used by a printer or rendered by the software do resolution requirements come into question.

This resolution independence saves on computer resources and imaging time. For instance, with fonts, it isn't necessary to save a family of **typefaces** in all possible sizes. Only the shape (or outline) is saved on the **hard drive**. Then, the user tells the software what size it should be when it is displayed or **output**.

Software such as **illustration** programs, or high resolution **samplers** like Xres, are also resolution-independent, which means that there is no (or a minimal) delay between a user-applied edit or **brush** stroke and seeing the result on the screen.

Resources are those portions of your computer that are used for processing and which, when occupied by one activity, are not available for others. This includes **memory** (**RAM**), **hard drive** space and **virtual memory**. For instance, suppose you are **outputting** a large file to your **desktop printer**. Memory (both RAM and virtual) will be occupied with processing the image and **queueing** it up for output. And some hard drive space will be needed for any **temp** (°.tmp) files that are generated by the process. Therefore, the resources involved in the printing processes will not be available for other work you might want to do on your computer. If the printing uses up all your resources, for the moment you won't be able to do anything.

Imaging is a resource-intensive process. That's why you will need a computer with lots of memory and hard drive space.

Revert to saved is a command that is found in the File **pulldown menu** in many programs, and it is used as a backdoor exit for a series of foul-up edits.

When all else fails and you have messed up your **image** beyond fixing, you can return it to the state it was in when you last saved it. The revert to saved command throws away all the work you have done on the file since it was last saved to the **hard drive** (or whatever storage device you are using).

Revert to snapshot is a command similar to **revert to saved** in which the user can return the **image** to a previous state, wiping out all recent edits. However, the file is reverted to a point in the editing where the user said, "I like what this picture looks like now," and tells the software to remember everything that has been done to it by taking a **snapshot**. That snapshot is not permanent, can be overwritten by future snapshots or completely lost when the software or the computer is closed out. We prefer saving interim versions of our pictures on our **hard drive** or other storage device. However, snapshots and revert to snapshot are useful if you want to quickly try out a couple of different kinds of edits to decide where to go next with your editing.

RGB is short for red, green, blue, which are the primary colors of one of the most important **color models** in **digital imaging**. RGB is a **subtractive** model used to describe and create **transmitted** colors, such as those that are displayed on a computer monitor.   SEE **Reflective color, Color management, HSB, CIE, CMYK, L*A*B**.

Rhapsody is the code name for **Apple Computer**'s high powered, next-generation **operating system**, being developed for both **PowerMacs** and **PCs**.

Ribbon bar is a horizontal strip of information or options relevant to the current tool or command. However, few programs use the expression *ribbon bar*. A more commonly used phrase for a similar site that displays such information is **status bar**.

Right mouse button, or **right mouse click,** relates only to **PC** (and not **Mac**) pointing devices, which have at least two buttons. The left button is the selector and is used in the same manner as the Mac mouse button. But the right button activates additional options. For instance, using a right mouse click when text or an **object** is selected will usually display a menu of options, including **cut, copy** and **paste**. Then, the user clicks with the left mouse button to choose the option he or she wants. Compared to the bother of finding a command in a **palette** or **pulldown menu**, or using **keyboard shortcuts** (**hot keys**), the right mouse button can save time and effort, and it doesn't interfere with the flow of drawing, painting, writing or other creative endeavors.

RIPping stands for **raster image processing**, which is the transformation or mapping of computer-based **data** that define an **image** or **document** into the specific **dots** that a printer or other **output** device can use to create **hard copy**.

Each of the many hundreds of thousands or millions of dots must be precisely placed in the correct position and told what color and/or density to print. RIPping can take anywhere from a few seconds to many hours, depending on the size and complexity of the file, the speed of the computer's **processor**, the amount of available **RAM**, the output device's software **driver**, the speed of the **port**, and the ability of the device to accept the volume of data or the rate of **dataflow**.

There are specialized **hardware** and **software** schemes, called *RIPpers*, which are supposed to speed up and increase the accuracy of the output. In higher end systems, RIPping may be done by **offloading** the data to a separate dedicated computer, or by tapping the **resources** (RAM, **hard drive** space, etc.) of other computers on a network.

Ripple is a **special effects filter** that jars the **pixels** of an **image** or a **selected** area of an image, so that the result looks like a pond's ripples or like a jagged rush of wind. In most **raster**-based programs, the user can define the number and the extent (amplitude) of the ripples, as well as see the effect of these option choices on a **preview** image.

RISC (*Reduced Instruction Set Computer*) is a high speed, stripped down **CPU**, or **central processor unit**. Its performance is boosted by switching various CPU functions, such as screen controls and keyboard, to **software** rather than burden the CPU with them. This makes the chip simpler than the more standard **CISC** (*Complex Instruction Set Computer*), in which most functions are performed within the CPU itself. Because of the way they deal with mathematics, RISC chips are particularly well suited for **vector graphics** and consistently outperform comparable speed CISC chips.

The Apple/Motorola/IBM **PowerPC** CPU is the best-known and best-selling RISC CPU, although there are others such as MIPS and Alpha. At present, all Intel chips are CISC chips. It is expected that most graphics computers will be RISC powered by the end of the century. Practically all **workstations** currently use RISC chips.

Robust is another of those wonderful words that are now so overused, especially by computerists, that they have become nearly meaningless. When a salesperson or reviewer describes **hardware** or **software** as robust, they are saying that the product is powerful, comprehensive and stable (i.e., supposedly bomb-proof).

Roll-up palette is a special kind of **dialog box** or **palette** found in some programs. It can be minimized to take up less space on the computer screen. However, it is still right there, whenever you need it. In effect, it rolls up into its title bar. Usually, this is controlled with mouse clicks onto a tiny box which may or may not have an arrow in it and which is typically in the right corner of the title bar. When the roll-up palette is fully open, clicking on that box telescopes it down in size. When it is displayed as only a horizontal bar (with the palette's name on it), clicking on the box will open it up fully.

ROM, or **Read-Only Memory,** is a chip with a permanently etched set of instructions burnt into it. It is placed by the manufacturer onto a **motherboard, peripheral board** or other device. The ROM contains coded instructions, or a mini-program, that tells the computer or the device how to function and how to process **data**. Unlike **RAM** (Random Access Memory), this information (which is called *firmware*) cannot be changed or erased by the user. It remains part of the computer or device even when the power is turned off.

For instance, the ROM on a **PC**, called the **BIOS** (*Basic In/Out System*), contains all the information your computer needs to power up and go to the **operating system** on the **hard drive**. The **Mac** ROM actually contains part of the operating system. The

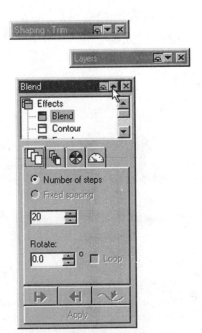

ROLL-UP PALETTE B

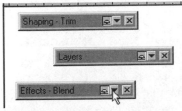

ROLL-UP PALETTE A

Roll-up palette: Some floating palettes can be rolled up into their title bar to save space on the screen. If you see a bar with a down arrow, click on that arrow to open up the palette more fully.

ROMs on a printer may hold **fonts**, as well as information on how to place text and graphics onto the printed page.

Usually, ROMs are a permanent part of the motherboard or the device, but sometimes, the information must be periodically updated (such as changing film **profiles** for a **film recorder**). This is done by burning the new ROM onto a user-replaceable chip, which is swapped for the old chip.

There are other types of ROMs, such as an EPROM and an EEPROM that can be reprogrammed from the computer, typically by using a diskette sent by the manufacturer.

Rosettes are the tight groups of **dots** of the primary ink colors that form from the overprinting of those colors, using **prepress halftone screens**. When the screens haven't been created correctly, these rosettes can create **moiré** patterns or other kinds of visual **noise**. But when the screening is done correctly, rosettes are usually not very noticeable, unless you use a loupe or magnifying glass to study the print.

Rotate is a command or an **interactive** tool that turns an **image, object** or a **selected** area of an image around on a pivot point.

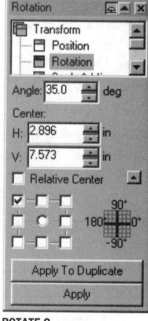

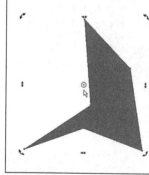

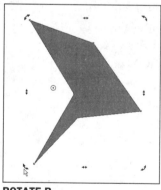

ROTATE A   **ROTATE B**   **ROTATE C**

Rotate: Rotation can be done in most programs either interactively or by dialog. **(A)** When you see an *x* or a circle with a dot in the middle of the interactive rotation, that is the center of rotation, which can be moved by a mouse click and drag. **(B)** The interactive rotation is done by clicking and dragging on a corner or control point, until the object or selected part of an image looks the way you want. In some programs (such as CorelDRAW from which this illustration is taken), you can also click and drag on other points along the sides of the bounding box to skew the object. **(C)** On the other hand, when you use a dialog to rotate, you can define the exact angle, as well as other precise parameters.

Generally, the user can set the command to any degree, clockwise or counterclockwise. However, automatic options may include a quick rotate with a single mouse click at 90 or 180 degrees, clockwise or counterclockwise.

The interactive rotate tool generates a **bounding box** around the area, object or image, and the user clicks and drags on the corners to rotate it to any arbitrary position. In many programs, the interactive tool also allows the user to change the location of the pivot point.

Rotation angle is the measure of direction and degree of a **special effect**, including but not limited to rotation. It is often an option in a **filter dialog box**, and the best way to see how different angles will affect your picture is to type different numbers in that option box. Then, look at the **preview** of the effect.   SEE **Rotate**.

RTF, or Rich Text Format, is a Microsoft file format that retains the various user-defined styles, such as bold or italicized letters, margins and line spacing. It is supposed to retain this information regardless of the program or the computer that generates or reads it.

Rubberstamp   SEE **Clone**.

Ruby mask   SEE **Quick mask**.

Rulers are measurement references that may be displayed on the sides of **images** or on the edges of the **workspace**. In most programs, they can be turned on or off.

In one valuable use for rulers, **guidelines** may or may not be accessed by clicking on the ruler and dragging out from it. As you drag, a line is pulled out that is parallel to the ruler. When you release your mouse button, the guideline is put in place.   SEE **Snap to . . .**.

Even in many programs that don't have **click and drag** pullout guidelines from the rulers, pointers or lines will show the cursor's position, as it relates to the two rulers.

Rulers: To display rulers along the edges of your image, use your program's Show Rulers (or similar command), which may often be found in the View or Window pulldown menu. You can adjust where the zero point of the rulers line up, by clicking on the box where the horizontal and vertical rulers meet and dragging to the point in your image where you want the zero point to be. Then, when you work in the image, most programs will show a line in the rulers corresponding to the location (or coordinates) of your cursor. This can be useful for precise drawing.

Run . . . is the Windows command that will start a program. In Windows 3.x, it is located in the File **pulldown menu**. In Windows 95, 98 or NT, it is found in the nested commands at the lower left corner, that are opened by clicking on the word Start. Choosing Run . . . brings up a **dialog** in which you can type a program's name or executable file, or through which you can browse for the right file name.

Sampling, in **image editing programs**, is the process of taking portions of an **image** or **document** and considering them as representative of the entire image or document. Therefore, when a **high resolution** image is sampled down, every few **pixels** are chosen to be displayed, captured or **output**. The rest are ignored for the moment, so that they don't clog up or slow down **processing**, or they may even be thrown away, if the purpose of the sampling is to **resize** or shrink the image.

Sampling is also called *resampling* in some programs.

In addition, sampling is done to sound and animation files, to capture real-life sound or motion and reduce it to a practical file size and format that the **hardware** can handle, while attempting to hold enough information for realistic replays.

Sans serif is a style of **typeface** that doesn't have extra lines (called *serifs*) as part of the characters. It is considered a clean, modern look. Sans serif is usually used for screen **font** displays, for printed **documents** that impart information, and in **pages** that already have enough graphics and finesse, so that you want some less-complicated elements in the **layout**.   SEE **Serif**.

Sapphire is the brand name of Management Graphics' low end 35mm **film recorder**, which is, in quality, actually better than many other manufacturer's high end recorders.

Saturation refers to the degree or density of color in an **image**. The lower the saturation, the closer to gray the color gets. High saturation color is a vibrant, intense statement that takes more ink to print.

S

Saturation is also one component of the **HSB** (**HSL**) **color model**, in which any color is identified by its **hue** (position within the spectrum of colors), **brightness** (or **luminance**, which is a measure of light), and saturation (the density of color).

Save is a command that records the current file (**document, image** or whatever) to the **hard drive** (or any other **storage device** you are using), using its current name and location on the **storage device**. In doing so, it overwrites (replaces) the original file. If you don't want to overwrite the original file, or if you want to put it into another **folder, directory** or storage device, use the **Save As** command.

If you don't save the file, any work you do on it will disappear when you close it, because what you see on your screen is only in **RAM** (random access memory) or **virtual memory**, both of which are emptied of all **data** when the program is closed. Remember to save your work early and often, if it is important to you, as an important defense against losing data, edits, beautiful paint jobs, etc.

Save As is a **Save** command that opens up a **dialog** in which you can name (or rename) your file (**image, document**, etc.) and/or change the location where it will be saved (**folder, directory, storage device**). Use the Save As command when you want to control where the file is being stored, if you want to change its name and/or if you wish to change the file format.

Scalable refers to the fact that **vector fonts, objects, images**, etc., can be **output** or displayed at any size, with no degradation of quality. That's because vectors consist of mathematically defined shapes, which don't have any size or dimension. Therefore, when the user designates their size, the math formula is recalculated to create the best shape possible at that size for the current display or output device.

Scale is a command or **interactive** tool that **resizes** an **object, image, selected** area of an image, etc.

In some programs, the Scale command opens up a **dialog** in which the user can type the new size in actual measurable

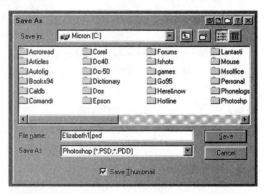

Save As: The dialog that opens up when you use the Save As command allows you to choose the location where you want to save the file, type in its name (if you want to change it—otherwise you'll overwrite or remove the original), determine what file format it should be saved in, and other options, depending on the program and the machine that you are using.

dimensions (such as 4 × 5 inches or 490 × 780 pixels) or as a percentage of the current size (50%, 120%, etc.).

In other programs, the command and/or an interactive tool places a **bounding box** around the object, image or selected area. Then, the user **clicks and drags** on the handles or corner squares of that bounding box rectangle, until the item is the size desired.

Scan is the process of **digitizing** items (photographs, documents, anything) from the real world, so that they can be read and used by a computer. Several devices are used for scanning (**flatbed scanners, film scanners, scanner back** cameras and **drum scanners**), but they all function in essentially the same manner. A beam of light is reflected off or transmitted through the **media** (paper, film and other items). The information that is read from that light is fed to a **CCD** (charge coupled device) or **PMT** (photomultiplier tube), which then hands it off to another internal chip that converts the **analog** to **digital data**. These digital data are then fed directly to the computer. The result is an **image** that you can view on the computer monitor, save to your **hard drive** (or other **storage device**), edit and **output**. However, how each kind of scanning device achieves this basic scenario is what separates the various technologies.

Scanner is a device that captures **pages**, pictures, slides and other material from the real world, **digitizes** it and feeds it to the computer. SEE **Scan, Film scanner, Drum scanner, Scanner back, Flatbed scanner**.

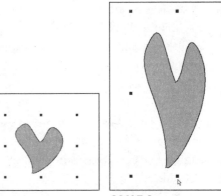

SCALE A   **SCALE C**

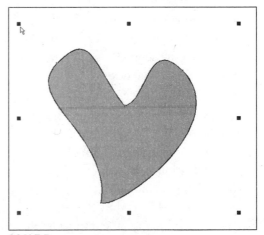

SCALE B

Scale: Generally, if you pull on the corner points or handles with a mouse click and drag, the object or selected area will maintain its aspect ratio as you scale it interactively, as in figure **B**. (In other words, its proportions, or how its length relates to its width, will remain the same.) But, if you pull on side handles or nodes, you will be able to enlarge or make smaller a single dimension, in the way that we stretch our heart in figure **C**. In addition, most programs will allow you to scale an object or selected area through a dialog in which you can be very precise regarding the new measurements and/or the percentage of the original that the area will be scaled.

Scanner back is a device that fits on the back of studio-type cameras (such as a Hasselblad or Sinar). It uses scanning technology to capture what is seen through the camera lens onto the scanner's **CCD** (charge coupled device). That information is then **digitized** and fed to the computer.   SEE **scan**.

Scanner backs can't capture objects in motion, such as players in a sports game, because the scanning can take from 15 seconds to 15 minutes. The longer the scan takes, the **higher resolution** the **image** will be and the larger the image file.

Scanner back cameras capture the highest resolution of any digital camera technology.

Scene, in **3-D** and **animation** programs, refers to the "world" that the user designs. It's where all action takes place . . . **objects** are placed and have spatial relationships to each other; lights cause hot spots, shadows and **highlights**; the **camera** pans and **zooms**; etc. It is what the camera will see, when the scene is **rendered**, plus anything else that is created by the user that exists outside the camera's **view**. Therefore, a scene is more than a stage setting, because it includes the actors—people, animals, animated objects, etc. That's why the expression *world* is such a popular and apt synonym.

For instance, a scene could be a living room, with its furniture, windows (through which sunlight or stars may be seen), a cat and dog, a fireplace, walls, floor, ceiling, fixtures, people, etc. All that must be created (or imported) and placed by the user.

Scitex is a multinational corporation that makes high end **scanners**, printers and machinery for **prepress. Leaf Systems** is a division of Scitex.

Scitex CT is a **file format** that is sometimes used in the prepress process.

Scratch Disk is an area of **hard disk** space (**virtual memory**) that an **application** reserves for editing, **undos** and other functions. That is where the program squirrels away information that it thinks it may need again, soon. This is supposed to speed up **processing**.

Scratch disk is invisible to the user, until it gets filled up. Then, if the program doesn't release the scratch disk memory, the user won't be able to do anything more (including **save** a file) until and unless he or she tells the program to release that area of memory (if the software allows it) or closes the program.

When setting up some **imaging** programs, the user is asked to define how large the scratch disk should be. The problem is to find that sweet number that will give optimum performance, without tying up too many computer resources. With some programs, it's best to have a small scratch disk, or none.

This is especially common among **Windows** programs, because Windows has its own somewhat efficient **memory management** which conflicts with application-based scratch disks.

Scratch Pad is the same thing in the computer as it is in the real world—a place for doodling and playing with color. In some programs, it is where the user can mix colors (as an artist does with a palette) until he or she has just the right one. It is sometimes called a *scratch **palette***.

Screen is the computer's monitor, where the user can view anything and everything that is in the computer, and where edits and painting are done.

In an entirely different vein, screen is a **halftone screen**, in which the **color separated files** of an **image** destined for the printing presses are converted to the **dots** that will define where the ink will fall on the paper.

Screen angle refers to the placement of dots on **halftone screens**. The dots of each color are angled in a different direction. Proper angling will help to avoid **moiré patterns** and other kinds of undesirable **noise** that may occur when the colors are combined by the printing press.

Screen capture is the process of grabbing whatever is displayed on the monitor and saving it as an **image** file that can be reproduced. It is often used to illustrate discussions about software. For instance, we used screen capture software to take snapshots of various program **interfaces, dialogs, pulldown menus, palettes**, etc., to create many of the illustrations in this dictionary.

Screen fonts are the **typefaces** that are used by software to display text on the computer monitor. When you are weeding out fonts from your **hard drive** (because fonts are often the worst space hogs on a system), be careful not to remove the screen fonts. Otherwise, your display will look all wrong.

Screen frequency is a measurement of the **lines per inch** (**lpi**) of a **halftone screen**.

Screen gamma measures light and color that is displayed by a computer monitor and how it needs to be changed to better represent the actual colors in an **image** or **document** file. SEE **Gamma**.

Screening is the **prepress** process of defining and applying **halftone screens** to **color separated** files.

Screen resolution is the measure of the amount of data a computer monitor can display. SEE **Resolution**.

Screen saver is a small program that displays a slide show of pictures, **animations**, logos, etc., whenever the keyboard, **mouse** or other pointing or **input** device hasn't been used for a length of time.

In the early days of computing, having an unchanging display on the screen could actually burn the monitor phosphors. That would result in a permanent ghost image on your screen. So, screen savers were developed to frequently change what was on the monitor, whenever the user wasn't inputting **data**. As soon as the user began typing or pushing around the mouse, the screen saver would disappear and the file that he or she was working on would be revealed again.

Now that monitor technology has improved, savers are used more for entertainment and to keep associates or others from snooping at what you are working on. After a delay with no input, characters from Star Trek, slides of impressionist master paintings, flying dinosaurs, or whatever will hide the display of your current file.

Incidentally, it is now possible to make personalized screen savers from photographs of the new baby or any other **images** you may have. Such screen savers, which are composed of low resolution pictures, can make some nice self-promos for **digital artists**, photographers and other **graphics** specialists.   SEE **Lo res**.

Scroll is the process of moving through a **document** or an **image** to see portions that are not displayed, because the entire document or image is magnified or too large for the window.

Scrolling is achieved in several ways: by using the hand icon (if the program has one) and **clicking and dragging** through the window; by using a **scroll bar**; or, in some cases, by pulling your cursor with your mouse outside the edges of the window (without clicking or dragging).

Scroll bar is a graphic that is automatically displayed on one side and the bottom (or

SCROLL BAR A

SCROLL BAR B

Scroll bar: When we moved the vertical scroll bar (on the right side of the picture), new areas of the picture were displayed. *(Photo from the Corel Stock Photo Library.)*

sometimes the top) of a **window** that is holding a **document, image** or whatever, that is too big to be fully displayed within the window. The scroll bar usually consists of arrows on either end and a box in the middle. The user either clicks on the arrows or **clicks and drags** on the box to move about, or **scroll** through the image.

Similar to scroll bars, boxes and arrows are also often used in **dialogs, palettes** and elsewhere in software to change values or select among options.

SCSI (*Small Computer System Interface*) is a kind of **port** (or **interface**) that is used to connect **peripherals** and high performance **hard drives** to the computer, and which is quite common among **imaging systems**.

To connect a SCSI peripheral (drive, scanner, film recorder, etc.) to your computer, you must have a SCSI **port** on your computer. Otherwise, you'll need to add a SCSI controller board and plug it into one of your computer's **expansion slots**.

Theoretically, depending on the type of SCSI your system has, from 7 to 16 devices can be daisy chained (added one after the other, on the same chain of cables) and connected to the same port on the computer. However, the more devices you put on the chain, the weaker the signal to each becomes. What's more, with SCSI and SCSI-2, the total length of cables on a SCSI chain shouldn't be more than 18 feet—though we've had failures with much shorter chains.

If devices on your SCSI chain don't work, there are various things you can do to try to fix the problem. First check the connections (is everything really plugged in properly?) and make sure that the last device has what is called a *terminator* on it. The terminator (aka *terminating resistor*) lets the computer know that it has reached the end of the chain. Without a terminator, the whole computer will be flaky or will stop working altogether (and you might never know why).

You can also try using new cables. Another possible solution would be to cut back on the number of devices you have attached. (You can add another or several SCSI boards to your computer, to provide additional SCSI ports.) Finally, consider using higher quality cables and a powered terminator.

There are various flavors of SCSI. SCSI-2 is faster and uses a more compact connector. Supposedly, SCSI-2 and 3 can handle up to 18 devices, but we'll believe it when we see it working in real studio conditions. Then, there is wide SCSI and fast SCSI and wide fast ultra SCSI. The manufacturers keep trying to make SCSI better, easier to use, more powerful and faster. That's because they know how important it is, and how frustrating.

We once had an editor tell us that he didn't understand why we were making such a fuss about learning how to tame and control SCSI. That's when we realized that he had little or no personal **imaging** studio experience. Whether you have a **Mac** or a **PC**, when you start adding important peripherals, such as **scanners** or **storage devices**, you'll quickly learn that SCSI is a 21st-century curse word. The only thing is . . . when it works, it's fast and clean. What's more, it is necessary, until something better comes along.   SEE **FireWire, USB**.

Search parameters are the **keywords**, names, dates or other **data** that you input, when you are seeking a file, **image**, document, etc. The program will then look for any data whose description would include those same keywords, names, dates that you indicated. For instance, if you maintain an image **database** (highly recommended), you will probably end up with hundreds, thousands or, even, tens of thousands of images in it. When you want to find that one picture that you took in Cancun at a nightclub, of the native dancers, you would search on those specific parameters: Cancun, nightclub, native, dancers. However, it is necessary to first save those keywords with your picture, to allow you to use them in your search parameters.

Select is the command or process of identifying an **object**, group of text, area of an **image**, or other items on the screen, and telling the software it is what you want to edit, apply a command or **filter** to, or change in some way.

In **illustration, 3-D** and other **vector**-based programs, selecting simply involves clicking your mouse on the item with the **Pick tool** (the arrow icon). If you want to select a group of items or a series of characters, then use a **click and drag** over or around the items. Until it is selected, the item (or items) is uneditable.

In **raster** programs, it is necessary to use special **selection tools** to identify the area of the image that you want to edit. When the selection is active, anything you do (apply a filter, brush on some color, use an **orientation** tool, etc.) will affect only the area that is selected.

Once selected, depending on the program, the item(s) may or may not be interactively resized, rotated or otherwise have its orientation or shape changed by pulling on handles or corner squares.

Select All is a command that **selects** or chooses everything (including hidden items) in the active window or **image**. It's a useful command that avoids the bother of having to pick or draw around each individual item.

Selection box refers to two different but related things.

When you **click and drag** with the **Pick tool** in a **vector**-based program, a rectangle forms that will **select** all the items within it, on the release of the mouse button. The rectangle that you draw for this purpose, and which disappears when you release the mouse button, is often known as a *selection box.*

The selection box is also the rectangle or the group of small-handle boxes that surround a selected **object** or group of objects, in some programs.

Selection marquee is the outline that is formed around a **raster image** or an area of the image, to identify it (or **mask** it) as the area that you want to edit, manipulate, **paint** on or otherwise change. Also called **marching ants**, the marquee is drawn using any of the program's **selection** tools.

In many programs, the selection outline (or marquee) can be hidden from view by the user, to keep it from interfering with his or her ability to see all of the picture. If you forget that a marquee has been hidden, you will have difficulty—lines that you paint, filters that you apply, and/or any other edits you do will affect only those **pixels** inside the marquee (even when it is hidden). Just use the command Show marquee or Show outline to see it. Or, you could use the Select None command (or click in the image with any selection tool) to remove it.   SEE **Marching ants, Marquee, Mask**.

Selection palette is a floating **dialog box** that provides access to all of a **raster** program's various **selection tools** and their **options**. Not all **image editing programs** have a selection palette. The tools may also often be found in a **pulldown menu** at the top of the screen, which is usually called *Select,* and/or in the **toolbox**.

Selection tools are those tools (which are usually identified by rather universal icons) that allow the user to **select** or **mask** areas, **objects** and other **image elements**.

In **raster**-based **image editing programs**, the typical selection tools are rectangle/square, ellipse/circle, **lasso, freehand, color** or **magic wand**, etc.

In **vector**-based programs, there is usually only one selection tool—the **Pick tool**.

Send to back, Send to front   SEE **Move to front, Move to back**.

Separate is a **vector** command that **breaks up objects** into component objects. For instance, a simplified house may be made up of a triangle for the roof, a square for the body of the building, and various rectangles, squares and circles for windows, doors, doorknobs, etc. If all these objects are **linked** or **combined**, then they can be edited and moved together, keeping their spatial relationships. But if you want to edit one of them, independently, say, to make the door a different color, then you would need to separate the door from the rest of the house.

Separation is the **prepress** process of breaking up an **image** into its **primary colors** and saving those component colors as separate files. For instance, if the printing press will be using **CMYK** inks, then the image is separated into four files—one each for the four component primary colors of cyan, magenta, yellow and black. The purpose is to provide the separated information needed to make **halftone** printing plates, each of which will define where each primary color ink will be placed by the printing press.

Separation setup is a **prepress** process (and a **software dialog box**) that defines how **images** will be separated or divided up into component **primary color** files. It provides information about the use of the inks on the printing press, whether **UCR** (*UnderColor Replacement*) or **GCR** (*Gray Component Replacement*) will be used and to what degree, the angles of the **halftone screens** and other specifics. This is one of the areas of prepress that requires finesse, as well as expertise to achieve good results in the final print.

Separation tables are used to define the percentages or amount of **primary color** inks that will be used to generate a picture and/or document on a printing press. Generally, they are used by **imagers** and **graphics** specialists that may use more than one printing house, press, type of paper or inks, but will use each kind of **setup** on a regular basis. Since each such situation requires a different **separation setup**, it can be useful to save the setup for future use.

Serial interface is a **port**, usually built into the computer, that is used for medium-speed **peripherals**, such as a **mouse, drawing tablet, fax/ modem, hand scanner** or **entry level digital camera**. Most serial ports have 9 pins, though older ones have 25 pins and may require a convertor plug to use with the newer smaller port. Serial devices can be positioned up to 50 feet away from the computer, but they transfer data only 1 bit at a time.

Serial ports used to be popular for attaching printers, but because of the size of graphics files and the greater speed of other interfaces (**parallel, SCSI, Ethernet**, etc.) few manufacturers make serial printers any longer.

Most computers have at least two serial ports, but it is possible to add more. The technocrats' terms for the serial interface protocols are RS-232 (**PC**) and RS-422 (**Mac**).   SEE **USB**.

Serial port SEE **Serial interface**.

Serif are the tiny, decorative extra lines on the main strokes of **typefaces**. Serif type tends to look more elegant and old-fashioned than **sans serif** (which doesn't have those extra little lines). A design rule of thumb is to not use more than one serif typeface on a **page**, if you want a clean look.

Server is a computer within a **network** that is dedicated to keeping the network running and the various computers communicating.

A **print server** is a special type of server that is connected to a printer on the network and which handles and **queues** all the print jobs sent to that printer from the various computers on the network.

Other servers may be a dedicated computer used for **rendering**, holding files, etc.

Service bureau is the **digital** age's equivalent to a photo lab and/or print shop. Depending on the organization, it may offer a variety of services—**scanning, color separations**, printing, **outputting** to film, retouching, etc.

The equipment and **software** used by service bureaus may or may not be superior to what the average **digital artist** may have in his or her studio. But a good service bureau is an important partner and aid for the **imager** who is interested in producing quality pictures. The problem is that there is little, if any, regulation regarding who can call themselves a *service bureau*. So, the only assurance you will have is to check reputation and give them a test job.

Setup is the process of defining, installing and/or organizing **software, hardware**, tasks, etc. In other words, you are setting up how the computer or program will run and what you want it to do.

Shadow is an area of a **raster**-based or **bitmapped image** where there is less light than in the rest of the picture. One of the tests of quality is how much detail can be discerned in shadowy areas.

Shareware is software that may be provided for free, but for which you are expected to pay a (usually very reasonable) fee, if you plan to use it. The developers of shareware are often generous individuals who believe in the kindness of strangers. The nice thing to do is go ahead and send in that fee. After all, it will connect you with the people who can help you get the most

Sans Serif

Serif

Serif: Notice the Serif's extra lines on the ends of the *S*, the bottom and top of the *R*, *I* and *F*. Sans Serif fonts do not have these extra bits.

from the program (including, sometimes, documentation), will provide access to upgrades, and, besides, they're the folks who spent all that time creating the program. For those of us who are creators, it makes sense to support the rights of other creators.

Sharpen is a **filter** that attempts to increase the focus of a **raster**-based **image** (including photographs) by analyzing the areas where relative darkness and light are adjacent and increasing that difference. That's because the computer and **imaging** software see focus where such differences between light and dark are strongest.

Shear is an **orientation** tool that tilts an **object** or a **selected** area of an **image**, so that it looks like it is being pushed over. Essentially, two opposite sides are kept at the same original angle; the other two sides are tilted to a new, user-defined angle.

Sheet-fed refers to a printer that **outputs** onto individual pages of paper (or sheets of **media**) rather than using rolls that must be cut (usually by a blade within the printer).

It also refers to **scanners** that can automatically **input** pages that are fed in one after the other by some sort of roller mechanism. (For many practical reasons, serious **graphics** professionals don't use sheet-fed scanners.)

Shift key, in **imaging**, is much more than just a keyboard button that you push to capitalize a letter. It can also be used to access options for a tool, command, **brush**, etc. When using a tool, just hold the Shift key to see what happens. Often the **status bar**, or information bar, at the bottom of the screen will tell you how it will change the tool. In other programs, you need to play with it, to see what happens.

The Shift key is often used in conjunction with other **constraining** or **modifying** keys, such as the **Alternate** (ALT), **Command, Control** (CTL), **Option** (OPT), etc., to access other options and to form **hot keys** (shortcuts to commands and tools).

Shortcut key   SEE **Hot key**.

Show . . . is a command that displays **palettes**, hidden **image elements, toolboxes** and other items. Because the **imaging** screen can become cluttered, most artists choose to show only that which they need at any one time. The rest remains hidden, until they are brought up with a Show . . . command, which is usually found in one of the **pulldown menus** at the top of the screen. Another way of uncluttering the monitor is to minimize **rollup palettes**, if the program has them.

By the way, in some programs, to show a tool's palette or options, just double-click on the tool's icon in the toolbox.

Shrinkwrapped refers to the clear plastic that envelops brand new boxes of **software** and **hardware**. If it is shrinkwrapped, it is new and a shipping (as opposed to a **beta** or test) version.

Shrinkwrap also refers to self-contained ready-to-use software and/or hardware that does not need additional programming or work (other than installation) to perform correctly.

SIMM   SEE **RAM**.

Simplify is a command that reduces the number of **nodes** that are used to defined a **Bezier** or **spline** curve. Extra nodes (or points of definition) can cause a curve to be less accurate and will take up more **memory** and other resources for **saving** and **outputting**. Therefore, the ideal would be to have only the number of defining points that are needed to describe that unique shape—no more and no less.

Size   SEE **Resize, Scale**.

Skew is an orientation command that tilts a selected object or an area of an image. It usually works interactively, with the user pulling on **handles** or corners placed by the **selection tool** or by the command. To set the change, you often have to click inside the **bounding box** or selection area. Otherwise, the area or object may return to its original orientation when you are finished. Also, skew is when paper is fed at an angle through a printer or scanner and produces sideways or distorted results.

Slide printer is another name for **film recorder**, a device that captures a digital image from a computer and puts it onto traditional film.

Slider is an **interactive** tool for choosing the level or value of an option of a command, **filter, palette, dialog**, etc. As with a **scroll bar,** it can be adjusted by either clicking on arrowheads or by clicking and dragging on a bar or box that can be moved within a larger bar.

Slot   SEE **Expansion slot**.

Smudge is a **raster** tool that is usually represented by a pointing finger icon. It mushes the colors of adjacent **pixels** together. Using it is like fingerpainting on your computer monitor.

Smudge: We used the smudge (or fingertip) tool on a hard straight line and then magnified it to show what the tool actually does. Notice that it not only pushes color from one area of the picture into another, but it also softens (or feathers) the effect by introducing transparent values of that color around the new area. That's what creates the blur.

Snappy is a brand-name **video capture device**.

Snapshot is a command (usually found in the File **pulldown menu**) that puts the current version of an image into **memory**. That way, you can try out an editing idea and, if you don't like it, you can use the command **revert to snapshot**, which will restore the image to the status it was when you squir-reled it away into memory.

However, like anything saved in memory, a snapshot is impermanent and can be wiped away. If you really like that version of the picture, we recom-mend saving it to a unique name on your **hard drive** or elsewhere on a **storage device**.

Snap to . . . is a command, usually found in **illustration, 3-D, desktop pub-lishing** and other **vector** programs, which tells the program to **align** an **object** or other **image element** to another object, **grid, guideline**, etc. In many programs, you can set up all objects and elements to automatically snap to the grid and/or guidelines.

For instance, suppose you draw a rectangle. If the Snap to grid is turned on, then the first corner and side of the rectangle will automatically move to the closest grid or guideline. And, as you draw the shape, the last placed edge or corner will jerk toward the next grid or guideline and the next, until you release the mouse button. On the release, that side and/or corner will automatically snap to the closest grid or guideline.

It is also possible to set up objects so that they snap to each other at a specified point or line. Therefore, a circle that is being drawn might connect automatically to the right side of a triangle.

Snap to is a user-definable and controllable option.

SneakerNet is the sarcastic name given to computers in the same or adjacent offices that need to share **data**, but which are not connected via a **network**. The data needs to be saved to a **floppy** or some other removable **medium**. Then, the user is supposed to put on his or her sneakers and run the file over to the other user.

Soft fonts are **typefaces** that are provided as **software** and saved on the com-puter's **hard drive** or other **storage device**. When the user wants the printer to use a soft font, the program from which he or she prints will send the font to the printer. The opposite are hard fonts, which are built into the hardware of a printer. Soft fonts are also called *downloadable fonts*.

Software are the **programs** and other code that make computers do what they do—**image editing, word processing**, sending **e-mail**, organizing **folders**, communicating with **printers** or **scanners**, optimizing **hard drive** performance, etc. This is in opposition to **hardware**, which are the physical **components** of the computer and its peripherals. You can't physically touch software, as you can hardware. The **floppy disks, CDs** and other **storage media**, which you can touch and which hold the software, are simply containers for the code and not the code itself.

Software driver   SEE **Driver**.

Solarize is a **special effects filter** that alters a **pixel**-based image in a manner similar to having a light turned on for a short moment at a crucial point while developing film in a darkroom. The result is that the **highlights** and brighter colors are reversed (as in the print's negative), but the **shadows** and **midtones** remain the same.

Solitaire is the brand name of a high end **film recorder** manufactured by Management Graphics, Inc.

Sound board is a peripheral that transforms **analog** music into **digital data** that can be reproduced, edited, played and stored on a computer. Most computers come equipped with sound boards or built-in sound circuitry that permits CDs to be played. Also, when used in conjunction with a **CD-R, CD-RW** or **DVD-W** drive, it allows music to be recorded for playback on a corresponding stereo system.

Source point is the **pixel** on which the user clicks with the **clone tool** (or **rubber-stamp**) to define the area from which the clone tool should pick up color, **luminescence**, etc., with which to paint at the **destination point**.

Special effects are changes made to an **image, selected** area of an image, an **object**, a **scene** or an **animation**, which alters its **orientation**, shape, composition, colors, lighting or other definitive elements. Just think of Holly-

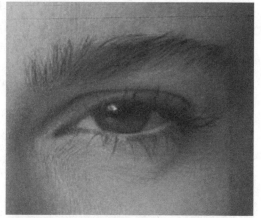

SOLARIZE A

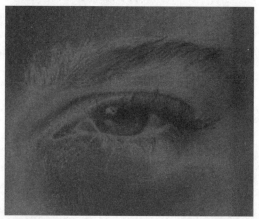

SOLARIZE B

Solarize: Though at first glance, the solarized version of this picture **(B)** may look like a negative, if you look closely, you'll realize that many of the colors (especially among shadows and midtones) are identical to the original **(A)**. For instance, look at the pupil. Solarizing a color image can create some interesting, almost psychedelic effects—changing bright colors to opposite hues on the color wheel.

wood's cinematic special effects, and you'll have the idea. For instance, moving words that break up into fireworks would be one kind of special effect.

Many of **imaging's** special effects are created using **filters** (**subprograms** or **macros** that work from within an **application**). These filters may ship as part of the program, or may be **plug-ins** that are sold by a separate manufacturer and which can be added to (or plugged into) the primary program. For instance, a photograph can be made to look like a sketch, with a **Find edges** filter, or like a bas relief with the **emboss** filter.

Another kind of special effect is the strange way that scenes or slides can be made to transition to the next one. The popular page curl special effect looks as though the current scene or slide is turning at a corner, to reveal the next one.

Just about every **imaging** program has some special effects shipped with it and/or available as plug-ins. However, other special effects, such as **morphing**, may be the whole purpose of a specific program.

Speckles is a type of image **noise**, or **artifacts**, that look like dust on a picture.

Spectrum is the full range of **hues**, or the many wavelengths of color, as they melt from one to the other, seamlessly. Think of a rainbow; that's a type of spectrum. However, a real spectrum doesn't have a beginning or an end, because every hue will blend into the next, as the wavelengths gradually change.

The **color wheel** is one type of software representation of the spectrum. In it, red flows into orange, to yellow, to green, to cyan, to blue, to magenta and back to red. Though the color wheel may show all the hues in the spectrum, it doesn't display all colors. The reason for this is that a color may be more-or-less saturated, more-or-less bright or dark. That's the basis of the **HSB** (**HSL**) **color model**, in which any color can be defined by its hue, **saturation** and **brightness**. Therefore, a color wheel **dialog** may have a **slider** that increases or decreases saturation or brightness.

The spectrum (or rainbow) options in **gradient** (or **fountain**) **fills** actually fills an **object, selected area**, type or whatever with all the hues that stretch between the starting and ending colors, within the color wheel. But if the starting and ending colors are at different levels of brightness or saturation, the gradient will concurrently travel along those continuums, too. SEE Color pages.

Spherize is a **special effect filter** that alters a **selected** area of an **image** so that it looks as though it were stretched over a three-dimensional globe. This is done by pressing out and enlarging the center, adding a highlight and

Spherize: A Spherize command was used on a circular selection of this New York cityscape, to create this bubble effect. *(Photo from the Corel Stock Photo Library.)*

keeping the outer **pixels** essentially the same (or bringing them in closer, depending on the specific filter). Some versions of spherize will allow the user to define where the highlight will be; others are arbitrary.

Spike is a sudden and sharp increase in the amount of electrical current pushing through your lines and into your equipment. A spike can be destructive to both **data** and **hardware**. That's the reason we recommend putting a **surge suppressor**, line stabilizer, **uninterruptible power supply, standby power supply** or any combination of these gizmos that are designed to flatten spikes before they can kill your data and/or your hardware. Because it's estimated that up to 90% of all unexplained computer glitches are due to "dirty power" (mostly spikes), the more you spend on protection, the safer your equipment and data will be.

Spin box is a graphic used by many programs as a method to set the value of a variable. In it, the user can either type a number into a box, or use the up and down arrows to spin through incremental numbers. It's similar to **Slider**.

Spline is a **vector**-based tool for defining curves, which, like the **Bezier**, uses **nodes**, or **control points**. These user-placed nodes direct where the curve will be, turn, arch, etc.

There is a difference between the Bezier and the spline tools. Using the Bezier, the curve line will always intersect with every node. (That's why you can get jagged shapes using it.) But, with the spline tool, the curve will be a best-fit, smooth line among the nodes. For those readers who are mathematically inclined . . . the spline's node controls (which, in turn, control the direction of the curve) are invisible tangent lines that go through the nodes and just touch the curve, at one point.

Both the Bezier and spline are invaluable tools for the accurate drawing of irregular shapes—so much so that at least one of them is provided in just about every professional quality **imaging** program (**vector-** and **raster-** based).

Split bar is a horizontal or vertical line that divides a **window** into two parts. Though it is seldom used in **imaging**, support software (such as **operating systems**) will often allow the user to set a split bar, to increase the amount or type of information being displayed. For instance, in **Windows** machines, the **File Manager**, File Explorer or the **File Navigator** will split windows, so that you can view all the **subdirectories** or **folders** in a drive on one side, and all the files in a specific subdirectory or folder on the other side.

Split channels is a **prepress** command that **separates** a color **bitmapped**, or **raster**-based, **image** into **grayscale** images, each of which represents a **primary color**. While many **image editing programs** don't use the name *split channels* for the command, it is the same thing as **color separation**.

Sponge is an **image editing** tool that picks up or removes color **saturation**, much as a real world painter's sponge is used to dab at just-applied paints to soften them or remove some of their density.

Spool is the process of feeding **data** and/or files to a **queue**, which holds them until the final destination is ready to receive them.

For instance, a **printer spooler** receives **images, documents** and other data when a program's Print command is used. Then, the spooler feeds the pictures, files, etc., to the printer as it is finished with the previous job. This is necessary because the **software** that creates the print jobs is much faster than the **hardware** that does the printing.

The hardware or software scheme that allows spooling to take place (that is, it has the **memory** to temporarily hold the data) is sometimes also called a **buffer**.

Spot color is an ink that is used on printing presses, which isn't defined by the various amounts of its **primary colors** (as in **process color**). Instead, it is identified by its brand name and reference number.

Each manufacturer (such as **Pantone**) sells an entire spectrum of spot inks to print shops and **service bureaus**, and each individual ink is named and/or numbered. The same companies that sell the inks to the printing companies also have software **palettes** or **swatches** which can be plugged into just about every professional-level **imaging** program. In fact, many programs come with major manufacturers' spot colors already part of the programming. Whether you **plug in** a swatch or it comes with your software, the colors are usually accessed as a palette option or **import**.

It's the comparison of colors in these digital palettes to a printed **swatch book** from the same manufacturer that gives the user some control over the appearance of the spot color in the final print job. When the user wants to choose a specific color, he or she chooses it from a printed **swatch**, looks at the name and number, then chooses that particular spot color from the software palette to use in the **digital** design. When the **service bureau** receives the file of the image, all the spot colors are (or should be) identified by name and number. Therefore, there should be no doubt what color the designer meant.

Spot color is usually used in print jobs that don't require too many colors, since each one necessitates a separate print run. For instance, it may be used to give the headlines of a newsletter and the logo a bit of visual boost. Photographs and other **bitmapped images** are seldom printed using spot color, since **process colors**, or **color separation**, printing can provide a much wider range of colors. On the other hand, spot color is very popular in **vector**-based images, such as those created using **illustration** or **desktop publishing programs**.

Spotlight is a **lighting effect** that emulates a stage spotlight. In other words, it has a narrow beam, tends to be rather bright and casts strong shadows.

Spreadsheet is a **document** that handles **data** (text and numbers), which are laid out in the columns and rows of a table. Calculations may be performed automatically (or as needed) by the spreadsheet software, which relate that data to each other. For instance, in a row that expresses the cost of rent over a time period, the first column may be the monthly rate. In the next column, the monthly rate may be multiplied by 12, to get the yearly rate. And, in the next column, the yearly rate may be multiplied by the three years of the rental contract.

Spreadsheets are useful for projecting "what-if" scenarios that may help you in pricing out the cost of an **imaging** job or project.

SPS (*Standby Power Supply*) is a device that consists of a battery and various electronic components that detect when the power from the wall outlet dips below a certain point. It then usually emits a sharp sound and/or sets off a flashing light, to let you know that it is switching your computer over to battery power. All this is done within 1 to 4 milliseconds. That's usually fast enough to keep the computer and monitor running without any interruption. The battery then provides enough time (5 to 20 minutes) for the user to finish the current task, save the **data** and close out the **software** and machine properly, before turning off. An SPS is valuable for any user who can't afford to have a computer freeze (which means losing all current unsaved data).

More expensive than an SPS is a **UPS** (*Uninterruptable Power Supply*) in which the computer and monitor are continuously running off the battery which is, in turn, continuously being recharged.

SRAM   SEE **RAM, Volatile memory**.

Stand-alone program is **software** that doesn't need any other program (besides the computer's **operating system**) to function. This is in opposition to an **applet, subprogram, plug-in** or other software that runs inside or dependent on another **application**.

Standard mode is the status of any command, tool, **filter, brush** or whatever whose options are set at their defaults, or the most common setting.

Standard Web Offset Publication   SEE **SWOP**.

Standby Power Supply   SEE **SPS**.

State-of-the-art is an expression used to indicate that a piece of **software, hardware** or any other technology is the most modern, up-to-date and includes the newest features—at least as many as the competition.

The problem with state-of-the-art products in **imaging** is that they become yesterday's news so quickly (sometimes while the item is still in the dealer's showroom). We prefer to stick with the best that we can afford at the time that we are buying, which does what we need it to do. And, we accept the fact that something faster, better, newer will certainly come streaming by, very soon, much sooner than we will be ready to buy again.

Even so, state-of-the-art is one of the many useful criteria to use when purchasing equipment and **programs**. It forestalls the inevitable obsolescence just a bit longer.

Status line (or status bar) is usually displayed toward the bottom of the program window. It provides often useful information about the selected area, tool or current command.

Steps are the incremental transitions of a **color gradient** or an **object blend**.

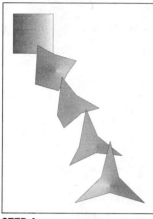

STEP A

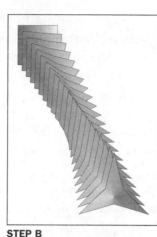

STEP B

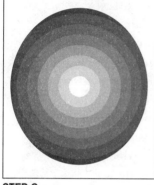

STEP C

STEP D

Steps: When we set this rectangle and star to blend (or morph) into each other, we tried it at two different settings—**(A)** 3 steps and **(B)** 20 steps. The number of steps determines how many intermediate objects will be created between the two original objects.

The number of steps in a gradient blend determine how smoothly the colors will change from one to the other. In picture **C**, the steps are set at only 10, which creates prominent banding. But when the steps are set at the highest you can go—255—the color transitions are smooth and seamless **(D)**. However, the greater the number of steps, the more resources the picture requires. Therefore, the trick is to find the lowest number of steps for a smooth gradient, without being so low that it will band.

If it is referring to a color gradient, then the steps are the number of colors that will be used to move the gradient from the starting to the ending color. The larger the number of steps, the smoother the gradient will be. A lower number of steps may result in undesirable **banding**, or obvious stripes of color.

When defining a blend between two objects, the user-designated number of steps refers to how many interim shapes will be used to **morph** or change the shape of the first object into the ending one.

Still video camera is a **filmless camera** that saves the captured **image** as **analog** rather than **digital data**. To get the image onto a computer, it must first be converted using an **analog-to-digital** device or chip.

Because they are analog, still video cameras can feed their images directly to television sets for immediate viewing. But when the still video's digitally converted images, that are fed to and **output** from the computer, are compared to the same picture captured by a **digital filmless camera** in the same price range, the still video camera's images are nearly always inferior to that of the digital camera. Recognizing the advantages and disadvantages of both technologies, many digital cameras incorporate both digital and still video functions (or **video-out** capabilities). That way, you get the image quality of a digital filmless camera (when you feed the picture to your computer), plus the convenience of being able to immediately display the picture on a TV monitor.

Stochastic screening is a comparatively new method of creating the dot patterns, or screens, that are used to determine where ink will be placed by the printing presses. Also called FM (*frequency-modulated*) screening, the placement and the size of the **dots** may be varied. While it is a more cumbersome and technologically intense (and, therefore, more expensive) process, the lack of **halftone screens** and the tiny dots of stochastic screening often produce smoother skintones, brighter metallics and other finer tones. What's more, stochastic printing has the potential for a higher **resolution** picture, using the same size image file. It is also said to help to avoid **moiré** patterns.

However, it is not the final solution for printing, because it has some inherent drawbacks that retard its general acceptance. Not all subjects are reproduced better, and it is easier to make mistakes in the setup which can cause the printed page to look inferior to offset printing. Still, with proper management of the **setup** and when used for the right subjects, a stochastic print literally shines when compared to a traditional halftone print of the same subject.

Some manufacturers are saying that they will be bringing stochastic printing to the desktop. It would be a nice development that would add even more options to the **print setup**. In the meantime, it is available in **PostScript imagesetters**.

Stock photographs are pictures that tend to be very generic in subject and can be used for various purposes. The **license** to use the photographs is sold by agents who generally work for or with the photographer, though some buy all rights from the photographer and then try to recoup their costs. SEE **License, Copyright**.

Storage device is a piece of hardware that can save **images, documents**, settings and **drivers** for your **peripherals**, and other **data** and **software**. The information remains in the storage device, even when the power is turned off.

There are many kinds of storage devices, each of which may be used in various ways. The **hard drive** on your computer is a storage device, as is the floppy disk drive (with a disk). **Removable storage devices** such as **SyQuests, CD-Rs, Zips, Jaz** and others are used for archiving, sharing, delivering and otherwise **offloading** images and other files from the hard drive. SEE **Archival**.

Without storage devices, it would be impossible to save your **imaging** work.

Storage media are those materials that are used by **storage devices** to save and backup **images, documents** and other **data** or **software**. For instance, a tape drive's medium is the tape. A **SyQuest**'s medium is the **cartridge** that is inserted and removed from the drive. SEE **Removable storage device**.

Streaming tape is the reel-to-reel tape that you see on the computers in the old sci fi movies. They were used to hold systems' information, **programs** and **data**. While **service bureaus** and other companies that have large mainframe computers may still use magnetic streaming tape, it is generally unnecessary (and overkill) for **desktop imaging** systems.

Stretching is the process of pulling an **object** or a **selected** area of an **image** in one direction. The resulting distortion makes the item look as if it were, well, stretched. SEE **Distort**.

Stroke is a command that draws a line where there is a **selection marquee** (outline) or a **path** (curve). The color and the size of the line are usually chosen by the user.

Style is a predefined (by the user or by a program) formula for the appearance of a **page** or **document**. It sets up the margins, **typefaces**, placement of pictures, columns and all other graphical or text elements. In many programs, it is done using what are called *style sheets* or **templates**.

For instance, in the now popular greeting card programs, the user is given several style sheets for different occasions, into which he or she may drop a personal photo or some **clip art**, and add personal text. The result is a fully customized birthday or Valentine's Day card, with a picture of Fido or your last vacation together, and both the recipient's and the sender's names.

Styles are also developed for magazines, newsletters and other publications, to make sure that each issue has the same look and feel as the last.

There are other definitions for style, such as the style of text, which may be normal, italics, underlined, bold, etc. Or the style of a paintbrush, which may fade as you stroke with it, or it might have a calligraphic flare.

Style sheet SEE **Style**.

S

Stylus is a pencil-shaped **pointing device**, which augments or replaces a **mouse**. It is used with a **digitizing tablet** and provides a greater level of control for the **digital artist**. That is because it is a more natural shape for drawing, usually can be set to an **absolute position** in relation to what is on the screen, and, in many cases, is **pressure-sensitive** (reacts to the pressure of the artist's hand, as a real brush would).

When working with **natural media emulating software**, a stylus is almost necessary. However, using it for anything other than actually drawing or painting on the computer (such as for selecting options in **pulldown menus** or in **palettes**) can cause hand cramping. That's why many artists, who are used to working long hours, will often use a stylus in addition to a mouse or a **puck**.

Subdirectory is an **operating system** division of the hard drive in computers that use **Windows 3.x** or **UNIX**. It's similar to the **folders** on **Macs**, and on machines that use **Windows** 95, **98** or **NT**. To make it easier to find programs and files, the user designates directories and subdirectories.

The common analogy to explain directories, subdirectories and folders is a room filled with filing cabinets. Each filing cabinet holds specific kinds of documents. Think of each of those cabinets as a directory. Each cabinet may have two, three or four drawers. Now, consider those drawers as subdirectories. Furthermore, each drawer is filled with dividers—in the computer, they would be the same as subdirectories within subdirectories.

For instance, suppose you divide your **hard drive** so that each **program** has its own directory (with its installed subdirectories). One other directory you may have could be where you save all your **images**. The subdirectories of that image directory may be one for each project. Inside the project subdirectory may be subdirectories containing: original **scans**, color corrected files, **composites**, etc.

The way a user organizes directories and subdirectories is a very personal choice—just as the way you arrange your desk drawer. The most important guiding rule is to be sure that it is logical to you, so that you can find the file you need whenever you need it.

Subprogram is a small routine subset, or bit of programming, that runs within another, larger **application**, and it is called up by that application when it is required or requested. For instance, a **scanner driver**, which activates the scanner from the **Acquire** command in the File **pulldown menu** of an **image editing program**, is a subprogram.

Subroutine is a portion of a program designed for a specific task. It is not separate from the main program and is invoked only where that particular function or **data** are required. For instance, a **desktop publishing program** may include a subroutine for converting all lowercase letters to uppercase.

Subscribe   SEE **Publish and subscribe**.

Subscribe and publish   SEE **Publish and subscribe**.

Subset   SEE **Subprogram**.

Subtract is a **vector** command that reduces

Subtract: When you subtract an overlapping circle from the shown rectangle, the result is the irregular shape on the right.

the area of one object by the area of another object. For instance, suppose you have a circle intersecting with the corner of a rectangle. If you subtract the circle from the rectangle, the resulting shape would be a rectangle with a curved indent at one corner.

Subtractive color is the **color model** that is used to describe **reflective**, real world color. That is, it deals with the colors that we see because they are reflected off objects, pages, etc. According to this color model, black is created when pure cyan, magenta and yellow are mixed in equal parts. However, pragmatically, it is necessary to add some black ink to the mixture when printing.   SEE **CMYK, RGB, Additive color, Transmitted color, Color management**.

Suite is a group of **programs** from the same **vendor** that are sold as a package. The purpose is to provide what is called a *complete solution*. Each of the programs deals with a different kind of task in a (usually) related field.

For instance, a **graphics** suite may include an **illustration** program, an **image editing program**, a **presentation program** and a **desktop publishing program**. Depending on the suite and the manufacturer, the programs may be so well integrated to each other, that you can just **drag and drop image** elements from one to another, as well as read and write each other's **file formats**. Other suites are just a marketing mishmash of unrelated programs. As a rule, most suites are less expensive than the total price of the individual programs would be, if purchased separately.

Sun Microsystems is a major manufacturer of high end **graphics workstations**, which run under **UNIX**. They are also the inventors of **JAVA**, which is a programming language for graphics on the **Internet**.

Surge is an electrical power anomaly, very similar to a **spike**, but usually longer lived and not as intense. It can seriously affect your **hardware, software** or **data**. As we have said before, do whatever you can to protect your system from electrical problems.   SEE **Surge suppressor**.

Surge suppressor is an electrical device designed to dampen or absorb **surges** and **spikes** in the electric current that runs your computer equipment. While many manufacturers promise complete protection, the truth is that surge suppressors have no effect on brownouts, blackouts and, often, major spikes and surges. Also, surge suppressors can age and lose their effectiveness. So, they should be periodically tested and replaced.

The best thing to do is buy those surge suppressors that carry $25,000 insurance policies, so that you have someone to call, when and if your equipment is damaged. Obviously, those suppressors do a pretty good job, because they don't have to pay off very often.

SVGA (*Super Video Graphics Adapter*) is a midrange PC **graphics** display standard in which the **resolution** on a screen is projected at 800×600 or 1024×768 **pixels**, in 32,000 or 256 colors.

Monitors that display above 1024×768, or **24-bit true color** (**16.7 million colors**), are called XGA.

S-Video is a standard for transmitting video signals from a Hi8 or super VHS videotape or camera. It is used in some **frame grabber boards** to capture **images**.

Swap file is an area of the **hard drive** in which **Windows 3.x** places information about currently active programs and files. Because it is a scheme for freeing up **RAM** space, it is a type of **virtual memory**.

When you set up your swap file, you have the option of making it permanent or temporary. A permanent swap file takes control of a contiguous area (a solid empty area) of the **hard drive**, in which there are no other **data**. A temporary one puts pieces of files and **software** wherever there happens to be room on the drive. Generally, the permanent option creates a faster swap file, because the computer doesn't have to go looking in nooks and crannies for pieces of **data** and, then, stitch them back together. By the way, permanent is a relative expression. As with anything in virtual memory, data in a swap file disappear when the program is closed.

Well, that isn't always true. Whenever a program or Windows isn't closed properly, pieces of the swap file can be left on the hard drive. These are useless data that take up space. If you are sure you know which files are important and which ones aren't, you can get rid of these bits and pieces (sometimes called *fragments* or *lost clusters*) of old swap files. Do a search for °.tmp (any file with the extension .tmp). Then, if you are sure that the .tmp files found are ones that you don't need, delete them.

Swatch is a representation of a series of colors, based on some defined standard. Since the colors are thus standardized, it helps with developing color consistency through the entire design/prepress/printing process.

Swatches are made available in several formats. Two are important to **imagers**: as a booklet, fan card or other paper-based display; or, as a piece of **software** that, in many cases, may be **plugged into** an **imaging** program's color **palette**. Both the **digital** and the printed version of the swatch relate to the same **spot** or **process color** inks.

Another type of swatch is used for **color calibration**, either as a **scanner** target (a transparency or card that is scanned in to establish an initial point of reference for **color management**) and/or as a card that is held up to the display of the same colors on the monitor (for some rather inefficient adjusting of monitor colors to a standard).

SWOP (*Standard Web Offset Publication*) are the recognized standards for generating **color separations** for **process colors**, which are destined to be printed on a **Web** press. In other words, it defines the handling of color for magazines, newspapers and other large volume print jobs.

SyQuest is a brand of **removable storage devices** and **media** that are used throughout the **graphics** industry for **archiving**, sharing and delivering **image** files. SyQuests range in size from 44-**megabyte** to 1.3-**gigabyte** cartridges. Unfortunately, SyQuest has many different formats, and one drive may or may not read a **cartridge** created by another. However, SyQuest is an industry standard for sharing files, whose speed is based on the fact that each cartridge is in reality a self-contained **hard drive**. It used to dominate the graphics field but has since been eclipsed by Iomega's **Zip** and **Jaz** drives.

Symmetrical node is a control point in a **Bezier** curve in which the line or curve on either side will mirror each other (be the exact opposite) in their behavior at that point.

System is the generic word for a computer and its attached **peripherals**.

System.ini is a file used by all versions of **Windows**, that defines what **hardware** and **software** is attached to it. If the **operating system** doesn't find a properly set up system.ini, when it starts up, it may not work properly or at all.

One of the advantages of system.ini is that it's a text file, which means it can be edited with any **word processor** or text editor, or inspected with any viewer software. However, if you don't know what you are doing, don't touch your system.ini, or, at least, make sure that you have a **backup** copy with a different name on your hard drive before you attempt any editing of it.

System 8.x is the primary **operating system** (OS) for **Mac** computers (just as DOS and/or **Windows** is the operating system for the great majority of PCs).

The *x* can be replaced by a number, depending on the incremental version of the OS. For instance, the current, newest Mac operating system is 8.1, though 6.5 is still commonly in use.

When the number to the left of the dot (the 8 in this case) changes, that represents a major **upgrade** or change in the **program**.

System color table is an option in the process of converting **24-bit color** to **indexed color**. When the system color table is used, the 16.7 million colors of the 24-bit **image** are **mapped** (or redirected) to the **256 colors** of the indexed version, using the computer's **operating system's color palette**. This is a useful option when you want to convert a series of pictures and have a consistency among them.

System requirements are the minimum computer configuration (amount of **RAM, hard drive** space, type of **graphics** display, kind of **processor**, etc.) needed to run a particular **program** or operate a certain **peripheral**. System requirements are usually published at the beginning or the end of the **documentation** of program or peripheral, as well as often on the box. If you don't have at least the minimum system requirements on your computer, you probably won't be able to run the device or program.

System resources   SEE **Resources**.

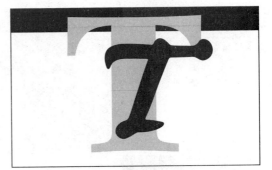

Tab key is used to jump the **cursor** or the **selection** to the next space, position or **object**. If you hold the **Shift** key while pressing the Tab key, the cursor will move to the previous space, position or object. It's generally used as a shortcut to replace moving your **mouse** or other **pointing device** and clicking on the new place you want your cursor.

For instance, let's say you are in a **dialog box**, setting various options for a **filter**. When you have entered the value of the first option, pressing the Tab key will put your cursor into the next option.

In **vector**-based programs, such as **illustration** software, you may be able to use the Tab key to **select** each object, in turn, in the order in which they were created. This is sometimes a last resort for finding a hidden object or selecting something whose defining lines and points overlap too many other objects.

Tabbed notebook is a graphic metaphor that displays groups of **icons**, options, commands, tools or whatever, so that it looks like a school notebook. Click on a tab, and the page associated with it is revealed. That way, a larger number of icons, commands, tools, etc., are more quickly accessible, while taking up less screen space.

In some programs, it is possible to "tear off" a tabbed page from the notebook. This is done by **clicking and dragging** on the tab, and its purpose is to expose more options, commands, etc., for immediate use. A torn off tabbed page can be clicked and dragged back into the notebook.

Tablet   SEE **Digitizer**.

Tagged Image File Format   SEE **TIFF**.

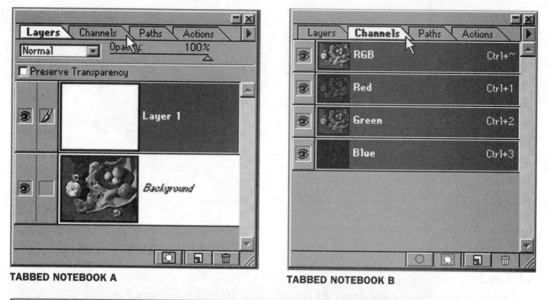

TABBED NOTEBOOK A

TABBED NOTEBOOK B

TABBED NOTEBOOK C

Tabbed notebook: (A) When you call up Photoshop's Layer's palette, you see other tabbed palettes nested with it. **(B)** Click on one of the other tabs—such as the one marked *Channels*—and another palette is revealed. **(C)** If you click and drag on any of the tabs—as we did with the Channels tab—you can "rip" off a page from the tabbed notebook. That allows you to view several of the palettes side by side at one time. However, to save space on your monitor, you can also click and drag other tabbed pages into a nest.

Take snapshot   SEE **Snapshot**.

Tape drive is a **storage device** that reads and writes **data** from and to magnetic tape. Tape drives are discrete devices; that means they read and write data sequentially and not randomly. So, it takes a lot longer to get to any specific data from the tape.

Think of the difference between listening to Barbra Streisand on a tape cassette and on a phonograph record. If you want to go from track 1 to track 12 on the tape, you have to fast forward through 2, 3, 4, etc., until you reach 12. With the phonograph record, you simply lift up the needle and move it to track 12. The tape cassette could be said to be a discrete device, while the phonograph can move about and read randomly (with a little help).

This is the reason tape drives are not suitable for everyday computing needs. However, their capability to record huge amounts of data, and at a cost of pennies per **megabyte**, make them useful **archival** and **backup** devices for permanent **image** and file storage.

The most commonly used tape drives are **DAT** (*Digital Audio Tape*) and **QIC** (*Quarter-Inch Cartridge*). The 4mm and 8mm DAT drives record **digitally** and can hold up to 8 gigabytes per tape. The downside is that the DAT drives and tapes are usually more expensive. QIC drives and tapes use more convenient cartridges and cost less, but they are not digital devices, and they generally cannot hold as much data. Obviously, between the two, the tape drive of preference for most professional imagers is DAT. However, CD-R and DVD drives may eventually replace tape as the preferred backup, because they are random access not discrete devices, and their cost is comparable.

Targa (*Truevision Advanced Raster Graphics Adapter*) is a DOS **raster** file **format**, whose **extension** is TGA. It is used primarily on **PC systems** that have a Truevision **video board**, but many professional **imaging** programs allow Targa files to be imported or exported, at varying levels of **resolution**—16-, 24- or 32-bit color.

Targa is also the name of graphics boards made by Truevision.

Tech support is the organization and group of people that a manufacturer sets up to provide technical assistance to **registered** owners of its **software** or **hardware**. They are there to help with **installation** and **setup**, getting the product to work with your particular **system** and **peripherals**, troubleshooting when something goes wrong or doesn't work, helping you **upgrade**, etc.

The level of tech support that a company offers is an important measure of the value of a purchase of their product. A decreasing number of manufacturers have toll-free phone numbers, which you can call whenever you encounter difficulties. Many of the toll-free services have been discontinued, requiring that you pay long-distance phone charges. In addition, quite a few companies are now limiting the number of calls, their length and/or the period of time from date of purchase (or your first call) during which you may continue to call for assistance. After your limit has been reached, tech support will cost money, based on either a contractual rate, a per minute cost or some other scheme.

Other kinds of tech support that are more often free is on the company's **Web page**, through their **BBS** or fax back. The fax back system works in combination with an automated voice phone, in which you press numbers on your touch tone telephone in response to questions. Out of that session, you should get to a point where you hear a description of a document that is supposed to provide the information that you need. If you want to receive that document, you again use the telephone handset to input your fax number. Then, you hang up. Not too long after that, you should receive a fax containing the full document that was described.

Tech support can also be provided by an entirely independent company that sells its services (by the minute or through an annual contract).

Technical support   SEE **Tech support**.

Tektronix is a Fortune 500 company, one important division of which manufactures high end **graphics** and business color printers. (They are also well known for their medical and scientific equipment.)

Temp files   SEE **TMP files**.

Template is a formatted **document** or **page**, which the user can customize by placing **text**, pictures and other material. Many **illustration, desktop publishing, word processing** and other **programs** include templates for newsletters, **letterheads**, posters, business cards, greeting cards, etc. SEE **Style**.

Terminal is a computer that is attached to a **mainframe** or **mini-computer**. Generally speaking, it cannot get much or any work done without using **data** and/or **software** that is stored on the larger machine. In an office or studio environment that is **networked**, everybody may work on a terminal rather than have individual **desktop computers**. A terminal can look just like a desktop computer, in that it has a **monitor, keyboard, floppy** drive and **mouse**.

Terminator (or terminating resistor)   SEE **SCSI**.

Test pattern is, typically, a graphic that contains **text** and lines of different sizes, and/or pure primary colors. It is used to test the **resolution**, color reproduction and other capabilities of **scanners**, printers and other **input** or **output** devices.   SEE **Calibration**.

Text is words, letters, numbers or other characters. It may be the body of a **document** meant to impart information, or it may be a design element in an **image**.

The text tool in **imaging** programs is usually represented by an icon that has a capital *A* or *T* on it. Using it, you can access and use any **fonts** that are on your computer.

Text editor is a primitive and limited **word processing program**, and is often a **subprogram** within an **operating system** or **application program**, in which text is used as part of layout, or as instructions to tell the computer what to do. It is also useful for quickly viewing and/or changing text files such as the readme files (that contain important information about installed **software** or **hardware** that didn't make it into the documentation).

Text tool   SEE **Text**.

Text wrap   SEE **Word wrap**.

Texture is **imaging**'s interpretation of real world surfaces, such as wood, cloth, metal, flower petals, etc. It is introduced into the computer either as a **digitized** photograph or as a drawn representation of the material, and It can be used in many interesting ways, depending on the **program** and the type of **software**.

At the most basic level, a texture is used to **fill** an **object** or area of an **image**. Therefore, a background may be filled with a cloudy sky or a crevassed marble surface.

Textures may also be used to create **bump maps**, in which the material pattern is used in the **alpha channel** of the image or object, to determine how light will react to it. The reason it is called a *bump map* is that the light acting on the texture can make the item look bumpy.

Libraries of textures may be included with **image editing, illustration, 3-D** and other programs. In addition, you may be able to add **scanned** or drawn textures, and/or purchase additional libraries that may be **plugged into** the program. It all depends on the software, its versatility and if it supports an **open architecture** (that is, allows **third-party** companies to develop and market add-ons to fit into the program).

Texture fill   SEE **Texture**.

TGA SEE **Targa**.

Thermal dye transfer SEE **Dye sublimation printer**.

Third-party describes a company that develops and sells additional **hardware** or **software**, designed to work with or inside an **application** or a piece of equipment. Usually, a third-party product won't work on your computer, unless the product that it is meant to enhance is also present.

    If the first party is the buyer (you), and the second party is the seller (the manufacturer of the primary program or hardware), then the third party would be a company that wants to somehow enhance or be included in that relationship between the first and second parties. At least, that's the origin of the phrase.

    For instance, third-party **filters** would include those **special effects** that **plug into** (work from within) programs such as **Photoshop, PhotoDeluxe** and **Picture Publisher**. Such filters are manufactured and sold by companies such as **MetaCreations**.

Threshold is a **raster** command in which the user defines a level of light within an **image**. Any **pixel** below that level is set to black, and any above it is set to white. In this way, color and **grayscale** pictures are converted to high contrast **1-bit** (black and white) images.

THRESHOLD A

THRESHOLD B

THRESHOLD C

Threshold: When we call up the Threshold command on this grayscale photo of the Statue of Liberty, a dialog opens up. At the center of that dialog is a histogram that shows the dynamic range (the spread between shadows, midtones and highlights) of the original photo. And you can choose the point in that histogram below which every pixel will turn black and above which every other pixel will turn white. As you can see, different points of threshold will retain different areas of detail.

Threshold may also be used in a similar manner to define what portions of an image will be changed by some effects. In that situation, threshold may also be called *tolerance.*

Thumbnail is a tiny representation of a picture, which gives the user just enough information to visually identify the image. It is too small to edit, **output** or do anything other than view.

Thumbnails are often displayed to show what pictures are stored in an image **database**, in a **digital camera**, on a **Photo CD** and elsewhere. Some **imaging** programs also create thumbnails for the open and **save dialogs**, which conserves effort and time.

Thumbnails are very useful; if you can see the picture before you open it onto your computer screen, you can know whether or not it's the one you need.

TIFF (*Tagged Image File Format*) is a **bitmapped** or **raster** file **format** that is used by all **image editing** and **paint programs**, on most **platforms** (including **Macs**, **PCs**, and **UNIX**-based **workstations**). Therefore, it is an excellent format for exchanging **images**.

Because it was originally developed by Aldus (which has since been gobbled up by **Adobe**) for the specific purpose of saving **scanned** images, it is particularly well suited for **photorealistic** pictures.

There are several kinds of TIFF, including one version that includes **LZW compression**. Be careful when you use LZW; not all the programs that can read, write, import and/or export TIFF can handle TIFF/LZW.

Tile is a command that is used to arrange **windows** on the screen, so that they fit together, edge to edge, as tiles on the floor do. This enables you to see all the **documents, images** and other windows that are open. It is useful if you want to do side-by-side comparisons, or if one window has been buried by all the others and you're having difficulty locating it.

Another Tile command arranges a **pattern** or **texture**, so that it repeats itself as it fills an **object**, an area of an **image** or a page.

.TMP is the **extension** for temporary files. They are created on the **hard drive** (or other **storage device**) by **programs** and the **operating system**, when **data** need to be put aside for the moment. The software doing this expects to need that data again, soon.

For instance, when **spooling** pictures to a printer, the software will create .tmp files to hold the **image** data, until the printer is ready to receive it.

Sometimes, .tmp files are left on the hard drive, taking up space, when they are no longer needed and can't be used anymore. So, it is important to do periodic hard disk housecleaning to sweep them away. There are several **utilities** for locating and deleting .tmp and other unused files.   SEE **Swap file** for one rather inelegant method of removing .tmp files from **Windows** machines.

Toggle is a switch or an option, in which there are only two choices—on or off, black or white, yes or no, etc.

In **software**, a toggle may be a **radio button** or check box in a **dialog box**, in which the user clicks to choose the "on" option.

In **hardware**, a toggle is a pin or a rocker switch, which has only two positions. Since it is often used in the **installation** and **setup** of the hardware, when the pin or switch isn't toggled to the correct position, the **peripheral** may not work at all, or work improperly.

Token-ring network is IBM's method of connecting computers and **peripherals** in a **local area network**. If you are using **Ethernet**, it is not compatible with token-ring.

Tolerance is a setting for the **magic/color wand** and **paint bucket** tools, which determines how extensively the tool will cover.

Both tools function based on color similarity, which starts with a single **mouse** click. The tool reads the color of the **pixel** under that click, and then seeks out all adjacent pixels that are similar in color to the one that was clicked. If the tool's tolerance is set at a low number, then the colors must be very similar to the one that was clicked on, to be included. (That, in turn, means that the magic wand will create a small selection, or the paint bucket will change the color of only a small area.) If the tolerance is set higher, more pixels will be included (the selection will be larger or the color change wider ranging), because the tool has a greater flexibility or tolerance regarding how close in similarity the color needs to be.

Tolerance (or threshold) is also a user-definable level of change that can effect or command will cause.

Toolbar is a thin rectangular grouping of **icons** that is often positioned to the side or

Toolbox: Photoshop's toolbox arrangement is very similar to many other programs, which is only natural, since Photoshop was a trailblazer in desktop imaging.

the top of the screen, though it may be placed or moved elsewhere (depending on the program). It is a narrow bar as opposed to the boxes that form **toolboxes**.

Toolbox is a grouping of tool **icons**, usually organized in a rectangle. It is a very useful arrangement, which places the most frequently used tools a mouse click away. While some software allow toolboxes to be hidden or put away to free up monitor space, the user can bring them up again with a **Show** or similar command.

Toyo colors is a brand of **spot color** inks.

Trace is a command or tool that can be used to "convert" **raster (bitmapped) images** to **vector**.

Actually, it isn't really a conversion, but the net result is that you end up with an **illustration** that is similar to a **pixel**-based picture. It works, because the software can place a translucent image **window** over the original picture, just as an artist might put tracing paper over a photograph. So, when the user

Trace: Tracing converts a bitmapped image (such as a photograph) into a vector by actually tracing the contours of the image, using vector (or illustration) tools. Here, we have used an autotrace utility (this one from Corel) to give us the starting point for our work. But now, we have to spend some time eliminating extraneous lines, nodes and objects. However, the end result, when filled with the appropriate colors, can be a rather good illustration. *(Photo from the Corel Stock Photo Library.)*

draws with the tracing tool (a **Bezier** or **spline** tool), he or she can follow the contours of the original picture, while drawing on a new empty canvas.

There are autotrace commands, in which the illustration software will attempt to create curves where it finds **edges** in the bitmapped picture. We have never been really satisfied with the results of autotraces, but they can be a good starting point, after which we do quite a bit of editing and **simplifying** (removing extra **nodes** and lines). The problem, as with any automatic command in **imaging**, is that computers are dumb, nonaesthetic machines, that make design decisions based on mathematics, not creativity.

Trackball is a **pointing device** that functions like a **mouse**, in that it is used to select and click on commands, to change the location of the **cursor** on the computer **monitor**, and to otherwise interact with objects on the screen. However, a trackball doesn't move about on your desk, like a mouse. Instead, a ball sits in a socket, and the user pushes the ball to rotate it within that socket, and that, in turn, moves the cursor, etc.

Transformation tools change the shape and/or **orientation** of an **object** or a **selected** area of an **image**. These include **rotate, skew, stretch, resize**, etc.

Transmission is the act or process of sending **data** from one computer to another, usually by telephone **modem** or **network**.

Transmit or send is the act or transmitting. It usually refers to **uploading** or **downloading** data via a **communications program** or over the **Internet**.

Transmitted color is that color which you see on a computer **monitor** or a TV. Its source is light that is sent directly from the monitor, TV, lamp or whatever. This is in opposition to reflected or **reflective color**, such as those colors on a printed page. Transmitted color is made up of the **primary colors** of red, green and blue, and follows the rules of the **RGB color model**.

Transparency is the quality of a color, **brush, layer, object**, etc., if what is under it can be seen through it. The level of transparency is often determined in a **palette** or **dialog box**, with a sliding scale, in which the extremes are full opacity and complete invisibility. The user then chooses a value between those two extremes, to set the level of transparency.

Trapping is a **prepress** technique used when two colors will be printed, so that they touch right next to each other. Because each color must be printed in a different print run, there may be **registration** problems, in which white paper may show

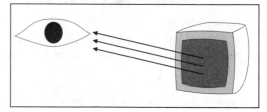

TRANSMITTED COLOR

through where the colors should be meeting. To avoid this, graphics artists will overlay the two colors, with one spreading out over onto the other, in the design. That technique (which is also called *spreading* and/or *choking*) is trapping.

Trash is where you throw unwanted material—**files, programs, images, folders**, etc., that you know you will never want again. On **Macs**, you literally drag it to a trash can icon. On Windows machines, you remove them by selecting the item with your mouse and, then, using the Delete key. In most cases, a final step is required—to empty the trash. Until then, it can be a relatively easy matter to restore trashed items. After you empty the trash, you need to use special **utility** programs to try to restore the thrown away items, but that isn't always possible. The more recently something was trashed, the more likely it is that you will be able to restore it. That's because the area on your **hard drive** where the **data** used to be is more likely not to have been overwritten if the data were trashed recently.

Trash can   SEE **Trash**.

Tri-linear array is a **charge coupled device** (**CDD**) in which all three **primary colors** are exposed simultaneously through a sandwiched red, blue and green filter pack. Most portable **digital cameras** use a tri-linear array technology, which is what allows them to capture action shots.

Trim has two different definitions, depending on whether you are in a **vector** or a **raster** program.

In **image editing programs**, the trim tool (or **crop** tool) is used to remove outer areas from a picture. After clicking on the trim tool **icon**, the user draws a rectangle (or **bounding box**) around the area he or she wants to retain. The rectangle may be **interactively** resized or edited by **clicking and dragging** on its corners or **handles**. Then, when he or she clicks inside the rectangle, everything that was outside the bounding box is thrown away, and the picture becomes only that which was inside the rectangle.

In **illustration** programs, trim is an **intersection** command that **subtracts** one shape from another. For instance, if you have a triangle **intersecting** with a rectangle, you can trim the triangle into a parallelogram, removing one of the corner points.

Trimetric view displays three-dimensional **objects** within a two-dimensional space (such as a computer monitor), without any of the **perspective** angling and shortening of lines that give the illusion that the back edges and sides are farther away than the front ones. In the trimetric view, if one side is supposed to be equal in size to another, regardless of whether they are closer to the front or not, they will be, literally and measurably, equal—you can even hold a ruler up to the monitor to measure them.

Trimetric view is an attempt by **draw** programs to emulate the ability of **CAD** software, to provide precise design models that can be used for actual manufacture.

Tritone is a **raster image** that is created using only three colors. This makes it reproducible using **spot colors** on an **offset** printing press, while still maintaining any **photorealism** that the picture may have.

True color is **photorealistic, 24-bit color**, which can generate up to **16.7 million** separate colors. Using the **RGB color model**, it is generated by 8 bits of information related to each of the three primary color channels of red, green and blue. True color is the closest the computer can get to the number of colors that the human eye can see, which is why it is called *true*.

TrueType are **Apple Computer** Company's **outline** or **scalable** fonts, which are saved on the **hard drive** as **vector** (mathematical) files, and which are generated at whatever size the user needs for viewing them on the screen or **outputting**. They are used on **Macs** and on **PCs**.

Trumatch is a brand of **process color** inks, for which printed and **digital swatch** books are available.

Tutorial is a lesson or group of lessons that will show you how to use a piece of **software** or **hardware**. The best are **interactive**, in which you actually do the work yourself, following instructions in a booklet, **documentation**, on a **CD-ROM** or elsewhere. Even experts will take tutorials to get to know a new product—especially software—because it is the quickest way to learn its special features, peculiarities and the way the engineers who created it think.

TWAIN is an acronym for, yes it's true, *Technology Without An Interesting Name*. It is a standard for attaching **peripherals** to computers and accessing them through **applications**.

Many **scanners** and **digital cameras** are TWAIN-compliant, which means that after you install them, you can use them directly from inside your **image editing, word processing** or **desktop publishing program**.

Twirl is a **special effects** filter that spins the **pixels** of an **image** or a **selected** area of an image around a center point. The amount of that spin is usually controlled by the user.

Type   SEE **Typeface**.

Type align is a command or a type of program that shapes **text** so that it follows a margin, **path**, curve or the outline of an **object**. For instance, when type is

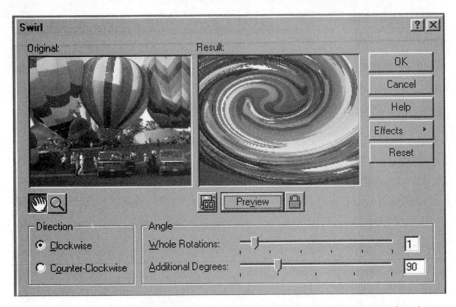

Twirl: A Twirl filter (which may also be called a *swirl*) can make an attractive, but unrecognizable, whirlwind of colors from a photograph or other bitmap image. Sometimes, when we want a pretty texture, we'll just paint different colors onto a blank canvas. Then, we'll apply a Twirl, followed by a Polar Coordinate filter. *(Photo from the Corel Stock Photo Library.)*

aligned to the right margin, the first character of every line fits right above and below other lines, as in a book or letter. But in many programs, you can also fit text so that it follows the shape of, say, a star or of the horizon.

Typeface is a family of characters that have a recognizably related style. Choosing the right typeface can change the entire feeling of a **page**— whether it is formal, lively, serious, etc.

A typeface is different from a **font**, in that the typeface is the family, and the fonts are the individual styles (normal, bold, italic, italic bold and other, sometimes fancy, variations).

Typeover is a **toggle key** that will cause what is typed to replace what is on the screen. When the toggle is in its other position—insert—whatever is typed fits into the position of the cursor, pushing everything that comes after it on the screen, further down.

Typo is a boo-boo, or mistake. Thank goodness for computers that make it so easy to proofread, spell check and correct. We hope that there are no typos in this book.

UBM stands for *Upper Memory Block,* an unused and unassigned **address** or **memory** location in the **PC operating system** where **peripherals'** software **drivers** are frequently loaded and managed.

UCR   SEE **UnderColor Removal**.

Undelete is a rather useful command that undos the last delete. In other words, if you use the Delete command to remove an **object, selected** area of an **image**, some **text** or whatever, you can use the Undelete command to restore it—if you haven't deleted anything else since then, and if the program has this command.

UnderColor Removal (UCR) is an important aspect of the **prepress** process, which is required because the **CMY color model** (which usually governs **offset printing**) generally won't work in the real world. To attain strong blacks and an overall crispness, it is necessary to add black ink to the mixture. But that requires that the amounts of cyan, magenta and yellow inks (**process colors**) also be adjusted to keep from using too much total ink (which increases costs, affects drying time, diminishes the durability of the paper, and can make a print job a literal mess). That's where UCR or **GCR (Gray Component Removal)** come into the picture (both of which are called **black generation**).

In the **color separation setup**, it is necessary to determine how much cyan, magenta and yellow to remove, and how much black needs to be added. Considerations that affect these decisions include the kind of composition it is, the printing press, the inks and the paper that will be used. Setup also requires not only expertise, but also an unquantifiable spark of insight and knowledge about how things work. That's the reason graphic arts is an *art* and not science.

UCR works mostly in the shadows of a picture, replacing the cyan-, magenta- and yellow-created dark grays with black ink. In opposition, GCR works wherever the process colors are at near equal levels and, therefore, make neutrals, including midtones, highlights and shadows. That overall effectiveness is why many professionals tend to prefer GCR for most compositions.

Be advised, black generation (whether UCR or GCR) is a complex and important issue that must be handled carefully, or an entire print job can be ruined. If you venture into this most meticulous area of prepress, be sure to work closely with the print shop and/or **service bureau**. In fact, try to work on a personal level, directly with the **pressman** who will be doing the actual printing and the **separation** expert who will be making the plates.

Underline is a style of **font** in which an underscoring line is placed automatically, directly below the **text**, as it is created. <u>This is an example of underlining.</u>

Undo is a command that cancels out the very last thing you did.

For instance, if you use a **brush** in a **paint program**, and you don't like the result, you can remove that brushstroke from your picture, using the Undo command or **icon**. But it works only if you haven't done anything else since you painted that stroke, or if the program has an undo list feature, which you have activated.

The Undo works by putting the most recent action into **memory**, along with information about what your **image, document, scene** or whatever looked like before that action. Since that takes up memory, it is usually replaced by the next action (and undo information). However, some programs do have undo lists, or multiple undos, in which they retain a long series of actions (and their related undos) in memory.

When you call up the undo list, it displays a description of your edits (the number of edits held in memory may be set by the user). You then choose at which point in that series things went wrong and click on it in the list. Your picture then reverts to the state it was in just before that clicked-on action.

Undo lists would be a great feature, if only they didn't take up so much memory. We tend to use interim **hard drive** saves to unique names, to protect variations of our images, to keep memory from filling up.

Undo list   SEE **Undo**.

Ungroup is a **vector** command that breaks up **grouped objects**. The user may group objects to keep them together in a certain spatial relationship; to add fills, textures or special effects to all of them at the same time; or for any of a number of other reasons. But eventually, he or she may wish to edit only one portion of the group. That is when the Ungroup command is useful.

Uninstall is a command that does much more than simply delete a program from the **hard drive**. It also seeks out any **subprograms**, pointers in the **operating system** and other bits and pieces of the application that were added to the computer (during the install or while using the program), so that the application could work properly and smoothly. If you just delete an unwanted program, all those extras will stay on your hard drive, cluttering it up and, possibly, interfering with the operating system and other applications.

There are several uninstall **utilities** (or separate programs) that work well on both **PCs** and **Macs**. Also, **Windows 95/98** and **Windows NT** have their own uninstalls. The way they work is by keeping track of all programs that are installed and the ways in which they change the **system**'s operating **environment**. Then, when the user chooses to uninstall the program, the utility is supposed to restore the system to a status in which there is no indication that the program was ever there.

Unfortunately, uninstall programs rarely work perfectly, so users will probably end up with some vestiges that cannot be deleted automatically. Either you must live with these remnants—which can interfere with other programs—or search and destroy them manually, a difficult and thankless task.

Always use *uninstall* rather than *delete* to remove a program.

Uninteruptible Power Supply   SEE **UPS**.

Union is a **vector** command that **combines** or **groups objects**. Generally speaking, when the command Union is used, the resulting complex shape will no longer be able to be broken apart into its component objects. On the other hand, grouped objects may be **ungrouped**.

Universal Serial Bus, also called USB, is a new kind of **port**, or **interface**, which establishes the connections and communication between a computer and **peripherals**, such as a printer, **pointing devices** and **scanner**. It differs from the traditional **serial** port (RS-232 or RS-422) in two ways: (1) it transfers **data** at much higher speeds, and (2) up to 128 devices can be attached or unattached—**hot swapped**—while the computer is running.

USB computers are just being introduced into the marketplace, as we write, and many industry experts predict that USB will supersede and eventually replace most serial and **parallel** ports, within a short time.

UNIX is an **operating system** that is used on high end **workstations**, mini-computers and mainframes. It is very powerful, complicated, convoluted and difficult to use, as well a being a **resource** hog. But people who use UNIX think that all other operating systems are toys for wimps. Don't be intimidated; plenty of top-notch, professional imaging is done on non-UNIX **desktop** systems.

Unload is a command that removes extra **typefaces**, color **palettes, clip art**, etc., from a **program, dialog box** or other **interface**. When such items are no longer needed, it makes sense to put them away, so that they don't take up monitor space, **memory** and other **resources**. You can always **load** them again, when needed.

Unlock   SEE **Padlock symbol**.

Unsharpen mask is actually a **sharpen filter** that increases the focus of a **pixel**-based **image** (such as a **digitized** photograph).

The reason for the seeming contradiction in the name of this filter stretches back to the non**digital** darkroom days of photography, when a negative of a picture would be reshot over a blurred print of the same picture. The resulting high contrast print would be sharper than the original. Like other sharpen filters, it works because it increases the differences between bright and dark areas, which is the way the human eye (and the computer) defines sharpness. But it makes these changes only where there is already a significant level of contrast, leaving other areas in the picture as they were.

In desktop **image editing programs**, the unsharp mask is the most precise of all the sharpen filters, and it requires the greatest amount of user control and decisions. There are three values that the user must set: amount, radius and **threshold**. The amount refers to how much the contrast will be increased. The radius defines

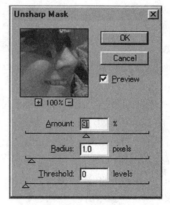

Unsharp: The unsharp filter dialog requires that the user decide at what values to set the radius, threshold and amount of the effect. Rather than worry too much about the meaning of those terms, experiment with how each changes the preview of your image. But remember not to believe everything you see on your monitor. Check the results as a print or whatever final display medium you will be using.

what areas will be changed, by setting the distance from the contrasting edge, where the filter will have an affect. And the threshold determines how different the dark and bright areas must be to be considered an area of contrast that can be improved.

Unzip is the process of uncompressing zipped files, so that they may be read. While *zip* and *unzip* are traditionally phrases that relate to any **compression** scheme, they are also used to specifically refer to files that have been compressed (shrunk) or uncompressed (re-inflated) using **PKzip** or WinZip **shareware** programs.   SEE **Zip**.

Update has several meanings that relate to computers and **imaging**. Essentially, anything that can be changed may also require updating.

When using **OLE** on a **Windows** machine or **Subscribe and Publish** on a **Mac**, if you change a file in its native **program**, it must be updated (made to reflect those changes) in the program where it is embedded or published. Usually, this is done automatically.

Update is also a synonym for **refresh**, that is, when information currently displayed on the screen doesn't accurately reflect the **data** in your computer. For instance, you may change floppy disks, but the files listed on your screen are those from the previous floppy. The screen needs to be updated or refreshed, so that it reads and displays the correct data from the new floppy.

Upgrade describes new versions or improvements in **hardware** or **software** just released by the manufacturer. This is often done by simply inserting a floppy or CD-ROM (provided by the manufacturer) into your drive and letting it do the job of seeking out what it needs to find and installing the new stuff. Or, it may require taking a **peripheral** (such as a printer or scanner) back to the store, so that new **firmware** can be programmed.

In software, there are major, minor and interim upgrades, and they are noted by the **version** number that follows the program name. For instance, an upgrade from Program 1.0 to 1.1 is usually a minor upgrade; but from 1.1 to 2.0 is a major upgrade, or a major revamping of what the program does, how it works, and what functions it offers. An interim upgrade, also called a *bug patch* (code that fixes mistakes in the programming), usually has a letter after the number, such as 2.1*a* or 2.1*b*. Bug patches or fixes are often downloadable from the manufacturer's **Web page**.

Upload is the act, process or procedure of sending or **transmitting data** from one computer to another, either by telephone **modem** or over a **network**. Its opposite function is **downloading**, which is receiving data from another computer.

UPS (*Uninterruptible Power Supply*) is a device that consists of a battery and various electronic components that feeds a continuous stream of "clean" power to your computer and monitor. It protects against power **surges, spikes, dips, brownouts, blackouts** and other power anomalies. If the supply of electricity that continuously recharges the battery drops below a certain point, or ceases altogether, the UPS usually emits a sharp sound and/or sets off a flashing light, to let you know that the battery will last only 5, 10, 30 or more minutes (depending on the size of the battery and the power draw of the computer and monitor) before losing power. That's more than enough time for the user to finish the current task, save the **data** and close out the **software** and machine properly, before turning off. A UPS is valuable for any user who can't afford to have a computer freeze (which means losing all current unsaved data). SEE **SPS**.

URL is short for *Uniform Resource Locator,* which directs the viewer to another file, document or page, generally on the **Internet**. For instance, a Web page may have a "click here" button or **hotspot**, which, when clicked, may access another **Web page**. An increasing number of imaging programs allow designers to embed URL hotspots into their pictures. Then, when the picture is used on the Internet, the URL hotspot becomes a "click here" point. The information that identifies the URL address is saved in an image map file. SEE **Mapping**.

USB SEE **Universal Serial Bus**.

User is a person who sits at a computer and finds something in it that he or she wants to do. It is a generic term that has no sex, no personality and no assumed level of competency.

User Defined is any command, **brush, filter**, tool or whatever that may be custom designed by the person using it. Therefore, the user may input values that can change how that tool, etc., will work.

Utilities are **programs** designed to keep a computer running smoothly and efficiently. They are technical in nature and do things like backing up your **data**, optimizing the **hard drive**, recovering lost or accidentally deleted files, rebuilding a damaged **FAT** (File Allocation Table), freeing up more **memory** for your programs, etc. SEE **Backup, Optimize**.

Although **Windows**, DOS and **System 8.x** come with a variety of utilities, there are many companies that sell **third-party** utilities that may be better or more extensive for working on those **operating systems**, than what Microsoft or Apple provide.

UV coating, or UltraViolet coating, is a spray, treated glass or laminate put on top or in front of a color print to protect it from deterioration. Most ink, dye and pigment colors, especially those produced by desktop computer printers, are inherently unstable, and over time and with exposure to light will change and/or fade. When a UV coating is applied to a print, it should extend its life.

V.32 bis and **V.34** are standards that set the speed of a **modem**. V.32 bis is a 14.4-**bps** modem. And V.34 is a 28.8-bps modem. When telephone companies change over to fiber-optics, expect modem speeds (and V numbers) to continue to increase.

Vanishing point is the position on the far horizon toward which lines reach to show **perspective**. For instance, the vanishing point is the point on the horizon where the sides of a straight highway meet. Of course, we know, logically, that the sides of the highway are parallel to each other. But the rules of perspective, which are based on the way the human eye perceives the world around us, has those parallel lines converge at the vanishing point.

Vaporware is **software** that is announced before it exists, and which may never be available for sale. Essentially, the would-be manufacturer tries to create an interest in an idea of a product, to see if there would be a market for it, to warn off would-be competitors and/or to get investors for his or her company. These announcements make it into news stories in magazines and newspapers, which is the reason it is important to look for information that tells you a product is something real and not vaporware. This information includes hard facts about its pros and cons (it has been tested), stories about people actually using it, if it's coming off the assembly line and when it will definitely be for sale in stores.

Variations is a method of viewing how changing the settings of a **filter** or some other command would affect the current **image**.

The Variations **dialog box** displays several small **thumbnail** versions of the image, based on different values for the filter or command. It is often

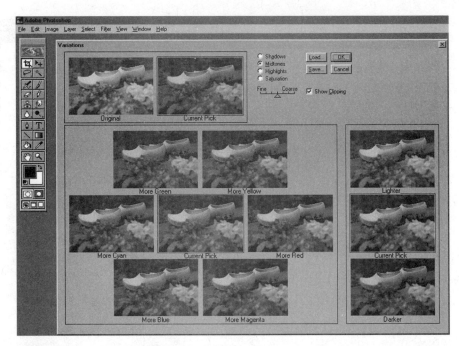

Variations: In this Photoshop Variations dialog, we clicked on the darker thumbnail several times. That altered all the other thumbnails, except the one representing the original image. We could, then, click on the, say, magenta thumbnail, which would make the current pick more magenta and less green (since green is the opposite of magenta).

possible to alter the range of variation, from wide to subtle differences among the thumbnails. Variations are also known unofficially as *Hollywood Squares,* because they are often displayed 9 at a time—3 rows of 3—just like the popular game show.

Depending on the program, you may or may not be able to click on the thumbnail that best approximates your choice. That, in turn, will change all the variations to show new ones, with your choice as the pivotal picture. Thus, with several clicks, the user can zero in on exactly the settings he or she wants without ever bothering to input any numbers or play with any sliding scales.

VDM (*Virtual DOS Machine*) creates a **window** through which **16-bit** application **software** can be used within a **32-bit operating system**, such as **Windows NT** and **OS/2**.

VDT is a *Video Display Terminal,* which is simply a fancy expression for a computer screen.

Vector is the overall term for any shape, **object, scene** or **font** that is defined mathematically. For instance, a rectangle is defined by its width, height, the position of its center point, the proportional width of the lines forming its outline, and the colors of its outline and **fill**.

This is in opposition to **bitmapped** or **raster**, in which all shapes are defined by the placement and color of thousands or millions of **pixels**. Raster images are capable of **photorealism**; vectors aren't (though complex vectors can come close). The major advantage of vector over raster is that vector requires less **memory, hard drive space** and other computer resources for creating, editing, **saving**, displaying and **outputting**.

Since the **dots** that are used to display and print vector shapes aren't designated until after the shape's size is determined, vectors and the programs that make them are said to be **resolution-independent**. That is, they are always output at the highest **resolution** that the printer, screen or any other **output device** is capable of providing.

Illustration (draw), **3-D, animation** and other **object-oriented** programs work with vector shapes.

Vector font   SEE **Vector, Resolution-independent, Outline font**.

Vendor is an organization that sells (and sometimes manufactures) computer **hardware, software** and/or **peripherals**.

Ventura is **Corel Corporation's desktop publishing program**.

Version number comes after the name of a piece of software and refers to the release, or when that particular edition of the program was manufactured. Generally, users want to have the most recent version, because it will have the most features and improvements.

Conventional wisdom suggests trying to avoid any program's 1.0 version, because there are certain to be interim releases, such as 1.1*a*, to fix the inevitable bugs.   SEE **Upgrade, System 7.x.**

Vertical alignment is a control over how an **object, text** or whatever is placed in relation to the vertical space on the **page** or to another object in the same **image** or **scene**.

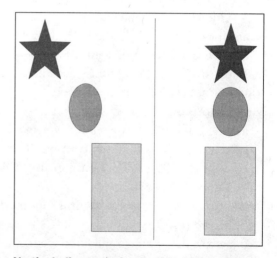

Vertical alignment: On the left side, the star, ellipse and rectangle are placed on the page wherever they happen to have fallen. On the right side, they are aligned vertically to each other. That means that the center point of each of the objects is now directly over each other.

VESA   SEE **Local bus**.

VGA (*Video Graphics Array*) is the current minimum graphics display standard on **PC** computers and minimum resolution for **digital cameras**. It's size is 640×480 pixels. **Windows,** DOS and every other current operating environment support VGA standard.   SEE **SVGA, Resolution**.

Video accelerator is an **expansion board** or chip designed to speed up how and when **graphics** are displayed on the computer monitor.

One of the slowest bottlenecks in working with large file and/or **high resolution** graphics is displaying the information as it is changed, **spooled** or **input**. A nonaccelerated video board relies on the computer's **CPU** to display the images, but the CPU is also doing many other tasks, such as minding the keyboard and/or accessing the **hard drive**. A video accelerator switches the responsibility for display and **redraws** to a dedicated high speed **coprocessor** chip and, sometimes, high speed video **memory** chips. In doing so, it can save seconds every time the screen changes.

Video adapter, also called a *video board* or *video card,* is a **graphics** board that can interpret **digital data** and display them as **dots** on a computer screen. Every computer must have some kind of video board, although some machines may have it built into the **motherboard**.

Video boards come in many sizes and flavors, but the one most appropriate for graphics applications displays **24-bit color** (**16.7 million colors**), at a **resolution** of at least 1024×768, 1280×1024 or 1600×1200 **pixels**. Expensive boards can display even higher resolution and at higher speeds.

Video board   SEE **Video adapter**.

Video capture is the process of "grabbing" a picture off a video device, such as a camcorder or a television, and converting it to a **digital image** that can be read, edited, **saved** and **output** by a computer. Devices that can do video capture are often called **frame grabber boards**.

Generally speaking, video capture will not produce as sharp or as detailed still prints as comparable **digital** capture devices (such as **digital cameras** or **scanners**). If you don't believe this, just look the next time your newspaper prints a photograph lifted from a network news program. It's fuzzier and more indistinct than what you are used to seeing on the front page. However, sometimes video capture is the only way to get a particular still image into a computer.

Video card   SEE **Video adapter**.

Videoconferencing is the technology that enables face-to-face real-time dialogs with other individuals, who are not in the room with you. The basic piece of equipment is a video camera that can **digitize images** and voices, and transmit them at high speeds over the telephone or **Internet** connection. However, at the current level of the technology, you have a Hobson's choice to make between jerky movements (15 frames per second) with greater image detail, or smoother live action (30 frames per second) at a lower **resolution**.

Video disc   SEE **Digital video disc, Laser disc**.

Video for Windows is a program that runs within **Windows** 3.x, 95, **98** and **NT**, which can run **AVI multimedia** (sound and pictures) files. If you didn't do a full Windows **installation**, it may not be on your hard drive. In that case, when a program needs Video for Windows, you will be asked to put your Windows disk or **CD-ROM** into your drive, so that it can be installed.

Video in is a **port**, either on a video **peripheral board** or built into the **motherboard** or a **digital camera**, that receives an **analog** video signal from a **camcorder, VCR** or other device, and displays it on the computer monitor as an analog picture.

Video out is a **port**, either on a video **peripheral board** or built into the **motherboard**, or a **digital camera**, that **exports** or **outputs** an analog video signal for display on a television set, as a broadcast feed, or to save to a **VCR**.

Video Toaster is the name of a very popular and successful professional video editing program (with a dedicated **expansion board**) that ran on the Amiga platform. It's still used in many newsrooms, even though the Amiga computer is no longer manufactured.

View is a series of commands that can change how the user sees an **image**, a **document** or a **scene**. When you realize that what you are really looking at on the screen is a **window** through which you can see a picture, document or scene, then it is easier to understand that there may be other windows or perspectives through which it might be visible.

In two-dimensional programs, such as **image editing, illustration** and **desktop publishing**, View allows the user to choose at what magnification or level of **zoom** he or she will see the current picture or document.

In **3-D** programs, View also relates to the direction from which the user may look at the scene—top, bottom, left, right, custom, etc.

Viewport is one of the names used for **window**, the area through which the user looks at the file (**image, document, scene**, etc.) displayed on the screen.   SEE **View**.

Vignette is a **special effect** that creates a circular blackout around the edges of a picture. Although it may be considered desirable in **digital imaging**, in photography, it is generally caused by using a lens that is too wide angle for the camera or lens shade, so that the lens (or shade) masks (covers up) the outer portion.

Virtual memory is an area of the **hard drive** used by **applications** and the **operating system** to temporarily hold **data** when there isn't enough **RAM** (**memory**). Unfortunately, virtual memory is much slower than RAM, which means that any time your computer uses it, all processing will slow down significantly.   See **Memory management**.

Virtual reality (VR) is the illusion that a computer-generated world is real, and that you are part of it. The technology consists of **3-D** graphics, special goggles that use stereoscopic vision, tactile and motion sensors attached to the various parts of the body and headphones with quadraphonic sound. Through all these devices, the computer feeds you **data**, so that as you move your head, or hands, it appears that you are moving within the space of the created world—the room spins, the wind blows, sounds come from different directions, you touch a surface, etc.

At present, virtual reality is somewhat crude and slow (when compared to our imaginations), but it is getting better every week, and it is certainly much more sophisticated that the original VR experiences. We may eventually see virtual reality interactive video replacing passive cinema and TV as our society's primary form of entertainment.

Virus is an artificial disaster area waiting to happen to your computer. It's a sophisticated bit of code created by mean-spirited destructive-minded **nerds**, whose only purpose is to wreck havoc and ruin other people's work. It is generally spread by attaching that code to an innocent-looking piece of **software**, or a **graphics** file, which when **installed** or **downloaded** onto your computer, will replicate itself and start doing its mischief. It may happen instantly, or it might be a time bomb–type of virus that will set itself off at a certain date, after a specific number of hours, or when a certain **program** has been run or accessed a set number of times.

The best protection against viruses is to know the source of the programs or **data** that you are putting on your computer. The next level of protection is to install a virus checker—software that will detect, eliminate or correct the damage from a known virus that may have infected your system. The last level of defense is to make frequent **backups** of all your data and programs, especially before any installation or addition of outside data. Then, if a virus is present and does damage to your **system** software, you can restore it to its original condition.

Visual database is an **application program** designed to organize and store images for easy retrieval. U-Lead's ImagePals is an example of a visual database.

VL-bus   SEE **Local bus**.

V-mail (video mail) is the process of sending a video file attached to an **e-mail** message.

Volatile memory is what your computer uses to perform all its functions. It's also called **RAM** (**Random Access Memory**), and the **data** in it last only as long as there is electricity powering it. It is called *volatile,* because as soon as the power is turned off, the memory is emptied of everything, forever. This is in opposition to the permanent saving of data on **hard drives** and other **storage devices**.

There is another type of memory called *nonvolatile* or *static memory* (SRAM) which doesn't lose data when the power is turned off. However, SRAM is slow and very expensive, and it is primarily used by certain devices for holding **user-defined** configurations. SRAM is usually not available to the user for image processing tasks.

Voltage regulator is a device that is placed between the computer and an AC wall socket, to govern the voltage flow of electricity to the computer. It is different from a **surge suppressor** in that it doesn't deal with electrical anomalies like **spikes** and **dips**. Instead, it attempts to keep the voltage within a very narrow range of normality. Voltage regulators are generally used in conjunction with surge suppressors, line stabilizers, **UPS**s, etc.

Volume, in **DOS** and **Windows NT**, refers to a **partition** of a **hard drive**, in which the partition is assigned a specific drive letter, like *D, E,* or *F.* In effect, the volume is treated as a separate physical hard drive, but it is only a virtual one.

The term *volume* is also used in Novell's popular NetWare **network software**, and it serves the same general purpose of partitioning hard drive space.

VRAM is short for video **RAM**, a kind of high speed **memory** used in better (i.e., more expensive) **graphics boards**. Because of its high cost, many manufacturers are now replacing VRAM with less-expensive **EDO** memory.

Wacom tablet is a well-known brand of **digitizing** or **drawing tablets** that use a **stylus** (pen) or a **puck** as the **pointing device**, instead of a **mouse**. These instruments permit more accurate and realistic drawing and painting. Wacom is the only brand of tablets in which the stylus or puck do not need batteries to operate.

Wallpaper is the background that a user selects to be displayed in the background of the **desktop**. Many different backgrounds may be selected or even created; however, wallpaper has no practical purpose, except as something aesthetically pleasing or to make a personal statement. If you are doing any color editing, we recommend that you forgo any wallpaper. Instead, use a neutral (18% gray is preferred) background that won't affect how you see colors.

WAV is a file format for digital sound files.

Wave is a **special effects filter** that pushes the **pixels** of an **image** or a **selected** area of an image into an undulating distortion. In most versions of this filter, the user can define the number of waves and how severe they will be. SEE **Distort**.

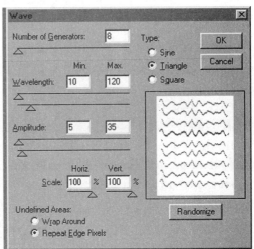

Wave: The original image to which we applied this Wave filter was made up of a series of straight horizontal parallel lines. You can see the result in the preview window just above the word *Randomize* in this dialog.

Wax thermal printers are **output devices** originally designed for the graphics arts industry, which produce **dithered** color **images** that can mimic the **output** from an **offset press** (the type of printing press most commonly used to mass-produce magazines, flyers, brochures, and other printed material). This makes them useful for producing **proofs, comps** and **FPO**s (For Position Only), to check how an image would look when reproduced on a commercial printing press. Generally, they are not used for making exhibition-type prints.

Wax thermals work by using heat to emboss dots through wax-coated cellophane ribbons of Cyan, Magenta, Yellow and blacK onto plain paper. The technology is similar to that used by **dye sublimation printers**, and in fact some models are capable of producing either dye sub or wax thermal prints, depending on the type of ribbons and the **drivers** being used. The difference is that wax thermal printers do not produce **continuous tone** or **photorealistic** prints, while dye sub printers do. Also, wax thermal prints are about ¼ the cost of dye sub prints. With the advent of inexpensive **inkjet** printers, wax thermal printers have declined in popularity among non-graphics arts professionals.

Web (Worldwide Web) is the public access portion of the **Internet**, which includes a multitude of information, services and images that are linked to each other and accessible to the general public through a computer **modem** and an Internet service. Many companies, organizations and individuals have personal **Web pages** through which they disseminate information about themselves, other points of interest, services or products. SEE **URL, Hotspot, Mapping, Web page**.

Web page is one of the most important advances in communications in history. It's the ability for anyone with access to the **Web** (and that's anyone with a computer, modem, telephone line and a subscription to an **Internet service provider**) to create and maintain an **interactive** communications with anyone else. Usually, it's in the form of a page (or pages), with color, text and graphics, that gives the reader information about the person, product or mission, and often provides the ability to exchange ideas, information or even execute commercial transactions. There are literally millions of Web pages instantly accessible from anywhere in the world, where users can buy, sell and trade products; read and leave opinions; check facts, figures and statistics; or have **real-time** chats with others. Be aware that just because something is published on a Web page doesn't necessarily mean that it's true. Anyone can put anything, accurate or not, up on the Web.

Web press is an **offset printing press** in which the paper is fed on very long continuous rolls. When you look at it in motion, it looks as though it were spinning a spider's web of paper. Web presses are most common for very large print runs, such as for newspapers.

Web service providers, also called *Internet Service Providers* (ISP), are the telephone companies of the **Internet** era. America Online, Prolog, Compu-Serve and many other companies provide the connections (for a fee) so that anyone with a computer and **modem** can access the **Web**.

Weight is another term for the width of lines, including those the make up **text** characters. A heavyweight line is thicker than a lightweight one. Within the same family of **typefaces**, bold text is invariably of a heavier weight than any of the nonbold fonts.

Weld is a **vector** command that **combines objects** in such a way that they cannot be **separated** again. Instead, they create a new shape that remains intact and reacts to all edits as a unity.

Well is a software graphic, usually rectangle in shape, into which the user **drags and drops** something with which he or she wishes to work. Wells are some-times used to designate the **view** of the picture, the **special effect**, the tool or style of tool, or various other things that the user wants to be active.

For instance, some **imaging** programs have color wells. The user chooses the color from the program's full palette and puts it into the well. That makes it the current **foreground** color, with which any tool will paint.

Only some **imaging** programs use the well metaphor, but it is becoming more popular, especially among **3-D, illustration** and **animation** programs.

Wet Edges is a **paintbrush** option that causes the color that is being laid down onto the **image** to bleed at the edges. It's a **natural media emulation** that is meant to look like watercolor or other real world paints that are wet by nature and which tend to bleed into the texture of the paper.

White matte   SEE **Black matte**.

White Point is a **color picker** or **eyedrop-per** tool with which the user designates

Wet Edges: Both of these curlicues were drawn with a black soft brush in Photoshop. However, the one on top was drawn with the Wet Edges option checked on. Different programs handle the Wet Edges effect differently. For instance, in some software, the edges will bleed more into the surrounding canvas, when the paint is set for Wet Edges. To see what using the Wet Edges option will do, just try it out.

which **pixel** in a **raster image** is to be the brightest point in the composition. Clicking on that pixel with the White Point tool sets not only it to white, but also all other pixels in the image that were originally brighter than the clicked-on point. Therefore, if used incorrectly, it can wipe out details in the highlight area.

However, the White Point is a valuable and easy tool for fixing exposure or color. If a picture has an unwanted blue tint, then setting the brightest point to white (instead of light blue) will also remap or set all the other pixels away from blue and toward a more neutral lighting.

Similarly, if a picture is too dark with no bright points in it, the White Point tool will correct the **dynamic range**, spreading out the pixels' values to include white.

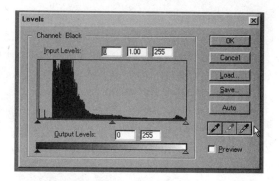

White Point: Notice the row of three eyedropper icons in this Photoshop Levels (histogram) dialog. The eyedropper on the far right is the white point; the one on the left is the black point. To use either, click on the icon in the dialog, then click on the point in your picture that you wish to set to black or white. But remember, this is a very dramatic tool that will change the tonal values of all pixels in your pictures. So, use it carefully.

Just remember, when using this tool, to be very careful which pixel you choose for the white point. It's so easy to use, that before you know it, you can be wiping out color and light information that you may need later. SEE **Black Point**.

White space is that area on a **page layout** where nothing has been placed. Therefore, it is empty, blank. The proportion of white space to type and images is an important design decision. A page with a lot of white space is said to be airy. One with very little may be tight, dense with information or too busy for the reader to easily wade through it all.

Widow   SEE **Orphan**.

Winchester is the original name given to the **hard disk drive**. Several decades ago, **IBM** marketed the first hard drive, a dishwasher-size monster with pizza-size platters. Each side of the platter was capable of storing 30 **megabytes** of **data**. IBM referred to the data platter as a 30/30, and since that's the size of the bullets in the classic Old West Winchester, the device popularly became known as a *Winchester drive*. Of course, most modern hard drives can hold far more than 30 megabytes of data, so the name *Winchester* has fallen into disuse.

Wind is a **special effects filter** that pushes the **pixels** in an **image** or a **selected** area of an image, as though a wind is blowing them in a user-specified direction. This filter is often used to give a person or an item in a **raster** image the look of motion. Usually, the user may choose between various levels—from a lovely little breeze that gently touches the pixels, to a hurricane gust.

Window is the area or box (on any computer, including **Macs** and **PCs**) in which a file (**image, document, scene**, etc.) is displayed. This is true regardless of what **operating system** or what computer **platform** you are using, since the display window has nothing to do with **Microsoft Windows** operating systems.

Several windows may be open at any time, but, as a rule, you can work in only one at a time—the **active** or current window. You can tell which is the active window, because its title bar (the top portion of the window's outline where the file's name is displayed) is a different color from all the other windows on your screen. If you apply a **filter** or any other edit, and it doesn't seem to work, it may be because the wrong window is the active one. Click on the title bar or inside the window of the one that you want to be active, before doing any editing.

In many **imaging programs**, it is possible to **drag and drop objects** and **selected** areas between windows.

Windowing is a technique that permits a user to rapidly jump between **active windows** within a **program** and among different programs.

Another definition of windowing is the process of extracting a small number of bits from a pixel, thereby taking out from an image file a portion of the data that defines each pixel.

Windows is the name of a series of **PC operating systems** that are sold by **Microsoft** and which run on the majority of **desktop** computers.

Windows 95/98 are **Microsoft**'s newest best-selling **operating systems** for PC-type computers. Both Win 95 and Win 98 are **32-bit operating systems** that permit faster operations and more versatility. They differ significantly from earlier Windows versions in their **GUI**, or Graphical User Interface (the way things appear on the screen) making it more orderly and logical (more Mac-like). Although Microsoft says that Windows 98 may be operated on a **486** computer with a minimum of 8 **megabytes** of **RAM**, practically speaking, it requires a minimum of 32 megabytes to function properly.

Windows NT is short for Windows <u>N</u>ew <u>T</u>echnology. Windows NT is **Microsoft**'s industrial-strength **32-bit operating system**, which is more powerful and versatile than **Windows 95** and **Windows 98**. It also requires more **resources**—a faster **CPU** (**Pentium**), more **RAM** (at least 32 **megabytes**, though 64 megabytes is the optimum minimum for proper functioning), etc. It is widely believed that Microsoft is slating Windows NT 5.0 as the operating system of choice for **networks** and **power users**, while Windows 98 is geared primarily for small businesses and amateur users. Some **graphics programs** are being written to take advantage of some of NT's advances, such as **multitasking** and networking. One important NT advantage is that it is available for a variety of non-Intel **platforms**, including **Alpha** and **MIPS** computers.

Windows 3.1 and **3.11** (aka Windows for Workgroups) are still current, but soon-to-be obsolete versions of **Microsoft**'s Windows **operating system**. They are **16-bit** operating systems that require the presence of **DOS** to work properly. What this means is that Windows 3.1 and 3.11 are generally slower and less versatile than **Windows 95/98** and **Windows NT**. For example, they cannot efficiently make use of more than 32 **megabytes** of RAM, which restricts the speed at which larger image files can be processed in an **image editing program**.

Windows 95   SEE **Windows 98**.

Windows explorer is the **file manager** program in **Windows 95, 98** and **NT**. In it, you can organize and create **folders; copy**, move or **delete** files, etc.

Windows for Workgroups   SEE **Windows 3.1** or **3.11**.

Win.ini is a file that holds all the basic information necessary to start up **Windows**, including **cursor** settings, **wallpaper** choices, **default** printer, **fonts** installed, **software** attached, etc. If Windows doesn't find a proper Win.ini file, it simply won't run. Win.ini may be changed with any **text editor** or **word processor program**, since it is a straight **ASCII** file.

A word of caution: We always make a **backup** of the Win.ini file, which we name *win.x*, before making any major changes or additions to Windows. Therefore, if the win.ini becomes corrupt or accidentally **deleted**, we can always start over again, without much angst.

Wireframe is a display option most frequently associated with **3-D software**. It shows **objects** as open gridwork made of polygons. Because wireframes include no color, **surface, texture** or **lighting** information, they require fewer **resources** and **redraw** more quickly.

When you want to see more details about your **scene** or **image**, choose another display option. Or do a **render**, which applies varying levels of your editing **data** to the basic shapes, depending on the program and which render option you choose.

The look of wireframes is something that sculptors and dress designers would recognize, because it uses the same skeleton-like structure on which the artist then applies materials.

Wizard is a question-and-answer session that guides a **user** through **installation, setups** and learning. In a wizard, each screen asks the user a question or to do something. How the user responds determines what the next screen will display and ask. This continues through to the finish of the task. It's a common sense, English language approach to cutting through the technobabble associated with documentation, installation and using computers.

Word is **Microsoft**'s **word processing program**.

WordPerfect is **Corel Corporation**'s **word processing program**.

Word processing composes text-based documents, using a computer. Word processing **software** is the **digital** replacement for typewriters, but enhanced with some **typesetting** and **graphics** capabilities. Popular word processing **programs** include **Microsoft Word** and **Corel Word Perfect**.

Word processor provides the tools and **environment** for **word processing**. The word is used both for word processing **software** that will install on any computer, as well as for a **dedicated** machine whose only function is word processing.

Word processor is any program devoted to creating, editing and printing text. Some high powered word processors, such as **Microsoft Word** and **Corel Word Perfect**, can also create and edit graphics, as well as **desktop publishing** documents.

WIREFRAME A

WIREFRAME B

Wireframe: (A) The wireframe or outline view of an object or scene takes fewer resources (and less time) to display and redraw on the screen. **(B)** But fills, textures, and other colors give a more realistic perspective of your art.

Word wrap occurs when a series of words or letters won't fit onto a single line. So, when it reaches the right margin, it automatically continues on to the next line below at the left margin.

Usually, it works by moving the word at the end of the line in its entirety to the next line. However, if you have automatic hyphenation turned on, the **software** will look for the natural break in the middle of that word. In many programs, the user may override the automatic hyphenation to create customized word breaks.

Each paragraph in this book has word wrap turned on, so that any sentence that is longer than a single line will still be readable, as it **wraps around** to the following line.

In many **imaging** programs, word wrap may be turned on or off. This is important, because the arrangement of text in an **image** is a design decision that may or may not be related to its readability.

Workflow explains how a project or job proceeds from concept, through each step along the way, to its finish. **Prepress** is an important workflow subject, because it involves a number of steps, numerous experts and, usually, several different locations. The study of workflow explores where the bottlenecks are and how to avoid them or improve performance so that they become irrelevant. Computer experts seem to love talking about workflow and how the newest gizmo or technology will improve it.

Workspace is that portion of the display within a **program**, where you actually work on your **image, document, scene**, etc. The rest of the display area is given over to **toolboxes, palettes, menus** and such.

Workstation is the name commonly given to an expensive, high powered **desktop** computer dedicated to **graphics**, engineering, design or some other professional task that requires lots of computing horsepower. Most workstations use a faster **RISC CPU** (the chip that acts as a computer's "brain"), and most also use an industrial strength **operating system** like **UNIX** or **Windows NT**. While the lines between desktop computers and workstations have blurred (as desktop systems became more powerful), workstations are still the platform of preference for many professionals.

WORM drive is a **storage device**, similar to a **CD-ROM** drive, designed to write **data** to a **disc** only once, although it can then be read many times. Hence its name, WORM (*Write Once/Read Many*). WORM drives are considered absolute, ultimate **archival** storage devices, since once written, nothing can ever be changed. One of their chief advantages is that they are proof positive of what was recorded and when. **CD-Rs** are a type of WORM drive.

Wraparound   SEE **Word wrap**.

Write protect is a method of preventing **data** from being overwritten by accident. On a **floppy disk**, pushing the little tab on the upper left corner open will turn on its write protection. Various other media have similar tabs, notches, etc., which **toggle** write protect on and off. It is also possible to write protect files through the **operating system** or **third-party utilities**. Write protecting your data is a good habit to get into, when there are vital, essential **images** that you don't want to accidentally delete or change.

WYSIWYG, literally, is an acronym that stands for *What You See Is What You Get*. It became a popular phrase with the advent of **desktop publishing**, because you could lay out pages on the screen that would look just as they would when printed out. (This is called a *layout*.)

   Unfortunately, WYSIWYG is a lie, when it comes to **imaging**, because of the problems inherent in translating the **transmitted colors** of a monitor to the **reflected colors** of a printed **page**.   SEE **Color management, RGB, CMYK, Absorptive color, Subtractive color**.

XA is a **CD-ROM format** that supports **multimedia** (text, animation and sound). Most current CD-ROMs have XA format.

Xaos is a group of **third-party special effects filters** that support Adobe's **open plug-in architecture**. That means they can be used from within most **image editing programs**, including **Photoshop, Picture Publisher** and **PhotoPaint**.

X-axis is an imaginary horizontal line that bisects two-dimensional space, and an imaginary horizontal plane that bisects three-dimensional space. When used in conjunction with the *y*- and *z*-**axes**, it gives the precise position of any point in **vector pages** or **scenes**.   SEE **X/Y/Z coordinates**.

XLS is the file format for Excel, **Microsoft's spreadsheet program**.

X/Y/Z coordinates provide the "address" of any point on a **vector page**.

Let's first look at a two-dimensional page (such as a drawing in an **illustration program** or a **newsletter** done in a **desktop publishing program**). Given that the *x*-**axis** is an imaginary horizontal line, and the *y*-**axis** is an imaginary vertical line, both of which bisect the page and meet in the middle, then when units of measure are used along those lines, any point can be referred to in terms of its relationship to those lines.

Think of it as a piece of graph paper that is placed over your illustration or desktop published page. The point where the *x*- and *y*-axis meet, in the middle of the page, is known as position 0,0. To the right of 0,0 on the *x*-axis, and above it on the *y*-axis, the units of measure are all positive numbers. To the left and down, they are all negative numbers. Therefore, if the unit of measure is inches, then point 1,2 would be 1 inch to the right of 0,0 and

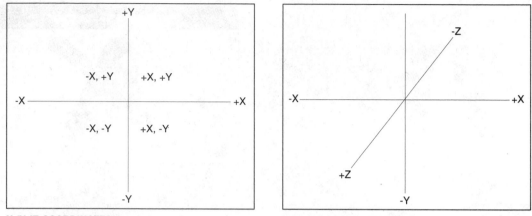

X/Y/Z COORDINATES A   **X/Y/Z COORDINATES B**

X/Y/Z coordinates: (A) Remember this schematic from high school math? Yes, Virginia, there is math.in art. It helps you locate points in two-dimensional illustrations. **(B)** Now add a third axis, for depth, and you have 3-D space in which you can locate anything. Imagine the z-axis going from in front of the page to behind the page, while the x- and y-axes live on the paper. Just as the x- and y-axes are 90° (at right angles to each other), so too is the z-axis at right angles to both the x- and the y-axes. The coordinate that identifies any point in x, y and z space is located by three numbers—in relationship to all three axes.

2 inches above it. Many 2-D programs show (by **default**) only the positive portions of the axes.

Now, extend that analogy to **3-D** space. The third dimension requires that we add another axis (called the **z-axis**) to describe positioning in a world that has not only height and width, but also depth. The negative portions of the axes become important in 3-D.

X/Y/Z coordinates are useful for precise placing and drawing of **objects** and other **image elements** in **vector**-based programs. Most illustration, **DTP** and 3-D programs have a **status bar** (usually at the bottom of the screen), where the current position of your cursor is displayed, according to these coordinates.   SEE **X-axis, Y-axis**.

Y-axis is an imaginary vertical line that is used in **vector**-based programs (such as **illustration, desktop publishing** and **3-D modeling**) to help the user arrange and draw objects according to precise positions.   SEE **X/Y/Z coordinates, *x*-axis, *z*-axis**.

YCC is a **color model** used by Eastman Kodak in relation to its multiresolution **PhotoCD file format**. Based on **luminance** and **hue**, it is supposed to be faster than other color models.

Zap or zapping is the act or process of eliminating or erasing files. SEE **Erase**. It also refers to the accidental erasure of anything, such as part of an **image**, a name in a **database** or a cell in a spreadsheet.

Zapf Dingbats is the name for a popular set of nonletter ornamental or decorative **fonts** or **characters**. Dingbats originally referred to a collection of miscellaneous printer's characters, and Zapf is the name of the designer who created them for computer use. Zapf Dingbats are usually part of the **fonts** built into most **PostScript** printers and are often used as **bullets**.

Z-axis is the imaginary plane that extends out into the distance in **3-D** space.

Think of a beach **scene** that is displayed on your computer monitor. While the monitor is only two dimensional, it has to provide all the information you need to describe and view three dimensions. Of course, it has no difficulty with displaying a telephone pole that is in the **foreground**, or the horizontal line where the ocean meets the sand. But the expanse of sea that goes off into the distance, a sailboat that is a few hundred yards offshore, and a cruise ship that is a few miles away, all need to be assigned positions in the area that supposedly extends from the foreground to the background.

In that scene, the telephone pole may be aligned to the vertical *y*-axis, the waterline to the horizontal *x*-axis, and the distance of the boat and ship from the waterline is measured along the plane that is the *z*-axis. SEE **X/Y/Z coordinates, X-axis, Y-axis**.

ZiffNet is the name of Ziff-Davis's **on-line forum** that allows authorized **users** with **modems** to access that computer publishing company's considerable database. ZiffNet contains the text of many magazines, libraries of **utilities**,

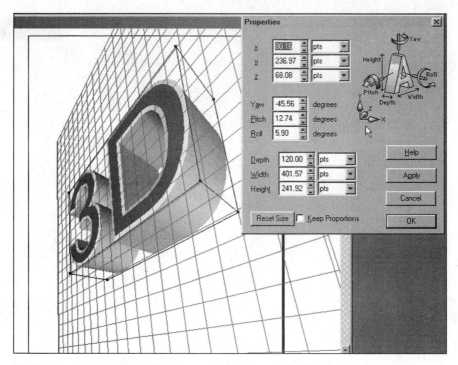

Z-axis: Locating a point in 3-D space, using the *x/y/z* coordinates and axes (plural of axis) is probably the most difficult aspect of working with 3-D. This is especially true because each axis may point in a different direction depending on your view—from the front, top, back, side, etc. But the basics are not so difficut, if you remember some primitive geometry. Notice the small schematic in this CorelDEPTH dialog that points in *x, y,* and *z* directions.

reviews and test results, and interactive communications with Ziff's editors, writers, reviewers and consultants.

Zigzag is a **filter** that radially distorts a **selected** part of an **image**.

Zip, or zipping, is the process of **compressing** or shrinking the size of a file. Files, especially **image** or **graphics** files, are frequently too large to save onto a single **floppy diskette**, or to quickly and economically **transmit** to another computer via a **modem**. Software engineers have developed a variety of methods for compressing data files, so that they will be anywhere from ⅜ths to ¹⁄₅₀th their original size.

Zipping, while a generic description for file compression, also refers to popular **shareware** programs called **PKZip** and WinZip.   SEE **Compression**.

Zits are unwanted **pixels** or **artifacts** in an **image**. They may be created by such diverse sources as electronic **noise** from the **CCD** in a **scanner** or electrical interference from any nearby device. While there are several methods to minimize zits (such as moving cables or devices further from the computer or scanner), the only way to completely eliminate zits is to edit them out of the image on the pixel level.

Zoom is a command and a tool (its icon usually looks like a magnifying glass) that allows a user to change the size of an area being viewed on the monitor. By clicking on the magnifying glass or accessing the Zoom pulldown menu, a user may zoom in or zoom out (increase or decrease magnification) in pre-set increments, such as 75% zoom or 200% zoom. Zoom is the most common way to enlarge a small area of an image, or to pull back to view the entire picture.   SEE **Zoom area**.

Zoom area is a rectangular selection drawn with the **zoom** tool, which then becomes the area that will be magnified to fill the **image window**.

Zoom box is the little square in the upper right-hand corner of a Macintosh folder **window**. Clicking on it either enlarges or reduces the size of the window.

In **Windows 3.x,** the equivalent of a zoom box is the box on the upper right corner of a window that has small up and down arrows. Clicking on it will either maximize, or enlarge the window to the full screen, or reduce it to a smaller window.

1-bit color is the simplest type of **image**. In it, every **pixel** is either black or white. There is no other color, no levels of highlight or shadows. When **output**, it looks like **line art**.   SEE **Bitmap**.

2-D stands for *two-dimensional*. It describes items, **scenes, objects, images**, etc., that exist on two planes only (*x*- and *y*-**axes**). Everything that is on a printed **page** is two-dimensional by definition. **Illustration, image editing, desktop publishing** and other programs work in two dimensions only, though they might use perspective tricks to try to make you think you see **3-D**.

3-D is *three-dimensional*. It refers to an item, **scene, object**, picture or whatever that has depth, width and height (*x*-, *y*- and *z*-**axes**). Everything in the real world—outside of computer monitors and printed **pages**—is 3-D.

For instance, a photograph of a watermelon is two dimensional. But the real watermelon is three dimensional; when you turn it on its side, your **perspective** or

1-BIT COLOR A

1-BIT COLOR B

1-bit color: This *grayscale* photograph **(A)** is converted to a 1-bit line art drawing **(B)**, which sets every *pixel* at either black or white (with nothing in between). *(Photo from the Corel Stock Photo Library.)*

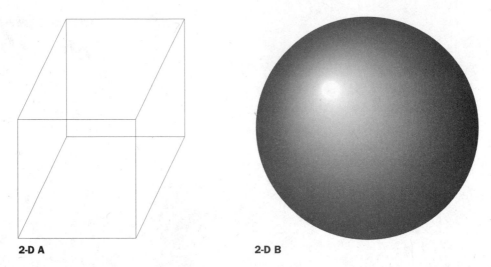

2-D A   **2-D B**

2-D: The 2-D box **(A)** uses very traditional tricks of the eye and the pen to create the illusion of *3-D*. In *imaging*, colors, *highlights*, and *gradients* are used to make you think you are seeing a *3-D object*. That's the way this circle **(B)** is made to look like a sphere. But it is, in reality, as flat as the box, a piece of paper, or any 2-D item.

view of it may change, but the essential size, shape, **texture**, etc., of the melon remains the same.

The difficult trick is to represent three-dimensional objects on two-dimensional monitors, in a realistic manner. That's the job of 3-D **modeling** programs. They construct 3-D objects and scenes so that they can be viewed

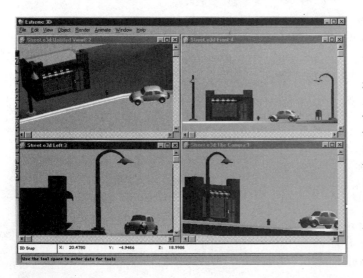

3-D: In *3-D*, all *objects* and *scenes* are defined by geometry that exists and has dimension from any angle, as can be seen in this four-view perspective of the same scene. Rotating or moving any object doesn't change any of its defining geometry, it simply alters the perspective from which you are viewing it and its relationship to other objects in the scene.

from any angle, rotated or whatever and still remain intact and whole. Thus, they give the illusion of real three dimensionality.

8-bit color is the same thing as **indexed color**, which can display, transmit or output a total of up to 256 different colors. It is useful for situations in which computer **resources** are limited, speed is important, images are to be displayed on the **Web,** and **photorealistic output** is not essential. Many older computers are incapable of greater **bit depth** color. So, if you are sharing **image** files with individuals who have such limited equipment, you need to downsize your **24-bit** photorealistic images to 8-bit. By the way, 8-bit color has become the standard for sharing **graphics** on the **Internet**.

16-bit data path   SEE **32-bit application**.

16-bit sound is the current standard for creating or reproducing audio on the computer. Most **sound boards** are 16 bits, in that they are capable of recognizing (or **sampling**) 65,000 different tones and volume levels, which can be saved in audio files or **output** on attached speakers.

32-bit sound is just beginning to hit the market, but should eventually replace 16-bit sound.

24-bit color is the *lingua franca* of professional **digital graphics**. It provides **8 bits** of color for each of the three **primary channels**, or a total of 256 colors of red, times 256 colors of green, times 256 colors of blue. The result is **16.7 million** different colors, which can be displayed, edited, **saved** and **output**. 24-bit color is also called **photorealistic** and **true color**, because it is the closest that the computer can get to the number of colors that the human eye can see.

32-bit application is software designed to take advantage of the greater speed, reliability and versatility of the more modern **operating systems** (which are also 32-bit), such as **Windows 98, Windows NT, OS/2** or **System 8.x**.

Older applications are generally written in 16-bit code, which means that they can process only half the amount of **data** at one time as 32-bit applications. While older 16-bit programs will run in 32-bit operating systems, the opposite is not true. That's why you should make sure that your software matches your operating system's maximum capability.

Incidentally, 32-bit applications and operating systems are said to process information using a 32-bit data path. In other words, they can handle 32 pieces of information at a time. That is in comparison to the older 16-bit data paths, that handled only 16 pieces of information at a time.

32-bit color provides **8 bits** of information for each of four **channels**. These four channels may consist of **RGB** colors plus an **alpha channel** (for opacity levels), or they may be cyan, magenta, yellow and black in a **CMYK** image.

32-bit color also allows **Windows 95, 98** and NT, and Mac System 8.x to provide what is known as the *packed pixel mode.* In other words, 24-bit data can be displayed faster and more efficiently when sent to the screen 32 bits at a time. If it sounds confusing, don't worry, it's all happening automatically, in the proverbial blink of an eye.

32-bit data path   SEE **32-bit application**.

32-bit operating system   SEE **32-bit application, Windows, System 8.x**.

32-bit sound is the newest standard for sound on the desktop. 32-bit sound boards are capable of recognizing, or sampling, millions of different tone and volume levels, which can be saved in audio files or **output** on attached speakers.

256 colors   SEE **8-bit color**.

286   SEE **80286**.

386   SEE **80386**.

486   SEE **80486**.

596   SEE **80586, Pentium**.

68000 is the name of Motorola's family of **CPU**s that power the Macintosh computers, beginning with 68000, through 68020, 68030 and ending with 68040. They have been made all but obsolete by Motorola/Apple/IBM's **PowerPC** (PPC) family of CPUs; however, the PPC can emulate the 68000 machines for compatibility with older software.

8088 is the **Intel CPU** that powered the original **IBM PC** introduced in 1981.

80286 is the name of the Intel **CPU** that powered the IBM-AT introduced in 1984. It was also known as the 286.

80386 is the **Intel CPU** that made a transition to **32-bit** processing, and made operating environments like **Windows** practical. Like the **286**, the 80 is usually dropped, so that the chip is called a **386**.

80486, or **486,** is the **Intel CPU** that was the first high speed **processor** which made **image editing** practical on the **PC**. Although largely obsolete (as are its predecessors), it is still a work horse throughout the industry.

80586, or **586,** is a **clone CPU** of **Intel**'s **Pentium**.

9 track tape is a largely obsolete reel-to-reel tape that is still used by some **service bureaus**, mini-computers and mainframes. It never became an important **format** for **desktops** or **workstations**.

16.7 million colors   SEE **24-bit color**.

About the Authors

SALLY WIENER GROTTA and DANIEL GROTTA are recognized as consummate digital imaging communicators. Authors of the acclaimed reference book *Digital Imaging for Visual Artists* (Windcrest/McGraw-Hill), they are also popular lecturers and journalists with numerous credits in national magazines and are contributing editors to *PC Magazine*. In addition, Sally Wiener Grotta is a highly respected digital artist and photographer. They are based in the Pennsylvania Pocono Mountains.